DATE DUE		
REF.	REF.	REF.	REF.
	REF.	REF.	
	REF.	REF.	

ENCYCLOPEDIA OF TERRORISM AND POLITICAL VIOLENCE

ENCYCLOPEDIA OF TERRORISM AND POLITICAL VIOLENCE

JOHN RICHARD THACKRAH

Routledge & Kegan Paul
London and New York

First published in 1987 by
Routledge & Kegan Paul Ltd
11 New Fetter Lane, London EC4P 4EE

Published in the USA by
Routledge & Kegan Paul Inc.
in association with Methuen Inc.
29 West 35th Street, New York, NY 10001

Set in Linotron Times, 9 on 10pt
by Input Typesetting Ltd, London
and printed in Great Britain
by T. J. Press (Padstow) Ltd
Padstow, Cornwall

Library of Congress Cataloging in Publication Data

Thackrah, John Richard.
    Encyclopedia of terrorism and political violence.
    Bibliography: p.
    Includes index.
    1. Terrorism—Dictionaries.   2. Radicalism—
Dictionaries.   1. Title.
HV64.31.T56   1987   303.6'25'0321   874304

British Library CIP Data also available

ISBN 0–7102–0659–3

CONTENTS

PREFACE

The first line of defence against terrorism is to learn as much as one can about terrorists, to understand their motivations and their methods, and to be able as a result to anticipate some of their targetting, or at least to limit damage if attacks cannot be prevented. The purpose of any revolutionary terror campaign is to build a new society; and thus members of the current global community need to take a realistic view of the threat of terroristic activity.

This encyclopedia will seek to fill a gap in terrorist literature in recent times. Much has been written about individual groups and incidents, but relatively little, certainly not in an encyclopedic format, on the ideas, theories and terms that are used in the rapidly growing academic study of terrorism and political violence.

International terrorism is a relatively new phenomenon on the world stage, although the use of terror has been around since Biblical times. Definitions of terms relating to terrorism are constantly changing, depending from which side of the ideological divide they are viewed. Some old terms have been discarded and some new ones have become part of our language. For example, for some time a major war of words has been taking place between those who have different views on when a terrorist becomes a guerrilla or vice versa, and about the difference between national and international terrorism. The author hopes this work may go some way to providing some solution to these problematic issues.

The countries chosen for some examination of the violence within their borders are, in the author's view, the main recipients or supporters of terror. Time and space does not allow for every country in the world to be covered, nor for each group within these countries to be analysed. A limited number of biographical entries of terrorists have been given because of the great emphasis given to their biographies in other literature about the subject. Space does not allow consideration to be given to many developments before the mid and late twentieth century. For obvious reasons of source material reliability, little attention has been given to the jargon of terrorists, which is virtually impossible to collate with any semblance of accuracy, as much of it is in the terrorist's mind only; and the attitudes are without apology Western-oriented. Examples have been given of certain events, incidents and persons to support the concepts and ideas.

The work will be useful for those persons working or studying in higher education, the services, government, business and law enforcement agencies.

It is hoped that readers will see that the essential facts and concepts have been included without over-simplifying, and that where entries touch current affairs they tend to reflect the views and judgment of the writer. Politicians vary even about the fundamental question of what constitutes terrorism, although variations are often over value judgments about how society should be organised rather than the material and language of politics. A single entry cannot tell the reader all there is to know about its subject matter because it is related to other entries. To know something about kidnap, for example, one has to know about finance, motivation, responses by the law, hostage negotiation, the mindset of the perpetrator and the types of political violence. Many entries could have been listed almost equally well under other entries.

The work could be seen by some as more of an encyclopedia than a dictionary. It is intended to be most useful as a handbook for constant reference, enabling the reader to look up a term he encounters about which he is doubtful, and find beyond a mere definition a satisfactory explanation of some matter of political interest, so that he can proceed directly in his reading without having to stop and search among numerous textbooks, commentaries, biographies, monographs, or eyewitness accounts. Everyone should be aware of the multivarious strands of ideas which contribute to the world's contemporary phenomenon.

I am grateful for having listened to, and read the writings of such authors as Paul Wilkinson, Richard Clutterbuck, Christopher Dobson and Ronald Payne, David Carlton, Brian Crozier, Peter Janke, Brian Jenkins, Grant Wardlaw, Ted Gurr, Edward Mickolus, and also of numerous researchers. These people have fired me with an unquenchable enthusiasm for this subject – and it has been a pleasure at various times to have talked with them, and exchanged views and ideas. To these people I offer heartfelt thanks. I am grateful to my colleagues and to students at the Police Staff College, who have accepted my desire to give vent to my interests in this area with my pen. The views expressed in this work are entirely my own, and do not represent any hint of government, Home Office or police policy on matters where this might be construed to be the case. My grateful appreciation also goes to my literary agent Michael Felgate Catt of the Catt-Wilson Agency in London; to Wendy Morris and Elizabeth Handford of Routledge and Kegan Paul, and to my typists, Mrs Jo Park and Miss Derilyn Park. Without them all, and ultimately without the constant support and encouragement of my parents, this work would not have been possible.

John Richard Thackrah
August 1986

MAIN ABBREVIATIONS AND ACRONYMS

AD	Action Directe (France)
ALF	Animal Liberation Front (England)
ANAPO	National Popular Alliance Party (Colombia)
ANC	African National Congress (South Africa)
ARDE	Alianza Revolucionaria Democrática (Nicaragua)
ASALA	Armenian Secret Army for the Liberation of Armenia
ATE	Anti-terrorism ETA
AZAPO	Azanian People's Organisation (South Africa)
BLA	Black Liberation Army (USA)
CCC	Cellules Communistes Combattantes (Belgium)
CGUP	Guatemalan Committee of Patriotic Unity
CLODO	Committee to Liquidate or Neutralise Computers (France)
DFLP	Democratic Front for the Liberation of Palestine
DLF	Dhofar Liberation Front (Oman)
DRIL	Iberian Revolutionary Directorate of Liberation (Spain)
EAM	National Liberation Front (Greece)
EGP	Guerrilla Army of the Poor (Guatemala)
ELAS	Greek National Liberation Army (military wing of EAM)
ELF	Eritrean Liberation Front
EM	Death Squad (Guatemala)
EPLF	Eritrean People's Liberation Front
EROS	Ealam Revolutionary Organisation of Students (Sri Lanka)
ERP	People's Revolutionary Army (Argentina and El Salvador)
ESA	Secret Anti-Communist Army (Guatemala)
ETA	Euskadi Ta Askatasuna (Euskadi and Freedom) (Spain and France)
ETAm	ETA military
ETAp-m	ETA political-military
EZU	Emiliano Zapata Unit
FAN	Armed Forces of the North (Chad)

ix

Main Abbreviations and Acronyms

FANE	Federation of National and European Action (France)
FAPLA	Angolan People's Liberation Armed Forces
FARC	Revolutionary Armed Force of Colombia
FARN	Fuerzas Armadas de la Resistencia Nacional (El Salvador)
FAT	Chad Armed Forces
FDN	Fuerzas Democraticas Nicaraguenses (Nicaragua)
FDR	Revolutionary Democratic Front (El Salvador)
FDR	Democratic Front against Repression (Guatemala)
FLN	Front de Libération Nationale (Algeria)
FLQ	Front de Libération du Québec
FNE	European Nationalist Alliance (France)
FNLA	National Front for the Liberation of Angola
FPL-FM	Fuerzas Populares de Liberación – Farabundo Marti (El Salvador)
FRAP	Frente Revolucionario Antifascista Patriótico (Spain)
FRELIMO	Frente de Libertação de Moçambique (Mozambique)
FRETILIN	Frente Revolucionária Timorense de Libertação e Independência (East Timor)
FROLINAT	Chad National Liberation Front
GARI	Gruppo de Accion Revolucionaria Internacionalista (Spain)
GPP	Guerra Popular Prologanda (Spain)
GRAE	Revolutionary Government of Angola in Exile
GRAPO	Gruppo de Resistencia anti-Fascista Primero de Octubre (Spain)
GUNT	Transitional Government of National Unity (Chad)
INLA	Irish National Liberation Army
IRA	Irish Republican Army
JDL	Jewish Defence League (USA)
JVP	Janatha Vimukti Peramuna (Sri Lanka)
KKE	Greek Communist Party
KNDO	Karen National Defence Organisation (Burma)
LTTE	Liberation Tigers of Tamil Ealam (Sri Lanka)
M-19	National Liberation (April 19) Movement (Colombia)
MCP	Malayan Communist Party
MIL	Iberian Liberation Movement (Spain)
MK	Umkhonto We Sizwe (Spear of the Nation) (military wing of ANC)
MNLF	Moro National Liberation Front (Philippines)
MNR	Movimiento Nacional Revolucionario (El Salvador)
MPAIAC	Movement for Self-Determination and Independence of the Canaries Archipelago
MPLA	Movimento Popular para a Libertação de Angola
MRLA	Malayan Races Liberation Army
NAR	Armed Revolutionary Nuclei (Italy)
NFN	New Nazi Front (France)
NICRA	Northern Ireland Civil Rights Association
NORAID	Irish Northern Aid Committee

NPA	New People's Army (Philippines)
OAS	Organisation Armée Secrète (Algeria)
ORPA	Revolutionary Organisation of the People in Arms (Guatemala)
PAIGC	Partido Africano da Independência da Guiné e Cabo Verde (Guinea-Bissau)
PCS	Partido Comunista Salvadoreño
PFLO	Popular Front for the Liberation of Oman
PFLOAG	Popular Front for the Liberation of Oman and the Arabian Gulf
PFLP	Popular Front for the Liberation of Palestine
PFLP-GC	Popular Front for the Liberation of Palestine – General Command
PIRA	Provisional IRA
PLA	Palestine Liberation Army
PLA	Popular Liberation Army (Syria)
PLF	Palestine Liberation Front
PLF	Popular Liberation Force (Eritrea)
PLO	Palestine Liberation Organisation
PNC	National Conciliation Party (El Salvador)
POLISARIO	Popular Front for the Liberation of Saquiet el Hamra and Rio de Oro (North West Africa)
PREPAK	People's Revolutionary Party of Kungleipak (India)
PSF	Popular Struggle Front (Palestinian)
RAF	Red Army Faction (Rote Armee Fraktion) (West Germany)
RZ	Revolutionary Cells (West Germany)
SLA	Symbionese Liberation Army (USA)
SNLF	Sandinist National Liberation Front (Nicaragua)
SWAPO	South West Africa People's Organisation
TELO	Tamil Ealam Liberation Organisation (Sri Lanka)
TULF	Tamil United Liberation Front (Sri Lanka)
TUF	Tamil United Front (Sri Lanka)
UDA	Ulster Defence Association
UDF	United Democratic Front (South Africa)
UNITA	Unido Nacional para a Independencia Total de Angola
UNO	Union Nacional O_positora (El Salvador)
URNG	Guatemalan National Revolutionary Unity
UVF	Ulster Volunteer Force
ZANLA	Zimbabwe African National Liberation Army
ZANU	Zimbabwe African National Union
ZAPU	Zimbabwe African People's Union

A

Abu Nidal It was reported in June 1984 that Mr Sabri Khalil al Banna, [the leader of the Revolutionary Council of Fatah (a Palestinian splinter organisation which was commonly referred to as the Abu Nidal group after Mr al Banna's code name)], had left Damascus for Baghdad for treatment of a heart ailment, and that the group's activities had been curtailed. Mr al Banna had been expelled from Baghdad in November 1983, and his readmission to Iraq was seen as being conditional on the cessation of the group's operations. Mr al Banna was again expelled from Iraq in November 1984, and relocated the headquarters of the group in Damascus.

The Abu Nidal group had claimed responsibility for the attempted assassination in June 1982 of Mr Shlomo Argov, the then Israeli ambassador to the UK, and also for the assassination of the moderate Palestinian leader, Dr Issam Ali Sartawi, in April 1983. The group had also been associated with terrorist activity in France and had recently supported the Syrian-backed rebellion by units of the PLO opposed to Mr Yassir Arafat.

In almost simultaneous actions in December 1985 by Arab gunmen at the international airports at Rome and Vienna, 20 people were killed, including four of the seven gunmen involved. Responsibility for the incidents was widely attributed to the Palestinian Abu Nidal group, acting with the support of Libya. The four gunmen who participated in the Rome operation had statements on them signed by the 'Palestinian Martyrs'; and the Arab Guerrilla Cells also claimed responsibility, stating that they 'hereby declare(d) the birth of a revolutionary and suicide group'.

A day after the atrocity a telephone caller to a Spanish radio station claimed responsibility for the attacks on behalf of the 'Abu Nidal commando'. A US presidential spokesman claimed all the evidence pointed to the Abu Nidal group. On the same day, Israeli officials began to refer specifically to the Abu Nidal group as the culprit. It had apparently erroneously been reported that Nidal had died in late 1984. The PLO itself had consistently condemned the activities of the group, and in his absence Abu Nidal had been condemned to death by the organisation. Unconfirmed reports from Arab diplomatic sources suggested that Abu Nidal might have been expelled from Syria to Libya following the June 1985 TWA Beirut hijack, as part of a secret agreement between Syria and the USA. A week later Arafat claimed that the Syrian and Libyan intelligence services were sponsoring terrorism in an effort to discredit the PLO, and he described Abu Nidal as a 'tool of Syrian and Libyan intelligence'. Israel tacitly acknowledged that the attacks were not the work of the mainstream PLO but affirmed that militant breakaway factions such as the Abu Nidal group were ultimately part of the same movement.

A joint meeting of Italian and Austrian security officials held on 1 January 1986 reportedly concluded that all seven gunmen involved in the December attacks were members of the Abu Nidal group and had been trained in Lebanon. One of the surviving gunmen had apparently confessed that the name 'Palestinian Martyrs' was a front for the Abu Nidal group. It was subsequently reported that the gunmen had travelled to Europe via Damascus and Yugoslavia. The US administration produced a report on 2 January listing 60 incidents which it claimed had involved the Abu Nidal group over the past two years. The report also asserted that the Libyan regime was actively supporting the group, a claim which Colonel Gadaffi denied. On 5 January 1986 he refuted allegations that Libya provided training camps or assistance of any kind to Abu Nidal, who, he said, did not live in Libya, although he admitted having met with him during 1985. He added that as head of state he did not regard the airport attacks as 'legal', but said that it was the duty and strategy of Palestinian guerrillas 'to liberate Palestine by all means'. At this time, due to a failure to locate any Abu Nidal power bases, the military option was not being seriously considered by the US forces.

On 13 January, an Abu Dhabi newspaper published what it claimed was an interview with Abu Nidal, during which he admitted that his group had carried out airport attacks, which he described as 'absolutely legitimate'. He praised Gadaffi as an 'honest man', and claimed to have visited the USA several times using forged passports, and to have undergone recent cosmetic surgery to avoid recognition.

On 20 January, the *New York Times* published an interview with Mr Ahmed Jabril, leader of the radical PLO group, the Popular Front for the Liberation of Palestine – General Command, which enjoyed close ties with Libya. Mr Jabril affirmed that the Abu Nidal group was responsible for the airport attacks, and added that the group received considerable material assistance from Iran, where Abu Nidal himself spent most of his time. He claimed that the group also received assistance from revolutionary organisations around the world as well as from conservative Arab states, and that it required relatively little money to carry out its activities.

An arrest warrant for Abu Nidal was issued by a Rome public prosecutor on 23 January 1986, and this is still in force.

Achille Lauro hijack The Italian cruise liner *Achille Lauro* was hijacked on 7 October 1985 en route between the two Egyptian ports of Alexandria and Port Said by four Palestinian guerrillas who, it later transpired, were members of the Tunis-based faction of the Palestine Liberation Front (PLF) – a constituent part of the Palestine Liberation Organisation. Under

A

the hijackers' directions, the ship, with 180 passengers and 331 crew on board (approximately 600 of the passengers having disembarked at Alexandria), circled in the Eastern Mediterranean. During the period of the hijacking the guerrillas demanded the release of 50 Palestinian prisoners and threatened to kill the passengers. Only one of the passengers, a disabled Jewish American named Mr Klinghoffer, was murdered – he was shot and subsequently thrown overboard. After lengthy negotiations over two days with Egyptian and Italian officials and two PLO members including the PLF leader Mr Abul Abbas, the hijackers surrendered, reportedly in return for free passage out of Egypt.

The identity and affiliation of those responsible for the *Achille Lauro* hijack remained unclear for some time. The Israelis believed the action was a deliberate attempt by Mr Arafat and the PLO to prevent further progress towards peace negotiations. The operation was widely denounced in Arab and Palestinian circles, with both the mainstream PLO and the anti-Arafat Damascus-based groups condemning it. The hijackers themselves said that they were members of the PLF, although Mr Arafat denied that members of any PLO groups were involved, and the Damascus-based PLF under Mr Talat Yacoub disclaimed responsibility. It was only after the surrender of the hijackers that it became clear that the operation had been mounted by the Tunis-based breakaway wing of the PLF, led by Abbas.

The PLF itself had originally been created by Yacoub as a breakaway from Mr Ahmed Jabril's Popular Front for the Liberation of Palestine – General Command (PFLP-GC). Abbas had joined the PLF on its formation but had led a breakaway pro-Arafat loyalist faction, which had subsequently based itself in Tunis when the main PLF declared against Arafat. A third PLF faction, led by Abdul Fatah Ghanem, was based in Libya. In September 1985 the Abbas-led group of the PLF had held its seventh congress in Tunis, and passed a resolution opposing the Arafat-Hussein reconciliation. In Tunis, Abul Abbas promised that the PLF would continue the struggle, trying to achieve PLO unity and legitimate leadership.

After the hijacking was over, Abbas confirmed earlier reports that the hijackers had been under orders to use the liner only as a means of transport to the Israeli port of Ashdod (where it had been scheduled to call), and had not intended to take it over. They had been precipitated into the hijack when they were discovered in a cabin cleaning their weapons. A senior PLO official said that the guerrillas were under written orders from Mr Abbas to carry out a suicide mission in Israel and that they had changed their minds out of cowardice and decided to hijack the ship; thus the PLF would be punished for the action.

After Mr Klinghoffer's death had been revealed President Mubarak of Egypt stated that the hijackers had left Egyptian territory, and were probably in the hands of the PLO. The PLO in Tunis denied that it was holding them, and said that they were still awaiting the arrival of the guerrillas, whom they intended to put on trial. President Reagan called on the PLO to hand the hijackers over to an appropriate sovereign state for trial.

On the night of 10 October, an Egyptian plane en route to Tunis with the hijackers, Mr Abbas and an (unnamed) PLO official on board was intercepted by four American planes and forced to land at a NATO base in Sicily, where the Palestinians were taken into custody by the Italian authorities. Mr Abbas later flew to Rome. The Italian government refused an American request for the hijackers and for Mr Abbas to be handed over to the US authorities. This policy of appeasement of the terrorists caused dissent within the Italian government. On 12 October Abbas flew to Yugoslavia, where the Yugoslav authorities rejected a US request that he be arrested. The US administration subsequently publicly criticised the Italian decision to allow Abbas to leave the country.

The US action in intercepting the Egyptian aircraft was praised by Israel and the UK and criticised by many Arab states. It provoked further anti-American demonstrations throughout the Arab world. The trial of the hijackers, together with a Syrian alleged to be their accomplice, on charges of illegal possession of arms and explosives took place in Genoa; they were convicted and received sentences of between 4 and 9 years in jail.

Action Directe Action Directe emerged in 1979 under the leadership of Jean-Marc Rouillan as a new revolutionary movement embracing elements of an anarchist group and a Maoist organisation. It attacked initially public and government buildings and property, but these events led to a French police anti-terrorist sweep which led to arrests and arms and explosives finds in many cities. Action Directe was in contact with the Basque separatist group ETA, as well as with militant Palestinian or pro-Palestinian groups operating in France. Former Brigate Rosse members and even Turkish refugees who had settled in France were attracted to membership of Action Directe. After a series of attacks of sabotage on computer equipment, it was proved that a group called Committee to Liquidate or Neutralise Computers (CLODO), was closely connected with Action Directe.

In September 1980, Rouillan and his female companion Nathalie Menignon were arrested in Paris; however, within months they and other terrorists benefited from a general amnesty for political prisoners declared by the incoming President Mitterrand. Soon the bombings restarted, coupled with robbing banks to finance the organisation's activities. Renewed arrests of suspected Action Directe members led to more arrests, which resulted in further bomb attacks which this time round were also directed at American and Israeli targets. As a result of this change of target, the French government announced the banning of Action Directe, adherence to which in itself thereby became a criminal offence. After further arrests the French authorities claimed to have firm evidence of links between Action Directe and militant anti-Zionist/pro-

Palestinian organisations with a presence in France. By 1983 the group had broken into factions, each with its own theoretical position.

By 1985–86 there were increasing threats to disrupt life in France, notably through bombings and shootings in Paris and other large cities. Notable successes of the group have included the killing of René Audran at the French Ministry of Defence in 1985, and in November 1986 the shooting of Georges Besse, the head of Renault, in retaliation for the killing by police of an AD member demonstrating outside the Renault car works in Paris earlier in the year.

Afghan guerrillas The world first became aware of the varied groups and strengths of the Afghan guerrillas after the Soviet invasion in 1979. This was rigorously opposed by a variety of Islamic and tribal movements and alliances. In spite of the strength of arms of the invading force, the guerrillas, or mujaheddin (holy warriors), have succeeded in conducting protracted warfare with very heavy casualties on each side. External support for the rebels has come from Pakistan, the United States and many Western European nations. By 1986 the mujaheddin controlled well over three-quarters of the country, including some of the towns. Soviet troops have suffered considerably at their hands and there have been large-scale desertions from the Afghan armed forces to the mujaheddin.

The mujaheddin alliances are varied in number and extent. The initial overall organisation of several guerrilla factions was the Islamic Alliance for the Liberation of Afghanistan created in 1980 but dissolved in 1981. The dissolution was due to deep divisions between the moderate factions, consisting of the Afghan National Liberation Front, and the National Islamic Front of Afghanistan, and the fundamentalist Muslim factions such as the Islamic Afghan Association and the Islamic Party. Another mujaheddin alliance consists of a merger of six guerrilla factions which first appeared in 1981 under the title of the Islamic Unity of the Mujaheddin of Afghanistan.

Mujaheddin organisations are as split and divided as the alliances. For example, the Islamic Party has two factions. One of these, led by Gulbuddin Hekmatyar, is the most well-armed and organised Peshawar-based guerrilla faction, which emphasises its own variety of a strict Sunni interpretation of Islam and is run in the style of an Islamic warlord. The other is led by Younes Khales, and is a group mainly supported by Pushtu tribesmen who have split from Hekmatyar's party. It is more traditionalist than fundamentalist. There is a group totally opposed to the Islamic Party, called Against Oppression and Tyranny, which has expressed opposition to Pushtu (Pathan) domination, especially in areas inhabited by ethnic minorities such as the Tadzhiks in Badakshan province in North East Afghanistan, who are Shia Muslims, distinct from the Sunni Muslim majority in Afghanistan. Two minor organisations are the Islamic Movement Organisation of Afghanistan, which seeks the establishment of an Islamic Republic of Afghanistan on the model of that of Iran; and the

Militant Front of Combatants of Afghanistan, a socialist front solely based inside Afghanistan (unlike other resistance movements which are represented in Pakistan). Rather unusually, there is a group of pro-Chinese communists opposed to the Soviet-backed regime in Kabul and also to the presence in Afghanistan of Soviet military forces.

Agca, Mehmet Ali Agca, a Turkish citizen, tried to kill the Pope in May 1981 in St Peter's Square in the Vatican City. Agca had been involved in a sophisticated programme for promoting destabilisation and terrorism in Turkey and elsewhere, with the ultimate aim of serving the political purposes of the Soviet Union and Warsaw Pact countries. Agca admitted that his goal was to fight against the Western democracies and destroy them. The reason for the terrorist activity was ideological.

In the summer of 1980 Agca had been brought to Syria by Teslim Tore, the head of Turkey's pro-communist People's Liberation Army. Here he was trained in the use of weapons, explosives, cold-war concepts, how to carry out coups d'état, and related revolutionary history. He met Bulgarian agents in Damascus, the capital of Syria (Bulgaria was seen as a country which could help Agca and his followers achieve their aims) and received money from them to deliver to two leftist labour groups in Turkey. The money was to be used to fund subversive activities. Working under the direct tutelage of Abuzer Ugurlu, a reputed Turkish mafia 'godfather' in Istanbul, Agca and his accomplices established an organisation with the specific political aims of undermining capitalism and of severing Turkey's ties with the West.

Agca developed a wide range of associations with a Turkish terrorist organisation, the Grey Wolves – both as a 'cover' and in order to draw rightist terrorists into supporting anti-Western goals. But he never became a Grey Wolf himself and did not join the outlawed National Action Party with which the Grey Wolves were associated (both are rightist groups led by Colonel Alpaslan Turkes). In spite of widespread leftist allegations that Agca had killed Abdi Ipecki, a liberal Istanbul newspaper editor, in 1979, at the instigation of the National Action Party, no link could be found. Ugurlu was in continual contact with Bulgarian agents working out of the Bulgarian Consulate in Istanbul. His alleged mafia operations involved the supply of arms to various factions throughout Turkey's political spectrum and to both right and left groups in Iran via Turkey. Along with Teslim Tore, one of Agca's closest associates in every phase of his activities was Oral Celik, a childhood friend who was also involved with the Bulgarians. Celik and Tore worked to place Turkey in the Soviet orbit. The Turkish Government reopened its case against Agca in early 1983, after the Italians had arrested Sergei Ivanov Antonov, a Bulgarian airline official living in Rome, and publicised the purported Bulgarian connection.

The Turkish investigation included detailed probing into the reputed Mafia operations of Ugurlu, who was extradited from West Germany to Turkey in March 1981 and was reported to have Bulgarian drug- and arms-smuggling connections going back to the 1960s. Only after some considerable time was a link suspected between Agca and Ugurlu, the Turkish mafia godfather.

Agca issued a threat against the Pope's life on his escape from prison in November 1979. Agca's explanation of the threat could help pinpoint when the plot to kill the Pope began to take shape. There is no reliable evidence that he was motivated by religion or Islamic fundamentalism in particular.

It is clear that Agca had close relations with the Bulgarians starting at least in 1978. Historical, inferential, and circumstantial evidence all tend to point in the same direction to explain the plot against John Paul II – towards Moscow. There is a strong probability that the Kremlin leadership and the KGB were the architects of the plot to kill John Paul II.

Algeria The Algerian civil war of the mid-1950s is often viewed as a model of guerrilla warfare. Over 1.5 million Algerians were killed or disappeared during the eight-year war of national liberation from November 1954 to May 1962. The war was fought with great cruelty on both sides. A third of the economic infra-structure of the country was destroyed during the war in the countryside and the vicious battles waged in the cities between the Front de Libération Nationale (FLN), a militant nationalist and originally only moderate Socialist movement founded in 1954, and the Organisation Armée Secrète (OAS). Over a million Europeans fled, immediately after the commencement of hostilities or during the last summer of the war in 1962, which meant the loss of many professional workers.

The French had ruled Algeria harshly for more than a century before the liberation war. French harshness toward, and degradation of the native population was compounded by the fact that military governors ruled the country for much of the nineteenth century, often using it as a testing ground of the army's prestige and as a vehicle of their own careers. The Colons, European settlers in Algeria many of whom were not themselves French, were constantly at odds with the military regime pressing for ever more exploitative policies toward the natives; and most of the Muslims refused to convert to Christianity or to assimilate fully the French culture, thus increasing the already lively disdain for them on the part of the metropolitan French, as well as of the Colons. These polarisations within Algerian society, which were accompanied by the expropriation of the best lands and retributive taxes, grew only more extreme when, during and after the First World War, the native labour force became deeply entangled in the French economy, the army and the factories and plantations of the Colons. The generations of stored resentment explain in part the savagery of the war and the harshness of the post-revolutionary regimes. Such an example of savagery occurred at the village of Melouza in 1957, where all the males were executed by the FLN for rebelling against FLN terrorism, supporting a rival nationalist group and also for co-operating with the French army. The FLN managed to

A

persuade most Muslims in Algeria that it was the French who had committed the murders in order to discredit the FLN.

The revolutionary theorist, Frantz Fanon (1925–1961), saw in his adopted country the need for violence as a cleansing force which unified the people, and he advocated terrorism as a tool for freeing the native from his feelings of inferiority, and from despair and inaction. Fanon argued that violence directed against oppressors made native populations fearless and restored their self-respect. He argued that when people had taken part in national liberation struggles they would allow no one to set themselves up as 'liberators'. Fanon was supported in his views by the FLN leader, Ouzegane, who suggested that terrorism fulfilled other functions internally, namely relieving the tension caused by inaction and controlling impatience among militants.

See also **Organisation Armée Secrète**

Angolan Civil War 1974–1976 In 1964 the wind of change had blown across most of black Africa, but Angola – the heartland of Portugal's African empire – appeared to be firmly and securely under Portugal's control. In Leopoldville (now Kinshasa), capital of what was then the Congo (now Zaire) were the rundown headquarters of what at the time appeared to be the chief Angolan liberation movement, the Revolutionary Government of Angola in Exile (GRAE). GRAE was run by Holden Roberto, whose brother-in-law was Joseph Mobutu, at that time commander-in-chief of the Congolese Army and soon to be the country's autocratic ruler.

Many members of the Portuguese Colonial Army and Portuguese settlers were killed in the early 1960s by Roberto's followers in the Bakongo tribe, who in turn suffered at the hands of the army.

Roberto had formed the first (forbidden) political parties in the Portuguese colony of Angola, and in 1962 had proclaimed the GRAE, with himself at its head. His advantage was that the Bakongo were a vigorous people who had tasted freedom and power in one part of their territories – Joseph Kasavubu, the Congo's first president, was a Bakongo – and were ready to struggle for it elsewhere. Kasavubu's disadvantage was that he represented only the Bakongo and the Bakongo were limited to the north of Angola. Only about one in ten of the six million Angolans were Bakongo. It was inevitable that other leaders should spring up elsewhere in that vast country to represent the other tribal or ethnic groups.

Jonas Savimbi defected from the GRAE in 1964, where he had been a close associate of Roberto, but was always playing second fiddle. He went to the south of Angola, to his own people the Ovimbundu, who were three times as numerous as the Bakongo in Angola; two years later he founded the Unido Nacional para a Independencia Total de Angola (UNITA). With the rival claim of UNITA it became hard for Roberto to maintain the fiction that he was leading a united government-in-exile. The GRAE gradually faded away, to be replaced by the more militant and

A

military Frente Nacional de Libertação de Angola (FNLA), also led by Roberto.

Another liberation movement on the Angola scene was a somewhat more sophisticated group, the Movimento Popular para a Libertação de Angola (MPLA). Founded in 1956, the MPLA was an urban movement, its greatest strength lying in the capital of the country, the port of Luanda, where half a million people (including 150,000 Portuguese) lived. It was a party of intellectuals and theorists, and very much influenced by marxism. There were many pure blacks in its ranks – led by a poet, Agostinho Neto. But there were many pure Portuguese in the party too, as well as *mestizos* (Angolans of mixed Portuguese-African blood), free from tribal links and loyalties.

Until 1974 the Portuguese hung on, but maintaining an army in Angola was a drain on resources. The FNLA was largely inactive and UNITA operated mainly in areas run by Portugal's white allies.

On 25 April 1974 the whole situation changed and in an almost bloodless revolution, the autocratic regime in Portugal was overthrown by the Armed Forces Movement and the anti-fascist 'Junta of National Salvation' took control of Portugal. Two months later Portugal offered independence to Angola, Mozambique and Guinea. Of the three, Angola proved a problem, and it was impossible to bring the warring factions together in a transitional government.

The Portuguese army had declined from its original position as a strong military force, and lost the will to fight – many of its soldiers supported the MPLA. The longer-established Portuguese, the settlers, artisans, tradesmen and rich minority of plantation owners, right-wing by both inclination and tradition, tended to support anyone who opposed the MPLA.

The Americans immediately gave direct and indirect support for the rival movements – Roberto's FNLA and, in the south, Savimbi's UNITA, to prevent at all costs another Western ex-colony being taken over by a pro-Soviet movement.

China gave support to the FNLA for anti-Soviet reasons; and in mid-1975, the Cubans became involved, with Soviet support, through a commando assault by sea on the UNITA-held port of Lobito and nearby railhead of Benguela. UNITA was pushed back into the interior. The Cuban leader, Fidel Castro, proceeded to pour in troops and money.

South Africa reacted by sending helicopters and troops across the border to protect the hydroelectric works at Ruacana. Fierce fighting raged in Luanda, where with Cuban help and Soviet arms, the MPLA attacked and destroyed the FNLA headquarters in the capital. The MPLA consolidated their hold and UNITA moved inland. Thousands of whites and *mestizos* fled the country; coffee, sisal and cotton crops went unpicked and the diamond industry collapsed. But the MPLA had perhaps reacted too soon, for Zaire gave more aid to the FNLA and South Africa gave more committed support to UNITA, and achieved success in the south. In the north, however, an FNLA move on the capital led to disaster. In the same month, November 1975, the MPLA proclaimed independence with Neto as President of the Democratic Republic in Luanda, while UNITA proclaimed independence at Nova Lisboa; and the FNLA proclaimed independence in Ambriz with Holden Roberto as President of the Democratic Republic. Despite South African-backed columns, and CIA intervention, Zaire still posed problems for the MPLA.

In despair Holden Roberto decided with CIA approval to switch tack, as he was concerned by the poor fighting qualities of the Zaireans, and hired sympathisers from Britain and America. These men showed great courage and ability in attacking the advancing Cuban and MPLA columns head on. Their leader Colonel Callan, a mercenary maintained discipline ultimately through execution; morale soon collapsed and Callan himself was captured. UNITA, under Savimbi, also suffered, and after a defeat at the hands of the MPLA the remnant retreated to the bush. By 1976 Roberto was safe in Kinshasa, but with all hopes destroyed; the Americans halted their operations and the South Africans withdrew from the Ruacana Dam.

The civil war was over and President Neto ruled the country. The captured mercenaries were put on trial and, amid a blaze of publicity, Callan and three others were executed. It was a triumph for the MPLA, for Castro and for the Russians; and a body blow not merely to Portuguese pride, but to South Africa, the CIA and the West in general.

Animal rights Increasingly, concern has been expressed by individuals and groups about the predicament of animals, especially those used in experiments. Groups can be concerned with general animal welfare, such as the Royal Society for the Prevention of Cruelty to Animals (RSPCA), or with animal rights, such as the Animal Liberation Front (ALF). The three main sectors within the animal rights groups are the established societies with huge funds which act within the law, the local animal rights groups existing in most towns, districts and universities, and extremist movements which are semi-clandestine and break the law. The leaders have motivation and ability – some are motivated genuinely for animal rights reasons, others are politically motivated and use animal rights as a means to an end; and lastly others are bored and frustrated and wish to make an impact on society. For this last group of people violence can become an addiction. Small demonstrations can be used as diversions for sinister activities by a larger group who desire to inflict economic damage on animal abusers.

Many of the groups have their own system of funding, often a newspaper, and are worth thousands or in some cases millions of pounds. In some groups there has been a radical challenge to seize control, and to become increasingly political.

The animal rights movement first developed on a wide scale in Western Europe and Scandinavia, and then spread to Britain and the United States.

Ultimately, members of some of these groups are willing to undertake widespread destruction and killing to try to achieve their aims. Some have sympathies with anarchists, and undertake widespread civil disobedience. The development of animal liberation groups in Britain represented a new and ugly extremist dimension in the operation of 'issue groups', prompting police to consider the establishment of a special squad to counter the increasingly violent activities of the groups. Extremist elements within the animal rights movement are actually indulging in acts of terrorism. Animal rights activists have used violence as a policy with the expressed intent of coercing the government to enact specific legislation. Fear is engendered by claims of poisoned sweets or other consumer goods, by abusive and threatening telephone calls, by the posting of letter bombs, the destruction of property, or even aggressive slogans painted on walls. Some members of the Animal Liberation Front do wish to change government policy by violent, undemocratic and illegal means. The Front believes in coercive intimidation, of which law-breaking has been an unavoidable consequence. Animal welfare is a popular cause, and there are few who are so inhumane as not to espouse its general aims. But the extremist animal rights movement provides an avenue for those who do seek to disrupt the stability of the nation. The Front is structured in a network of cells, each independent and in contact only by a liaison representative. It is secretive and conspiratorial. The style of dress worn during raids – hoods, camouflage smocks or coveralls – and the use of pickhandles and the hazardous items point to an emulation of urban guerrillas. Terror tactics are employed – breaking and entering in a violent manner and the flouting of the law. Front propaganda is disseminated by recognised terrorist groups. The outrages committed by extremist behaviour bring media attention and perhaps encourage recruiting.

The reality is that frustration evoked by perceived public apathy or revulsion could prompt the militant fringe to opt for a campaign of excesses, attacks and raids which could result in death. Future possibilities are varied. Amateur animal rights supporters wishing to become dedicated to the cause, or individuals who do not have formal association with the movement, could carry out illegal acts similar to those undertaken by the Animal Liberation Front membership. An individual could also act rashly merely on the basis that 'righteousness' of the cause permits it.

Anti-Semitic terrorism in Europe From being a particular problem associated with the creation of the Israeli state and attacks on Jews in that country, Palestine and other Arab countries, anti-Semitic terrorism has spread in the last decade to include a wide range of Jewish targets in Europe. Seventeen West European countries have been affected, with the highest proportion of attacks in Britain, France and West Germany. Most of the attacks have been targeted against Israeli facilities or citizens and the rest against local Jewish community institutions, or Jewish individuals. Well over a quarter of all attacks against Jews and Israelis in Europe involved people rather than property, and such attacks were

A

obviously intended to cause casualties. The greatest number of attacks have been carried out by perpetrators connected with Palestinian terrorist organisations.

Jewish communities in Europe tend to keep log books of anti-Semitic events and rely on the direct reporting of local organisations and private persons who may have received threatening phone calls, abusive letters or whose property might have been daubed with anti-semitic graffiti, swastikas, etc.

Jewish public awareness of the necessity to report every single anti-Semitic occurrence may differ from country to country; and many smaller incidents can remain unreported. The high number of reported general anti-Semitic incidents in the UK is probably due to a combination of a particular community awareness as well as a professional and conscientious attitude towards establishing a proper record of incidents. For instance, the daubing of synagogues and the desecration of cemeteries deeply affect the feelings of Jews. Unrelated spontaneous acts of simple prejudice, violent as they may be, are still of a different class from pre-planned terrorist atrocities requiring the acquisition of a weapon or the handling of explosive charges.

Only rarely in these anti-Semitic attacks have the perpetrators been apprehended on the spot. Armed attacks have almost always lasted less than four minutes, and the perpetrators have been able to use the public confusion in the wake of the attack to escape. Most of the more serious attacks have been carried out by the radical non-mainline Palestinian groups who oppose Arafat's ban on international terrorism, such as the operatives of Abu Nidal, the Lebanese Armed Revolutionary Faction, the Black June group, 15 May etc., who have increased their level of activity against Jewish targets. Whether some of the less conspicuous attacks, such as arson attempts on synagogues and Jewish-owned shops, which are often accompanied by night-time Nazi-type daubings, are necessarily of right-wing origin is only speculative. Theories have also circulated about the activities of the French group Action Directe, to the effect that a hard-core faction may indulge in deadly terrorism against Israeli or Jewish targets, whereas a more moderate faction would decide to hit only at 'economic' targets such as trade and banking agencies.

See also **Federation of National and European Action**

April 19 Movement (M-19) Formed in Colombia in 1974, the M-19 took its name from the date on which ex-President General Rojas Pinilla, the leader of the National Popular Alliance, had been defeated in the 1970 presidential elections. The M-19 claimed to be the armed wing of the ANAPO – the National Popular Alliance – although the latter rejected this claim. While ANAPO was a hierarchically organised party standing for 'Colombian socialism' on a Christian socialist basis, by the end of the 1970s the M-19 came to be regarded as left-wing and Marxist, and its leaders declared as its aim the achievement of a democratic and ultimately socialist state by political means. Initial operations included thefts and

A

kidnappings and it was reported to have declared war in 1978 on the government of President Ayala, which had introduced increased penalties for acts of violence such as armed rebellion, kidnapping and bombing. Seizure of weapons was a common feature of the M-19's activities.

Major M-19 operations in 1980 included the temporary occupation of the embassy of the Dominican Republic in Bogotá from February to April 1980, when M-19 guerrillas seized 57 hostages, including the ambassadors of 14 countries – among them those of Israel, Mexico and the USA – as well as the papal nuncio. The demands originally made by the kidnappers for the release of the hostages were in protracted negotiations involving, among other intermediaries, the Inter-American Human Rights Commission (IHRC) of the Organisation of American States, and were eventually reduced to payment of a ransom of $10,000,000 and the release of 28 political detainees. The guerrillas accepted assurances that the trials of M-19 suspects would be monitored by IHRC observers, and left by air for Havana on 27 April, taking with them the 12 remaining hostages (who were later released in Cuba). All other hostages had been freed in stages during the negotiations and one of the guerrillas was killed in a shooting incident at the beginning of the action. The ransom eventually paid amounted to $2,500,000.

Later the M-19 continued to engage in numerous acts of violence, including bomb attacks, hijackings and even the interruption of television broadcasts in 1980, and increased violence in Bogotá. Two amnesties announced by the government against the guerrillas were rejected, because such an amnesty did not include those who had carried out murders and kidnappings. Recommendations by a Peace Commission set up by the government that the government should enter into direct negotiations with M-19 leaders were rejected by the Government (owing to opposition by the armed forces and certain political sectors), and when they rejected another of the Commission's recommendations (to suspend sentences imposed on guerrillas), five of the Commission's members resigned.

In 1982 a further amnesty appeared to have more success, because it covered those convicted of sedition, conspiracy and rebellion. The political command of M-19 had talks with the Interior Minister with a view to obtaining a 'social justice guarantee' before M-19 laid down its arms. Kidnappings still continue to the present, including the kidnap of a banker's daughter in 1983, and more spectacularly in 1985, the holding in the Supreme Court in Bogotá of judges involved in justice trials against M-19. This resulted in the army storming the law building and the deaths of 50 people, including the leader of M-19 and the Chief Justice of Colombia.

Argentina The Republic of Argentina, like Peru, has been ruled by alternating military juntas and democratic governments since its independence in 1810. The juntas have taken particularly strong action against corrupt civilian rulers, students, trade unions and members of the Catholic Church. In 1970 the death penalty was reintroduced in Argentina for the first time since 1886, and can apply to those caught attacking the security forces, judiciary or public officials, as well as for the kidnapping and disrupting of transport if it had subversive motives or resulted in death or serious injury. With the restoration of democracy (after the Falklands War) in 1983, all political parties were required to re-register; to obtain official recognition each party was to have at least 35,000 members and adequate representation in at least five provinces, while all parties which denied human rights or advocated the replacement of the democratic system, the illegal and systematic use of force and personal concentration of power, were prohibited.

During the heyday of the right-wing juntas in the 1960s and 1970s, many thousands of people disappeared, and thousands more were deprived of legal rights or tortured. In this connection two human rights groups were set up: the Grandmothers of the Plaza del Mayo, and the Mothers of the Plaza del Mayo. The former pressed the government for information about children who had been abducted with their parents or had been born in prison; the latter protested against the absence of any official explanation for those thousands of persons who had disappeared. By 1983 the vigils in the Plaza del Mayo in Buenos Aires had developed into more pronounced anti-government demonstrations.

Of left-wing movements the Montoneros was the most active. It is a left-wing Peronist urban guerrilla group which acted from 1970 as an armed branch of the Argentinian Communist Party, and seeks a social revolution, while its ideological position is pro-Cuban. It once had some 5,000 members with 15,000 active sympathisers, but now numbers of supporters are below 400.

One of the first major actions of the Montoneros was the kidnapping of the two directors of the country's largest firm of grain dealers. They were released in 1975 after nine months' captivity, on payment of 60 million dollars in ransom and distribution of one million dollars worth of food and clothing to the poor; and the publication of a statement of continuing resistance to the government to expose its anti-popular, repressive and pro-imperialist stance. They have attacked the armed forces' equipment and personnel; kidnapped and assassinated foreign business executives; attacked the police academy; and after the arrest of many of their members, the Montoneros started to inflict casualties in ever increasing numbers on the military. In 1977 it was confirmed that a group of Argentinian financiers had been financing the Montoneros by investing 17 million dollars and securing interest of about 130,000 dollars a month on their behalf. The same year witnessed the arrest of a prominent newspaper editor on suspicion of being connected with the Montoneros – ultimately he was expelled from the country.

In view of these events, it was surprising that a pacification and liberation programme was announced by the government in 1977; it did not put an end to the armed struggle, but was an appeal to the common sense of all political and social groups. There was a call for a new economic policy, the restoration of constitutional rights, the rehabilitation of all political parties, the liberation of all political prisoners, the closure of concentration camps, the institution of proceedings against those responsible for torture, kidnappings and murder, and the holding of elections.

Despite declining numbers, by the early 1980s there was evidence that a small number of Montoneros were being trained in guerrilla warfare in Palestine Liberation Organisation camps in Syria and Lebanon. In 1980 a dissident faction, '17 October Montoneros' was formed, named after the date of the mass mobilisation which started the Peronist movement in 1945, and 'completely committed to insurrection'.

The People's Revolutionary Army (ERP) was also active in the 1970s as an armed branch of the Workers' Revolutionary Party, with a rural front in the Catamarca and Tucaman provinces in North-West Argentina. Initially the group killed businessmen as well as servicemen and newspaper editors; but in the mid 1970s changed its tactics from not attacking the government unless the latter attacked the people or repressed the guerrillas, to pursuing hostilities against foreign and national enterprises and against the counter-revolutionary armed forces. By the late 1970s ERP had increasingly suffered losses at the hands of the government, and a Trotskyite guerrilla movement also calling itself the People's Revolutionary Army was formed.

The chief right-wing organisation is the Argentinian Anti-Communist Alliance, established in 1973 and taking action against communists and all leftists. Until 1976 it killed many politicians named on its hit-list, but since then activities have declined. The anti-Semitic organisation, the Argentinian National Socialist Front, attributes the cause of Argentina's problems to 'Jewish-Bolshevist plutocracy'.

Armenian Secret Army for the Liberation of Armenia (ASALA)

Founded in 1975, ASALA is a clandestine Marxist-Leninist terrorist organisation structured on a cellular basis. The group wants to revenge the massacre of more than a million Armenians in Turkish Armenia during 1915–16, and to have Turkey admit responsibility for the killings. Specifically, it wants to end to Turkish discrimination against Armenians, official Turkish recognition of the Armenian language, and the creation of an independent Armenian state. Although ASALA's declared objective is the liberation of Armenia, many in the group believe that the Soviet part of Armenia, the Armenian Soviet Socialist Republic, is 'liberated' and constitutes no problem. ASALA is strongly anti-American and has described the Turkish state as having a 'fascist regime', and it seeks to co-operate with the left-wing Kurdish movement. It regards the Armenian question as a product of 'imperialist conflicts' and therefore attacks imperialism wherever it may be.

Its strategy has been to murder Turkish diplomats in Western Europe and North America; by mid 1982 it had killed 24 Turkish officials abroad and carried out over 100 bombings against Turkish targets in most major

European capitals. ASALA is deeply permeated by a spirit of revenge for the earlier massacre of Armenians. It probably has its headquarters in Beirut and its chief members are Ara Yenikomoushian and Hagon Hagonian, respectively the military leader and main spokesman. The latter probably died during the Israeli bombardments on Beirut in June 1982. In 1981 alone it carried out 40 attacks in 11 countries. Under cover names it has attacked Swiss interests in retaliation for the arrest of ASALA members, and, using the name Orly Organisation, it attacked French interests in retaliation for the arrests of Armenians carrying false passports in France.

See also **Armenian terrorism**

Armenian terrorism During the First World War, the Government of the Ottoman Empire decided in August 1915 to 'solve the Armenian question once and for all' by exterminating the (Christian) Armenians. The action which followed and which was later described by Armenians as systematic genocide, resulted in the deaths of some 1,400,000 people and the flight of the survivors from Turkey, half of them to the Russian part of Armenia and the remainder to Middle East countries, Europe and North America. By the mid 1980s the number of Armenians was estimated at 6,000,000, of whom some 2,800,000 lived in the Armenian Soviet Socialist Republic, about 200,000 in Lebanon, about the same number in France and some 500,000 in the USA. While many of these Armenians became assimilated to the peoples of the countries to which they had moved, others maintained their own culture and associations and their adherence to the Armenian Catholic Church. It was only in the third generation since the events of 1915 that a demand was raised by Armenians for the establishment of a united and independent Armenia (which some of them wanted to be socialist). In France the Committee for the Defence of the Armenian Cause was set up in 1965; and in Lebanon Armenians first began to commit acts of violence directly related to their cause in the 1970s.

The organisations subsequently formed to conduct 'warfare' against the Turkish authorities represent, however, only a minority of the Armenian people. Many Armenian organisations repeatedly condemn those of their fellow countrymen engaged in acts of violence. The Turkish Government, on the other hand, has not given in to the demands made by the militant Armenians and consistently refuses to accept any responsibility for the 1915 events.

The best known of the groups is the Armenian Secret Army for the Liberation of Armenia (ASALA), but there are other principally Armenian groups responsible for violent activities. The Armenian Liberation Army describes its objective as the restoration of autonomy for the Armenian areas of Eastern Turkey. The Armenian Liberation Movement was set up by Armenians in France to support ASALA. In 1982, in a clandestine radio programme, the newly-created Armenian National Liberation Movement declared 'the necessity of armed resistance against the enemy

– the Turkish Government', and undertook heavy attacks against alleged imperialists, Zionists and reactionaries.

Probably the most sinister of the groups is the Justice Commandos for the Armenian Genocide, established in 1975, which has claimed responsibility for the deaths of Turkish diplomats in various countries; and it also aims to denounce the callous indifference of the so-called civilised world to the fate of the Armenians.

The Republican Armenian Army, formed in 1970, has called for the liberation of all Armenian areas of Turkey and the Soviet Union, and for the creation of an independent Armenian state. This group has also pledged its solidarity with the Palestine Liberation Organisation in its struggle for the rights of the Palestinian people.

Switzerland in particular has come to face the wrath of a number of groups in view of its tough stance against Armenians captured for violent acts – groups involved here include the Committee for Aid to Armenian Political Prisoners, the New Armenian Resistance Group, the Organisation of 9 June, the Organisation of 3 October, and Suisse XV.

See also **Armenian Secret Army for the Liberation of Armenia**

Army-police co-operation In a liberal democracy when the subject of co-operation against terrorism is broached in army or police circles, the usual response is that an armed policeman is not a soldier and a soldier is not an armed policeman. Any response to terrorism must be acceptable to the government of the day, but it is also important that the response is acceptable to the public and the police, since the police function in a democracy rests on the consent of the citizens to be policed.

Effective police work against terrorism depends on intelligence, and intelligence depends on public co-operation. In Britain, the government has the power to requisition troops when a threat to order has developed beyond the capacity of the police to deal with it. In general, the police role is one of keeping the peace by the use of traditional procedures and legal machinery, whereby in a democratic society lawlessness is contained and processes are controlled by methods acceptable to the public as a whole. Conversely, the soldier is the embodiment of the ultimate sanction of force necessary to every government for protection from external attack or dealing with domestic extremist activities. The army does not act, as a police force does, on behalf of the community as a whole, but on the orders of its political masters to whom it is accountable through its command structure. In Britain, military aid to the police is restricted to very small numbers of troops, strictly limited in purpose and short-lived in duration. There is a consensus view that army-police emergency measures should be kept at a minimum as there are dangers of doing the terrorists' work for them by alienating the host community, escalating the conflict and eroding democracy in the cause of security. The military can never come to the aid of the civil power without the permission of the government of the day. Modern democratic governments prefer to rely on the police to handle disorder because it reduces the chances of

A

politicisation of the military. An army is not fitted or trained to sustain a police role at least not as a permanent function in conjunction with military duties.

There has traditionally been a dichotomy between civil and military relations. Free societies have faced the eternal balancing task of harmonising liberty and national security. Preserving such a balance has been complicated by the fact that the one institution indispensable to the nation's security, the military, exercises a power not necessarily in harmony with an open democratic society. Ulster shows that it is hard to deny that since the government in a democracy should have the monopoly of armed power, the military should be regarded as the backup to maintain the rule of law.

Democratic countries prove that a soldier can do nothing useful to combat terrorism, suppress insurrection and assist or substitute for the police unless he is given the necessary legal powers to do so. The army is conscious of its constitutional subordination to the law, and will do nothing that it is not authorised lawfully to do. If a soldier has to substitute for a policeman, he has to be given the powers to make this substitution effective.

There are differences between civil police forces and the armed services – in approach, and purpose, and accountability. There is a difference between counter-revolutionary warfare and keeping the peace. The military are necessary to prevent the overthrow of lawful government by force, for only they are fitted by equipment and training to suppress force by force. Police officers keep the peace using old, complex, and sensitive procedures whereby in a democratic society lawlessness is contained and excesses controlled by the avoidance of arbitrary force. In the West, such force can only be used with the approval of courts and public opinion. There are advantages to the state in having several police forces, which increasingly are more heavily armed, in particular that they enable most disorders to be contained without calling out the regular army.

Throughout the democracies, people reject the idea of a military-style police force (a third force) but believe small numbers of troops have to be involved in any plan for military aid where loss of life might be minimised in situations involving terrorists or political fanatics.

Populations in democracies clamour for the maintenance of a balance between civil liberties and efficient policing, and to draw distinctions between the right to protest and actions to undermine the government of the day. Mutual understanding in democracies between police and army is improved only by army acceptance that there can be no quick solution to the troubles, as has been experienced in Kenya, Cyprus and Ulster.

An army built up in a staunchly democratic society has a direct idea of its role in countering terrorism, and must tread the fine balance between over-reaction and pusillanimity, or effeteness. It would be hard for the civil power to become overdependent upon the army's presence, especially with all the constraints imposed by a democratic way of life.

States need constitutional organisation and policing laws that make mastery of terrorism possible. Modern governments prefer to rely on the police to handle disorder because it reduces the chances of disagreement with the military about their role.

ASALA
See **Armenian Secret Army for the Liberation of Armenia**

Assassination Assassination can be described as murder for a political end by the disinterested agent of a revolutionary cause. Throughout history – ever since it was first used in Persia in 1092 – it has been justified or even urged as a revolutionary means by a number of respectable and considerable authorities.

During the century before 1870 there were more than a score of revolutionary assassinations in Europe, but the high point in political, usually revolutionary, assassination began about 1865 and notable victims included three American Presidents – Lincoln, Garfield and McKinley, and a British Secretary for Ireland. Assassination tended to be used by revolutionaries chiefly when no other means of overthrowing the Establishment seemed open to them; it was favoured by anarchists and nihilists, but in general repudiated by socialists and communists.

Over the past decade there has been a large increase in assassinations and attempted assassinations. International terrorist groups have engaged in numerous types of acts to increase public awareness of their causes, and above all, they have been willing to assassinate government leaders for blatant political purposes.

In general, developed countries have tended to experience lower levels of political unrest and assassination than less-developed countries. Most of the assassination events in the 1960s and 1970s occurred in nations that are primarily agricultural. The United States and France appear as notable exceptions to this rule.

See also **Assassins**

Assassins As a political weapon, terrorism was first exclusively used during the twelfth and thirteenth centuries by a secret medieval dissident Islamic religious order, popularly known as the Assassins.

The term itself is derived from the Arabic and translates literally as 'hashish-eater', or 'one addicted to hashish'. This group of sectarian Muslim fanatics, who often acted under the influence of intoxicating drugs, was employed by its spiritual leaders to spread terror in the form of violence and murder among prominent Christians and other religious enemies. These zealots were, in effect, the first terrorist armed bands, and their fearsome activities entered European folklore by way of the returning crusaders and the writings of Marco Polo. Ultimately, they were destroyed by the Mongol invaders, but their use of murder as a political instrument provided a grim inheritance for the modern world.

Assassin is now a common noun in most European languages, and from the time of their enigmatic founder, the legendary 'Old Man of the

Mountain', they were the first group to make planned, systematic, and long-term use of murder as a political weapon – and their ideals and activities have since had many adherents.

They were able to turn their reputation to good account. Under threat of assassination they exacted payments from both Muslim and Christian rulers in the Levant in the thirteenth century. The end of the power of the Assassins came under the double assault of the Mongols and of the Mameluke Sultan of Egypt, Baybars.

The Ismaili Assassins did not invent assassination; they merely lent their name. Murder as such is as old as the human race. It is significant that in all their murders, in both Persia and Syria, the Assassins always used a dagger, never poison, and never missiles, though there must have been occasions when these would have been easier and safer. The Assassin was almost always caught, and usually made no attempt to escape; there was even a suggestion that to survive a 'mission' was shameful.

It was the loyalty of the Assassins, who risked and even courted death for their master, that attracted the attention of Europe and made their name a byword for faith and self-sacrifice before it became a synonym for murderer. The victims of Assassins belonged to two main groups – the first being made up of princes, officers and ministers, the second of *gadis* and other religious dignitaries.

Concerning the place of the Assassins in the history of Islam, four things may be said with reasonable assurance. Firstly their movement, whatever its driving force may have been, was regarded as a profound threat to the existing order, political, social and religious; the second is that they are no isolated phenomenon, but one of a long series of Messianic movements, at once popular and obscure, impelled by deep-rooted anxieties, and occasionally exploding in outbreaks of revolutionary violence. There was a reshaping and redirecting of the vague desires, wild beliefs and aimless rage of the discontented into an ideology and an organisation which, in cohesion, discipline and purposive violence, have no parallel in earlier or in later times. Ultimately the most significant point was their final total failure. They did not overthrow the existing order; they did not even succeed in holding a single city of any size. Yet the undercurrent of Messianic hope and revolutionary violence which had impelled them flowed on and their ideals and methods found many imitators. For these idealists the great changes of our time have provided new causes for anger, new dreams of fulfilment and new tools of attack.

Attacks by terrorists There are a number of criteria which are necessary for a successful terrorist attack or an incident fomented by a group.

Sufficient hardware, explosives and weapons are required, generally available from the United States and certain West European countries. Military and criminal skills, leadership or training are widely used and can be obtained in the United States. Intelligence and current knowledge of the target can be a weak point in the terrorist preparation. Inside assistance from someone who has knowledge of the target's schedule and routine (a fifth column type) is generally not available to terrorists. Ultimately, dedication, a 'do or die' attitude towards success, is not found among terrorist groups, with the exception of the Japanese Red Army.

The more popular motivation factors are the achievement of a political goal, the need for publicity and attention, the erosion of political stability, the need to redress grievances, the desire to liberate colleagues in foreign jails, and money to buy arms. The cost-effectiveness of attacks is mainly dependent on the chance of major publicity, the probability of gaining hostages, safe passage as sole demand, and of escaping punishment or death.

B

B

Basque nationalism Political violence is a constant in Spain's historical development. Francoism itself emerged as a result of the Civil War in Spain (1936–1939). Francoism was in its turn soon attacked by the communist guerrilla fighters of the *maquis*. Sporadic actions either of an anarchist character or of groups like DRIL (Iberian Revolutionary Directorate of Liberation) were also points of violent resistance to the dictatorship. But it was in 1959 that Euskadi ta Askatasuna (ETA), or Euskadi and Freedom, which would become the fatal protagonist of terrorism during the political transition, first began its activities on a small scale. Its French equivalent is Iparretarrak, formed in 1973. Although it became violent in 1976, its acts have been few and far between. Emerging from a generational changeover in Basque nationalism and carrying out a radical redefining of this nationalism, ETA planted their first bomb in July 1961. Both men and material were limited; but in May 1962 it celebrated its first assembly where it defined itself as the Basque revolutionary movement of national liberation created in patriotic resistance. It considered the armed struggle as the only possible action against Francoist repression. Insurrection was viewed as a rational weapon when the oppression eliminated all the other means. ETA believed that a critical moment in nationalism had arrived – namely millenarianism, which attributes an absolute value to the political objective of national independence.

In the view of ETA, the recourse to violence and terrorism had ideological justification. By 1970 the repressive policies of the state had caused ravage among the militants which, together with a lack of cohesion internally, provoked a situation almost of hopelessness. However, the power of Francoism shown at the Burgos trial made ETA rise from its ashes. This trial, in late 1970, tried 16 Basque nationalists accused of banditry, military rebellion and terrorism. Owing to the internal situation of the Franco regime, the national and international repercussions of the event were extraordinary. Francoism fuelled support for ETA, while quite a large part of Spanish public opinion felt a sympathy towards the clandestine organisation in the false conviction that it was a group of youths carrying out a stronger resistance against an ominous dictator. However, ETA was fighting against Spain and not just Franco, and this was highlighted by their greatest success in terms of publicity and propaganda: namely the murder of the Spanish Prime Minister, Admiral Carrero Blanco, in 1973.

Nevertheless, although the armed struggle was still not questioned in

ETA, the growing autonomy and importance of the military sector became unendurable for the pro-worker sector of the group. By late 1974 the break between ETA political military (ETA p-m) and military ETA (ETAm) became definitive. For the latter the armed struggle was the exclusive method, whereas for the former this was combined with other types of political action.

At this time FRAP (Frente Revolucionario Antifascista y Patriótico) proclaimed its existence, a left-wing Maoist group especially active in the 1970s. It had come from the Communist Party of Spain (Marxist-Leninist). Anarchist-inspired and short-lived organisations arose, such as the MIL (Iberian Liberation Movement), one of whose members was condemned to death and executed. Other extreme right groups also emerged in Spain: Warriors of Christ the King, ATE (Anti-terrorism ETA), Triple A, and Spanish Basque Battalion.

Political violence in the Basque country appears more and more connected not with movements proposing social-political change but with an organisation which pretends to be more and more openly military. The definitive separation between the two factions of ETA came about when the party supported by the military branch decided to present itself at the first general election in the post-Franco era in 1977. Some of the extreme militants at this time created a new terrorist group, Los Comandos Autónomos Anticapitalistas. Other groups, such as MPAIAC (Movement for Self-Determination and Independence of the Canaries Archipelago) and GRAPO (First of October Anti-Fascist Resistance Group), and the extreme right all added to the domestic problems. The gangster-like activity of these last mentioned revealed a plan for political destabilisation which reached its maximum point with the murder of five lawyers, specialists in labour cases, in Madrid. By 1977, with FRAP virtually broken up, GRAPO emerged strongly, with its declared objective to prevent the perpetuation of Franco.

With the onset of democracy, Spanish society became bent on conciliatory moderation. Violence became more and more associated with intransigence. With the foundations for Spanish political life set up, a new period of consolidation began. As the political transformations accelerated, terrorism became more FRAP-oriented. The Basque groups benefited from a broadening of the machinery for economic extortion and from other changes in methods of operation. The deaths of an army general and of senior police chiefs in 1978 began a strategy of provocation directed against the army and aimed at feeding the temptations of the hotheads in certain sectors of the army bureaucracy.

Throughout, the terrorism of ETA has been inseparable from the Basque question. From Basque nationalism, ETA extracted a delegitimising vision of the State, and the hostile attitude necessary for the will to fight. There would be no neutral non-belligerents, only patriots and traitors.

In practice the main difference between terrorism that is essentially nationalistic, and other versions is found in the degree of support from the population; active support, passive support or ambiguous neutrality.

23

Thus one had the Statute of Autonomy accepted by political-military ETA and rejected by military ETA.

See also **Carrero Blanco, Peaceful end to terrorism**

Beirut hijack The hijacking of a US Trans-World Airlines 727 plane en route from Athens to Rome by two Lebanese Shi'a Moslems on 14 June 1985, and the subsequent murder of one American passenger and the detention of others by Shi'a militiamen in Beirut preoccupied the US administration until the release of the last 39 hostages on 30 June 1985.

The crisis was seen as paralleling that which had confronted President Carter during 1979–81 when 52 US hostages were held for 444 days in Teheran, Iran, before their release on 20 January 1981, the date of Reagan's inauguration as President. As on that occasion, the crisis proved a subject of consuming interest for the US media; the administration, despite a deliberate intention to avoid creating the appearance of being unable to give effective attention to other issues, was forced largely to abandon other matters while it lasted. Nevertheless the early resolution of the Beirut crisis ensured that Reagan did not experience the loss of authority which Carter had suffered as a consequence of the Teheran affair and which had been seen as a principal factor in his electoral defeat in November 1980.

A notable feature of the crisis was the role played by the American television networks. These were criticised by some, including a number of eminent journalists, for having entered into a 'symbiotic relationship' with the Shi'a militiamen, exchanging access to the prisoners for publicity (which was seen as the lifeblood of terrorist activity), and broadcasting unedited interviews with the prisoners who were being held at gunpoint, in which the prisoners appeared to express gratitude to their guards for good treatment and to extend sympathy for their cause. Television journalists did not tax the militiamen with questions deemed likely to inflame the situation, and there were rumours, denied by the networks, that payments had been made to guards to obtain interviews with the hostages.

See also **Teheran Embassy Siege**

Beliefs of terrorists The actions of terrorist organisations are based on a subjective interpretation of reality that differs from the perceptions of the governments and societies they confront. The actions of terrorists are not governed by a consistency and reason that are based on accurate perceptions of reality; one of the aims of terrorist organisations is to convince their audiences to see the world as they do. An important aspect of the struggle between governments and terrorists concerns the definition of the conflict. Each side wishes to interpret the issues in terms of its own standards of political legitimacy. Belief systems composed of dominant images, symbols and myths contribute to perceptions (and misperceptions) which determine actions and expectations. The content and origin of terrorist beliefs affect why and how terrorist strategies are adopted, terrorist reactions to government policies, and the outcomes of terrorist challenges.

Systems of beliefs may be derived from numerous sources. The political and social environment in which the terrorist organisation operates comprises one set of origins. In this category can be included general culture variables (history, tradition, literature, religion), which are imparted to individual members of society through socialisation patterns, and formal ideologies, which are acquired in young adulthood and are consciously borrowed.

Sources of beliefs may also be internal. The situation in which terrorists operate is filled with stress and uncertainty, making particular beliefs relevant and satisfying and also persistent and hard to change. Both the mental stress and the ideological commitment inherent in terrorism encourage reliance on a rigid set of beliefs and inhibit flexibility and openness. Terrorists may be rational about convictions that the majority of society sees as deluded.

A significant element in the belief system is the image, which can be a mental portrayal of oneself, of another actor, or of the world. Images are frequently stereotypical, falling into preconceived and rigid categories that simplify reality. Dehumanisation and deification of the enemy dominate thinking. The enemy is perceived in depersonalised and abstract terms such as 'bourgeoisie capitalism', Communism or imperialism. The enemy is a monolithic and impersonal system. In a group such as the Red Army Faction (RAF), the present West German government is condemned by being identified indiscriminately with the Nazi regime. Right-wing terrorists seem less likely to see the government as an enemy, but instead are prone to class or ethnic attributions. In Latin America, intellectuals and professionals such as lawyers or journalists are lumped together as the Left, or Communists. Eurofascist groups in Western Europe struggle against 'capitalism' and 'Marxism'.

Most leftist revolutionary terrorists see themselves not as aggressors but as victims. Their self-perception is that they are representatives of the oppressed – workers or peasants – who are unable to help themselves. They are the enlightened among the mass of unenlightened; the elect, who recognise dangers that the masses do not. The struggle is an obligation and a duty, not a matter of voluntary choice. Often they think of themselves as morally superior, more sensitive, and more noble. In their self-definition, the term 'terrorist' has become a subjective label applied by the enemy, and as global values have changed in the aftermath of anti-colonial struggles the image of 'freedom fighter' or 'national liberation front' has become a superior legitimising device. Many terrorists define their role as that of sacrificial victim; whether or not this image accords with reality, the notion of being willing to die for a cause is important to the terrorist's self-perception. Revolutionary terrorists often see the enemy as much more powerful than themselves, with many alternatives to choose from; terrorists have no course of action but terrorism, which they see as a response to government oppression, not a free choice on their part.

Two other aspects of terrorists' beliefs about the nature of the conflict

B

are intriguing. The first is the tendency to define the struggle in elaborately legalistic terms. They do not see what they are doing as murder or killing – instead they perform 'executions after trials'. Their victims are usually termed traitors. If they are kidnapped they are held in people's prisons. A second feature of the terrorists' view of struggle is their military imagery and symbolism.

Although terrorists appeal to popular support and often seem to believe that mass revolution is their goal, little attention is devoted to the development of beliefs about the role of popular support. As exemplified by the Basque terrorist organisation, ETA, the inevitability of support is assumed. For terrorists, victims among the 'enemy' are not seen as individuals but as representatives of the hostile group. If terrorists admit that innocent victims exist, they may blame the government either for refusing to concede their demands or ignoring warnings. They often refuse to accept responsibility for violence. Any action in the service of the cause can be interpreted as a success. There can be no failure if all violence brings the desired change nearer.

A significant source for terrorists' beliefs is the political and social environment from which the group springs, and often its historical context. Ideology is a powerful influence – an international factor that cuts across national situations but may be interpreted differently in specific circumstances. The primacy of political ideas in motivating terrorism contributes to the resemblances one finds among terrorist groups from different cultural contexts.

In certain cases terrorism reflects social reality – in nationalistic groups individuals are already socialised into patterns of thinking that can make violence acceptable if it appears feasible and productive: Basque resistance to the Spanish state, Armenian opposition to the Turks, and Irish Catholic bitterness toward the British are integral parts of their respective political cultures.

With regard to ideologies, terrorists are not inventors of these, as they tend to be action-oriented rather than philosophical. Some terrorist leaders, however, have been intellectuals and many groups, such as the RAF, spend inordinate amounts of time debating ideological issues. The fact that nationalism and national liberation are now the greatest sources of political legitimacy in the post-colonial world has contributed to the growth of terrorism. Both Marxist-Leninism (with variants of Trotskyism, Maoism, Castroism or Guevarism), and Fascism have contributed to terrorist doctrine. Although the individual violence associated with terrorism is not condoned by orthodox Marxists, many contemporary terrorists feel obliged to aid the force of historical progress with violence.

Some commentators have argued that many terrorists are in fact ambivalent about the use of violence. This internal conflict may explain why it is necessary for terrorists to believe that they have no choice and that the enemy bears ultimate responsibility for violence. The structure of the terrorist belief system, portraying an all-powerful authority figure relentlessly hostile to a smaller, powerless victim may reflect early relationships with parents, particularly of sons with fathers. Their beliefs may reflect feelings of inferiority, low self-esteem and helplessness.

To many terrorists the neutralisation of guilt is important. The individual who becomes a terrorist is likely to experience guilt for violent acts, so it is necessary for terrorists to maintain the belief that someone else is responsible and that their actions transcend normal standards of moral behaviour.

Once established, belief systems are resistant to change. For example, terrorists deny that there are innocent victims, despite proof to the contrary. Terrorists tend to believe only information sources they trust. Certain types of images can help terrorists to avoid dealing with the complex values inherent in political decisions. The 'inherent bad faith' model of the enemy indicates that the adversary never acts in good faith. Any apparently conciliatory gesture is interpreted as an attempt to deceive.

In hostage seizures, terrorists are involved in making decisions that involve momentous consequences. Not only do they accept personal risk, but the fate of the organisation to which they are passionately committed is at stake.

The importance of the group to terrorism is well established. Tendencies towards cohesion and solidarity, present in all primary groups, lead to the suppression of dissent and the internalisation of group standards and norms. Members have to be totally obedient to group norms; and members of terrorist organisations have to accept not only a set of political beliefs but systems of social and psychological regulation.

Despite pressures for cohesion, disagreements exist within terrorist organisations. Factionalism is endemic in the Palestinian and Basque terrorist groups, for example. Factions of terrorist organisations seem to disagree over the best means to achieve collective ends. Variations in belief systems may account for differences in methods. The circumstances of a terrorist group – isolated from society, under constant threat and danger, lacking reliable information sources and channels – and their reliance on rigid and inflexible beliefs about their relationship to the world suggest that the terrorist's ability to adapt to reality is limited. Equally, terrorists are not capable of correctly anticipating the consequences of their actions. Understanding their belief systems enables governments to predict terrorists' susceptibility to communications. Forcing terrorists to accept the falseness of their beliefs or denying them any way out of a threatening situation may lead to their emotional breakdown and a resolution of a crisis.

See also **Psychological theories, Terrorist mindset, Terrorist roles**

Black June and Black September These are both hard-line Palestinian groups. The Black June group took its name from the Syrian intervention in the civil war in Lebanon in June 1976, after which the Palestinian-backed Lebanese Muslim Leftists were defeated by the combined forces of the Syrians and the Lebanese Christians. In September 1976, three

B

members of the group were tried and hanged for an attack on an hotel in Damascus with the object of enforcing the release of a number of persons arrested on charges of having committed acts of violence. The leader of the group was killed by Syrian troops and four persons held hostage also lost their lives in the attack.

Black September, under the leadership of Abu Daoud, took its name from the month in which Al-Fatah's forces were defeated by Jordanian troops in 1970. It broke away from Al-Fatah because it disagreed with the latter's emphasis on the need for political action as a 'national liberation movement'. The Black September group belonged to the minority group of 'avenging' Palestinians, members of which committed individual acts of violence. It was held responsible for the killing of Wasfi Tell (the Jordanian Prime Minister) in Cairo in November 1971 – in revenge for the killing of its former leader, Abu Ali Iyad, in July of that year. Other acts of violence atrributed to Black September included the hijacking of a Sabena airliner at Lod (Israel) in May 1972; the murder of eleven Israeli athletes at the Olympic Games in Munich on 5 September 1972; the seizure of the Israeli embassy in Bangkok in March 1973; and the murder in Khartoum of the US ambassador and the Belgian chargé d'affaires at the Saudi Arabian embassy in March 1973. In August 1973 two members of the group made an attack at Athens airport, killing five people and injuring 55 others – they were sentenced to life imprisonment.

Abu Daoud, the Group's leader, was among the 1,000 political prisoners released by King Hussein of Jordan under an amnesty in 1973, most of them having been held since the 1970–71 Jordanian action against Palestinian guerrillas. In January 1977, Abu Daoud was arrested in Paris while attending a funeral. Within days a French court released him after West German authorities had not immediately made their request for his extradition on charges of his involvement in the attack on the Israeli athletes at Munich in 1972, and as Israel was considered to have no right to ask for his extradition.

The Black September–June organisation was described as a merger of the Black September and Black June organisations, and the Abu Nidal group led by Sabri Khalil al-Banna (Abu Nidal). It claimed responsibility for killing the United Arab Emirates Foreign Minister in October 1977 in Abu Dhabi, instead of the Syrian Foreign Minister who was then visiting Abu Dhabi. The assassin, who was said to have been supported by the Iraqi regime, was condemned to death and executed. Yassir Arafat was quick to condemn the attack, as was the Al-Fatah central committee.

See also **Lod Airport Massacre, Munich Olympics Massacre**

Black September
See **Black June and Black September**

Brigate Rosse
See **Red Brigades**

C

Carlos Carlos (Ilyich Ramirez Sanchez) is a Venezuelan assassin, who has been described as the world's first truly transnational terrorist (or autonomous non-state actor) and millionaire. He spent some time at the Lumumba University in Moscow (used as a selection course for Third World students chosen for training as leaders of 'liberation armies'), before being expelled. However, he maintained close connections with the KGB, and with the West German Baader Meinhof group. The exposure of Carlos and the international ramifications of his network convinced many people throughout the world that the upsurge of bombing and assassination and the taking of hostages for political gain was no ephemeral affair, and no short-term aberration. In the early 1970s he operated in London on behalf of the Popular Front for the Liberation of Palestine. A series of errors, due to a mis-routing of information, prevented Carlos's arrest in London and enabled him to carry out his spectacular series of terrorist crimes, culminating in the kidnapping of OPEC oil ministers in Vienna in 1975. He is rumoured to have received a bonus from Gadaffi of nearly two million dollars for this operation, and other reports suggest that he took a cut out of the five million dollar ransom paid by Saudi Arabia and Iran for the release of their ministers. Carlos received support or approval, either covertly or overtly, from many groups, individuals, organisations and governments. He regularly operated out of France and became the Popular Front for the Liberation of Palestine's chief hit man there. He was dubbed the superstar of violence, and married a woman terrorist Magdalena Kaupp. Reputedly he now runs the Palestinian terrorist organisation known as the International Faction of Revolutionary Cells. It is derived from the West German Revolutionary Cell organisation, which was divided into two sometimes competing sections, one of which operated inside Germany and the other internationally. Ultimately, Carlos's future lies in receiving finance and support for these terrorist ventures.

See also OPEC **Siege**

Carrero Blanco, Premier Luis Carrero Blanco's death in December 1973 at the hands of terrorists was one of the most spectacular murders ever committed by any world group. The Spanish premier was assassinated in Madrid by six ETA members who planted a bomb in the street in which his car was travelling. His chauffeur and a police guard were killed in the explosion, which lifted their car five storeys off the street and into

29

the courtyard of a church where the premier had just attended Mass. ETA claimed that the attack was in revenge for the killing of nine Basque militants by the government, as well as to fight Spanish repression. Four terrorists who claimed to have been responsible for the assassination, had initially planned to kidnap Carrero Blanco, but were forced to change their plans after a lengthy surveillance. The preparation for the attack took approximately one year and involved digging a 25-foot-long tunnel leading from a rented basement room out under the middle of the street, where the explosives went off. In July 1975, two Basque nationalists were arrested and charged with transporting the dynamite used in the killing. Two months later, ETA's military chief – a key suspect in the assassination – was captured, and thirteen other suspects arrested in Madrid, five in Barcelona and others in Bilbao. The arrests came after the discovery of a plot to free forty political prisoners.

Cellules Communistes Combattantes
See **Fighting Communist Cells**

Chad The Republic of Chad is ruled by a Council of State whose leader since 1982 has been Hissène Habré. Of the principal political factions opposed to Habré's regime, only the National Peace Government with its National Liberation Army is still a fighting force. The country, a former French colony, is divided between the Black Christian and animist south, and the Muslim north, part of the latter, the Aozou strip, having been annexed by Libya because of its large deposits of uranium. It is here that the former president, Goukouni Oueddei has formed a National Peace Government with a National Liberation Army, supported by Libya. Since 1983 there have been occasional clashes between Oueddei and Habré.

The Chad Armed Forces (FAT), established in 1975, have suffered from mixed loyalties and defections. They are composed of Black Christians and animists and have opposed the various factions of the Chad National Liberation Front (Frolinat). When Habré came to power through civil war his Armed Forces of the North (FAN) gradually defeated the Chad Armed Forces. A new national Chad Armed Forces was formed in late 1982. The Democratic Revolutionary Council was established in 1979, and was one of the numerous factions of the Chad National Liberation Front. The Council took part in the formation of a Transitional Government of National Unity (GUNT), whose main base has been in the extreme north of Chad and partly also in the south east.

The National Peace Government is the strongest of the groups and was formed in 1982. Previously the Peace Government's leader, Goukouni Oueddei, had headed the Transitional Government of National Unity between 1979 and 1982, when it was overthrown by the forces of Habré. The National Peace Government was formed in Libya with the objectives of overthrowing the terrorist regime of Habré and the restoration of peace and unity in Chad. The National Liberation Army of this group has fought several battles against the Habré government since 1983. Habré blames Libya for these events.

Charter 77 After the Soviet invasion of Czechoslovakia in 1968, the activities of Czech dissidents centred on examining and monitoring the Soviet government's record of human and civil rights in terms of the international agreements signed by the Czechoslovak government. The chief instigators of the internal opposition to the activities of the Communist regime were the Charter 77 group, whose founders in January 1977 included Professor Jiri Hajek and Dr Vaclav Havel. They were chiefly concerned by the need for a right to education without political interference, freedom of expression of opinion and freedom of conscience, and they objected to the absolute power of the authorities.

The object of the Charter was to inspire a belief in the reality and truthfulness of civil commitments by a free, informal and open community of persons of varying convictions, religions and professions, joined by the will to work individually and collectively for respect for civil and human rights in their country and in the world. 1977 had been created the year of the rights of political prisoners, and in the course of that year the Belgrade Conference reviewed the fulfilment of the Helsinki accords signed at the Conference on Security and Cooperation in Europe in 1975.

The Communist government in Prague viewed the Charter as rabidly anti-communist. A number of the original group were caught; some were given long prison sentences while others were allowed to leave the country but at the same time were deprived of their citizenship. Many West European governments have since called for religious freedom in Czechoslovakia and the release of all prisoners.

China The People's Republic of China defines itself as a socialist state under the people's democratic dictatorship led by the working class and based on the alliance of workers and peasants. The power struggle within the Communist Party which followed the death of Mao in 1976 was accompanied by various manifestations of opposition to the government, although organised groups were largely confined to those seeking full observance of human rights in China. Externally, the regime in Beijing is faced with no serious threat except from the Taiwanese Nationalists who were driven to their island home of Taiwan (formerly Formosa) when the Communists came to power under the leadership of Mao Tse-Tung and Chou en-Lai in 1949. The Kuomintang regime in Taiwan claims it is the legitimate government of the whole of China.

In 1981 the Communist Party issued directives insisting that literature and art must conform to official policy and calling for a total ban on unofficial publications and organisations. These directives were aimed at such organisations as the Chinese Revolutionary Party formed in 1982, and advocating the establishment of a multi-party parliamentary democracy in China; and the Human Rights Alliance, which in 1979 published a manifesto calling for a constitutionally-guaranteed right to criticise state and party leaders, representation of non-communist parties in the

National People's Congress, and freedom to change one's work and to travel abroad. The Society of Light has been less successful than the Alliance in that since its inception in 1978 most of its leaders have been arrested. It complained that wages have not kept pace with prices, and has called for 'the fifth modernisation' – democracy, to complement the four modernisations of agriculture, industry, national defence, and science and technology advocated by the Communist Party in 1975. The Society's leader Wei Jingsheng was jailed for eight years in 1980 for 'counter-revolutionary' activities. Dissident activity has been reported in the Uighur autonomous region (Xinjiang, previously Sinkiang); and in Tibet, overrun by the Chinese in 1959, where some Lamas were executed in 1985 for alleged 'treason'.

Regulations on state secrets adopted in 1951 were reissued in 1980. State secrets are defined as secret information on all aspects of political, economic and military affairs – divulgence of which is considered a treasonable offence.

Civil disorders and terrorism Civil disorders are a form of collective violence interfering with the peace, security and normal functioning of the community. They are public in character even though like institutional disorders they may take place in a restricted setting. Although occasionally they begin with surprising suddenness and develop with alarming speed and intensity, mass disorders are always outgrowths of their particular social context. Civil disorders can develop out of legitimate expression of protest, lawfully organised and conducted. Many such are symptomatic of deep-seated tensions in community relationships, and when a precipitating event occurs, these tensions erupt into violence. The immediate, official response to disorder must restore order and permit the normal functioning of the community. Only a long-range strategy can remove the root causes of disorder and ensure that it will not recur when emergency constraints have been lifted.

Disorders and terrorism have common characteristics and specific differences. Both are forms of extraordinary violence that disrupt the civil peace; both originate in some form of social excitement, discontent and unrest and both can engender massive fear in the community. Disorders and terrorism constitute in varying forms and degree, violent attacks upon the established order of society. Nevertheless, the focus, direction, application and purpose of terrorism are different.

Civil disorders are manifestations of exuberance, discontent or disapproval on the part of a substantial segment of a community. They do not necessarily have political overtones. In many cases disorders are haphazard events rather than systematically staged and directed expressions of social or political violence.

Acts of extraordinary violence, such as terrorism, are the work of a comparatively small number of malcontents or dissidents who, their rhetoric notwithstanding, threaten the security of the entire community. Acts of terrorism are planned in advance, although their execution may be a matter of sudden opportunity. To be effective, terrorism requires a calculated manipulation of the community to which its message is addressed. In the case of civil disorders, the terror generated is incidental and spontaneous, though not always unexpected. In the case of terrorism, the fear is deliberate; it is the very purpose of violent activity. Civil disorders, and the fear and disruption incidental to them, are ripe for exploitation by the same dissidents responsible for acts of terrorism. When such exploitation takes place, the purpose is the same; the disruption of normal political and social life. Whatever the immediate or ulterior objective of the terrorist, his prospects for success depend to a large extent upon the involvement of the community in his purposes. Terrorism without an audience is an exercise in futility. In this respect, terrorism is as much a collective phenomenon as the mass disorder.

The nature of American society, unlike European society, has enabled it to absorb a great deal of undifferentiated violence without real damage to its political structure or the prospect of a true revolution.

Less organised forms of urban rioting precede or complement outbreaks of organised terror or guerrilla warfare in urban and rural areas. Such breakdowns in public security tend to be preceded or complemented by the development of a parallel or underground movement in direct competition with the threatened regime.

Stages in collective violence range from primitive communal brawls or gang fights, to reactionary violence, which is actively political, with a conservative desire to return social conditions to some previously achieved state, and finally to modern types of violence, which grew from confrontations between authorities and politically sophisticated groups.

Civil war Civil war occurs with the development of armed hostilities between two or more sections of society, both possessed of political organisations and claiming the right to rule the society, or in the case of one of the parties, the right to independent status. A civil war is distinguished from a rebellion by such claims to political power on the part of the insurrectionary party, and distinguished from a revolution by the approximate balance of forces on each side, though a revolution can precede, accompany or follow a civil war.

It is hard objectively to determine the boundary between the wanton destruction and death caused by terrorists, the guerrilla war (sometimes called low-intensity conflict) pursued by young national liberation movements, and the civil war fought by mature, stronger, national liberation movements. Yet in each of these cases the user of military capabilities as a tool or potential tool of violence is not a state. From this, non-traditional violence may be most simply defined as violence between any two international actors, at least one of which is usually a non-state actor, or receiving external support. Distinctions between war and peace have been blurred; civil wars, revolutionary wars, liberation wars, religious and ideological revolts and terrorism may all affect and be affected by the international system. Since 1945 state authority has been challenged more often from inside the state than from outside the state.

Civil wars rarely lack international dimensions, either because one or another of the parties involved in the war receives support from external sources or because an external actor is vitally concerned with the outcome of the war. During the twentieth century ideology, economics, power and religion have internationalised virtually every civil war.

Civil wars occupy a curious place in any typology of wars and violence. On one hand they are quite often violent. Because of their inordinate violence civil wars have been condemned as needless and senseless destroyers of life and property. On the other hand, civil wars have been defended as the last recourse of action against corrupt, outdated or unyielding social systems and governments.

Civil wars Defined as 'war between belligerent factions seeking by organised violence to acquire a monopoly of force and political power in a state', civil war is a type of conflict feared by most countries. It is by definition divisive and by its nature requires the channelling of energies and resources inwards to the detriment of trade, state development and international relations. It is extremely destructive, not just in the physical sense, but more importantly in the moral, creating deep divisions within society which may take generations to repair. It invariably creates a political vacuum as rival centres of authority emerge, and this invites foreign interference which may be difficult to shake off once the war is over. In short, civil war threatens the independence of the state and tears its fabric apart.

The world is divided into a number of 'states', geographical entities containing people ruled by a recognised form of central authority which enjoys at least a degree of independent decision-making – and each contains within its boundaries the seeds of conflict. The population is unlikely to be completely homogeneous, particularly if the borders of the state reflect the arbitrary decisions of outside powers (as is the case with so many ex-colonial members of the Third World) or result from a history of expansion by conquest in the search for security.

This means that there will always be groups within the state who do not owe natural allegiance to the central authority, preferring the traditions and beliefs of their own ethnic, tribal or religious backgrounds and this may lead to accusations of their disloyalty, as well as government-sponsored attempts to persuade or force them into conformity.

Similar divisions may result from an uneven spread of wealth or power within the state. Some areas may be starved of resources, growing resentful of the development of other, more favoured regions; others may hold a monopoly of a scarce resource and be loath to share their advantages with the rest of society unless they are given a corresponding monopoly of political power.

In some states these divisions may be controlled by a strong central government which exercises its power by means of accepted forms of democracy or effective totalitarian repression, but even then the potential for internal conflict remains. In extreme cases it may be manifested in the creation of an entirely new state through the secession of the disaffected areas – in 1971, for example, Bangladesh seceded from West Pakistan, with Indian aid, after years of being treated as a 'poor relation' by the central authorities in Islamabad – but the more common result is civil war.

Civil wars have affected many states, but they have increased in both frequency and importance since 1945. In part this is due to the simple fact that since that date the number of independent states in existence, and therefore susceptible to civil war, has more than tripled in the aftermath of European decolonisation, but there is more to it than that. The division of major parts of the world into two rival ideological camps has pitted communism against capitalism in even the most sophisticated states, deepening already-existing political divides, sometimes to the point of violence. Improved communications have shown people that other groups have attained a level of economic or political development that contrasts sharply to their own, leading to a questioning of government policies and a drift towards conflict. Such groups may, of course, be exploited by outside powers but whatever the background, civil war has developed with ever-increasing frequency.

Many of the more intractable and long-lasting of the conflicts that have taken place since 1945 bear the hallmarks of civil war, even though they are not normally described as such. The Vietnam War was fought mainly by members of the same Vietnamese culture, and until the intervention of US and North Vietnamese forces the combatants came from within the same state. In Northern Ireland, too, the 'troubles of the 1970s' often seemed a species of civil war, with the British Army almost an outside force.

Looking in more detail at the specific causes of civil wars since 1945, it is clear that the ideological clash between communism and capitalism has had a dramatic impact. It has been the direct cause of two of the most significant civil wars of the period, albeit with different results. In China the offensive launched by the communists under Mao Tse-Tung in 1946 was designed to destroy the Western-orientated government of Chiang Kai-Shek. Although the resultant war had its origins in the political chaos which had beset China since the overthrow of the Manchu dynasty in 1911, the fighting of 1946–49 was firmly based upon opposing political views. In the end the communists prevailed. A similar clash of ideologies fuelled the civil war in Greece between 1945 and 1949, with the communist-led Democratic Army fighting the Nationalist government, but in this case it was the Nationalists who won, not least because of Western commitment to their cause.

The fact that events in Greece almost led to a more general confrontation between the rival camps of East and West undoubtedly muted the degree of direct support offered by the superpowers to factions in subsequent civil wars, but this did not mean that ideology had ceased to play an important role, merely that the superpowers have been more circumspect, preferring subversion to open battle and using proxies to provide the necessary aid. Events in Angola in 1975 illustrate the point, with the communist MPLA receiving arms, advisers and equipment from the Cubans rather than the Russians in their struggle to defeat the South African-backed and CIA-funded forces of FNLA and UNITA.

In many cases, it is still local issues which cause civil wars, centred upon purely internal differences. In Nigeria, for example, the civil war of 1967–70 had its origins among the Ibo tribe of the eastern provinces, who felt that the federal government in Lagos was actively discriminating against them.

A similar pattern of events occurred in Chad after 1968, when the tribes of the northern and eastern provinces, convinced that their rivals from the south and west were enjoying a monopoly of political power, revolted under the banner of Frolinat (the National Liberation Front of Chad) and initiated a civil war which has yet to be completely resolved. In Sudan a civil war took place from the moment of independence in 1956 until a partial reconciliation in 1972 between the Christian and animist inhabitants of the south and the Muslim-dominated government in Khartoum, while the Lebanese Civil War of 1975–76 had its roots in the inevitable clash between the Maronite Christians of the governing elite and the disaffected Muslim majority.

If the causes of civil wars are many and varied, the results are often predictable. Although the superpowers may be deterred from offering direct support, it is one of the characteristics of the post-1945 period that few civil wars have remained self-contained. In an interdependent world, beset by problems of ideological and resource rivalry, too much is at stake to prevent outside interference and this can often be decisive in terms of the outcome or longevity of internal squabbles. The civil war in North Yemen was sustained by the fact that Egypt supported the republicans while Saudi Arabia backed the monarchists; in Lebanon the rivalries of 1975–76 have been fuelled by Syrian and Israeli intervention; in Chad it was the French and Libyans who offered aid.

In each of these cases, intervening states stood to make substantial gains from the victory of their chosen allies – in Chad, the French committed troops to protect their valuable stake in the mineral resources of the country – and this makes a peaceful or lasting solution extremely difficult to achieve. Local issues disappear beneath more global pressures, the degree of violence increases as more sophisticated weapons and even troops are made available, and the fighting drags on, achieving either stalemate (as in North Yemen and Sudan), or eventual victory for the faction which enjoys the most effective outside support (as in Greece, Nigeria and Angola). This pattern will continue.

Cominformists Cominformists were pro-Soviet Communists who opposed the 1948 break between Yugoslavia on the one hand, and the Soviet Union and the Cominform (the successor to the Communist International) on the other. They frequently attracted the attention of the Yugoslav authorities. At a secret conference in the mid 1970s, the Communist Party of Yugoslavia was reported to have been established at Bar on the Adriatic coast. This party condemned President Tito for having 'betrayed' the original Communist Party of Yugoslavia and having, by a coup d'état, opened the way to 'counter-revolutionary terror' and established 'a regime of personal dictatorship', under which 'more than 200,000 Communists had been expelled and arrested'.

The programme declared that the new party was an inseparable organic part of the international communist movement, and proposed a transitional regime leading to a 'genuine people's democracy': the formation of a united National Front of all socialist and democratic parties and groups opposed to Tito; the formation of a provisional government of all parties; the disbandment of the secret police and the counter-intelligence organisations in the army and militia, and the abolition of all concentration camps and political prisons; the abolition of the Presidency of the Republic; the nationalisation of the principal means of production; a new electoral law giving every adult the right to vote, irrespective of his political views, and Yugoslavia's withdrawal from agreements made with Western governments. Many alleged Cominformists were brought to trial in the late 1970s. Their brief hope for revived support upon the death of President Tito never materialised and the Cominformists became a spent force.

Contra insurgency in Nicaragua Almost immediately after the Sandinista victory in 1979, former Somoza National Guardsmen began to regroup as the Contras to carry on a guerrilla war against the new regime from bases in Honduras, while training camps were set up in Florida and Guatemala. They received extensive support from the United States, particularly after the inauguration of President Reagan in 1981, and in 1982 their attacks upon economic targets in Nicaragua led to the declaration of a state of emergency there.

As a result of American support, the Contras were able to mount air attacks on targets inside Nicaragua and carried out the mining of Nicaraguan harbours from American support ships. Nevertheless, they were unable to establish 'liberated zones' on Nicaraguan territory, and US pressure for the unification of the Honduras-based Fuerzas Democraticas Nicaraguenses (FDN) with the Alianza Revolucionaria Democrática (ARDE) which operated from bases in Costa Rica, was resisted by the ARDE leader, former Sandinista guerrilla Eden Pastora.

The Contras suffered a major set-back in mid 1984, when the US Congress voted to halt all covert financial assistance to the rebels. The Sandinistas, meanwhile, were able to consolidate their regime and expanded their armed forces with aid from Cuba and the Soviet Union. An election held in November 1984, although boycotted by some opposition parties, confirmed popular support for the Sandinistas, and helped win them wider international backing in the continuing war against the Contras.

See also **Sandinist National Liberation Front**

Costs of terrorism Apart from the direct costs of terrorism – the dollar damage due to bombings, armed assaults, arson and sabotage, the amount of ransom paid in hostage situations, dollar losses due to thefts and dollar losses due to extortion payments – one also has to take into account the flight of foreign capital from nations experiencing terrorist campaigns, as well as decisions not to invest in those countries in the first place. The opportunity costs for hostages, and opportunities lost while a given corporation consolidates its losses after an attack should also be included. The costs of security measures taken to prevent attacks is also high and must include the costs of metal detectors, sky-marshals, bodyguards, security training for corporation people and embassy staffs, as well as more intangible costs, such as randomly re-routing airline flights, ships, motorcades and home to office travel to evade attacks. Another intangible cost is the personal anxiety faced by victims and possible victims of attacks, as well as whatever anxieties are faced by the terrorists themselves. Finally, one can include the costs of all academic and governmental research on terrorism, as well as the costs of policy staffs assigned to develop national responses to terrorism.

Strategically, terrorist groups aspire to control the apparatus of state. As far as can be determined, no campaign of terrorism by itself has ever led to the fall of a government, although the independence of Algeria and Israel can be attributed in part to pressure on colonial authorities by the sustained attacks by the FLN and the Irgun respectively. At a somewhat lower level, many groups seek policy changes, ranging from greater autonomy for a province of the country to increased wages for union members.

At a tactical level, terrorists have sought changes in sentences, elimination of torture, or the outright release of specified political prisoners including members of their own groups. Money ransoms and extortion payments frequently occur.

Where terrorism has proved to be overwhelmingly effective is in the securing of publicity for groups' actions and views. Dramatic actions are able to attract sensation-seeking television and newspaper coverage, which tends to give an impression of strength that the group does not possess. They attempt to embarrass the government and corporations viewed as exploiters by releasing damaging information secured in interrogation of hostages or by theft of documents, as well as by clever manoeuvring of hostage negotiating situations. For example, the terrorists may demand that the government donate food to poverty-stricken peasants, casting themselves in the role of Robin Hoods, while forcing the government into the position of refusing a charitable demand or giving in to a group of criminals. Corporations refusing monetary ransoms are portrayed as caring more about finance than the lives of the hostages.

It is the government's task to demonstrate that official duties to society can be carried out in the face of the terrorist threat and to decrease whatever amount of influence the terrorists have. The government can work with the press to alter public perceptions of the might of the terrorists. It can make the perpetration of a particular type of incident so costly to the terrorist that he or she will be deterred. It can abide by a publicly stated policy of not granting concessions in the face of terrorist threats, and the government may engage in a nation-wide crackdown on the terrorists by enacting emergency measures that severely limit civil liberties. However, indiscriminate repression of society is often precisely what the terrorists seek – and the government thus temporarily cures a symptom, while adding to the cause of the infection of terrorism. Death Squads, vigilante organisations with or without extra official support, arise often in the face of terrorist threats to security. They add to the general feeling of dread in the society brought on by increasing disregard for normal non-violent legal measures for dealing with political demands. However, they are viewed by others as doing the job of the police, in rooting out terrorists who have led the country to this situation. Often political violence cannot be eliminated completely and governments are fundamentally forced to resort to these repressive measures.

Counter-insurgency is the term for measures taken by governments against insurgents or those people who take part in an uprising against incumbent governments, usually in the form of an armed insurrection.

Good government is the best method to avoid insurgency, and effective counter-insurgency must involve political action by civilians as well as military action by soldiers. Soldiers have to act in a political context and civilians, for their own safety, have to accept military rule. There are a wide range of political situations in which insurgency occurs, or may occur, depending on the nature of the arena chosen (urban or rural), and the status of the territory in which it occurs (a province, a dependent territory, a protectorate or a friendly state), as well as on the political order of the state that is combatting the insurgency (liberal democracy, authoritarian government or dictatorship).

The main lesson of counter-insurgency is the importance of maintaining the primacy of civilian government. In the case of insurgency in a colonial territory, best results have been achieved where the colonial government has had the option open to it of handing over power in the medium term to an elected civilian government that can command popular support and has been prepared to embrace this opportunity. Counter-insurgency forces operating in a friendly state are always liable to be regarded by the local inhabitants as anti-national, if not indeed as an occupying force. The perceptions and attitudes of the opposition have to be understood.

Success in counter-insurgency depends on certain conditions being met: planning is an essential prerequisite, and lack of planning has led to more serious trouble than any other omission. A government confronted for the first time with armed insurgency threat tends to give a panic response.

The first response to an armed threat should be through the police and not the armed forces.

The history of counter-insurgency in the twentieth century has shown a natural tendency to develop in parallel with developments in the concept of insurgency itself. From 1945 up to the mid 1960s, the main theatre of insurgency was the countryside. Emphasis was given to guerrilla warfare, which as a development of partisan warfare was well understood to be dependent on an infrastructure of civilian support for motivation, the supply of food and other material resources, and the provision of disguise. In Malaya, for example, psychological warfare was aimed primarily at the small number of active terrorists with the aim of encouraging them to surrender. The combined effects of isolation, fear and hunger led many to do so, once they knew that they could surrender in safety.

After 1967, counter-insurgency was to evolve into the 'justification' for what was later known as the 'national security state' in the 1970s and 1980s. The 'national security state' was typically a Latin American military government obsessed with the overall objective of permanently eliminating foreign 'subversion' by the imprisonment, torture and execution of political opponents, many of whom had no connection with any form of insurgent activity. Fuelled by inter-service rivalry, such military establishments built up vast intelligence organisations whose functions had little enough to do with real intelligence – the gathering and evaluation of information. Four steps can be discerned in the nature of any counter-terrorist intelligence. Firstly, *direction* – the determination of intelligence requirements, preparation of a collection plan, insurance of orders and requests to information collection agencies, and a continuous check on the productivity of collection agencies. The second step is *collection* – the systematic procurement and selection of information relevant to a specific intelligence problem. Thirdly, *processing* is the step whereby 'information' becomes 'intelligence' through evaluation, analysis, integration and interpretation. Fourthly, there is *dissemination*, the conveyance of intelligence in suitable form (oral, graphic or written) to agencies which need it.

Counter-terror forces need to be aware of the type and nature of the terrorist operation, its relationship to the revolutionary process, its organisation, ideology, type of propaganda, tactics, weapons, targets, audience and media coverage.

Projections can be made in relation to the purpose, reason or cause of the planned event, the nature of the situation, groups or individuals involved, the number of persons expected, locations affected, the time and duration of the event or situation, the potential for disorder, the effect upon the law enforcement agency, the wider significance of the event or situation and the evolving patterns and trends.

Counter-intelligence functions are needed to strengthen the counter-insurgency operation, and to combat the surprise effects of terrorism, which can be used to

- create a situation for which police and security authorities are unprepared;
- force security authorities into hurried or ill-considered actions;
- dislocate or disperse security forces;
- allow deployment of terrorist elements in unexpected strength;
- allow assault from an unexpected direction;
- facilitate exploitation of unexpected timings;
- capitalise on the use of unexpected tactics.

See also **Insurgency**

C

Counter-nuclear terrorist strategy In terms of mounting an effective counter-nuclear strategy, governments must organise their activities according to the three sequences of responsibilities.

These are: appraising the terrorist group under scrutiny for the purpose of identifying leadership elements; appraising the leadership elements for the purpose of identifying predominant patterns of risk calculation; and examining decision-making in order to determine the appropriate type of counter-nuclear terrorist strategy, i.e. the strategy that corresponds with the identified pattern of risk calculation in the terrorist group.

Governments have to develop rationally conceived 'behavioural technology' which distinguishes contingencies of reinforcement according to the particular type of terrorists involved. To deal with the problem of nuclear terrorism one has to correlate deterrent and remedial measures.

The optimal counter-nuclear terrorist strategy is one in which effective counteraction leaves the prevailing network of citizens' rights and privileges unimpaired. Barring this possibility, the need for effective strategies must be tempered by concern for those freedoms which are assured by humanitarian international law.

There are distinctive decision-making criteria which governments can adopt in developing appropriate strategies of deterrent and remedial measures. The criteria evolve round the principal types of terrorist groups. The first group is characterised by a high degree of commitment to political objectives and an absence of criminal activity. Deterrent efforts have to focus on the terrorists' threats to obstruct political objectives. Efforts have to be directed at convincing the group that its resort to nuclear violence would militate against political objectives because it would both stiffen government resolve and alienate vital bases of popular support. Another group can be characterised by a high degree of commitment to political objectives and by its use of criminal tactics. Governments have to try to create a bad press for the group among political adherents and supporters by spreading the news about the group's ordinary criminal tendencies.

The third group is characterised by a moderate degree of commitment to political objectives and by an absence of criminal activity. Here the group's primary rationale and concern is still manifestly political, but there is no evidence of self-sacrificing values and the group does not secure funds through 'expropriation'. Closely related to this group can

41

be one characterised by a moderate degree of commitment to political objectives and a use of criminal tactics. Governments have to focus on a strategy of threats and promises and efforts to broadcast and publicise the group's ordinary criminal activities.

The next group is characterised by a low degree of commitment to political objectives and by the absence of criminal activity. Here the group's *raison d'être* is only nominally political and the group does not secure funds through threats or extortion. This group looks upon violence as its own end rather than as an instrument. Violence is viewed as a romantic and creative force that is self-justifying. In ordering of priorities for action against this type of terrorist group, deterrence should be abandoned as a counter-nuclear terrorist strategy. Since personal safety is unimportant in this type of terrorist group's risk calculation, governments have the dilemma of having to apply appropriate sanctions, but at a reasonable level, consistent with the society's basic commitment to decency and essential human rights.

The last group to mention is characterised by a low degree of commitment to political objectives and by the use of criminal tactics. While this type of terrorist group may also exhibit nihilistic or psychopathic traits, its primary characteristics come closer to those of ordinary criminals or bandits. Government effort should focus on threats used to counter orthodox criminality and these need to be augmented by preventive measures.

Counter-nuclear terrorist strategies within states require sanctions to be differentiated according to the particular type of terrorist group involved. Since nuclear terrorism might take place across national boundaries, the basic principles of these strategies must also be applied internationally. It is critical for them to harden the target and soften the adversary. The problem in counter-nuclear terrorism is allowing international law to serve the interests of international order without impairing the legitimate objectives of international justice.

See also **Nuclear terrorism**

Coup d'état A coup d'état is a change of regime brought about by illegal and unconstitutional action on the part of a holder, or group of holders, of some political and military office. It involves limited forms of violence. It can be preceded by a conspiracy, concerned with obtaining certain political offices for sympathisers. Unlike a revolution, it does not call on mass support to effect such changes, though it may seek legitimation of the changes by a plebiscite or mass demonstration. A putsch is a form of coup d'état. Figuratively speaking, a coup d'état has the same effect as binding the eyes, ears, mouths, hands and feet of the persons who exercise recognised controlling political power, making impossible resistance, flight, calls for help or movement of armed forces or police on behalf of the person captured.

The conditions which appear to be most conducive to coups d'état are centralisation of political power in the hands of a small number of individuals, minimising the number of arrests required; failure to take adequate preventive measures, whether physical, psychological, economic or political; and non-responsiveness to changes in the domestic and international situation or to the climate of public opinion. In the matter of internal security, critical attention must be paid to the attitudes and actions of professional military officers or paramilitary leaders, who may be in a position to effect a coup. In the matter of responsiveness to public opinion, governments have to be aware that riots and mob action are a weapon not infrequently used to frighten persons possessing political power into abdicating the power, leaving a void which conspirators may fill.

C

A coup d'état differs from a revolution in that the latter is effected by the people, or at least by those who hold no power under existing arrangements, and perhaps represent themselves as 'leaders of the people' in order to gain it. Some observers consider a coup d'état to be part of an inevitable and socially-based revolution.

Crisis management A terrorist action is generally well organised and part of its plan will be to catch the target unprepared. This surprise may prevent the target from taking effective action so that it therefore has to accept the only alternative of complete and prompt compliance with all of the terrorists' demands.

The term crisis management means a planned efficient response to a crisis, that is, any event that significantly disrupts the operations of the organisation. In this case, crises are categorised as actions directed against the executives of the organisation and perpetrated by terrorists.

Crisis management plans furnish guidance and a list of resources which facilitate a co-ordinated and effective response to terrorists' actions against business. A crisis has to be anticipated against threats of kidnapping, ambush, assassination, harassment and extortion.

To counter these events, plans have to contain organisations' and businesses' stated policy with regard to crisis management. This will include whether or not to pay ransom, designations of responsibility, executives covered by the plan and criteria for the implementation of the plan. Crisis management teams have to include those individuals with authority to implement and carry out policies and procedures in the crisis management plan, i.e. decision-makers or those in direct communication with decision-making authority. A typical team for crisis management has to include a co-ordinator or security director, an assistant to the co-ordinator, legal counsel, and negotiators, special analysts and consultants.

The purpose of the crisis management centre is to serve as the focal point for directing a co-ordinated, planned response during a crisis situation. The centre has to be located within the particular organisation. Management centres have all the equipment, documents and supplies needed during a crisis. Plans give precise instructions concerning who does what, when, how and by what authority. Once a businessman has been kidnapped, threat has to be verified, and there has to be proof that an executive actually has been abducted. Verification of the threat is not always a simple matter of locating and confronting a supposedly abducted executive. An attempted extortion could be based on the fact that the extortionist knows the executive would be hard to locate. Criteria for a crisis management programme have to be based on past experience of extortion threats, and the current terrorist or extremist activity in the area.

The threat is a coercive tool of an extortioner; the validity of the threat, and who is doing the threatening are questions threat analysis seeks to answer. Threat analysis of terrorist activities has both long-range and immediate applications. Such analysis, based on pre-event information, is a long-range, constantly updated process that provides a current threat profile of the corporation, key facilities and key personnel. It provides a barometer of the seriousness of the threat.

Threat analysis has to verify the validity of the threat – does it in fact exist? Is the threat as serious as the creators of the threat would have the organisation believe? Is the threat delivered by an individual or group that presupposes that a response will be a specific action? Is the threat from a terrorist group, or from a criminal group posing as terrorists?

Any demands of the terrorist, whether they take the form of threats, physical actions, or the holding of a hostage, have to be communicated by oral or written messages. Verification of the level of threat in a hostage situation can often be obtained from the victim if he is allowed a rudimentary form of communication. Case history files have to be maintained, storing available information of previous events by category. Liaison with other individuals or organisations is a support to threat analysis because it allows different perspectives to be obtained about specific crises. Propaganda analysis is important to crisis management. The majority of ransom demands come from persons who have a full-time commitment to terrorist activity. In a kidnap situation, negotiations are most successful when the negotiators have a clear understanding of the level of threat and the personality of those who are threatening.

The purpose of threat analysis is to turn any form of threat into a manageable problem that can be analysed and neutralised by the crisis management team. The crisis management process involves pre-planning, threat perception, threat verification, threat analysis and threat response. However, no two negotiating situations are alike. Kidnapping can be defined as extortion with abduction; and extortion is often used as the encompassing term for threats and attacks. Perpetrators of extortion include the professional criminal, the psychotic or mentally disturbed, and the terrorist.

The objectives of hostage negotiation plans are to save lives. The professional criminal will normally grab a hostage as a shield or as someone he can bargain for his getaway, and he is more apt to view his situation rationally, as a clear exchange of the hostage for his freedom. Conversely, a mentally disturbed hostage-taker can have any number of motives for his act, thus negotiating with this type can be far trickier than with the professional criminal. The mentally disturbed individual tends to be irrational and unpredictable. Taking a hostage may be for him a way of acting out a fantasy or to feel power, or it may be part of a suicide plan.

Terrorists are different from criminals or the mentally disturbed. There are criminals and psychotics in the ranks of terrorist organisations, but that does not alter the basic premise. A terrorist seldom acts alone, he is part of a group; even though there may be a leader of the terrorist group, the group code of conduct will influence him since his motives will be dominated by the objectives of the group. Several individuals have to be worn down to save the hostages, and efforts at establishing contact and rapport have to be aimed at more than one person.

The terrorists will be indoctrinated with revolutionary political ideology, and have a sense of the total 'justice' of their cause. For the hostage negotiator, this means the terrorists' negotiators may be immune to many of the psychological techniques employed against the mentally disturbed or the criminal. However, like the professional criminal, terrorists are rational in their views of alternatives; life and freedom in exchange for hostages is usually a prime negotiable demand.

As with hostage negotiations, no two negotiating situations with terrorists will be alike. Demands will differ, strategic objectives of the terrorists will vary and terrorist negotiators will come to the negotiations with different sets of skills. Any trick leaving the terrorists empty-handed could have disastrous consequences, especially in a kidnap situation. Terrorists do not normally kidnap somebody to kill him because once he is dead, they have lost their bargaining lever. Terrorists will execute their captive without hesitation if they believe their just cause has been slighted.

Terrorists may enter negotiations with demands that differ from the original extortion threat, or there may be additional demands. Terrorists' demands and objectives fall into several categories: to obtain ransom money in exchange for the safe return of a kidnapped executive or a member of his family; medical supplies in exchange for their captive; public recognition of the terrorist organisation; release of fellow terrorists jailed by the authorities; protest at national politics or policies or those of the organisation; and to embarrass the target organisation. Terrorist demands can be presented as non-negotiable, specifying that all demands are to be met in full within a specified time period; or the consequences will be a prompt carrying out of the threat if demands are not met. Depending on what information is available to them, negotiators can ask for proof that the victim is still alive and for the exact time and place of the executive's release and for time to study the demands. Negotiations can be effectively concluded only when reasonable guarantees can be given as to when and where the executive will be released; and when there is agreement that acceptance of the terrorists' conditions means no future extortion threats against the organisation.

Given the special nature of a crisis it is mandatory that it can be analysed and the resources employed to cope with it reviewed. It can be defined as a situation in which there is an uncertain outcome; as a period of tension and time pressure in which decisions must be made; and as a situation involving threats to personnel or to the organisation.

A crisis calls for innovation, and in a very real sense a crisis must be treated as a crime to ensure all relevant information to the case is collected, preserved and evaluated.

Clues about a terrorist group's propensity to violence can be revealed by the types and number of the weapons they carry or have stockpiled. The terrorists' degree of discipline is also shown by the way they handle weapons and how they respond to orders or the mere presence of certain individuals. Outright statements or unconscious slips by the terrorists could reveal a strategy of trying to force the organisation out of the host country, or of wanting the organisation to remain so that the terrorists could extract an annual extortion tax to help fund activities. Thus the keys to successful negotiations are a clearly defined strategy, knowledge of the opponent, experience as a negotiator, and careful preparation.

Croat separatism For decades the firm rule of President Tito in Yugoslavia masked the ethnic, religious and nationalistic stresses to which the Yugoslav Federation has been exposed almost since its inception at the end of the First World War. Pre-eminent in the problem of nationalities are the Croats, whose nostalgic yearnings for restoration of their ancient statehood have led to terrorism. In 1918 most Croats opted to join in a common state with the Serbs, provided they were accepted as social partners and allowed to manage their own affairs, but a small but vociferous minority totally rejected the whole Yugoslav concept. This minority of separatists consisted of Zagreb intellectuals and supporters of the former Austria-Hungary. They emphasised the Croats' Central European and Catholic affiliations and looked back nostalgically to the ancient Croat state which they wanted to see revived in republican form. They were prepared to accept financial and other backing from any foreign circles who wished to see the destruction of Yugoslavia.

In the 1930s a violent pro-Fascist Croat organisation – the Ustashi, led by Gustav Percec – was formed. In 1934 the group murdered King Alexander and the French Foreign Minister, Barthou, in Marseilles. During the Second World War they were loyal to Hitler and Mussolini, who both recognised the need for an independent Croat state. In the late 1940s they increasingly sought Western help by stressing that they were merely anti-Communist refugees, persecuted dissidents and social democrats who wanted to exercise their own independent Croat state. Many Croats emigrated to Australia, where over a period of years they set up terrorist organisations to overthrow the Yugoslav government.

Stalin's break with Tito in 1948 presented the separatists with new ideas, but soon the group was split into pro-Soviet and anti-Soviet factions. Due to the problems with the Soviet Union, any residual feelings or fresh stirrings of regional nationalism have been sternly repressed.

The federal aspect of the new Yugoslav state has consequently been largely cosmetic, and authority has emanated from the government and party centre, Belgrade. Economic grievances have been more freely ventilated. By the late 1960s even the Croat League of Communists found itself explicitly advocating Croat national interests to Belgrade, and it consequently enjoyed unprecedented popular support.

Though heartened by developments inside Croatia, the separatists abroad could claim little credit for promoting them. In addition to the ideological differences between anti- and pro-Communists, they remained divided on the main national issue. The émigrés aimed to establish an independent Croat State: the nationalists in the Croat League of Communists wanted a larger measure of autonomy and independence within Yugoslavia. Whereas the émigrés were quick to make capital out of what was occurring in Croatia and felt themselves no longer so isolated from their territorial base, the nationalists in Croatia had more to lose than to gain from closer association with them.

In 1971 there was a widespread purge of the state and party apparatus in Croatia following increasing industrial unrest centred on Zagreb. The separatist activities during the 1970s and early 1980s took specific forms. There were bomb attacks and sabotage inside Yugoslavia, including the planting of time bombs on international trains. An attempt was made on Tito's life in Zagreb in 1975. There were armed incursions from abroad, especially from Croat émigrés in West Germany and Australia. Attacks have occurred on Yugoslav institutions and representatives abroad – Australia, the USA, France, Austria, Norway, Belgium and particularly Sweden and West Germany have been the main theatres for such operations. There have been hijackings of Yugoslav planes, and occasionally of foreign airliners from Sweden and the USA.

Yugoslav countermeasures against the separatists' activities abroad have centred on diplomatic pressure against the host countries; stricter administrative surveillance over expatriate Yugoslavs; and direct action by counter-intelligence and security agencies.

Separatist militancy shows no sign of abating in the era of collective leadership representing the country's constituent nationalities. Extreme nationalists inside and outside Yugoslavia are hoping to exploit the centrifugal forces and tensions and tilt the balance to their advantage. This can provide new incentives and opportunities for the separatists.

Many factors militate against the separatists' cause – they enjoy little or no co-operation from other international terrorist organisations, whose Marxist ideology they do not share; they lack any generally recognised leader and remain at odds among themselves; apart from the wish to see Yugoslavia destroyed, the separatists have no practical political programme; and their cause still suffers from the stigma of the crimes committed by the Ustashi before and during the war.

Cuba Since 1961 the Republic of Cuba has had a Government which has been designated as Communist under Dr Fidel Castro, the First Secretary of the Cuban Communist Party, receiving the 'fraternal friendship, aid and co-operation of the Soviet Union and other socialist countries'.

Political opposition to the Castro regime has found most of its support among Cuban refugees, several hundred thousand of whom have settled in the United States. Some of these refugees have joined a group called Omega Seven, which is an underground paramilitary wing of the Cuban Nationalist Movement, an above-ground anti-Castro movement based in Miami and Union City in Florida. According to the FBI it is the most dangerous terrorist group in the USA. Over the past decade many other anti-Castro refugees from Cuba have made their home in Florida and undergone clandestine training in guerrilla warfare and the use of sophisticated weapons, even though the latter is a contravention of American law.

In 1961 the newly formed Cuban National Revolutionary Council was involved in an attempt made by a force of Cuban exiles to land in the Bay of Pigs area on the north Cuban coast. This was repulsed by the Cuban army and militia with heavy losses. At the same time the activities of anti-Castro guerrillas inside Cuba were also suppressed by Cuban forces. A similar attempt at landing exiles to overthrow the Castro regime was made by another group, Cubans United, in 1981 but this was frustrated by a tropical storm. The Alpha 66 Group also tried in 1970 and 1981 to land members in Cuba, but many members were caught by the Cubans. The United Revolutionary Organisation Co-ordination, founded in Chile in 1975 by an anti-communist Cuban has the objective of trying to undermine all links between Cuba and other American states.

In 1980 the Inter-American Human Rights Commission of the Organisation of American States (from which Cuba has been excluded since 1962) claimed that Cuba ill-treated political prisoners, of whom there were over one thousand, some held without trial. The United States, and in particular the administration of President Reagan (1981–1989) believe that the Cuban government gives direct support to communist insurgents in many Central and South American states – especially El Salvador, Honduras, Costa Rica, Chile and Peru.

See also **Guevara**

D

Data, miscellaneous With regard to the criminality of terrorism, there are a number of sources which can be used. Court proceedings leading to the trial of terrorists are an underused but potentially rich source. Local newspapers give ample coverage to court proceedings, but initially one would use first-hand police records and court proceedings, which provide a narrative account of incidents. Psychiatrists and psychologists have shown that interviews with terrorists in prison are also a valuable source if convicted terrorists are willing to talk. However, in this context the interview situation can be seen as more of an interrogation, perhaps even combined with the threat of torture. Therefore on moral grounds this information is often unusable. Interviews in the real-life environment in which terrorists operate perhaps yield more genuine information but are difficult to obtain. Even more useful are the writings of ex-terrorists who have stayed underground and who keep equal distance from former colleagues and adversaries. Some insight into the style of terrorists can be gleaned.

Memoirs of former terrorists are easier to obtain as a data source, but one has to be aware of the degree to which reminiscences are useful and of the element of self-justification. Terrorists are neither born as terrorists nor condemned to stay terrorists for the rest of their lives. Some became adherents of violence or became statesmen. Most importantly, memoirs can tell us something about when and why terrorists gave up terrorism or switched to another tactic. The study of post-terrorist careers of terrorists can even yield policy results.

Memoirs are personal histories, often more informed but also more biased than other accounts. Indeed the study of past terrorist organisations and movements can increase our understanding of contemporary terrorism. On regime or state terror of a repressive nature, there is very little systematic material. The only sources of information on state repression are reports and documents issued by Amnesty International. Their reports form an account of state terrorism and violations of human rights in more than two-thirds of all the countries forming the United Nations. While the overlap between state terrorism and genocide is only partial, persecution and genocide are social warning indicators which can be made relevant to the study of state terrorism.

For research on terrorism to become cumulative there has to be some uniformity in collected data. Problems exist in getting access to data collected by a variety of government agencies. Data is needed on a wide range of issues, all of which can be classed as worthwhile. Data from public opinion surveys for various countries over time, using comparable incidents in order to assess public attitudes and reactions is invaluable. Data about non-negotiation techniques, terrorist demands and the target of demands, concessions and their relationship to non-violent solutions of incidents and to future demands and concession policies is all of use. Furthermore, data on terrorist victim selection patterns and threat perceptions in audiences sharing victim characteristics, data on counter-measures taken by governments against insurgent terrorism and on counter-measures taken by populations against regime terrorism can lead to build up patterns on the terrorist scene.

Social scientists, who are the principal users of the data bases have to decide whether terrorism is a function of larger ambitions and aims, thereby making it a dependent variable; they have to distinguish types of violence and injury perpetrated against persons and places, in order to help establish some qualitative measures of terrorism and counter-terrorism, and to provide empirical assistance to the efforts to develop international legal measures to combat terror of guerrillas and counter-terror of the state.

See also **Data on terrorism**

Data on terrorism The collection of data on terrorism can be based on both subjectivity and objectivity. Systems for data collection were developed initially in the United States. Definitions have to be used to establish a basis for the facts and theories have a place in deciding the relevant aspects. If a data collector is interested in terror he will concentrate on the data relating to terrorism, guerrilla warfare and political violence. A data collector alone accepts or rejects the material which he uses – but it has to be remembered that the data obtained is only as good as the reliability of its source. For example, the media is used as a popular source for building up data on terrorism and yet one is only too well aware, in democracies at least, of their political proclivities.

The gathering of data for analysis first began in the early 1960s in the United States – the primary source of comparative political violence being the Index of the New York Times – and the only problem was deciding whether an entry under 'bombings' or 'assassinations' could be classed as terrorism. The early databases in the United States tended to cover four main manifestations of terrorism – political assaults against persons and things; political assassinations and executions; political hostage-taking and kidnapping; and hijacking of aircraft. The data was not very specific and was uneven for many countries.

Chronologies of incidents are the more common form of data collections. Sometimes they are based on the type of incident and are global in scope, such as in the case of hijacking data. Nevertheless, they more commonly concentrate on incidents of certain terrorist movements or cover the domestic events within a nation. The national framework for data collection is still most widespread in countries like West Germany, the United Kingdom, the Netherlands and the United States.

Apart from country-based chronologies there are also a number of incident-type-based chronologies, both national and international. The United States for example, produces a list of hijacking attempts worldwide, and the first data to cover international conflicts was based on the Palestinian problem and published in 1977. The Rand Corporation chronology has been the prototype for most other chronologies of incidents, and was developed by a think-tank, RAND in California for the State Department and the Department of Defence, and concentrated primarily on international terrorism. The RAND chronology covers all incidents of terror with international repercussions – incidents in which terrorists went abroad to strike their targets, selected victims or targets that had connections with a foreign state (e.g. diplomats, foreign businessmen, officers of foreign corporations), or created international incidents by attacking airline passengers, personnel and equipment. Their first public report was issued in 1975 and thousands have been produced since that time. RAND has looked into such research areas as the potential for nuclear action, hostage survival chances, the profile of a typical hijacker and a typical terrorist. Using statistical methods, these quantitative studies led to findings which apparently have had influence on the US government's antiterrorist policies – for instance, most members of a kidnapping team will escape death or capture whether or not they successfully seize hostages; and more terrorists have died during assaults by security forces than from cold execution for deviance by other terrorists. RAND and other organisations have used chronologies to analyse trends in terrorism, yet due to the flexible definition of terrorism it is questionable whether overall assessments are possible.

A chronology similar to RAND was developed at the University of Oklahoma using a data collection based on clear-cut incidents of kidnappings, armed attacks involving hostage-taking, hijackings and assassinations. From their data they came to the conclusion that when confronted with a situation involving terrorist demands, few nation states show any evidence of constant and coherent response strategies, and that terrorists do not usually comply with time limits they have imposed on various authorities for meeting their demands.

Another company, Risks International, produces an Executive Risk Assessment in which the database covers incidents within the United States as well as abroad, and the information is derived from the foreign and English-language press, American and foreign government and police reports. The data is grouped by the type of activity; the categories used are kidnapping, hijacking, assassination, maiming, attack against facilities, and bombing.

The most ambitious publicly accessible data-gathering effort has been undertaken by the Central Intelligence Agency. The data system ITERATE – International Terrorism: Attributes of Terrorist Events – covers a wide range of attributes, including the educational level of members of the terrorist group, the rank of hostages involved, the demands, the attitudes of the groups to life and death, the type of negotiator, the negotiating behaviour of the terrorist, the reliability of warnings and the organisations claiming or denying responsibility for an incident.

Such data can be used for studying global diffusion patterns of transnational terrorism over time; for terrorist trends analysis; to improve hostage negotiation techniques; to compare terrorist campaigns; to evaluate policies for use in crisis management; to evaluate possibilities for deterrence of terrorism; and to evaluate the effects of publicity on terrorist behaviour.

Policy considerations in general over the past decade appear to be playing a bigger role than scientific criteria in determining the inclusion or exclusion of incidents of political protest and violence. A largely American source which is internationally accessible to researchers is the Clandestine Tactics and Technology Data Service of the International Association of Chiefs of Police's Bureau of Operations and Research, which distributes documents to selected applicants relating to analyses on terrorist groups' activities, tactics and countermeasures. Microfiches of terrorist incidents are compiled by the US National Criminal Justice Reference Service. The results of the work of Congressional committees on terrorism to which national and foreign experts were invited as well as representatives of various government agencies, and the numerous statistics and chronologies on all aspects of insurgent terrorism so gleaned are held at the library of Congress – one of the best libraries in the world for the study of terrorism literature. The terrorist events in the early 1970s brought an international awareness of the need for the study of terrorism. National and international bodies and study groups were created, generally being integrated into existing bureaucracies. The US Office of Combatting Terrorism was formed within the State Department, while the United Nations formed an ad hoc committee to study the question of international terrorism. There are also many monitoring and operative agencies usually linked to policy-making bodies.

Dawson's Field In September 1970 Leila Khaled of the Popular Front for the Liberation of Palestine (PFLP), and Patrick Arguello (a Latin American working for the PFLP), tried to hijack an El Al plane en route from Tel Aviv to New York, which they had boarded in Amsterdam. They were overpowered by armed Israeli sky marshals, who had been placed on all El Al planes after a spate of attacks in the late 1960s, and Arguello was fatally wounded. Leila Khaled did not press home the attack, failing at the vital moment to pull the pin from her grenade. Arguello did pull the pin from his grenade, but it had a weak spring and failed to explode.

In spite of this failure, other similarly equipped PFLP squads forced a TWA 707 and a Swissair DC8 to land at Dawson's Field, a former RAF landing strip in the desert, 40 miles north of Amman in Jordan. A British vc10 on route from London to Bahrein was also forced down there and held hostage for the release of Leila Khaled, who was then being held at Ealing police station in London after the El Al flight had made an emergency landing at Heathrow. Finally, in this series of hijacks, a TWA plane flying from Amsterdam was seized, taken to Cairo and blown up.

Five governments (the UK, Netherlands, Israel, USA and Switzerland) became involved in lengthy negotiations with the Palestinians for the release of the hostages; the Palestinians were then able to claim that they were operating on a nation-to-nation basis and that their cause had thereby been officially recognised.

As in so many acts of terrorism, the very success of the act brought about a violent reaction. King Hussein of Jordan unleashed his Bedouin army on the Palestinian guerrilla bases; there was a minor civil war in and around Amman in 1971, and finally the Palestinian guerrillas fled to Lebanon to set up new bases. After the Dawson's Field fiasco, Palestinian groups turned their attention to attacking El Al planes on the ground.

Debray, Regis Debray was a French revolutionary theorist who was active in the urban and rural guerrilla activity in South America in the 1960s. He believed that intellectuals were invaluable to the success of any revolutionary cause – but that when they took part in such activity they had a bad conscience. The struggle against oppression was his over-riding concern and approached the status of a fight for a sacred cause.

Debray regarded the urban working class (not excluding the Communist parties) as an essentially conservative element. In Castro's view, the city was the grave of the guerrilla, and Debray was even more outspoken. Life in towns was for him tantamount to an 'objective betrayal', for in his view the mountain proletarianises the bourgeois and peasant elements, whereas the city embourgeoises the proletarians. Living conditions in the towns were fundamentally different from those prevailing in the countryside. Even the best comrades were corrupted in the cities and affected by alien patterns of thought. Debray's arrest shortly after the death of Guevara highlighted the ultimate failure of rural guerrilla practice in South America.

To Debray the guerrilla *'foco'* or nucleus was composed of foreign career revolutionaries and selected indigenous participants. Jungle and mountain reconnaissance amidst maximum secrecy helped to adapt guerrillas to the environment. This allowed for small training operations against the regime.

The guerrilla base would now be established with regional guerrillas and urban squads, which would increase in numbers from natural evolution. The people's army would then go on the offensive. Regional and urban groups would keep government forces tied down, and the mobile force would attack selected targets. A general strike would then precede a conventional offensive on the capital.

Definition: issues and problems A definition is basically an equation. It says what a word is meant to mean. However, with regard to the concept of terrorism the emotive nature of the subject matter, the term's derogatory thrust and the political discourse are all major contributory factors to its complexity. Although there is hardly a definition which does not contain the word violence, the concept, rather than being considered as a technique of applying violence which in principle can be used by anyone in all sorts of conflict situations, is linked to certain actors only for certain types of conflicts. Often the well-worn phrase 'one man's terrorist is another man's patriot' is used, proving that the concept has been subjected to a double standard, and an 'in-group, out-group' distinction.

In spite of the spread of terrorist incidents throughout the world, terrorism has neither a precise definition nor one which is widely acceptable. Like many political terms it is pejorative. Some governments are prone to label as terrorism all violent acts committed by their political opponents, while anti-government extremists claim to be the victims of government terror. The imprecise nature of the term means that it can be applied to almost any set of fear-producing actions to serve a variety of purposes. More generally it can apply to similar acts of violence – kidnappings and hijackings – which are not intended by the perpetrators to be terror-producing. Political sociologists argue that no definition can, in principle, be reached because the very process of definition is in itself part of the wider contestation of ideologies or political objectives. Definitions support the argument that the perspectives change according to when and where the terrorist act takes place. The question of the definition of terrorism is central to an understanding of the phenomenon and to the success of any rational measures directed against it. To many observers almost any act of violence may be included under the rubric of terrorism. Others would not label as terrorism violent acts carried out within a revolutionary context which a number of people would recognise as terroristic. Confusion can arise over a seeming similarity of behaviour when a violent act is carried out by a politically motivated individual, a criminal or the mentally unbalanced.

Terrorism is also a moral problem, and attempts at definition are predicated on the assumption that some classes of political violence are justifiable whereas others are not. For instance, students of terrorism find some difficulty in labelling an event as terrorist without making a moral judgment about the act. Governments and lawyers and politicians find themselves unable to take such a detached view. Hence, violence has been defined in terms of force, coercive power, authority and legitimacy. One of the problems of implementing criminal sanctions occurs in the case of acts of terrorism that produce a terror outcome by threats of violence, without actual physical injury to any human or non-human targets. A generally accepted definition of terrorism requires an element of terror and coercive purpose. All terrorist acts involve violence or the threat of violence, often coupled with specific demands.

The word terrorism is often used with qualifying terms – 'often', 'mainly', 'generally' and 'usually'. These qualifiers allow for the injection of personal views in deciding whether a particular act is or is not 'terrorist'. Conversely, defining terrorism by focusing on the nature of the act rather than on the identity of the perpetrators, or the nature of their cause makes a substantial degree of objectivity possible. The Central Intelligence Agency distinguishes between transnational terrorism or terrorism carried out by basically autonomous non-state actors, whether or not they enjoy some degree of support from sympathetic states, and international terrorism, which is terrorism carried out by individuals or groups controlled by a sovereign state. So far the General Assembly of the United Nations has been unable to agree on a standard definition, and if the time ever comes when there is general agreement that international terrorism must be curbed, any definition adopted will have to be couched in universal, and not pro-Western terms. International terrorism can be distinguished from purely domestic terror-violence by the presence of an international jurisdictional element. Transnational terrorism, a term often used erroneously as a synonym for international terrorism, can be considered a sub-classification with specific reference to non-state non-political actors.

D

Although specially constituted UN committees have continually condemned acts of international terrorism in principle, they have exempted from their definition of such acts those activities which derive from the inalienable right to self-determination and independence of all peoples under colonial and racist regimes, and in particular the struggle of national liberation movements in accordance with the purposes and principles of the Charter and the relevant resolutions of the organs of the United Nations.

In the absence of an international definition, the West has tended to go it alone as a community and to act as a group against terrorism. Governments in both East and West often use the word terrorist to describe their opponents, even when these opponents have not used violence. Guerrilla groups refuse to let themselves be seen by governments as terrorists and will prefer to call themselves guerrillas. While it is easier for governments than for terrorists to legitimate their activities, terrorists often strive for legitimacy. Governments are often seen as having substantial resources, and as rational beings whose actions serve a longer goal, while individuals have little social claim and are typified by meagre resources and limited modes of violence coupled with an irrational drive and a deranged mind.

Terrorism, by definition, is an act that seeks to influence a population significantly larger than the immediate target. The quality of the public's understanding and its response to terrorism of all varieties is highly significant. One of the prime purposes of terrorist activity is to put a grievance on the public agenda. Terrorism is a strategy whereby violence is used to produce certain effects upon a group of people. With special reference to political sub-state terrorism, this strategy is one of four 'ideal type' strategies whereby a group out of power can effect violent social change, the other three being the coup d'état, insurrection and guerrilla warfare.

Definition: issues and problems

Many of the definitional problems plaguing analysts of terrorism can be found in the scientific and ideological discourse on violence. Terrorism has been defined in terms of violation, violation of the corporal integrity of the state, violation of territorial or special integrity, of moral and legal decency, of rules and expectations and even as violation of self esteem, dignity and autonomy. It has been defined in terms of force, coercive power, authority, legitimacy, behaviour, motives, intentions, antecedents and consequences. In relation to the differing perceptions of violence, terrorism can be seen as an easily recognised and undesirable activity, subjectively determined and shaped by social and political considerations.

Terrorism can be committed for several purposes. Individual acts of terrorism may aim at wringing specific concessions such as the payment of a ransom or release of prisoners. Terrorism may seek the deliberate provocation of repression, hoping to induce the government to self-destruct. It may be used to enforce obedience and co-operation and as in the Irish troubles, it is frequently meant to punish. Terrorists often declare the victim of their attack is somehow guilty.

No one desires to have the appellation terrorist applied to his activity. Terms such as freedom fighter or liberator are attempts to mitigate what is in fact an ugly profession. A fine line can be encountered between terror and terrorism, with attempts to legalise or justify the former being made while proscribing the latter. Terror practised by a government in office appears as law enforcement and is directed against the opposition, while terrorism, on the other hand, implies open defiance of law and is a means whereby an opposition aims to demoralise government authority. While the terrorist group makes no pretence at legality, legitimate government must at least formally adhere to law. A definitional struggle has thus arisen between those who claim an exception at law for certain manifestly harmful forms of conduct and those who will not admit it.

The difficulty that surrounds accurate definitions of terrorism presents itself again in dealing with typologies. It can be viewed in three ways; terrorism committed or taking effect outside the territory of a state of which the alleged offender is a national, terrorism intended to damage the interests of a state or an international inter-governmental organisation, and terrorism committed neither by nor against a member of the armed forces of a state in the course of military hostilities.

The International Chiefs of Police see terrorism as a purposeful human activity primarily directed toward the creation of a general climate of fear designed to influence, in ways desired by the protagonist, other human beings and, through them, some course of events. If the word 'political' is inserted between the words 'human' and 'activity' one avoids mixing terrorism with gangland intimidation or similar acts. In describing an act of terrorism there must be a terror outcome, or else the process could hardly be labelled as terrorism. The judicial dividing line between fear and intense fear is very small. Terrorism can occur at an instant and by one act. Definitional approaches which relate merely to acts of violence, the threat or use of violence, repressive acts, and similar categorisations are incomplete and unhelpful in terms of meaning and effective guidance for decision. These types of approach ignore the critical need for a focus upon the use of intense fear or anxiety for coercion of a primary target into behaviour or attitudinal patterns sought in connection with a demanded power outcome. Terrorism's success is measured not only by the ability to topple the social order but also to loosen that order in symbolic terms; by weakening the law-making capacities of elected officials and casting doubt on the concept of rights in society and the obligations of the state.

There is a popular belief which terrorists perhaps wish to hold of their actions, that violent or lawless acts, from skyjacking through indiscriminate bombing to ritualistic murder and politically inspired kidnappings, assassinations and the destruction of property, are simple manifestations of man's basic aggressive and destructive nature.

D

Terrorism is not a universal phenomenon, but it is a historical one, emerging only at particular times and associated with particular developments in people's consciousness. Terror can be seen as a counter value campaign, depending on the target attacked, and a guerrilla campaign can be judged in terms of what is being defended. To a large number of observers terror is by definition political. Changes sought by terrorists short of total revolution, have to be achieved within a given political context, i.e. the government institutes reforms, the government falls, or alternatively the government represses the terrorists.

Although terror is in part political violence, not all political violence is in fact terrorism. Vague generalised definitions can mean that the scope of the analysis is too broad and so the findings may be meaningless. Too narrow a definition means there is little opportunity for comparative analysis which can show patterns common to a variety of acts of terrorism. Vague generalised definitions can mean that the scope of the analysis is too broad and so the findings may be meaningless.

A terrorist campaign that causes a significant level of fear among the target population may achieve its aims. Not all the violence espoused by terrorists is mindless. In some instances terrorism is potentially more effective especially from a cost-benefit strategy than conventional or guerrilla warfare. Unlike other forms of warfare, the goal of terrorism is not to destroy the opposing side but instead to break its will and force it to capitulate. The response to an act of terror or guerrilla activity can vary greatly depending on the danger of repetition and the degree of identification with the victim. If the observed identification is not with the victim but with the target of terroristic coercion, it is unlikely to be terror or guerrilla activity, and if the identification of the observer is with the terrorist himself, it might even be euphoria.

Definitions of terrorism have to be studied within the overall subject matter of terrorism and related to its history, philosophy, psychology, sociology, politics, statistics, language and law. In the field of terrorism there is no agreement about any single definition; but there is considerable agreement about the elements which definitions should contain. Open-mindedness and objectivity can be some help in the problem of definition.

Terrorism is a purposeful human political activity directed to the creation of a climate of fear and designed to influence, in ways desired by the protagonist, other human beings and through them, some course of events. It is an unacceptable challenge to the principles on which organised society rests.

See also **Definitions**

Definitions Terrorism manifests itself through distinctive deployment of a variety of criminal acts calculated to harm human life, property and other interests. The ultimate test is the examination of the differing circumstances and events which terrorism is designed to classify. Definitions become standards by which each set of circumstances are judged. In the following set of definitions terrorism is defined solely in terms of its ultimate objectives, rather than in terms of ideology and manner of action. It is easier to identify that which is not terror than attempt to label exactly that which is terror.

The following range of definitions and issues illustrates the difficulty faced by people, groups and organisations who seek to solve the problem of terrorism in the contemporary world.

'Terrorism is a method of combat in the struggle between social groups and forces rather than individuals, and it may take place in any social order.' (Hardman 1936)

'Terrorism is a method of action by which an agent tends to produce terror in order to impose his domination.' (Waciorsky 1939)

'Terrorism is a method of action by which the agent tends to produce terror to impose his domination on the state in order to transform it.

Political terror is the planned use of violence or threat of violence against an individual or social group in order to eradicate resistance to the aims of the terrorist.' (Chisholm 1948)

'Terror can strike without any preliminary provocation, its victims are innocent even from the point of view of the prosecutor.' (Arendt 1951)

'Terrorism is the threat or use of violence for political ends.' (Crozier 1960)

'Sociologically, terror is a person or thing or practice that causes intense fear or suffering, whose aim is to intimidate, subjugate, especially as a political weapon or policy. Politically, its main function is to intimidate and disorganise the government through fear, and through this political changes can be achieved.' (Roucek 1962)

'Terrorism may gain political ends in one of two ways – by mobilising forces or by immobilising forces and reserves sympathetic to the cause of the insurgents, or by immobilising forces and reserves that would normally be available to the incumbents.

A process of terror is the act or threat of violence, the emotional reaction and the social effects; whereas the system of terror may be defined to include certain states of war as well as certain political communities.' (Walter 1964)

'An action of violence is labelled terrorist when its psychological effects are out of proportion to its purely physical result.' (Aron 1966)

'Terrorism is an atmosphere of despair.' (Leiden and Schmitt 1968)

'There is an element of arbitrariness both in the decision-makers' ability to disregard any binding legal norms and in the calculability of the application of terror as perceived by the citizen.' (Dallin and Breslauer 1970)

D

'Terrorism as an element in the process of violent change can be defined as the use of physical violence. It is a complementary tactic to both guerrilla and conventional warfare. Terrorism differs from guerrilla warfare in as much as its purpose is to influence the opponent and any third parties rather than annihilate him. The purpose of the act, not the nature of the act itself is the essential characteristic which distinguishes terrorism.' (Silverman and Jackson 1970)

'The basis of terror tactics is the threat; and terrorism is a form of guerrilla warfare. The basic tactic for guerrilla warfare is to hit and run and hide, hit, run, hide. Guerrillas conceal themselves in mountains or rural areas; and terror tactics are employed in urban areas as well.' (Mallin 1971)

'Terrorism is the systematic use of intimidation for political ends.' (Moss 1971)

'Terrorism is part of a revolutionary strategy, it is manifested in acts of socially and politically unacceptable violence. Terrorism's attractiveness and significance for revolutionary organisations are due to a combination of economy, facility and high psychological and political effectiveness.' (Crenshaw Hutchinson 1972)

'Events involving relatively highly organised and planned activities on the part of small but cohesive groups are the chief characteristics of terrorism.' (Morrison 1972)

'The definition of someone who is a terrorist is purely a labelling device.' (Horowitz 1973)

'Politics by violence and propaganda by the deed are the hallmarks of terror.' (Neale 1973)

'Terrorism is the most amoral of organised violence.' (Wilkinson 1973)

'What distinguishes terrorism from both vandalism and non-political crime, is the motivated violence for political ends.' (Crozier 1974)

Definitions

'The peculiarity of the horror of terrorism is what people remember.' (Fairbairn 1974)

'Terrorism is the coercively intimidatory weapon of revolutionary movements.' (Wilkinson 1974)

'International terrorism is politically and socially motivated violence.' (Bite 1975)

'Terror is violence used to create fear, but it is also aimed at creating fear in order that the fear, in turn will lead somebody else.' (Fromkin 1975)

'The threat of violence, individual acts of violence or a campaign of violence designed primarily to instil fear – to terrorise – may be called terrorism.' (Jenkins 1975)

'International terrorism embodies an act which is essentially politically motivated, and it transcends national boundaries.' (Fearey 1976)

'Transnational terrorism is carried out by autonomous non-state actors, whether or not they enjoy some degree of support from sympathetic states. International terrorism is carried out by individuals or groups controlled by a sovereign state.' (Milbank 1976)

'The use of terrorist violence is based on the assumption that the intended victim is unreasonable and incapable of seeing the viewpoint of the terrorist.' (Qureshi 1976)

'Political terrorism can be defined as a strategy, a method by which an organised group or party tries to get attention for its aims, or force concessions toward its goals, through the systematic use of deliberate violence.' (Watson 1976)

'Violence, in order to be terrorism, must be political.' (Weisband and Roguly 1976)

'Political terrorism is a special form of clandestine undeclared and unconventional warfare waged without humanitarian restraints or rules.' (Wilkinson 1976)

'Terrorist strategy aims not to defeat the forces of the incumbent regime militarily, but to bring about the moral alienation of the masses from the government until its isolation has become total and irreversible.' (Wolf 1976)

'Terrorism is the recourse of a minority or even of a single dissident frustrated by the inability to make society shift in a desired direction by what that society regards as "legitimate" means.' (Clutterbuck 1977)

'The selective use of fear, subjugation and intimidation to disrupt the normal operations of a society.' (Horowitz 1977)

'Individual terror is a system of modern revolutionary violence aimed at leading personalities in the government or the Establishment.' (Iviansky 1977)

'Terrorism is used to create fear and alarm and gain attention.' (Jenkins 1977)

'Terrorism can be used to create an atmosphere of despair or fear, to shake the faith of ordinary citizens in their government and its representatives.' (Leiser 1977)

'As a military arm terrorism is a weapon of psychological warfare.' (Mallin 1977)

'Terrorism involves the intentional use of violence or the threat of violence by the precipitator against an instrumental target in order to communicate to a primary target a threat of future violence.' (Paust 1977)

D

'Terrorism is a state of intense fear which threatens the most fundamental human drive – the will to survive intact.' (Silverstein 1977)

'Two facets are incorporated in terrorism – a state of fear or anxiety within an individual or group, and the tool that induces the state of fear.' (Singh 1977)

'Terrorism involves both the use and the threat of violence.' (Smith 1977)

'Political terrorism can be defined as coercive intimidation, and is one of the oldest techniques of psychological warfare.' (Wilkinson 1977)

'The systematic components of a definition of revolutionary terrorism are a systematic and purposeful method used by a revolutionary organisation; it is manifested in a series of individual acts of extraordinary and intolerable violence, a constant pattern of symbolic or representative selection, and is deliberately intended to create a psychological effect on specific groups of people.' (Crenshaw Hutchinson 1978)

'Terrorism consists of planned acts of violence employed for explicitly political purposes directed against an established state or organisational power; and involving a relatively small number of conspirators.' (Hamilton 1978)

'One man's terrorist is everyone's terrorist. All terrorist acts are crimes and many also would be violations of the rules of war, if a state of war existed.' (Jenkins 1978)

'Terror is the use of force in a context which differentiates the victim of the violence employed from the target of the action.' (Kaplan 1978)

'Terrorism may be defined as systematic and organised violence against non-resisting persons to create fear in them for the purpose of retaining or gaining governmental authority.' (Karanovic 1978)

'The use or threat of use of anxiety, induced by extra-normal violence for political purposes by an individual or group, whether acting for or in opposition to established governmental authority.' (Mickolus 1978)

'Politically motivated behaviour of a non-state group without electoral prospects in a democratic context which aims by means of violent acts against persons and or property to coerce people in order to obtain its will thereby.' (Schwind 1978)

'Political terrorism is the threat and or use of extra-normal forms of political violence in varying degrees with the objective of achieving political objectives and goals.' (Shultz 1978)

'The apex of violence is terrorism.' (Zinam 1978)

'Terrorism is every method of political struggle that fulfils three conditions – namely the involvement of the extreme use of violence against innocent people, and is not a legitimate method of struggle.' (Pontara 1979)

'Political terrorism is the systematic use of violence for political ends directed against outsiders in a political conflict. Its increase can be seen in terms of four factors – arms, mobility, communication (publicity) and money.' (Tromp 1979)

'The United States government have a widely used definition, which is the threat or use of violence for political purposes when such action is designed to influence the attitude or behaviour of a target group wider than its immediate victims and its ramifications transcend national boundaries.
Terrorism is a special mode of violence which may be briefly defined as coercive intimidation. It involves the threat of murder, injury or destruction to terrorise a given target into conceding to the terrorists' will.' (Wilkinson 1979)

'Terrorism is the use or threat of extraordinary political violence to induce fear, anxiety or alarm in a target audience wider than the immediate symbolic victims. Terrorism is violence for political effect as opposed to military impact.' (Heyman 1980)

'The use, or threat of use of anxiety-inducing extra-normal violence for political purposes by any individual or group.' (Mickolus 1980)

'An act of political violence, but terrorism escapes definition when it becomes embellished with value-ladened political meaning.' (Miller 1980)

'Terrorism may be described as a strategy of violence designed to inspire terror within a particular segment of a given society.' (Bassiouni 1981)

'Terrorism occurs both in the context of violent resistance to the state as well as in the service of state interests.' (Crenshaw Hutchinson 1981)

'In the West, terrorism is distinguished from guerrilla warfare in that the latter term refers to paramilitary combat carried out against regular military forces. However, almost all guerrilla movements make use of terrorism at one or another stage of their development, and some rely on it.' (Francis 1981)

'Terroristic actions are demonstrative, spectacular and theatrical, and the victims are mere pawns in the terroristic game.' (Hacker 1981)

'Terrorism relies for its effects not so much on any general unpredictability, but rather on its specific unexpectedness as well as on the eruption of violence into environments normally free from it.

Non-governmental terrorism is the considered and systematic use of widespread offensive violence, murder and destruction aimed at governmental employees and the general population as well as public and private property, to force individuals, groups, communities, economic entities and governments to modify or change their actual proposed behaviour and policies so as to concede to the terrorists' political demands.' (Herman 1981)

'By terrorism, one means a series of intentional acts of direct, psychological violence, which at indeterminable points but nevertheless systematically, with the aim of psychic effect, are conducted within the framework of a political strategy.' (Hess 1981)

'Terrorist acts are severe bouts of violence directed at non-combatants by the contending sides of a political struggle.' (Sederberg 1981)

'The process of terrorism consists of the act or threat of violence, the emotional reactions to such an act or threat and the social effects resultant from the acts and reactions.' (Stohl 1981)

'Terrorism is seen as the resort to violence for political ends by unauthorised, non-governmental actors in breach of accepted codes of behaviour.' (Lodge 1982)

'Terrorism is an organised system of extreme and violent intimidation to create instability within democracies. International terrorists seek to launch indiscriminate and unpredictable attacks on groups (police, army, multinationals or nations) to change the politico-economic balance of the world.' (Thackrah 1982)

All these authors of definitions of terrorism have tried to contribute toward the understanding of a complex subject, and their definitions are the result of varied academic backgrounds and attitudes to research on terrorism. The concepts of terror and terrorism are slippery and much-abused, and their relation to other forms of political violence and to criminality is often ambiguous. It is the interplay of subjective factors and responses within terror and terrorism that makes them difficult concepts for social scientists to define.

See also **Definition: issues and problems**

Dhofari guerrillas The Omani province of Dhofar is ideal guerrilla country. It is in the west of the sultanate and is bordered by broken terrain leading into the People's Democratic Republic of Yemen (PDRY), by the Arabian Sea and in the north and east by inhospitable desert known as the Empty Quarter. Within these boundaries the province is dominated by the Jebel, a belt of mountains which act as backcloth to a thin coastal strip around Salalah, isolating it behind steep-sided escarpments and virtually impassable wadis. Even the weather favours the guerrillas; between June and September much of the province is subject to the south-west monsoon, producing plant growth to mask guerrilla movement; for the rest of the year the high temperatures hamper counter-guerrilla operations.

The population of Dhofar is divided between those living on the agriculturally rich plains and those in the mountains. It was among the latter tough, nomadic and intensely religious tribesmen, collectively known as Jebalis, that resistance to the rule of the sultan emerged in the early 1960s. The sultan governed his country with heavy-handed repression, refusing to sanction any policies of modernisation or reform – and their aims initially were intensely nationalistic, specifying independence for Dhofar and an end to foreign (predominantly British) interference. Formed in 1962, the Dhofar Liberation Front (DLF) instigated a low-level and weak campaign of sniping, sabotage and ambush. By the mid 1960s few DLF fighters were active.

In late 1967 the situation changed dramatically, for when the British withdrew from Aden Protectorate the newly-emergent PDRY offered support to the DLF and sent its own 'advisers' into Dhofar. At a special congress in June 1968 they ousted the nationalist leadership, replacing it with a communist dominated General Command, dedicated to the spread of Marxism. Renamed the Popular Front for the Liberation of the Occupied Arabian Gulf (PFLOAG, amended in 1971 to denote Popular Front for the Liberation of Oman and the Arabian Gulf), the new movement strengthened its hold on the Jebel, often by means of intimidation, and it initiated a guerrilla campaign which by 1970 had forced the Sultan's Armed Forces (SAF) to withdraw.

In July 1970 the Sultan was deposed by his son Qaboos, who immediately introduced reforms, but it was to take another five years of hard fighting before the SAF, led and inspired by British officers well-versed in the minutiae of counter-insurgency, could claim a victory. During that period the PFLOAG (renamed yet again in 1974, this time as the Popular Front for the Liberation of Oman) achieved a maximum strength of about 2,000 guerrillas. Equipped with Soviet and Chinese weapons, the guerrillas exploited their local knowledge and perfected the techniques of ambush, hitting the SAF units at long range before melting back into the Jebel to escape air and artillery response.

Fortunately for the SAF, the communist leadership, following policies which undermined both the Moslem religion and the tribal system, alienated many Jebalis, while government 'civil development' centres offering advantages of water, medicine, education and protection attracted tribal settlement. Moreover, as guerrillas surrendered, they were recruited into British-organised 'firqat', or counter-insurgency patrols, and sent back into the mountains to try to win over the allegiance of the Dhofaris. It was a successful exercise in the exploitation of the natural fighting abilities of tribesmen in ideal guerrilla terrain.

Direct Action
See **Action Directe**

Dissidents in the Soviet Union Although there are no officially recognised opposition organisations, a number of groups have been established from time to time to campaign for the observance of civil rights based on the 1948 Universal Declaration of Human Rights which the Soviet Union did not sign, and the final act of the 1975 Helsinki Conference on Security and Co-operation in Europe which was signed by the Soviet Union. The government in Moscow has always believed that rights can be restricted in the interests of internal security, public order and public health or morals.

Apart from the Helsinki Group, other organisations include independent trade unions, groups propagating autonomy for national minorities and the prevention of their russification, e.g. the Georgian rebels and Crimean Tartars, those demanding freedom of religious worship such as the Free Seventh Day Adventists, the Council of Churches of Evangelical Christians, and Pentecostalists; and groups in particular among Jews calling for freedom to emigrate, such as Aleyeh and the Refuseniks. A number of intellectuals have proposed various forms of changes in the country's political and social system and demanded freedom of expression for writers and artists – for example, the Free Interprofessional Organisation of Workers, the Democratic Popular Front of the Soviet Union and the Trade Union for the Defence of the Workers. An important role in the activities of the dissident writers and artists has been played by privately produced typescripts circulated as unauthorised publications, known as *samizdat*.

Dissidents have suffered greatly at the hands of the authorities. Some have been expelled from official bodies; others dismissed from employment, and at a more drastic level, sent into internal exile, imprisonment in penal institutions including labour camps of varying degrees of severity and to internment in psychiatric hospitals. In a few notable cases, dissidents have been deprived of their nationality, and allowed to emigrate or even expelled from the USSR.

Andrei Amalrik, an historian and dramatist, was sentenced to three years in a strict regime labour camp for defaming the Soviet state in 1970; six years later he was allowed to emigrate, dying in France in 1980. Vladimir Bukovsky, a biologist and poet, was committed to a mental hospital in 1962 after he had published a poem in a clandestine magazine; and after further periods of detention in psychiatric hospitals and labour camps, was exchanged in 1976 for Luis Corvelan the Chilean Communist leader, who had been held in prison in Chile. Subsequently Bukovsky settled in Britain and studied at Cambridge University. Yuli Daniel and Andrei Sinyavsky, translators and authors, were given five year labour camp sentences in 1966 for smuggling and publishing abroad works used in the ideological struggle against the Soviet Union. Both were expelled from the Writers' Union. Alexander Ginsburg, a writer, was sentenced to seven years' hard labour in 1968 for collecting information and distributing anti-Soviet literature for the People's Labour Organisation, and in 1978 was given eight years in a special regime labour camp for anti-Soviet activities and propaganda. Yuri Orlov, former chairman of the Helsinki group, was given seven years in a hard labour camp in 1978 and five years in internal exile for anti-Soviet agitation and propaganda. Another member of the Helsinki group, Anatoly Shcharansky, a computer specialist, was sentenced in Moscow in 1978 to three years in a close confinement prison and a further ten years in a strict regime labour camp for high treason and espionage. He was exchanged in Berlin in February 1986 for Communist bloc personnel who had been spying in the West.

Alexander Solzhenitsyn, a writer, who after gallant war service criticised Stalin in a private letter, served eight years in a forced labour camp in 1945–53, followed by exile in Siberia until 1956. The novels he wrote about his experiences and those of others, notably *One Day in the Life of Ivan Denisovich*, and *Gulag Archipelago* earned him worldwide renown and the Nobel Prize for literature, but also expulsion from the Writers' Union and in 1974 expulsion from his country and deprivation of Soviet citizenship. One of the chief civil rights activists in the Soviet Union has been Andrei Sakharov, an eminent physicist involved in the foundation in 1970 of the Committee for Human Rights and the Helsinki Group. He has taken part in efforts to obtain the release of political prisoners and for the rights of national and religious minorities. Unfortunately, although he wishes to leave the country, his occupation prior to retirement was as a nuclear physicist and the Soviet government insists he knows too many state secrets to be allowed to emigrate. After several open letters to Russian papers and to individuals and organisations abroad he was, along with his wife Yelena Bonner, banished to internal exile in Gorky in 1980. His wife spent six months in the USA in 1985–86 receiving treatment for a heart condition – but this was allowed by the Soviets only after her husband had been on a well-publicised hunger strike.

Dissent and dissenters have always featured in Soviet history, but due to the nature of the Soviet regime, and its limited interest in freedom and the rule of law, they have failed to arouse the masses to try to overthrow the regime.

Dynamics of terrorism Case study analysis of terrorists and their life patterns is still very much in its infancy. However, empirical estimates of model parameters have been obtained from data on international terrorism since 1968. Some evidence suggests that the tendency of acts of terrorism to incite further violence is more easily reversed in less democratic, poorer and less well-educated societies. It appears that reversal of a terrorism 'epidemic' is more likely under conditions which facilitate repression rather than reform, and more open societies face particular difficulties in responding to terrorism effectively.

Quantitative empirical studies have consisted of tabulations or attempts to fit models of 'social contagion'. Theoretical formulations have concentrated on issues of definition and typology. Many controversies have been raised on historical, ideological and tactical concerns, but these have not been formally addressed in quantitative social research. The concern that the main effect of terrorism is increased police repression is a common theme among a number of leftist warnings. Marighella (1971) argued that terrorism leads to repression, but made this relationship the foundation of terrorist strategy. Hyams (1974) sees liberal reform as the ultimate consequence of terrorism. Terrorism, says Hyams, improves the climate for reform and brings about a more just society. Moss (1971), Clutterbuck (1975) and Laqueur (1977) dispute the claim that terrorism is primarily a weapon of the miserable and oppressed, and they point out that it is often the work of idle élites, particularly students and intelligentsia. Terrorism is much easier and safer in more open societies; and the terrorist faces surprisingly low risks of harsh punishment or even arrest (Wilkinson 1978). Writers from a variety of liberal and conservative perspectives maintain that reform becomes less likely, and repressive reaction more likely in the climate of insecurity and violence produced by a terror campaign. Terrorism is usually unsuccessful in bringing about social changes sought by terrorists and it has a good chance of making those changes far more difficult to attain. The overall message of writers is that society has difficulty in responding to terrorist acts. Whereas authoritarian states opt for straightforward violent situations, states founded upon liberal democratic principles have to find other approaches.

Thus a new model of terrorism, adopted among others by Heyman and Mickolus (1980), considers the view that terrorist incidents may encourage further violence through a process of imitation or diffusion, giving rise to a dynamics of terrorism similar to that observed in the spread of a contagious disease. If terrorism is contagious between countries, then commonalities of culture, circumstances and personnel and the ease of rapid communication make the phenomenon of contagion even more visible within countries. Thus the number of incidents observed over a fixed time period would have a Poisson distribution (see p. 68). This model, however, does not cover the key element of controversy in the political and ideological literature on terrorism, namely, the sorts of circumstances in which the terrorism 'epidemic' can give rise to a change in conditions which leads to the eventual reversal of the epidemic.

Chronology data can be useful, especially if it is comprehensive and current. However, the necessary dependence on news service sources for incident reports creates inevitable biases in favour of countries with well-developed and unrestrained news media. Incident counts for less-developed countries, or countries with highly restricted information tend to be deflated relative to counts for the more public industrial democracies. Such data often refers only to incidents of international terrorism in which two or more states were somehow involved. The great majority of terrorist acts are purely domestic in character, but reliable domestic terrorism chronologies are available for very few countries. Much of the literature on terrorism does not distinguish between domestic and international terrorism, or sees the latter primarily as an extension of the domestic struggle.

Contagion terrorism at some point can be reversed, when the cumulative number of incidents begins to decrease, rather than increase the probability of future incidents. Reversals can result from a tendency of terrorism to generate successful repression, which destroys the terrorist organisation or makes rebellion too dangerous; or a tendency for terrorism to generate social reform, which undermines the grievances that produced the terrorism in the first place. Terrorism is least reversible in relatively open and affluent societies, which proves that concerns about the dilemma of the liberal state are well founded. Terrorism seemingly confronts citizens of open societies with a no-win choice between tolerating terrorist violence on the one hand, or accepting loss of basic freedoms and important restraints upon government behaviour on the other. The middle ground can be narrow and dangerous, and whatever the goals of terrorism, by its nature as a means it is likely to have malignant effects. Autocratic, poor and uneducated countries do not seem to suffer from these effects.

The Poisson model of terrorism appears to be the best of the models for analysing the occurrences of terrorist events. It has three bases: the probability that an event of terrorism will occur during a time interval increases with the length of the time interval; the probability is almost negligible that two events of terrorism will occur in a very small time interval (with the exception, of course, of co-ordinated efforts); and generally the vents of terrorism which occur during one time interval are independent of those which occur in any other time interval. However, with regard to the latter point, it is conceivable that an event of terrorism, if given sufficient publicity, will generate a climate which is conducive to other events of terrorism.

The study of international terrorism has been the domain of the psychologist, political scientist, sociologist and those in the legal profession for many decades. Analytical attempts to study the problem suffer from the lack of hard data. Thus more research has to be undertaken of a quantitative nature in the field of terrorism. Simple hypothesis testing of the theories of the qualitative researchers would be of interest.

Dynamite terrorism Dynamite terrorism was undertaken by Irish revolutionaries in the last quarter of the nineteenth century. It was important and indeed perhaps politically and psychologically necessary for them to endow dynamite's power with the broadest theoretical and philosophical meanings. Super-explosives were interpreted to represent 'power to the people' for use against the state. The state used raw power and violence against the people – so they should do likewise in return. Secondly, super-explosives represented scientific power. To some terrorists it seemed proper for science to enable man to unleash the forces of nature against the state. They believed that the highest form of revolutionary terror should utilise the most advanced science and technology of the time.

Super-explosive terror represented a moral form of power because it elevated violence above the level of common criminality. Conventional weapons might have been easier to use, but they aroused conventional prejudices and lacked grandeur. Super-explosives were claimed to constitute a humane form of power. Since the state was the chief source of inhumanity and immorality, according to some terrorists, the quicker it was destroyed the better for humanity – even though some people were killed or harmed in the process.

Lastly, super-explosives were seen to impart a mystical, magical kind of power – useful at least to charm the audience and perhaps to create an apocalyptic breakthrough to a new millennium.

The threat potential and tactical applications of dynamite were often greatly exaggerated by both terrorists and defenders.

D

E

East Timor Following the April 1974 revolution in Portugal, several political groups manoeuvred for power in the small Portuguese colony of East Timor. After a short civil war, the left-wing Frente Revolucionária Timorense de Libertação e Independência (Fretilin) proclaimed independence on 28 November 1975.

On 7 December, East Timor was invaded by Indonesian troops who expelled Fretilin from the capital, Dili. Guerrilla fighting continued, even though East Timor was formally annexed by Indonesia on 14 August 1976, and Fretilin was able to survive repeated Indonesian offensives. Negotiations took place between Fretilin and the Indonesian authorities in March 1983, but fighting was renewed in August 1983, following the ambush of a group of Indonesian soldiers.

Casualty figures on both sides are unknown. Indonesia has long claimed that resistance to its occupation is insignificant while the East Timorese claim that a 'hot' war is under way between Indonesian regulars and Fretilin guerrillas.

Indonesia has consistently feared that a successful independent government in a small state in the midst of its far-flung inland territory would set an example for parts of the country beset by secessionist rumblings.

Indonesia's denial of strong resistance from the East Timorese has been challenged by photos and tape recordings smuggled out by guerrillas, which show that the ceasefire took place in 1983. Fretilin forces were organised into companies and operate in ten military zones in the central and eastern districts. There is evidence that the most wanted of the guerrillas are still fighting. There are new names in the leadership, including veterans from the first phase of the war, who have rejoined the guerrillas after having surrendered to the Indonesians in 1979. Indonesian activity is focused in the east, where the strategy since 1983 has been to build a cordon across the island to contain the guerrillas.

Efficacy of terrorism To some people and nations terrorism works. Terrorism without efficacy would be only an expression of some destructive pathology. By definition terrorism works when the target of terrorism acts in such a manner that it either loses public support for its political position or it lessens its own political capabilities. Terrorism is the strategy of the weak. If those wanting to weaken a hated political authority were strong, they would not use terrorism as their main strategy because successful terrorism depends entirely upon the actions of the target. The target, in effect, has control of the situation. If those wanting to weaken a hated political authority are strong, they will use strategies for which the outcome is more within their own control. If successful terrorism depends on the target's action, then to explain successful terrorism one has to study the behaviour of the target and not the behaviour of the terrorists.

Targets can take responses that will weaken their political authority and give credence to the terrorist – namely, overreaction, power deflation, failed repression of moderates, appeasement of moderates, and massive intimidation. Key variables can explain each of the five responses – the target's perception of self, of the terrorists and the relative capabilities between self and terrorists.

Overreaction by a target, whether subject to regime or insurgent terrorism, is a familiar pattern of behaviour. The loss of public support is inevitable – and the target is seen to have acted to transform a country's political situation to a military one. If the target overreacts with ostentatious protective measures, it magnifies the political stature and threat of the terrorists. Overreactions can result in the target lessening its own capabilities. Counter-terrorism can be very expensive in money, attention, equipment and labour. Overreaction usually entails ever greater costs. When insurgents are the target, regime terrorism denotes that it is the regime that is weak. The regime then uses terrorism to provoke the opposition to overreact, to use formidable state measures so as to reduce its popular support, or to deplete the force capabilities of the insurgents. Regardless, overreaction is made more likely when the target sees itself as powerful and able to inflict a lesson upon so unworthy a foe.

A target that is incapable of responding to terror will find public support decreases and its capabilities and confidence to fight terrorism will recede. If either a regime or insurgent group cannot protect its people, then it will lose legitimacy. The same result occurs when terrorists can choose the timing and victims of their strikes without hindrance, and then successfully collect ransom, release prisoners, have manifestos read or printed in the media, destroy symbols of state authority or injure or kill victims. Since the function of political authorities centres on protecting people and controlling the policy-making process, those authorities who fail in these tasks lose their legitimacy as authorities. The more failures, the more their power deflates. Terrorists are serious, dedicated fighters who skilfully match the target's action with spectacular reaction. The terrorists create situations where options for actions all have greater costs than benefits. The first difficulty may be identifying and finding the terrorists. Usually the anti-terrorist service is hampered by a public which gives the terrorists sanctuary and anonymity. This allows the terrorists to surprise the target, striking where it is least prepared to respond and where the terrorists enjoy multiple options while the target does not – these issues were evident in the British experience in Palestine.

The terrorists' target chooses to attack not only the terrorists but the moderate, non-violent opposition as well. If the target is a regime, it can ban political parties, institute censorship, increase surveillance, arrest and incarcerate protestors and even kill moderates as an example to others of the costs of opposition. If the target is an insurgent group, it can kidnap, bomb, and assassinate the moderates, both in the regime and in the non-violent opposition to the regime. Moderates conclude that moderation is untenable and to protect themselves from the target they go to the side of the original terrorists, usually as the lesser of two evils. Examples of insurgent targets repressing moderates include the Tupamaros in Uruguay, the Black Panther Party of the USA and the Sendero Luminoso (Shining Path) of Peru. Whereas target overreaction may be seen as an act of omnipotence and self-confidence, repression of moderates stems from frustration, anger and anxiety. These emotions lead to irrationality and desperate actions.

Vigorous political reforms, which appease moderates, alienate the avid supporters of the old order. These supporters can move into the camp of the irreconcilable opposition. For example, when Prime Minister Pierre Trudeau made major reforms on behalf of French Canadians on the issue of language and political appointments, a substantial number of English-speaking Canadians considered these actions as nothing more than outright appeasement of the Front de Libération du Québec (FLQ). Concessions seemed to be a reward for planting bombs and blowing up Canadians. Reforms remove the injustices that stimulated the terrorism in the first place. Removing grievances will not end terrorism, but it isolates the radical and habitual terrorists from the mass of the people who do not like the risks of disorder and violence, especially if they bear them for no apparent cause. Yet the hated political authority is weakened and weakened in line with the professed aims of the terrorists. Terrorism has worked even though the terrorists are dead, in jail or struggling to stay alive.

Those who are intimidated into inaction or obedience will not keep or build public support because those who do not act cannot serve others – cannot protect, provide or promote. Intimidation works when the target experiences fear and feels vulnerable. Strong convictions inhibit intimidation, notably when the upholding of them has public attention.

While the causes of terrorism, that is of the terrorist's behaviour, are largely sociological, the success or failure of terrorism, which is determined by the target's behaviour is largely dependent on psychological factors. Terrorists must know or manipulate the target's psychological perceptions to induce it to act in the way it is predisposed to act. Successful terrorism changes the relative capability of the contestants. The target is weakened and the terrorist strengthened. Political strategies are always dependent upon relative capabilities. A large moderate, non-violent opposition movement in tandem with a terrorist movement forces the target to deal with the issues behind the opposition. Repression radicalises and militarises the moderates. The only other option is to appease the moderates via reforms. Targets who usually avoid using strategies of violence are forced to reform, while targets that like violence will not be moved to reform by non-violent protests.

Egypt The Arab Republic of Egypt is a 'democratic and socialist state' with a limited system of party pluralism. The franchise was restricted in 1978, specifying that the right to belong to political parties and engage in political activities did not apply to those who had been involved in political corruption before the 1952 revolution or to those convicted of political offences who had subjected the national unity or social peace to danger.

The Muslim Brotherhood has been the most powerful opposition group against the regime, and its Islamic fundamentalism has been supported by many small militant groups intent upon destroying the state's leadership, one of them being responsible for the death of President Sadat in 1981. Communist and other left-wing groups have been involved in acts of violence protesting against the Camp David agreements with Israel of 1978. Some former politicians and military personnel have called for the abandonment of Egypt's pro-Western policies and a return to close relations with the Soviet Union.

In its sixty years of existence, the Muslim Brotherhood has had a chequered history of banning and rehabilitation at the hands of many governments. For example, the Wafdist government legalised the Brotherhood in 1951; the Neguib government ordered its dissolution in 1954 and then restored it a few months later. President Neguib was then deposed by Nasser in late 1954 after it was alleged that he had been involved in a conspiracy by the Brotherhood. Many members of the Brotherhood were condemned to death or imprisoned. In 1964 an amnesty was declared and many Brotherhood members were released. In order to counter the influence of communists, a number of Brotherhood members were appointed to official posts and some played a leading role in anti-government plots. Others were accused of plotting to assassinate Nasser – and death sentences or imprisonment resulted.

In the late 1960s, the Brotherhood was revived in Egypt and President Sadat from 1970 gradually came to regard it as a natural ally against the Nasserite socialists and communists. Sadat's pro-Western policies led to renewed opposition by all Islamic fundamentalist organisations, including the Brotherhood, who harshly criticised the President's policies and offered a detailed political alternative based on Islamic Law. Considerable support came from the universities and its influence was further strengthened by the social disruption caused by the increasing westernisation of Arab countries, the growing strength of the Arabs through oil wealth and later the Islamic revolution in Iran.

After Sadat's assassination in 1981, hundreds of Islamic fundamentalists were arrested and suspected Brotherhood sympathisers purged from the armed forces. Over the last three to four years, security clamp-downs on Islamic fundamentalists have tended to be concentrated on an array of smaller groupings rather than on the Brotherhood in particular. The government appears to have adopted a policy of encouraging the Brotherhood as a moderate alternative to the more extreme fundamentalist groups.

Another strong fundamentalist group is the Repentance and Holy Flight, which is sizeable, highly organised and spread horizontally and vertically throughout Egyptian society. Their goal is to topple Egypt's present social order and to establish an Islamic order. There are up to 5,000 active members and about 300 of these are professionally trained, heavily armed and financed by a foreign power.

The Egyptian Communist Party, although illegal, has maintained close relations with other pro-Soviet Communist parties and has posed a security threat to Egyptian governments in periods when the latter have pursued a Western-aligned foreign policy.

In 1986 dissident servicemen on national service caused considerable violence and panic in Cairo in which over 100 deaths were reported. The current leader, President Mubarak, has many dissident elements opposed to him.

El Salvador The root of the social conflict which led to the outbreak of open civil war in El Salvador in 1979 went back over a hundred years. Between 1879 and 1882 three successful land reforms abolished collective ownership of the land from which the peasants scraped a subsistence living, and substituted a free market in land and labour. The result was the emergence of an economy based upon the export of coffee, and an extremely unequal pattern of land ownership. It made possible the creation of a powerful landed élite usually known as 'the fourteen families', which controlled a densely settled peasantry. Many confrontations occurred between the peasantry and the élite.

Between 1961 and October 1979, El Salvador was ruled by the army-dominated Partido de Conciliacion Nacional (PNC). There was a growth in the urban working class, and growing pressure on densely settled land. There was a dramatic increase in the number of landless peasants, from 12 per cent of the population in 1961 to 65 per cent by 1981.

There was a growth in political mobilisation and electoral competition. The 1970s started with the army asserting that it was not prepared to lose power through the ballot box, and this process of radicalisation continued throughout the decade. The Union Nacional Opositora (UNO) was founded in 1972, uniting the social-democratic Movimiento Nacional Revolucionario (MNR) founded in 1968 and the Union Nacional Democratica, a front for the banned Partido Comunista Salvadoreño (PCS) – against the military. In the 1977 elections fraud kept UNO out of power yet again, and substantial elements of the democratic opposition responded to the increasing repression and the blocking of all democratic change by deciding to take up arms against the regime. The relative complexity of the guerrilla alliance which emerged was explained by the diverse political origins of the various groups, and by the different stages at which they joined the armed struggle.

The communist PCS had been involved briefly in an unsuccessful guerrilla campaign during the early 1960s, from which it had drawn the lesson that it would be more profitable to pursue its goals through electoral alliances. But in 1970, a group led by Salvador Cayetano Carpio broke away from the PCS to form the first of the guerrilla groups, which emerged in 1972 as the Fuerzas Populares de Liberación – Farabundo Marti (FPL-FM), operating from a base in the north west (Marti had been a leading member of the PCS, who had been executed during the 1932 uprising).

Radicalised urban supporters of the Christian Democrat PDC, disillusioned by the events of 1972, formed the Egercito Revolucionario Popular (ERP), which though initially committed to a Guevarist strategy of revolution carried out by a small guerrilla élite, subsequently adopted the aim of a mass insurrection. A dissident faction of the ERP formed the Fuerzas Armadas de la Resistencia Nacional (FARN) during the mid 1970s, and became increasingly committed to the creation of a broad opposition alliance. FARN quickly got involved with a series of lucrative kidnappings.

Yet another group emerged in 1979, the Partido Revolucionario de los Trabajadores Centroamericanos, founded in 1975 and making its existence as a fighting force known in 1979. The army of guerrilla organisations was completed in 1980 when the PCS abandoned its stubborn faith in the electoral process and opted for armed struggle.

By the late 1970s the ruling military had continued to pursue its policy of repression, but also introduced a number of limited reforms. These contributed to a gathering crisis and provoked the development of a number of extreme right-wing political and paramilitary groups, determined to resist change. Under General Carlos Romero, the hardline right-wing military leader, and former head of a paramilitary rural security network, right-wing death squads such as the Union Guerrera Banca extended their operations, and the poor human rights record in El Salvador deteriorated.

A reformist coup led to a brief political honeymoon, but the security forces soon decided to block all reform. Reformers were driven out and replaced by individuals prepared to collaborate with the hard-line approach of the armed forces.

By 1980 the civil war was well underway. The unarmed opposition groups had been progressively radicalised by the brutal repression of peaceful political activities. The Archbishop of San Salvador, Oscar Romero, was murdered in his cathedral, and even his funeral was a violent incident. Faced with these outrages, the MNR and the Christian Democrats joined with other opposition groups linked to student and trade union organisations to form the Frente Democratico Revolucionario (FDR).

The PCS issued a joint communiqué with FPL and FARN in 1980, calling for an armed popular revolution. Guerrilla groups united on a permanent basis on 21 October with the formation of the Frente Farabundo Marti de Liberacion Nacional (FMLN). The FDR pledged support to armed struggle when six of its leaders were assassinated later that year during

E

severe repression which followed a series of general strikes it had organised.

Fighting increased, and allegations of direct Cuban and Nicaraguan backing for the FDR-FMLN led to a rapid increase in US military assistance to El Salvador. Bombing and sabotage increased and electricity supplies were badly affected.

Allegations were widespread that army units were massacring innocent peasants whom they suspected of sympathising with the guerrillas. While US backing for the El Salvador government prevented the FDR-FMLN from successfully launching the all-out offensive which brought the Sandinistas victory in Nicaragua in 1979, the government forces were unable to prevent guerrillas from consolidating control of many areas, especially in the north and north-east.

Casualties of the war and murder campaigns of right-wing death squads mounted, and a systematic FDR-FMLN campaign of economic sabotage hit El Salvador severely – especially the attacks on bridges.

In spite of American assistance, the El Salvador army was unable to seize the strategic initiative and continued to react to guerrilla activities by launching large, clumsy and generally unsuccessful search and destroy operations which did little damage to guerrillas, but alienated peasant support. The army kept reoccupying previously-held guerrilla territory but with little effect on long-term progress in the war. On several other occasions, guerrilla units inflicted heavy casualties on government troops.

Napoleon Duarte – a long time UNO supporter – emerged as President in 1983. This improved the national image of El Salvador, and the US Reagan administration was able to counter criticism of its Central American policy and continue the supply of equipment to the regime. President Duarte, backed by Washington, opened peace negotiations with the FDR-FMLN in 1984, but the depth of conflict made any permanent solution to the crisis unlikely.

England Until the end of the Second World War, from the British perspective, violent insurrection and guerrilla warfare were phenomena experienced by foreigners. All has now changed. Britain has had a vital concern in curbing the spillover of international terrorism from the Middle East and Europe and the internecine strife between groups in the Asian sub-continent into London's international diplomatic and business community. The terrorist campaign in Ireland has been a cancer in the British body politic for over a decade, and Britain also has to help safeguard British persons, property and interests overseas. The fight against terrorism has not been without difficulty from a legal point of view, for instance in comparison between a civil law state like France and a common law state like the United Kingdom. In the UK, where extradition is a judicial procedure, the courts have not in practice utilised their power to challenge conduct by reviewing, say, grounds upon which a decision to deport is made. Britain pioneered a compromise whereby either party to an extradition treaty might in absolute discretion refuse to surrender its own subjects. Unlike France, neither British nor American law recognises a 'political murder' and Britain has made it plain that it is not prepared to negotiate if any government minister is abducted. A number of trends can be discerned over the years: the waxing and waning of nationalism in Scotland and Wales, in comparison with the increasing virulence from Middle Eastern and Asian separatist groups. Tactics can range from the kidnap of industrialists to bomb attacks on government premises. So far, state and government targets have been entirely buildings. There has been a decreasing impact of the ultra-left compared with the growth of nationalist terror and attacks on American interests.

Of all European countries, Britain suffered least from the student revolutions of 1968, due to the weakness of the New Left. Furthermore, although the Vietnam War was hotly debated, the issue never led to prolonged riots. Race has provoked continuing violence, and led to clashes in a number of cities. For a brief period, Celtic separatism in Wales and Scotland bred the prospects of violence, but the issue subsided with the debate on devolution, so that no conflict arose.

Movements with extremist factions in them exist on both the Right and the Left. The National Front, formed in 1967, despite divisions and defections, including the formation in 1980 of a New National Front, has remained the major extreme right-wing party in Britain. The British Movement, founded in 1968 by Colin Jordan, is an anti-Semitic and anti-immigration movement which encourages military training and has its own leader guard providing uniforms and special training. Some of its members have been accused of arson attacks, and the possession of arms and ammunition. Column 88, formed in 1970 from remnants of the National Socialist Movement, has members well versed in intelligence work, arms handling and the use of explosives. It has carried out a number of postal bomb attacks and raids on left-wing bookshops and guerrilla training programmes. Contacts have been maintained with active terrorist right-wing groups in Italy and with Palestinian groups. There is then the little-known SS Wotan 71, a terrorist group first known in 1976, which has been active against minorities and left-wing organisations.

Anarchist groups in England have been few in number, but in the case of the Angry Brigade its influence was considerable. It was produced out of the free-thinking ideas which led to the 1968 disturbances in France and the development of Baader-Meinhof terrorism in Germany. In a four-year period until 1971, the Brigade was responsible for 125 bomb and machine gun attacks in the London area. Their most spectacular attack was at the home of the Secretary of State for Employment, Robert Carr, in 1971. However, many of their attacks were symbolic, and the trial of the leaders in 1972 largely eliminated the Brigade, although the title Angry Brigade again was ascribed to two incidents in 1982–83, perpetrated by a woman. Other extreme left-wing groups have called for radical industrial reform, union power and an intensification of the industrial struggle. England's nationalist groups are extremely weak and virtually non-existent. An Gof 1980 Movement is a Cornish nationalist group, and the English People's Liberation Army has undertaken isolated bomb attacks.

See also **Ireland**

Entebbe raid 1976 In June 1976 an Air France plane carrying 257 people, including 12 crew members, from Tel Aviv to Paris, was hijacked out of Athens by seven members of the Popular Front for the Liberation of Palestine (PFLP). Nationals from France, Greece, the United States, Canada, New Zealand, Britain, Jordan, Lebanon, Cyprus and Japan had boarded at Athens.

The plane landed in Benghazi for refuelling, and later flew to Entebbe in Uganda. The West German leader of the hijackers announced that the hijackers were the Che Guevara Brigade of the PFLP. At Entebbe, the hijackers were provided with additional weapons by the Ugandans, who also guarded the hostages. Three additional terrorists joined the original seven here.

The release was demanded of 53 terrorists imprisoned in Israeli, Swiss, West German, French and Kenyan jails. The hijackers demanded that Air France bring these 'freedom fighters' to Entebbe Airport to be exchanged with the hostages and the aircraft. None of the governments gave in to the demands. On 30 June, three days after the hijack, 47 elderly women, sick persons and children were released. The Israeli Cabinet then announced it was willing to negotiate for the release of some of the prisoners in return for the hostages. On 1 July the terrorists released 100 more hostages and it was learned from this group that a selection had taken place; the non-Jewish hostages were separated from the Israelis or persons of dual nationality. A day later, the terrorists increased their demands, adding five million dollars in compensation for the return of the Air France plane. The Israelis also learned from the tapped telephone of Wadi Haddad (the PFLP's planner of terrorist operations), in Somalia, that he had ordered the deaths of the Jewish hostages regardless of the response of the Israelis.

As a result of this message, planning began for Operation Thunderbolt, a daring rescue of the hostages. The plan called for flying several C130 Hercules transport planes 2,500 miles to Entebbe from Tel Aviv, securing the release of the hostages and returning to Israel. The Israelis claimed that no other nations were involved in the rescue operation, although many reports held that the Kenyans allowed the planes to refuel in Nairobi, and it was noted that the Israelis were allowed to treat the wounded there with a medical team of 33 doctors.

Because of superior intelligence, which many believed was derived from questioning the released hostages, overhead photography and Israeli agents on the scene in Entebbe, the Israeli mission was a success. Flying low to avoid hostile radar, the planes landed at a deserted section of the airfield. A black Mercedes led the first group of commandos who raced to the airport lounge where the hostages were being held. A second group set off bombs in another section of the field, creating a diversion. They later destroyed 11 MIGs of the Uganda airforce so that their planes would not be attacked while returning to Israel. A third group secured the airfield entrance gate, holding off a squad of Ugandan soldiers. In the gun battle, the terrorists were taken by surprise and did not have a chance to shoot any of the hostages before they were all killed. A few hostages were killed or wounded when they stood up in the crossfire. The operation lasted 53 minutes, and all the planes returned successfully to Israel, with a stopover in Nairobi.

Reports conflicted regarding casualties. Israeli authorities believed seven of the terrorists were killed and three who were not present at the airfield escaped. Eleven other Israelis, civilian and military, were wounded. The Israelis believed 20 Ugandan soldiers were killed. Idi Amin, the Ugandan leader, later admitted that 20 Ugandan soldiers were killed.

Several governments condemned the Israeli action in press statements and during a United Nations debate. Amin later telephoned the Israelis to add his own congratulations, to request weapons and military spare parts and to announce that he had broken relations with the Palestinian terrorists. Amin was ignored by the Israelis.

Amin was reported to have engaged in a widespread purge of individuals connected with the guarding of Entebbe airport, with some claims that 245 were killed by Amin's troops as punishment. Among those killed was Dora Bloch, an Israeli-British citizen who was left behind in a Ugandan hospital where she had been taken after choking on some meat at the airport lounge. It is believed she was strangled in hospital on the direct orders of Amin.

The identity of the terrorists was difficult to ascertain – although it is believed the initial leader was Wilfried Böse, an associate of Carlos, closely aided by high-ranking members of the military branch of the Popular Front for the Liberation of Palestine. It was learned that the terrorists had flown on Singapore Airlines to Athens from Kuwait and had taken their weapons on board the plane because they stayed in the Athens transit lounge, where they were not subjected to searches. The Air France plane was returned by Amin, who unsuccessfully demanded several million dollars in compensation. The whole episode buoyed the Israelis' spirits and aided the domestic popularity of their government.

Eritrean Liberation Front An Eritrean Liberation Front (ELF) was set up in 1958 in Cairo, and from 1961 onwards became increasingly active in preparing for armed struggle inside Eritrea, with weapons brought in from the Sudan. In 1969 and 1971 acts of sabotage were committed and Ethiopian airliners hijacked. The ELF also undertook guerrilla warfare inside Eritrea, with the result that a partial curfew was imposed by the Ethiopian army in 1969 and a state of emergency declared over the greater part of the province in December 1970.

The onset of guerrilla tactics coincided with the younger militants accusing the leadership of being 'feudalist' and 'capitalist', and beginning to shift towards a socialist commitment. Radical Arab governments in Iraq, Libya and Syria championed the new political stance, as did the Palestinian Al-Fatah guerrilla movement.

Ideology also caused the ELF to split in 1975, and if this had not happened they might well have been in a position to seize independence on the fall of the Emperor in 1974. In July 1974 the PLF, the new and more radical group formed by the split asserted that Ethiopia and Eritrea were two separate countries and different at every level – historically, ethnically and culturally. It also expressed readiness to negotiate with the Ethiopian Government provided the latter recognised the PLF as the sole legitimate representative of the Eritrean people and also their right to self-determination and independence (i.e. not a return to federal status, which was out of the question).

In the latter part of 1974, both the ELF and PLF intensified their military activities and greatly increased their influence in the countryside, holding two mass meetings. In 1975 the ELF and PLF reached agreement on the formation of a common front, and thereafter the two organisations gradually coalesced into one movement based on non-Marxist principles. In the 1970s a Popular Liberation Force and an Eritrean People's Liberation Front (EPLF) were created.

In the vacuum created by the collapse of the former Ethiopian Empire, separatist forces increased rapidly in number. Estimates in 1977 put the ELF at 22,000 guerrillas, who engaged in full-scale warfare with the revolutionary forces of the new government under the control of Mengistu Haile Mariam. That year the ELF took control of a number of towns, but was unable to hold them in 1978 when the government launched a counter-offensive backed by massive Soviet armaments. Reduced again in 1979 to controlling the rural areas, the ELF sustained vigorous resistance throughout 1980, only to be wasted in battles with its rival body the EPLF, in 1981. At that time the ELF – PLF split into two factions when a group led by Osman Agyp (who was based in Iraq) broke away in opposition to the leadership of O. S. Sabeh (who was based in Egypt and Dubai). After the fiercest in-fighting for years, the EPLF was left as the strongest rebel group. From the start of the struggle, the ELF had found considerable support for its pretensions amongst Islamic countries, by whom it sought to be recognised as the 'legitimate representative of the Eritrean people'. After the mid 1970s, the Soviet Union no longer saw its interest in supporting separatism, but worked instead to secure the revolutionary government of Mengistu. The Cubans, too, changed sides although they declined to fight in Eritrea on behalf of the central government and against their former friends.

ETA

See **Basque nationalism**

Ewart-Biggs, Sir Christopher The IRA was suspected of detonating a remote-controlled land mine that exploded under the car of the new UK ambassador to Ireland, Christopher Ewart-Biggs, and his secretary in July 1976. The blast ripped the car apart, and two others riding in the car were injured. The explosion occurred as the car drove over an estimated 50 to 100 pounds of explosives, 150 yards from the official residence near Dublin. Ewart-Biggs was going to a meeting with the Irish Foreign Minister, Garret Fitzgerald. The Irish government offered a reward of £20,000 for information leading to the arrest of the killers. Ewart-Biggs had been in the post only twelve days, and had planned to engage in a high-profile diplomatic campaign, although he had taken several security precautions, including varying his route each day and having two security vehicles follow his car. In October 1979 Michael O'Rourke, an IRA man (who had previously escaped from jail) was arrested in the USA as being linked to the Ewart-Biggs case.

Extortion and product pollution Product extortion has increased rapidly in Western Europe and the United States over the last decade. There is generally a high yield and low risk provided the extortioner is not too greedy and has secured the means of receiving payment.

There are a number of dilemmas for any company subjected to extortion. Commercially and managerially it can be seen to be cheaper to pay and hush up and get rid of the problem quickly. Morally the company must maintain a publicly defensive position, and avoid failure to warn the public of possible risks, and failing to recall or destroy suspect stock. Possibly there can be long-term implications for the corporate image. Legally there is liability for failure to warn of a known risk, and there is a public policy of responsibility not to reward or encourage crime. The dilemma for the police is that they have the responsibility to protect the public from risk even though the threat may be a hoax. Publicity can inflict huge losses on the target company, but the police have the responsibility to make arrests and to prevent or deter future crime. So far mainly small-time criminals have been involved, but this could easily escalate to include criminal gangs and political groups.

The cost of product contamination and extortion can be enormous. In 1982 in the United States the pharmaceutical company Tylanol suffered a $500 million loss in profits; in Britain in 1984 the Mars confectionery company suffered a loss of sales of £15 million, a loss of profits of £2.5 million and had to destroy 3,000 tons of stock. A few months later, a confectionery company in Japan suffered a 43 per cent loss of sales in the first month after contamination of their product, followed by a disastrous fall in share prices. Extortioners threatened to contaminate beer and lager produced by the Heineken company in 1984 and demanded £500,000. Supermarket chains throughout the world have occasionally suffered at the hands of extortioners.

Extradition Extradition is part of the process of criminal justice – the acquisition of custody of the accused for trial or, where the person has escaped from prison, for completion of his sentence. The extradition process is generally spelled out in bilateral treaties, supplemented by statutes or provisions in codes of criminal procedure. The ultimate decision about whether an accused person should be surrendered is a matter for the government of the country concerned, but the actual determination of whether a valid claim for surrender has been made by the requesting state is a matter for the courts, so that the factor of a strict or moderate interpretation of a given treaty may advance or inhibit the grant of extradition.

In connection with the extradition of terrorists, policy considerations can be a substantial bar. Even where a treaty exists and diplomatic relations obtain between parties, extradition may be denied on the ostensible grounds that the charge against the accused is political in nature, or that extradition formalities have not been complied with, or that the accused is being tried in the requested state, whereas the real grounds for the denial of extradition may lie in daily relations between the requested state and other countries with which it desires to be on cordial terms.

Policy considerations also include economic considerations, ranging from concern for the protection of air transport franchises and other trade advantages in a given geographical region, to maintaining a bargaining position in regard to foreign economic, technical and military assistance. The extradition process is fraught with opportunities for carelessness or genuine error in the paperwork and in communications between the requesting and requested states – and Britain has experienced such problems many times in claiming the return of suspected terrorists from the United States and the Republic of Ireland.

In terms of treaties for the control of international terrorists, governments have to decide whether in contemplating the apprehension of offenders 'extradition' is the term that is wanted, or whether the concern is for 'lawful return', and whether, in supplying an alternative to apprehension, 'submit to prosecution' is recognised as being a concept that is open to widely varying interpretations, reflecting particularist moral principles, legal precepts, political practices and other considerations.

A state may determine not to prosecute an alleged offender as required under the universal jurisdiction measure, but to extradite the person to a requesting state, especially one with preferred jurisdiction. This measure is subject to international concern for safeguards on human rights. This means at least that the extraditing state must be assured that the requesting state will grant the alleged offender due process. Considerations of fairness dictate that a person should not be extradited to the state that was the object of the terrorist attack.

Extradition is the prerogative of the requested state and in the absence of a bilateral treaty between the requesting and the requested state, there is no international legal duty to extradite. Even where there is an applicable extradition treaty, the scope of the duty to extradite may be narrow. Extradition may be requested only for offences listed in the treaty, and the political offence exception may determine whether the alleged offender will be returned to the requesting state or granted asylum by the requested state.

Traditional international legal measures have lacked established procedures for international co-operation in preventing and punishing violations of diplomatic inviolability. States that are parties to anti-terrorist conventions have an international obligation to prosecute the offender, whether prosecution follows lawful return or takes place in the state where the offender was found.

Thus, extradition is a difficult and complex process – differences in criminal codes procedures and judicial traditions have to be taken into account, and so far only a small minority of terrorist suspects have been successfully extradited.

See also **International humanitarian law and terrorism**

E

F

FANE
See **Federation of National and European Action**

Fear Today any person can become a victim of a terrorist, regardless of his or her innocence or neutrality. Fear is deliberately used as a weapon to achieve social change in a Western society, where other legal means of change are available. The legal systems of a democratic state regard a terrorist as just another criminal; but the terrorist, on command of his superiors, will kill without hatred people in whom he has no personal interest, while claiming to be a patriot and a soldier. The terrorist tries to show that his actions are a response to the denial of basic freedoms.

Gaps between people (persons in positions of power, the establishment and discontented elements) have always existed, and continue to separate management from labour, power élites from students, and the urban areas from the countryside. Much of this discord has existed without serving as a catalyst for terrorist campaigns. The contemporary terrorist has identified these issues, and does not act until he has made a careful and rational analysis of the general conditions and manipulative causes which are latent within his society – as well as of the present and potential strength of his group. The organisation and extension of a terrorist campaign are predicated on a supportive propaganda message to attract and condition people to serve as followers and supporters of an extremist organisation. Terrorists search for people who are hurt by fate or nature – the ugly, those suffering from an inferiority complex, craving power and influence but defeated by unfavourable circumstances.

Today's terrorist tries to influence behaviour by extra-normal means through the use or threat of violence while simultaneously creating an atmosphere of perpetual and escalating terror, conducted by patriots whose only options are the bullet or the bomb. Although the terrorist avoids undertaking any action which might fall beyond the ambit of a real or a contrived popular cause, he is ultimately nothing more than a criminal who tries to exploit any available natural social pathology.

See also **Terrorism and terror**

Federation of National and European Action (FANE) was formed in France in 1966 as an amalgamation of two former factions of the extreme right-wing Occident Movement (itself officially banned in 1968). After the organisation had been linked with an intensification of attacks on Jewish and left-wing targets from early 1980, the French Government ordered its dissolution on the grounds that it had an expressed aim in the installation of a new Nazi regime. FANE spokesmen maintained they opposed the French Jewish community 'as a powerful pressure group rather than individuals'. As part of FANE's aim of building a pan-European neo-fascist movement, contacts had been established with the extreme right-wing Armed Revolutionary Nuclei (NAR) of Italy.

Young Jewish militants attacked FANE members as a warning to neo-Nazis that they could not act with impunity.

After FANE was banned, its followers regrouped under differently-named organisations, notably the European Nationalist Alliance (FNE) and the New Nazi Front (NFN). Early in 1981, a grouping calling itself the 'Fascist New Generation' issued a text under the ex-FANE symbol proclaiming its belief that 'Adolf Hitler is the only god', and listing sixty Jewish personalities as apparent potential targets. The group's ultra-rightist sympathies and involvement in political violence and terrorist acts have provoked left-wing attacks.

The European Nationalist Alliance group has been held responsible for numerous anit-Jewish attacks and incidents, including bomb explosions outside synagogues. The New Nazi Front has been responsible for daubing slogans on tombstones.

See also **Anti-Semitic terrorism in Europe**

F

Fighting Communist Cells (CCC) This is a group of Belgian left-wing terrorists, who since 1984 in particular have perpetrated a bombing campaign. While there is no solid evidence of direct collaboration between the Fighting Communist Cells and terrorist organisations in other European countries, there clearly have been contacts. In December 1985, heavily armed plain-clothes police in Namur arrested the suspected ringleader of the terrorist group, a former printer named Pierre Carette, and three alleged accomplices. In the same month, the police found what is thought to have been the headquarters of the Fighting Communist Cells in Brussels. The discovery turned in a hoard of terrorist hardware, complete with six kilograms of dynamite, a Colt .45 pistol, maps, leaflets and magazines on weaponry. But more important was a list in code of fifteen presumed members of the organisation, which is commonly known as the CCC (Cellules Communistes Combattantes).

The organisation first surfaced in October 1984, where it claimed responsibility for an explosion that caused heavy damage at a subsidiary of the American company Litton Industries in Brussels. Since then, by its own admission, it has perpetrated over two dozen bomb attacks against NATO related targets, banks, public buildings and multinational corporations. Two people – both fire-fighters who had been called to the scene of a bombing – have been killed in the terror campaign. Several persons have been injured.

The CCC has outlined its aims in communiqués found after almost every attack, and usually accompanied by a photograph of the target. 'We are the party of social revolution!', one communiqué said. 'The exploitation of our work by bourgeois sharks has lasted too long! We are fighting for social revolution, for the future, for humanity, for communism!'. Other communiqués said the group was waging a 'war on NATO'. But despite the strong rhetoric, the CCC has taken precautions to avoid injuring people deliberately. The group has issued warnings of impending attacks, so that buildings could be evacuated, and most of its attacks have taken place in the quiet pre-dawn hours. This strategy has differed sharply from Euroterrorist groups in France and West Germany – Action Directe and the Red Army Faction – which have clearly sought to harm human beings on several occasions and succeeded.

Freedom fighters In historical terms freedom fighters, unlike terrorists, were bound by certain rules of behaviour which form the cornerstone of ethical behaviour. These draw a distinction between soldiers and small children, between repressive authorities and helpless women, between governmental agents and ordinary citizens, between a military outpost and a house. Thus a terrorist kills civilians while a fighter for freedom saves lives and fights on at the risk of his own life until liberty wins the day.

Nevertheless, since the Second World War these distinctions have changed. Freedom fighters or national liberation movements have all, or nearly all, practised or continue to practise pure terrorism – that is acts of violence in which innocent members of the public are the sufferers, whether deliberately or through callous disregard for the risks of death or injury on the part of the perpetrators.

A reason that freedom fighters make efforts to present themselves effectively as terrorists is that freedom fighters have generally not achieved government recognition and response.

G

Gadaffi, Colonel Muammar Colonel Gadaffi has maintained himself in power for sixteen years, longer than most leaders in the Arab world. Although he is considered by some to be the archproponent of international terrorism, his position has become increasingly insecure, and indeed after the American air raid in April 1986, Gadaffi failed to appear in public for several months. He has carried his interpretation of Islamic law to unprecedented lengths in flouting diplomatic conventions, for example by ordering his diplomats to shoot Libyan demonstrators in the streets of London from his embassy windows in 1984. The only crime of these demonstrators was that they were anti-Gadaffi.

To many millions of people throughout the world, Gadaffi is a direct sponsor of Islamic funamentalist terrorism. Diplomatic privilege has been abused through the use of the diplomatic bag to smuggle weapons with which to kill anti-Gadaffi Libyans in European countries. Because of its involvement in world affairs and its liberal traditions Europe will always attract exiles. Unscrupulous states such as Libya under Gadaffi and Iran under Khomeini seek them out, so that European states will continue to suffer from political conflicts and disputes to which they are not a party. Gadaffi has provided supplies of weapons, usually obtained originally from the Soviet Union, to Irish republicans.

In 1980 Gadaffi sent his hit squads to seven different countries. They carried out 14 separate attacks abroad against Libyan exiles in 1980 alone, murdering 11 people.

Since he came to power Gadaffi has concentrated on killing Libyan exiles opposed to his regime, destabilising the governments of neighbouring Arab countries and supporting violence, particularly by funding and arming small, violent groups which might otherwise be unable to survive. However, although he has castigated the West and his Arab enemies and made much of his support for revolutionary movements including support for more than thirty terrorist groups in the past, from the Red Brigades to the IRA and Abu Nidal, none of his protégés has ever been wholly dependent on him for survival. Support for Nidal, however, does represent a new and radical step for Gadaffi. His global ambitions have been fuelled by his oil wealth, and as the cash supply increased, so he began to influence small terrorist groups more for political ambitions than as a dedicated terrorists' patron.

Gadaffi's relations with the Palestinians have been mercurial, which has led him to become one of the least popular of the Palestine Liberation

Organisation backers. While the recruiting of terrorists has fallen off in recent years, there are still training camps in Libya, although Gadaffi owes the Soviet Union considerable cash sums for arms. During the 1980s Gadaffi has supplied almost no money to terrorist groups and his global ambitions have had to be contained within budgetary constraints. Nevertheless Gadaffi has become the bogeyman of international terrorism, despite others who arguably could be considered more supportive of terrorist groups, such as Ayatollah Khomeini or Abu Nidal.

Gadaffi is credited with ordering the murder of Moussa al Sadr, the founder of Amal (Hope), the minority Shi'ite group in the Lebanon, who disappeared in mysterious circumstances on a visit to Libya in 1978. This was as a result of a quarrel between Moussa and Gadaffi over the Palestinians, whose presence in Lebanon was resented by the Shi'ites but supported by Gadaffi. Gadiffi was a proven source of money supplied to the IRA from abroad, in a cargo aboard a ship, the *Claudia*, which contained weapons and explosives.

Gadaffi has consulted with Abu Nidal, a PLO rebel and renegade controlling bands of hitmen who travel the world to kill their victims, and has worked closely with the transnational terrorist, Carlos, especially in support for the raid on OPEC headquarters in Vienna. He has also been involved in a series of hijackings, allowing the hijackers to land in Libya, make their deals and then disappear into the terrorist underground. Gadaffi has backed anti-government groups in many countries and has threatened to support urban terror groups of a number of countries if their governments do not fall in with his wishes. The United States above all is most concerned about the possibility of Gadaffi-inspired terrorism, and this has accounted for their acts against Libya in the Gulf of Sirte in August 1981 and March 1986, and for the bombing raid on Tripoli in April 1986. The April 1986 raid raised arguments on the subject of what the West can do about international terrorism.

Generational terrorism and refugees Terrorism, an ageless phenomenon, has begun to exhibit a new energy and a new dimension.

The new energy is the emergence of a second generation of antagonists in protracted conflicts, whose unusual psychological experience and lifelong rage have altered the focus and calibre of political violence in the Middle East. The new dimension is religious extremism, which has moved into a second, more ominous phase in the region since the 1979 Iranian revolution. It is no longer exclusively Islamic.

These new trends are most visible in Lebanon, where the ongoing eleven-year civil strife is increasingly being played out in car bombings, kidnappings, and other indiscriminate violence.

'There is a high probability that young people who have been socialized in a climate of intergroup violence, and who have identified with their anger . . . will be attracted to membership in organizations that advocate violent action in pursuit of their "just cause" ', says Rona Fields, a psychologist who has studied the impact of violence on children in Lebanon, Israel, Northern Ireland, and South Africa.

United States experts on terrorism say that the spate of recent knifings and other attacks on Israeli troops and settlers on the West Bank are the work not of trained Palestine Liberation Organisation cadres, but of local youth who have grown up under nearly twenty years of Israeli occupation and who are acting on their own initiative.

At least four factors come together to produce terrorists among a generation that has known nothing but bloodshed and enmity, according to psychologists. This is known as the 'rejuvenation' of violence.

(1) An environment of conflict makes it difficult for normal educational, familial, and environmental exposure to suppress instincts of aggression in children, according to psychologists. Instead, those instincts go unchecked or are further encouraged by the violence.

(2) Those who grow up in conflict consider violence a justifiable means of expression, not a last resort as their parents view it. They define justice and power differently from their parents, often by the calibre of a gun.

(3) The sense of being a victim is conditioned, since the second generation feels it is blameless for the conflict's outbreak. And a victim has special rights in the fight for survival.

(4) The normal dynamic of adolescence – the moulding of an independent identity through rebellion against authority – becomes closely associated with the political situation. Carrying a gun or being inducted into a militia is often a rite of manhood.

Government response to terrorism General conclusions on effective government response can be drawn from selective experience. Concessionary policies and failure to extradite terrorists are associated with an increase in terrorist activity. The establishment of a tough policy following a period of softness appears to require consistent actions applied over a period of time. A period of soft, concessionary policies may result in the establishment of a terrorism infrastructure. Isolated policy events, regardless of events and regardless of intensity, have no impact when they run counter to general policy implementation. A constantly applied, increasingly tough policy toward incident management is associated with significant decreases in all serious events. Ultimately, the failure to adopt and implement a tough, consistent incident management policy during a specific period of time can be associated with increases in terrorist activity.

Greek Civil War This war was not only a desperate struggle between the forces of left and right to secure power in Greece, but marked the first round in the Cold War. After the invasion of Greece by the German armed forces in April 1941, a number of resistance movements developed in the Greek mountains. Varying greatly in political outlook, the Greek resistance groups fought as much amongst themselves as they did the Germans, and in October 1943 open warfare broke out between the left-wing National Liberation Front (EAM) with its military wing the Greek National Liberation Army (ELAS), and its centrist and right-wing opponents. In the early stages, ELAS had the slight edge, being the most powerful of the guerrilla-political factions and claiming to have two million supporters and 50,000 fighting men, who clashed with British troops. The latter arrived on the withdrawal of German troops in October 1944, and two months later the second round of the civil war began. The central committee of the Greek Communist Party (KKE) was confident that the time was right to strike – the Papandreou government was weak and far from popular, and ELAS was at the height of its power. Fighting broke out all over Greece but the main action was centred in Athens, where fierce street fighting developed. The British slowly gained control and short-lived peace terms were agreed in February 1945, based on the demobilisation and disarming of ELAS. The general election a year later was boycotted by the KKE.

Britain remained in Greece but took no part in subsequent fighting, confining its role to training government forces. There was a lack of progress by the Greek government in combatting the guerrillas. Maintaining a military presence became increasingly expensive to an impoverished post-war Britain. The Americans as a result became initially reluctant defenders of Greek freedom. The result was the Truman Doctrine, which promised United States support for any European country liable to communist subjugation.

The war continued, and the government's plans for a series of winter operations were abandoned, leaving the guerrillas in virtual control of northern Greece. The strategic problem facing the army was that if it engaged in clearing the guerrillas across the mountains, a force would be needed to provide a static defence of towns and villages. There were also bands of armed civilians. Although the British and Americans strongly disapproved of such civilians, the Greek government tolerated them. The armed civilians were right-wing bands which had fought ELAS. Guerrilla numbers were never large, but besides the difficult terrain, the greatest asset possessed by the guerrillas was the attitude of the people. Supplies for the guerrillas came from Yugoslavia, Albania and Bulgaria. As a result of the split between Stalin and Tito in 1948, the pro-Soviet policy of the KKE came unstuck – and both Stalin and Tito for different reasons withdrew support and Albania and Bulgaria isolated the KKE.

The National Army's victory was total when the left-wing and communist groups split into feuding factions, while the triumphant government was free to carry out its policies without opposition.

The war witnessed the gradual progression from a bandit war to a civil war. Firstly, the guerrilla tactic of killing isolated officials and making threats to prominent right-wing citizens in small villages led to a government response of getting the gendarmerie to disperse its units and extend patrolling to protect villages and maintain public morale. Secondly, the guerrillas launched raids against small villages left unprotected by the gendarmerie; this forced the government to confine the gendarmerie to larger towns in the affected areas, and to call in the national army. Thirdly, the guerrillas created large safe areas and harassed the civilian population to create a refugee problem for the government. The government had to respond by full-scale campaigns against safe areas, bringing world recognition that civil war was in progress.

Guatemalan insurgency For over two decades a civil war has existed in Guatemala. The country's four principal left-wing guerrilla organisations have been active since the 1960s in both rural and urban areas, waging an assassination campaign against government personnel, judges and members of the armed forces. In 1982 they established a 'unified military command', believing that the creation of the Republic of Guatemala in that year had merely produced a change in the façade of the regime and that no reforms were possible without revolutionary changes.

Overtures were made by the new regime to the guerrillas, but the guerrillas rejected an amnesty and an offer of negotiation. The killings continued unabated and anti-guerrilla operations intensified with the assistance of newly recruited and trained paramilitary peasant militias.

Conflict has generally continued at an undiminished level with the advent of active right-wing terrorist groups apparently sponsored behind the scenes by the Guatemalan authorities themselves to counter the long term grip of left-wing guerrilla insurgency. Throughout this century the Guatemalan military has received some form of assistance from the United States. This has not always won 'purchased affection' for the United States, for not only have many of the Guatemalan militarists resented their dependence upon US aid, but it has become a constant source of irritation to national pride. In the Guatemalan military there have been many officers who were just as fiercely anti-American in private as they were anti-Communist in public. They were willing, with some shame, to take American assistance, but wanted to use it as they pleased when and wherever they could.

The majority of the Guatemalan proletariat (this includes Indians, Ladinos and Mestizos) are caught between two choices. The worker must either protect his subsistence level, or he must organise to fight for better choices. Those who take the first road acquiesce silently in primitive socio-economic conditions. Those who opt for the second road risk reprisals that include death. The trauma of this fearful impasse created a consciousness which inspired many Guatemalans to join guerrilla movements. The Guatemalan conflict has its genesis in the incompatible requirements of a series of 'estates' within a state, i.e. the Indians, the pariah Ladinos, the economic oligopolists, the military establishment with its foreign supporters and the reformist intelligentsia.

Most fear perhaps is engendered by those groups who adopt frontier society tactics; namely, the paramilitary groups. They single out victims as pro-Marxist and death squads of ten or more men kidnap, interrogate and murder the victims. These death squads usually operate at night and often pretend to be legal 'authorities' making routine investigations.

G

Of the numerous left-wing movements, the chief ones include the Democratic Front against Repression (FDR) formed in 1979, whose objects are defined as the denunciation at national and international level of all repressive actions committed in Guatemala against any popular and democratic sector and the provision of aid to widows and orphans of the victims. Both the Guatemalan Committee of Patriotic Unity (CGUP) formed in 1982 and the Guatemalan National Revolutionary Unity (URNG), also created in 1982, have similar programmes: an end to repression and a guarantee of life, peace and fundamental human rights for all citizens; provision for the basic needs of the majority of the people; equality for the indigenous and White-descended (Ladinos) people; the creation of a new society in which all sectors of the population would be represented in the government; and alignment and international co-operation. Closely linked with URNG is the Guerrilla Army of the Poor (EGP) which emerged in the 1970s, and is active in the mountainous provinces and composed predominantly of the country's landless peasants. The Revolutionary Organisation of the People in Arms (ORPA) was established in 1979 as a political and military movement to be built up secretly at first in rural areas and later among all sections of the people. It was anti-racialist and stood for the development of the indigenous people's culture, in this way coming close to the aspirations of URNG, whom it joined in 1982.

In retaliation for the killings and other acts of violence perpetrated by left-wing guerrillas numerous extreme right-wing organisations, some of which were alleged to enjoy government support or to work in close association with the police, have engaged in attacks on left-wing leaders, including journalists, trade unionists and lawyers. The loss of life has run into tens of thousands – for example, in 1981 alone over 11,000 people lost their lives. The Death Squad (EM) has for many years been involved in killings of alleged left-wing activists or sympathisers. In 1976 the Secret Anti-Communist Army (ESA) came into existence and has been responsible for the killing of numerous politicians and officials, as well as trade unionists and student leaders whose names appeared on regularly published 'death lists'. Similar tactics have been pursued by the White Hand, a group active since 1970 when its headquarters were said to be in the police building in Guatemala City.

Guerrilla warfare in history The team 'guerrilla' was originally used to describe military operations carried out by irregulars against the rear of an enemy army or by local inhabitants against an occupying force. Tactics are based on enemy harassment, cutting off communications and carrying out surprise attacks.

Primitive people in general had an aversion to open fighting; for example, Jiftah and David in the Bible. The Maccabean revolt in 166 BC made use of guerrilla tactics in the early phase, but guerrilla units played only a minor role in the Jewish war against the Romans. The Romans made use of guerrilla warfare, as an invasion battle attempt to wear down the enemy, to attack small detachments in ambush by day and larger units by night.

Few guerrilla acts took place in the Middle Ages because of the development of new tactics; great emphasis was placed on cavalry and the use of missile weapons. The Hundred Years War was originally a dynastic conflict between Britain and France, but guerrilla tactics soon developed. Peasant revolts spread throughout Europe between the fourteenth and seventeenth centuries; and the Balkans became the main banditry area from the fifteenth to the late eighteenth century. Partisan warfare played a notable part in the American War of Independence – it was not a crucial factor between defeat or victory, but did have a delayed influence on military thinking.

In post-Napoleonic Europe, guerrilla warfare developed in the south and east of the Continent. The Carlist wars showed that guerrilla tradition had become deeply rooted in Spain, while the Greek War of Independence, genocidal in character, was essentially a series of uncoordinated operations by irregular troops. Polish insurrections in 1793, 1831 and 1863 were a blend of regular and guerrilla war. During the period of Italian unification, the elements of political propaganda and indoctrination foreshadowed guerrilla wars of a later age.

The Spanish war against the French in the early nineteenth century first produced a solely guerrilla war; and South America was the area where guerrilla warfare occurred on a vast scale. Guerrilla warfare was the high road to political and economic power, and yesterday's brigand could be tomorrow's government minister. In South America, and indeed in many other parts of the Third World, guerrilla warfare has taken many forms – wars of national liberation, the struggles of landless peasants and small farmers against large landowners, and fighting between local chieftains for political power.

Guerrillas have been active in the periods of imperialist expansion by European colonial powers, and indeed in three wars in the nineteenth century, guerrilla warfare played some role; in the American Civil War 1861–65, the Franco-Prussian War of 1870 and the Boer War 1899–1902 – the latter being a three-year war of attrition.

The demarcation between guerrilla warfare and banditry has been unclear. Most guerrilla movements have included members of semi-respectable professions – such as smuggling and poaching. Guerrillas and bandits have lived off the land, with horses and food provided by the local population, without having to pay for them, e.g. during the guerrilla phase of Chinese Communism recruits were drawn from robber bands.

Guerrilla warfare has been successful only if the enemy army was not large enough to occupy the whole territory. The essential element of success in guerrilla warfare is surprise, followed by retreat before the opponent could recover. A partisan unit had no lines of supply and communication and success depended on surprise. Their actions had purely strategic significance, and the contribution to warfare was to weaken the enemy without making a special contribution to any major battle, e.g. in the Russian Civil War 1918–19, and in the fight against the Germans in Yugoslavia in the Second World War.

Essential differences were evident in the nineteenth and twentieth centuries between guerrilla warfare on the fringes of European colonial empires, which were long drawn-out affairs in which success was neither sought nor achieved, and revolutionary uprisings in West European capitals which could only prove victorious by rapid and decisive action. In the First World War guerrilla operations were restricted to two theatres – Arabia and East Africa, under the leadership of Lawrence and Vorbeck. To both men, guerrilla doctrine became an exact science if pursued properly. If the enemy could be encouraged to stay in harmless places in large numbers, the enemy could be permanently weakened. Warfare could be adapted to local conditions, human and geographical.

Lenin maintained that guerrilla warfare should be waged by worker combatants, although he was aware of the ambiguity in connection with his desire for iron discipline and central control. Trotsky maintained that guerrilla warfare was the true peasant form of war. The secret services attached importance to the role of the guerrilla in the Soviet Union between the two world wars; guerrilla groups formed just one aspect of intelligence and sabotage work behind the enemy lines. Ireland earlier this century witnessed an urban insurrection rather than a guerrilla war. In Macedonia in the Balkans from 1910 to 1912 there was separatist activity beset by splits; in Mexico in the civil war from 1912 to 1920 under Pancho Villa, bandits gave support but provided no political leadership. Resistance in Mexico was regional and wanting in organisational ability and necessary minimum political sophistication.

By the end of the Second World War, guerrillas were faced with changing circumstances. Due to a shift in public opinion, the chief powers in the world could not act with the same degree of ferocity as on past occasions. The development of modern weapons favoured the guerrillas more than those operating against them. There were difficulties in combatting guerrillas in populated areas. Europe's decline after 1945 led to deep economic and political unrest and revolutionary situations the world over. The Second World War had been the guerrillas' opportunity – and the political impact of partisan activity had been far greater than its military contribution. The relation between communist and non-communist partisan units always had been strained. The Warsaw Uprising of 1944 was the chief urban insurrection of the Second World War; while in France resistance was dogged by betrayal. For the Communists in the Cold War 1945–1950, guerrilla activity proved excellent cadre training, a school for the mobilisation of the masses and a tool for the seizure of power. In China, Mao Tse-Tung argued that guerrilla operations by themselves could not win a war; nevertheless the Communists achieved victory in 1949 and instigated a new social and political order after a 15-year guerrilla war.

Vietnam proved to be longest of the guerrilla wars (1954–1970), and provoked a deep moral crisis in the Western world, especially the United

States. The Vietcong stressed political propaganda and indoctrination, while the Communists were enthusiastic, determined and dedicated.

Three stages in the development of guerrilla warfare occurred in the post-Second World War period – firstly, to the end of the Malayan insurgency, the lull in Indo-China and the defeat of such groups as the Huks in the Philippines and Mau Mau in Kenya; secondly, in the 1960s the scene of operations shifted to Vietnam and Latin America, and from the late 1960s urban terrorists replaced rural guerrillas. The main problems facing guerrillas have been the necessity to establish rural bases, in which many have failed, and the internal splits between nationalists, pro-Moscow Communists, Trotskyites and Maoists. Lessons were learnt – for example, from the Cuban revolution. Popular forces can win a war against the army; it is not necessary to wait until all conditions for making a revolution exist – insurrection can create them, and ultimately, as Latin America showed, the countryside is the main area for armed fighting.

Counter-insurgency theorists agree that guerrilla warfare is cheap, but the fight against it is costly. It is a form of warfare by which the strategically weaker side assumes the tactical offensive in selected forms, times and places – it is a weapon of the weak, and usually only decisive when the anti-guerrilla side puts a low value on defeating the guerrillas and does not commit full resources to the struggle.

In connection with guerrilla activity, some important assertions can be made. The geographical milieu is important, for example the bases. Guerrilla wars generally occur in areas in which such wars have occurred before. There is a negative correlation between guerrilla war and the degree of economic development. It has undergone profound changes and can never be seen as apolitical. Peasants have formed the traditional mass basis of guerrilla movements and motives are generally manifold for joining the guerrillas. Guerrillas are very dependent on the terrain, the size and density of the population, and the political constellation. During the 1970s and 1980s urban terrorism has been more frequent than rural guerrilla warfare, and guerrilla movements have become increasingly beset by internal strife in their own ranks or between rival movements. Guerrilla warfare is perhaps on the decline because colonialism and liberal democracy are also on the decline.

See also **Urban guerrillas in Latin America**

Guevara, Dr Ernesto 'Che', 1928–1967 Che Guevara was a Latin American revolutionary and guerrilla, a fighter of Argentinian origin.

As Fidel Castro's right-hand man in the guerrilla campaign against the Cuban Batista regime, after its victory in 1959, he analysed the theory and practice of guerrilla warfare in his book *The Guerrilla War*, which introduced basic modifications into hitherto accepted Marxist-Leninist theories. He disappeared from Cuba in March 1965 in order to organise guerrilla wars in other Latin American countries. In December 1966 he launched a guerrilla campaign in Bolivia, where in October 1967 he lost his life when he was captured by Bolivian government forces. Since his death, 'Che' has become the legendary hero of a growing cult among left-wing students and other young radicals in the Western world.

Guinea-Bissau War of Independence, 1963–1974 In 1956, the Partido Africano da Independência da Guiné e Cabo Verde (PAIGC) was founded by Amilcar Cabral, who began to prepare for a guerrilla war against the Portuguese after they repressed a dock strike in the capital, Bissau, in 1959. The main PAIGC base was in neighbouring Guinea-Conakry, and it was from there that the PAIGC launched its first military operations in January 1963, with attacks on three towns.

The small Portuguese garrison soon was forced onto the defensive and by the end of the year the PAIGC claimed control of 15 per cent of the colony. Guerrilla operations expanded throughout the late 1960s, and in 1967 the PAIGC began to operate from bases in Senegal. By 1971, they had some 6,000 men under arms and administered 'liberated zones' comprising a claimed 80 per cent of the colony. The Portuguese were increasingly confined to the safety of their firebases, and in March 1973 the guerrillas for the first time challenged Portuguese control of the sky by deploying Soviet surface-to-air missiles.

In January 1973, however, Cabral was assassinated, and his brother Luiz assumed the leadership of the movement in 1974. The Portuguese revolution of April 1974 soon led to a negotiated Portuguese withdrawal from Guinea-Bissau and the last troops left in October. About 1,900 Portuguese troops were killed in the war, as well as an unknown number of black auxiliaries, and any number from 6,000 to 12,000 PAIGC guerrillas may have died.

H

Herrema, Teide In October 1975 a man posing as a policeman kidnapped Teide Herrema, the Dutch manager of a metal plant in Dublin, a few yards from his home as he was driving to work. There was no struggle. Four terrorists took part in the kidnapping, with four or five other renegade IRA members providing safe haven and cars. He was taken by his kidnappers to a nearby house where he was kept for eight days in a small room, during five of which he was tied up, blindfolded, and had cotton stuffed in his ears to deprive him of sensory detection. Eventually he was moved to a house in Monasterevin.

The kidnappers demanded that three IRA terrorists were to be released within 48 hours or Herrema would be executed; that the metal plant was to close for 48 hours as an act of good faith; and that police were not to search for the kidnappers or set up road-blocks. The company agreed and offered to pay a ransom. The Irish government refused all the kidnappers' demands. The group later demanded safe passage out of the country.

The kidnappers used the code word previously employed to identify IRA members, although the Provisional Sinn Fein leader, Ruari O'Bradaigh, said at the annual conference of his group in Dublin that the kidnapping served no useful purpose and his group condemned the attack. The three prisoners whose release was demanded included Bridget Rose Dugdale, who had been the leader of a group which had stolen nineteen valuable paintings from the home of a British millionaire. These three collectively were being held for attempted murder and possession of explosives. Four thousand Irish police searched for the kidnappers and the deadline passed without incident. A Capuchin priest served as an intermediary but was unsuccessful in obtaining Herrema's release. Two weeks after the kidnap Herrema broadcast a statement in which he claimed to be alive and noted that his captors threatened to cut off his foot if police continued to demand proof that he was being held by them. Four days later, the police discovered the house where the kidnappers were hiding. They attempted a rescue by storming into the house, but the kidnappers fired five shots and retreated to an upstairs room, holding a gun to Herrema's head. Gallagher (Dugdale's lover) claimed to have explosives tied to himself and to Herrema. Police used a listening device to monitor conversations between Herrema and his captors. Gallagher offered to surrender but Coyle refused. The police continued to put pressure on the terrorists to release Herrema, making loud noises and shining spotlights in an attempt to prevent sleep. On 7 November, Gallagher became ill and called out to police that he would release Herrema. Within hours Gallagher, Coyle and Herrema walked out of the house. In March 1976 an Irish Court sentenced Gallagher to 20 years in prison, and Coyle received 15 years. In September 1986 Herrema himself made it known that he would like to see Gallagher released since his continued detention served no purpose.

Hindawi, Nezar Hindawi, a Jordanian journalist, was sentenced to 45 years' imprisonment in London in October 1986 for his part in trying to blow up an El Al jet carrying 380 people (including his pregnant girl friend, who unknowingly carried the bomb), on a flight from London to Tel Aviv in April 1986.

There was a strong Syrian link with the attempted attack – Hindawi travelled on an official Syrian passport in a false name; his visa applications were twice supported by official notes from the Syrian Embassy, and he went to see the Syrian Ambassador in London after the bomb was discovered. It was particularly on this evidence that Britain severed diplomatic relations with Syria. Hindawi had been given the bomb by Syrian security agents posing as members of Syrian Arab Airlines crews. He said he had been recruited in Damascus by the head of Syrian military intelligence to carry out attacks on Israeli targets. His cousin was arrested by the Italian authorities in Genoa (a hotbed of Palestinian terrorism) on suspicion of being involved in terrorist activities.

It is difficult to pinpoint Nezar Hindawi's exact affiliation because the various Arab terrorist organisations change their names regularly, but he is thought to have belonged at one time to the May 15 Organisation (named after the date of the founding of the state of Israel), which in recent years has left its original Iraqi backers. It is believed that Hindawi also acted as a professional mercenary – he was given 12,000 dollars to carry out the El Al plot. He could be seen as the ideal terrorist – ruthless, cold-blooded and with no humanity.

The Hindawi episode gave added impetus to the views of terrorist experts who believed that Syria had been behind most of the hijackings and bombing attacks carried out in Europe during the previous two years. In April 1985, 18 people were killed and 82 others injured when a bomb exploded in a Madrid restaurant used by American personnel; the attack was carried out by Islamic fundamentalists. Three months later, Syrian-backed terrorists struck when two bombs exploded in a United States airline office in Copenhagen. Then followed the Rome and Vienna airport attacks, the *Achille Lauro* hijack, and an attack in West Berlin in April 1986 when a bomb blast occurred in a packed discothèque which left 2 dead and 230 injured. This resulted in tougher American actions towards terrorist-sponsored states, especially Libya and Syria.

President Assad of Syria had intended to wash his hands of responsibility for the London bombing. As a leader of one of the big regional powers in the Middle East he has a key role in any attempt to make peace in that area, and as such has greater power than Colonel Gadaffi.

History of terrorism Terrorism has always engendered violent emotions and greatly divergent opinions and images. At the end of the last century, the popular image of the terrorist was that of a bomb-throwing alien anarchist, dishevelled, with a black beard and a smile, fanatic, immoral and sinister. His present-day image is very similar. Those practising terror have certain beliefs in common – they can be on the left or right, nationalist or internationalist, but in many respects their mental make up is similar.

There is widespread belief that terrorism is a new and unprecedented phenomenon, one of the most important and dangerous facing mankind today. Since it is a response to injustice, the only means of reducing the likelihood of terrorism is a reduction of grievances, stresses and frustration. Terrorists are fanatical believers and terrorism can occur anywhere.

Terrorism was first used as a word during the French Revolution as a synonym for a reign of terror, and later developed to mean the systematic use of terror. Many varieties have appeared throughout history: peasant wars, labour disputes and brigandage accompanied by systematic terror, general wars, civil wars, wars of national liberation, and resistance movements against foreign occupiers. Terrorism was often a subordinate strategy in many of these cases. Terrorism has emerged from political protest and revolts, social uprisings and religious protest movements. One of the early examples of a terrorism movement was the Sicarii, a highly organised religious sect consisting of men of lower orders active in the Zealot struggle in Palestine around 70 AD. They attacked targets in daylight, using a short sword. Messianic hope and political terrorism were the prominent features of the Assassins sect, an offshoot of the Ismailis who appeared in the eleventh century and were suppressed by the Mongols in the thirteenth century. Secret societies like the Thugs in India did not wish to terrorise the government or population, but rather the individual. Political assassinations of leading statesmen were relatively infrequent between the sixteenth and eighteenth centuries in the age of absolutism, once the religious conflicts had lost some of their acuteness. Monarchs, whatever their personal differences, had no thought of killing one another. Systematic terrorism began in the late nineteenth century and there were several distinct categories from the very beginning.

The Russian revolutionaries fought an autocratic government from 1878 to 1881, and again in the early twentieth century. Radical nationalist groups, such as the Irish, Macedonians, Serbs and Armenians used terrorist methods in their struggle for autonomy or national independence. Lastly, there was the anarchist 'propaganda by the deed' during the 1890s in France, Italy, Spain and the United States.

The three waves of Russian terror were the Narodnaya Volya between 1878 and 1881, and their notable successes included the head of the

Tsarist political police and Tsar Alexander II. The second wave of terror was sponsored by the Social Revolutionary Party, and their victims between 1902 and 1911 included two ministers of the interior, a Grand Duke and some provincial governors. Finally, the third small wave occurred after the Bolshevik coup in 1917.

The achievements of Irish terrorism have been less striking, but it has continued on and off over a much longer period. Armenian terrorism against Turkish oppression began in the 1890s and has continued at varying levels until the present day – with church dignitaries, political leaders and Turkish diplomats being the popular targets. Another revolutionary organisation directed against the Turks was the Macedonian IMRO, which started out as an underground civilian propagandist society and turned into a military movement, preparing for systematic terror and a mass insurrection. Polish socialists and some Indian groups, particularly in Bengal, developed anarchist traditions which were to continue well after independence had been achieved.

The high tide of terrorism in Western Europe was the anarchist 'propaganda of the deed' in the 1890s, in which bomb-throwing by individuals coincided with a turn in anarchist propaganda favouring violence. The expected international conspiracy never existed. However, there were many attacks on the lives of leading statesmen in Europe and America until the First World War.

There were no systematic terrorist campaigns before 1945 in Central and Western Europe, although they did exist on the fringes of Europe, in Russia, the Balkans and in Spain. Labour disputes in the USA were more violent than in Europe almost from their beginning. Up to the First World War, terrorism was considered to be a left-wing phenomenon, even though the highly individualistic character of terrorism did not quite fit the ideological pattern.

After 1918, terrorist operations were mainly sponsored by right-wing and national separatist groups. Sometimes these groups were right-wing and separatist, as in the case of the Croatian Ustashi. The Croatians wanted independence and had no compunction about accepting support from any quarter. The Romanian 'Iron Guard' was a budding Fascist movement which resorted to violence. Assassinations were few but spectacular, such as those of Liebknecht and Luxemburg (both German Communists), in 1919 and of the British commander-in-chief of the Egyptian army in 1924.

Individual terrorism played a minor role in the European resistance movement during the Second World War – a few high-ranking Nazis, notably Heydrich, the governor of the Czech protectorate, were killed.

For many years after the war, it was chiefly in the urban regions such as mandated Palestine (1945–47), and later in Cyprus (1955–58) and Aden (1964–67) that the terrorist strategy prevailed. Urban terror was overshadowed by large-scale guerrilla wars.

Urban terrorism was regarded at best as a supplementary form of warfare, at worst as a dangerous aberration. It was only in the mid 1960s that urban terrorism came into its own as a result of the defeat of rural guerrillas in Latin America, and following the emergence of urban terrorist groups in Europe, North America and Japan.

Terrorism has always been justified as a means of resisting despotism, and as such its origins can be traced back to antiquity. Plato and Aristotle believed tyranny to be the worst form of government. Tyrants never worked alone, they could not function without assistants, and thus it was necessary to attack the system on a broad front. The proponents of armed insurrection rather than of individual terror, such as Blanqui and Baboeuf, nevertheless influenced later terrorists through their advocacy of violence, scant regard for human life and belief that a few determined people could make a revolution. Occasional terrorist acts were perpetrated by the Carboneria in Italy, but these did not amount to a systematic campaign.

The idea of an alliance between the revolutionary avant-garde and the criminal underworld was a feature of nineteenth-century terrorist movements, e.g. the Narodnaya Volya in Russia, and among American and West German New Left militants of the 1960s. The Russian revolutionary Bakunin was a great enthusiast for merciless destruction, especially of members of the Church, the world of business, the bureaucracy and army, the secret police and even royalty. Thus for Bakunin there was an irrepressible need for total revolution, and for institutions, social structures, civilisation and morality to be destroyed root and branch. The revolution in Russia developed in stages, starting with sporadic acts of armed defence in resisting arrest and as a reaction against individual police officers who had maltreated arrested revolutionaries – and ending with total revolution and paralysis of the state. Russian revolutionaries believed that terrorist operations were far more effective in promoting the revolution, if only because of the tremendous publicity they received – very much in contrast to illegal propaganda and organisational work, which had no visible effect. Some Russians believed that terrorism was not only effective, but humanitarian. It cost fewer victims than a mass struggle, and was the application of modern science to the revolutionary struggle.

By the last decade of the nineteenth century there were active terrorist operations in Spain, Italy, France, India, the USA, Poland and among stateless groups such as the Armenians. Despite their approval in principle of a direct bomb-throwing approach, both Marx and Engels condemned the foolishness of conspiracies, denounced the purposeless 'propaganda by deed' and dissociated themselves from individual actions. Communists have shown ambiguity in their approach to terrorism. It might be rejected in principle, but on certain occasions the practice of terrorism has not been ruled out.

In history, terrorism has been practised as much by right-wing and nationalist groups as by left-wing groups. Terrorism in India had a strong religious base; the Clan-na-Gael in America stood for bloodless terrorism directed against buildings; whilst in Ireland in the 1880s the Invincibles practised individual terror such as the Phoenix Park murder of a British minister. Some Irish groups were keener on gimmicks – such as spraying the House of Commons with osmic gas, and collecting money to purchase poisoned stilettos, lucifer matches and other unlikely weapons.

Assassinations of political opponents carried out by the Black Hundred in pre-1914 Russia are also examples of terrorism as carried out by the extreme right. The Fascists under Mussolini in Italy tended to intimidate opponents rather than eliminate individual enemy leaders; the Nazis showed the tremendous use which could be made of political violence to maximise publicity in the mass media. The composition of right-wing terrorist groups varied greatly from country to country, ranging from criminal elements to young idealists. Terror carried out by individuals was infrequent; instead there was terror of incitement – of speech, and of the written word.

Generally in the inter-war years, the decision by a group to adopt a terrorist strategy was taken on the basis of a detailed political analysis. An initial sense of grievance and frustration would later be supported by ideological rationalisation – ranging from a systematic strategy to imprecise doctrines.

See also **Assassins, Terrorism in the 1960s, Terrorism and terror**

Hizbullah Hizbullah, or the Party of God, was formed in 1982 in Baalbek and is considered the largest radical movement in Lebanon, although its strength cannot be accurately judged because it has no official structure or membership list. Any Shi'ite state which adheres to Islamic tenets is, in theory, a member of Hizbullah. The movement, which was started by militant local clerics, is aided by the Iranian Revolutionary Guard, which had deployed in Lebanon's eastern Bekaa Valley after the Israeli invasion.

Within a year Hizbullah had infiltrated Beirut. At first, it did not publicise its presence, but gradually militant posters and the return to conservative Islamic dress by Shi'ite women revealed the strength of Hizbullah. Now the group has at least three offices in West Beirut.

Hizbullah addresses its message to the downtrodden, opting for religion, freedom and dignity over humiliation and constant submission to America and its allies. The movement is loyal to Ayatollah Khomeini and has listed three goals in Lebanon: firstly, to expel the US, France and the influence of any imperialist power from the country, and the expulsion of Israel 'as a prelude to its final obliteration from existence' and the liberation of 'venerable Jerusalem'; secondly, the submission of the Christian Phalange Party, and trial of its members for crimes against Muslims and Christians; and thirdly, to give people the opportunity to determine their faith (although Hizbullah has an overriding commitment to the rule of Islam).

Hizbullah has become the umbrella cover for a host of smaller factions, including Islamic Amal, the Hussein Suicide Squad, Dawah (the

Lebanese branch of the Iraq-based al-Dawah al-Islamia), and other smaller movements.

Hostage negotiation This often devolves down to a policy debate on whether deterrence deters, and to a 'no ransom' versus negotiation argument.

On the general question of deterrence, those who demand prisoners' freedom focus adverse publicity on the government. Those who demand ransoms put targets in a bad light. Many attacks are made in retaliation for governmental moves against terrorist organisations. Groups may engage in kidnapping to publicise an overall ideology. Some kidnappers hope to disrupt society's expectation of security and order. Terrorists hope to provoke government repression against themselves. A hostage may be of some value to those who have seized him. An incident may represent an individual's personal affirmation of solidarity with the norms of a terrorist group. Many observers believe that if a tough policy stopped terrorist incidents – terrorists would engage in other types of violent action which did not involve hostages.

The 'no ransom' position is centred on certain basic approaches. Terrorists are all the same – with a leftist ideology, and employ the same tactics. Due to their links, there is perhaps the creation of a terrorist international – with the same funding sources, holding worldwide meetings and with joint operations. While capitulation encourages others, in isolated incidents the opposite is true. The temptation to kidnap diplomats can be removed by denying rewards. The no ransom view maintains that it is morally wrong to give in to the demands of groups engaging in terrorist acts. Governments have responsibility to protect political prisoners; and ultimately a stated policy cannot countenance giving in to terrorist demands.

The flexible response position is perhaps more complex. Primarily, terrorists are not all the same and do not react in the same way in hostage situations. They differ in ideology and purpose in the choice of terrorism, differ in tactics, and do not have the same views on the sanctity of life, and rarely double-cross bargainers. Links between groups do not lead to a commonality of tactics, strategy, perceptions of motivations. Rarely do terrorists attend relevant international meetings. Some groups, notably the Palestine Liberation Organisation, are split on the sanctity of life, tactics and strategy. Many terrorist groups fight primary terrorist groups – and nation states have many links – including trade and communications. Examination of the site of incidents provides clues on how to conduct negotiations. The contagion hypothesis rests on shaky evidence. Governments have a moral duty to protect nationals. Terrorists care about what happens to them after an incident. Ultimately, granting asylum is a time-honoured practice, and the politics of desperation is the last refuge of the weak.

Hostage-taking In recent years hostage-taking has become a favourite tactic of political terrorists, largely because of the intense publicity surrounding terrorist situations where hostages are involved. Hostage-taking has also burgeoned as a tactic of mentally unstable and criminal individuals. Because of its high profile and the attendant publicity, and the extreme actions which governments have been prompted to take as a consequence of hostage situations, they exemplify many of the policy issues surrouding anti-terrorist operations.

Three broad groups of hostage-takers exist:

(1) *The mentally ill hostage-taker.* Primarily because of the high media exposure given to hostage and siege situations, it has become increasingly apparent to mentally unstable individuals that taking someone hostage guarantees individual recognition by the news media, the opportunity to exercise power and to put the police into a defensive posture. For those with suicidal tendencies a hostage or barricade situation is often seen as a spectacularly successful method of bringing about one's demise. It is important for the negotiators who communicate with the hostage-taker to try to understand that individual's world. The individuals involved are people with limited personal power who feel their problems occur because they are being persecuted by the world or significant segments of it. Their feelings of frustration, helplessness and lack of worth may overwhelm them so that they feel they must strike back by taking power and control over someone or some organisation that symbolises their problems.

(2) *The criminal hostage-taker.* Criminals take hostages usually as a last resort. Sometimes the police response to a crime in progress may be sufficiently rapid that the offender is trapped with what appears to him to be no alternative but to take a hostage in an attempt to bargain his way out of custody. While criminals are generally rational when committing a crime, they obviously do not want to be arrested and may display somewhat less than their usual reason when the police corner them.

(3) *The social, political, ethnic or 'religious crusade' hostage-taker.* Such a hostage-taker is generally a member of a group which can be defined as terrorist, and will have a strong sense of commitment to or belief in a particular idea or cause. Terrorist groups are usually small, but extremely dedicated, even to the point of dying for the furtherance of their beliefs and ideas. Whatever the goal of their particular movement, professional terrorists have usually studied revolutionary tactics and effective methods of promoting and broadcasting the basis for their ideology or cause. Terrorist groups are most difficult to deal with because of their total commitment. Although rational, they often enter a situation with set demands and identified limits as to what they are willing to do in the furtherance of their cause. Frequently members of these groups are committed to the extent that they will kill or die if necessary. Although situations involving terrorists are complicated by their determination, extensive planning, and ability to exert power effec-

tively, experience has shown that alternatives to the original demands can often be worked out, frequently ones which concede little in political terms.

Since hostage and siege situations are a major form of terrorist activity (not necessarily in terms of frequency, but certainly in terms of impact), security forces around the world over the past decade have been developing special negotiating procedures to cope with these situations in order to prevent the killing of innocent hostages or the granting of significant political concessions to the terrorists. The leaders in this field have been the British and the Dutch in dealing with political terrorists, and the New York City Police Department in dealing with criminal hostage-takers. The development of hostage negotiation techniques is an evolving process, with new approaches becoming necessary as new types of hostage situations emerge or as hostage-takers become aware of negotiating techniques and seek to minimise their effects. Terrorists do change their tactics in response to information about what factors swing the balance of the negotiating situation in favour of the authorities.

See also **Hostage negotiation**

H

India In terms of terrorism and political violence in recent times in India, the world thinks of the Sikhs and their demands for an independent state, especially after the Golden Temple incident in June 1984 and the assassination of Mrs Gandhi in October that year. Nevertheless, there are other illegal movements, many of which are separatist , and mainly represent communities or are extreme left-wing. There is also a profusion of legally existing political parties, both at national and at state level. Divisions of existing parties, defections from these parties and formations of new parties have been frequent.

Hindu movements are well-established in origin. The All Assam People's Struggle Council was set up to oppose the inclusion of aliens, or Muslims who had fled from East Pakistan in 1971, when that territory seceded from Pakistan and became Bangladesh. Many atrocities have been committed against Bengalis and three massacres were reported in 1985. The All Assam Students Group actively campaigns against Bengali immigrants in Assam. On a broader scale many Hindus have been attracted by the paramilitary nature of the National Union of Selfless Servers. It is a communal group functioning as a secret society offshoot of the Hindu Jan Sangh sect which provoked street violence with Muslims. It is estimated to have up to ten million members. Less paramilitary but equally extremist is the left-wing Hindu group known as Ananda Marg. It wishes to establish global unity on the basis of a new social economic theory, and regularly uses suicide as a way of expression. It has been active in Australia against Indian diplomats. The political wing of this movement is the Universal Proutist Revolutionary Party. The word Proutist is derived from the 'progressive utility' theory developed by one of its members, P. R. Sarkar.

The most well-known of the left-wing movements are the Naxalites – who originated from an armed revolutionary campaign launched in North Bengal in 1965. This extreme faction of the Communist Party of India (Marxist-Leninist) was formed as a result of disagreements over operational strategy for the spread of communism in rural India. The Naxalites are committed to Maoist principles of people's liberation warfare. A decade ago some members led by Satya Singh rejected revolutionary Marxism and now support parliamentary democracy. Nevertheless, extremists continue to carry out attacks in over half of India's provinces, with a membership strength of around 15,000. The Naxalites support the upholding of both armed struggle and all other forms of struggle complementary to it. The other chief left-wing movement is the Dalit Panthers, who appeared in the late 1960s as an organisation of young militant untouchables which took its inspiration from the Black Panthers in the United States. They have been active in encouraging conversions of Harijans to Islam, as a means of escaping from the caste system.

In addition to the Sikh separatists, other separatist groups are active in other parts of India. In Kashmir there is Jamaat-i-Tulaba, a student wing of the pro-Pakistan political party, planning an Iran-type revolution for the liberation of Kashmir from 'illegal occupation and enslavement by India'. The Jammu Kashmir Liberation Front is based in England, – with branches in Ajad, Kashmir, the Middle East, Europe and the United States and a good number of sympathisers in the Indian-held part of Kashmir. In Manipur the People's Liberation Army is active. It is a Maoist organisation operating mainly in Manipur, but advocating independence from the whole north-eastern region of India. Support comes from tribes who have rejected Hinduism as a faith identified with the cultural domination of New Delhi. Like the People's Liberation Army, the People's Revolutionary Party of Kungleipak (PREPAK) has been active in the state of Manipur, whose secession from the Union of India it seeks.

In Mizoram, and in particular in the Mizo Hills district in southern Assam, the Mizo National Front is active, as well as around the borders of Bangladesh. The Naga separatist movement has had a history of armed and non-violent resistance to the incorporation of Nagaland in the Union of India, of which that territory became a constituent state in 1972 – but in recent years factional groups have been formed which have reduced its effectiveness.

Also in North East India in Tripura, one finds armed extremists campaigning for an independent Tripura. The radical, cultural and social organisation of Tripura hill youth has links with the Mizo National Front in terms of weaponry, training and logistical support.

See also **Non-violence, Sikh extremism**

Indoctrination and skills Many observers believe that terrorists have to be aware only of political indoctrination. However, the likes of Marighella and Debray believed one could become a good fighter only by learning the art of fighting which involves everything from physical training to the learning of many kinds of job, especially those involving manual skills.

According to Marighella and Debray , the accomplished terrorist has to know something of the mechanics of radio, telephones and electronics, and should be able to make maps and plans, measure distance and locate his position on the ground by use of a compass. Forgery arts and first aid skills were considered important. Above all, the recruit to the terrorist group had to prove himself in action before being given complete training and there are many examples among the Germans, Palestinians, and Latin Americans of this process. In some Latin American movements, the raw recruit, as an act of good faith, has to kill a policeman or soldier before being fully accepted into the band. A terrorist needs discipline and has to be taught the virtue of obeying orders, but after that the need is more for grounding in intelligence work than in strictly commando-type assault operations. There is a need primarily for small-arms instruction, plenty of range practice and a thorough knowledge of explosives and detonators. Training can be of a low level; but what the recruits lack in this respect they make up for in zeal and cruelty.

Terrorists pay much attention to the use of disguise and in successful groups international figures who have reappeared several times look quite different on each occasion. To use explosive devices requires considerable training, and it is the bomb work which divides the pros from the amateurs. To explode a device demands not only technical ability, but a cool head and a steady hand.

Only by taking part in a raid and by a baptism of fire can a terrorist prove himself. In several groups criminals have been welcomed into the movement for their technical skills, and sometimes for the doctrinal satisfaction the participation of genuine working-class outlaws gives to young middle-class or well-to-do terrorists beset by guilt. Criminals can provide experienced help in how best to go about specialised forms of fund-raising.

The reason for the primacy attached to the act of killing is that it binds the would-be terrorist irrevocably to the organisation. Up to that moment he or she could back out, but once the candidates have killed they are committed. Those terrorists who wish to quit give the reasons of wishing to lead respectable lives, the acknowledgment that the terrorists have won, the hatred of killing, reduced opportunities and fewer targets. They are not necessarily fanatics, but some are irrational or crazy. At different stages they are happy in their calling. Terrorists join a group without considering the fateful step and anxiety sets in when the entry trap closes; there is an extreme penalty for defection, and individuals in the same group often do not trust each other. Tensions are many and very severe, with strong emphasis on differences of opinion. Leadership, discipline, planning and execution of actions can be very lax. Terrorists are unable to cope with any government's declining to take an initiative on abductions and intimidation, and are sensitive to perceived loss of sympathies, especially if they see their task as consciousness-raising.

Insurgency In its most general sense insurgency is a struggle between a non-ruling group and the ruling authorities, in which the former consciously employs political resources (organisational skills, propaganda or demonstrations or both) and instruments of violence to establish legitimacy for some aspect of the political system which the ruling authorities consider illegitimate.

Legitimacy and illegitimacy refer to the public perception of whether existing aspects of politics are moral or immoral. Insurgents seek through violent means to separate themselves from existing arrangements and to establish a separate political community.

Dissidents can grant legitimacy to the regime but reject individuals in power. This is exemplified by coups in which insurgents seize the key to decision-making offices without changing the regime of their predecessors. Basically, it is a crisis about political legitimacy.

Six types of insurgent movements have been isolated from the general theories of political violence. Secessionist insurgents reject the existing political community of which they are credibly a part and seek to constitute an independent organisation. Revolutionary insurgents seek to impose a new regime based on egalitarian values and centrally controlled structures to activate the people and change the social structure. Restorational insurgent movements wish to displace the regime and the values and structures they champion are identified with a recent political order. Reactionary insurgents seek to change the regime by reconstituting a past political order, but their vision relates to an idealised golden age of the distant past in which religious values and authoritarian structures were predominant – e.g. the Ayatollah in Iran seeks to recreate the seventh-century Islamic society, as perceived by Shi'a Muslims. Conservative insurgents seek to maintain the existing regime in the face of pressures on the authorities to change it, as exemplified by Protestant organisations in Ulster who wish to retain the regime in Northern Ireland which they see as threatened by the Irish Republican Army. Reformist insurgents such as the Kurds in Iraq have attempted to obtain more political, social and economic benefits without necessarily rejecting the political community, regime or authorities.

Insurgent movements use both political resources and instruments of violence against the ruling authorities in order to accomplish their objectives. Organisation can be of two types – conspirational, where small élite groups carry out and threaten violent acts, or internal warfare where insurgent élites attempt to mobilise large segments of the population on behalf of their cause. Internal warfare cases are widespread and include Vietnamese, Cambodian, Chinese, Algerian and Portuguese colonial conflicts. Ample cases of conspirational insurgencies exist, such as those led by the Bolsheviks in Tsarist Russia, the Red Army in Japan, the Red Brigades in Italy and the Muslim Brotherhood in Egypt.

Different forms of warfare can be associated with the violent aspects of insurgency, notably terrorism, a form of insurgent warfare conducted by individuals or very small groups; and guerrilla warfare, a form of violence based on mobile tactics used by small, lightly armed groups who aim to harass their opponent rather than defeat him in battle.

Insurgents need to maximise the effectiveness of political techniques and violence. Popular support can be divided into two categories – active and passive. Passive support includes those who merely sympathise with the aims and activities of the insurgents, and active includes individuals who are willing to risk personal sacrifices on behalf of the insurgents. Active supporters are individuals who provide insurgents with supplies, intelligence information, shelter, concealment, liaison agents and carry out acts of disobedience or protest which bring severe punishment by the government. Insurgents seek to gain support and recruits by charismatic attraction, esoteric or private appeals, public appeals, terrorism, the provocation of government counter-terrorism and a demonstration of potency. The latter includes meeting the needs of the people through social services and a governing apparatus and obtaining the military initiative.

Popular support is often crucial for the success of an insurgency. The co-ordination of a campaign is complex and its outcome can be influenced by other major variables, most especially the government response and the insurgent's organisational dexterity.

Insurgency can be seen as more of a political phenomenon than a military one. The analysis of an insurgent organisation involves scope, complexity and cohesion, and assessing whether services and channels for expressive protest are being provided by the government. 'Scope' refers to the number of people who either play key roles in the movement or provide active support. If there is a need to supplement membership, an insurgent organisation will increase its activity and demands and through the efforts of its political cadres penetrate hamlets, villages and cities, especially in areas in which neither the government nor insurgents have firm control. In many cases insurgents have established parallel hierarchies to compete with government institutions. What can occur is the penetration of the existing official administrative structures by subversive agents, or the creation of autonomous insurgent structures to take over full administrative responsibility when military-political conditions are deemed appropriate. For greater support, new branches can be created, such as youth groups, peasant organisations, workers' groups and women's organisations.

Insurgents engaged in a lengthy armed struggle can diversify their military organisation by creating logistics units, terrorist networks and guerrilla forces with the last mentioned divided between full-time and part-time fighters. Full-time guerrillas can operate from secure bases, attack government military units and installations on a continual basis and constitute a nucleus for a regularised force in the event that the movement gets involved in mobile conventional warfare. Part-time guerrillas stay in their communities and provide a number of invaluable services – collecting intelligence, storing supplies and protecting political organisers. For the individual, participation can yield material benefits, if the organisation has the resources, and it can generate psychological satisfaction by virtue of the new sense of identity which stems from the perception that one is engaged in common endeavour.

To achieve unity, insurgent movements stress common attitudes, sanctions and organisational schemes. Organisational formats are important in establishment of cohesion – control by politicians, independent political and military commands and control by the military. Rival movements can still continue to exist and operate and as a result insurgents may attempt to co-ordinate activity by creating a unified command for a particular operation, by arriving at a division of labour among various groups or by establishing a unified command for all operations.

The most publicised aspect of insurgent strategy is its frequent stress on external support as yet another means to offset the government's advantages. Moral support is the least costly and risky for a donor, for all it involves is public acknowledgment that the insurgent movement is just and admirable. Political support advances a step further as the donor nation supports the strategic goal of the insurgent movement in the international arena. Material assistance is more concrete and risky for an outside power, and includes money, weapons, ammunition, medical supplies, food, training and perhaps the provision of military advisers, fire support or combat units. It is valuable as the insurgents can increase the scale and intensity of violence, since such a development necessitates greater logistical support. When external logistical inputs are essential, the role of sympathetic major powers can be important. External states may be important as sanctuaries in which guerrillas can be trained, arms stockpiled, operations planned, leadership secured and ultimately a provisional government established.

Societal cleavages such as ethnicity, religion and language, may be helpful to dissident elements. In situations where the government displays the ability and willingness to resist and the military is not demoralised, the insurgent movement has to prepare itself to wage a prolonged conflict. Governmental response is crucial in insurgent conflicts, because where its response is poor or uneven the insurgents can tolerate shortcomings in popular and external support organisation, in their internal cohesion and in the environment. Where the government manifests strength, such failings can spell defeat. Governments countering insurrections have to deal with insurgent propaganda relating to organisational activity, terrorism, guerrilla warfare and mobile conventional warfare. The execution of a counter-insurgency programme requires co-ordination of political, administrative, military, police and intelligence efforts. To counter the terrorist campaign the government has to seek to destroy the political-military structures of the insurgent organisation by locating and detaining its members. Facing large-scale guerrilla actions, the government has to consolidate areas it holds and expand from these with the objectives of gaining control of the population, food and other resources, while inflicting losses on guerrilla units and defending vital lines of communication.

In terms of conceptual sophistication, insurgent strategies range from the carefully articulated to the chaotic.

Insurgents who adhere to a Leninist strategy believe that a small, tightly knit, disciplined and highly organised conspiratorial group that has obtained support from major disconnected social groups, such as the military and working class, provides the most effective means for achieving the goal of the movement. The Leninist approach assumes a government that is alienated from its population, hence one which will surrender when confronted by low-level terrorism, subversion of the military and the police and the final seizure of radio stations, government offices and other state institutions. Leninist strategy is conspiratorial organisation combined with active support from selected social groups.

The most elaborate insurgent strategy is expounded by Maoist theoreticians who ascribe great significance to popular support, extensive organisational efforts and the environment as resources necessary for a prolonged conflict with an enemy perceived as being in a superior position prior to hostilities. The Maoist approach unfolds in distinct steps, each of which is designed to achieve part of the goal and is dependent on the outcome of the step before it. These stages of political organisation are terrorism, guerrilla warfare and mobile conventional warfare. Initially, the insurgents stress esoteric and exoteric appeals as well as the social services and mutual help aspects associated with demonstrations of potency. Guerrilla warfare is a 'social' stage – the earliest part of this stage is characterised by armed resistance carried out by small bands operating in rural areas where terrain is rugged and government control weak. Civil war, the final stage of a Maoist-type insurgency, involves regularisation of guerrilla forces and mobile-conventional warfare. Maoist insurgent strategy emphasises three inter-related elements; popular support, organisation and the environment. Environmental characteristics are important in the Maoist strategy. However, external support has an ambiguous place in the framework of Maoist strategy. Although self-reliance is the overriding consideration, in practice, moral, political, material and sanctuary support have played a key role, especially in offsetting similar assistance to the government.

An alternative to the Maoist protracted warfare strategy is provided by the Cuban model. Guevara believed that the mere fact of taking up arms in situations where grievances existed would create suitable conditions for revolution. Regis Debray believed that one of the major characteristics of the Cuban revolution was the rejection of the idea that the guerrilla force should be subordinated to the party and rather that primary emphasis should be placed on the guerrilla force as the nucleus of the party. Under the Cuban revolution, certain conditions were vital to success. The political and the military were not separated but formed one organic whole, consisting of the people's army, whose nucleus was the guerrilla army.

The vanguard party existed in the form of the guerrilla force itself, and the guerrilla force was the party in embryo. It has to be pointed out however that it is questionable whether Castro could have achieved his aims if the Batista government had not been in a state of profound decay.

In recent decades insurgents have found the urban terrorist model to be attractive. Emphasis is placed on popular support and erosion of the enemy's will to resist, rather than on defeating the enemy in classical military engagements. Unlike the Maoist and Cuban examples, the focus of conflict during initial phases is in the cities rather than the countryside, because of the assumption that the increased size and socio-economic differentiation of urban centres makes them vulnerable to terrorism and sabotage. For an urban strategy to be successful it would seem the regime would already have to be on the brink of collapse.

Within the general rubric of insurgency, terrorism emerges as but one means of achieving political ends. As a decisive strategic technique there is little to undermine its efficacy. However, insurgents do have political and military weaknesses, and the prolonged use of insurgent activities is normally counterproductive, in that it galvanises governments to greater efforts and outrages the previously apathetic public.

See also **Counter-insurgency**

Insurrection Insurrection is armed resistance against government authority and its chief policy-forming agents for the purposes of resisting the imposition of legal constraints, overthrowing the government or weakening its authority.

Intelligence roles Generalised measures are never sufficient to stop terrorists, even though they may be very effective in drying up the potential bases of popular support for the terrorist movement. Authorities have to be prepared for the attacks and campaigns of varying duration and intensity launched by numerically tiny groups which may entirely lack popular sympathy or support.

Widespread support is rare, and groups are usually based on a structure of cells or 'firing groups' of about six persons. They exercise a degree of operational independence and initiative and are obsessively concerned with the security of their organisation and lines of communication. This cell structure is designed to enhance secrecy, mobility and flexibility while at the same time facilitating tight overall central control by the terrorist directorate. Paramilitary command structures and discipline are fostered to ensure unswerving obedience to the leadership; offenders against the terrorist code are ruthlessly punished, often by death. Experienced terrorists develop sophisticated cover against detection and infiltration. They are adept at hiding in the anonymity of the urban landscape and at swiftly changing their bases of operations. Terrorists are constantly engaged in training new 'hit men', bomb-makers, small-arms specialists and assassins. In a protracted and carefully planned campaign certain individuals and cells in the terrorist movement will be strategically placed as 'sleepers', to be actuated later in the struggle as and when required.

The terrorists' small numbers and anonymity make them an extraordinarily difficult quarry for the police in modern cities, while the ready availability of light, portable arms and materials required for home-made bombs makes it difficult to track down terrorist lines of supply. Yet once the key members of a cell have been identified it is generally practicable to round up other members. On the basis of information gleaned from interrogating a relatively small number of key terrorist operatives it is possible to spread the net more effectively around the whole organisation.

A crucial requirement for defeating any political terrorist campaign therefore must be the development of high-quality intelligence, for unless the security authorities are fortunate enough to capture a terrorist red-handed at the scene of the crime, it is only by sifting through comprehensive and accurate intelligence data that the police have any hope of locating the terrorists. Government and security chiefs need to know a great deal about groups and individuals that are seeking rewards by terrorism, about their aims, political motivations and alignments, leadership, individual members, logistic and financial resources and organisational structures.

The greatest weakness of modern liberal states in the field of internal defence is reluctance or inability to see subversion as a problem until it is too late. The primary objective of an efficient intelligence service must be to prevent any insurgency or terrorism developing beyond the conceptual stage. Hence a high-quality intelligence service is required long before the insurgency erupts. It is vital that such a service should have a national responsibility, and be firmly under the control of the civil authorities and hence democratically accountable. In a liberal democratic state the most appropriate body for the tasks of intelligence-gathering, collation, analysis and co-ordination is the police Special Branch or its equivalent. It is normally the case in a liberal state that the police service enjoys at least some public co-operation. The routine police tasks of law enforcement and combatting crime at every level of the community give the police service an unrivalled bank of background information from which contact information can be developed.

The development of a reliable, high-quality intelligence service is not easily accomplished. There are serious pitfalls. The police may lose the confidence and co-operation of certain key sections of the population. This is especially probable where the police have been controlled, administered and staffed predominantly by one ethnic or religious group and are hence regarded as partisan by rival groups. In such conditions it often becomes impossible for the police to carry out law enforcement functions, let alone develop high standards of criminal investigation and intelligence work. In extreme cases, as in Ulster 1969–70, when the police system was faced with almost total breakdown, another agency, the army, has to be brought in to provide the intelligence system as well as exercising the major constabulary functon.

The breakdown of normal policing due to political and communal conflict is a rare occurrence in liberal states. Police and intelligence services are costly to establish and maintain and their breakdown creates grave internal dangers. But armed forces are even more expensive and no liberal state can view with equanimity the diversion of large numbers of expensive military personnel, some with very sophisticated technical training, away from their vital external defence role and into what are essentially internal police functions. It is certain that Britain's small, professional, all-volunteer army cannot afford the manpower, time or special training required for such tasks.

If the state is faced with the breakdown of civil policing and the total collapse of law and order either nationally or in a particular region, the army then has an absolutely crucial though unenviable role as a weapon of last resort. It has the duty to restore order in such cases. The tasks of intelligence in an incipient civil or inter-communal war are onerous in the extreme, and the routine work of gathering and building up contact information consumes reserves of time, training and manpower that an army can ill afford. A recurrent problem for the police forces of liberal states is the difficulty of co-ordinating and gathering intelligence on a nation-wide basis. This has particularly adverse effects on anti-terrorist operations.

Crucial preconditions exist for effective co-ordination of intelligence at national level. The continuing confidence and co-operation of political leaders and the general public must be maintained. Hence it is vital that such agencies are seen to operate within the law and that constitutional safeguards against the abuse of their powers should be seen to be effective. There has to be constant and close liaison and co-operation with the military and state security services in intelligence matters. Access to the very latest technologies of intelligence-gathering, communications and surveillance is essential. A most important need is for centralised intelligence data computerisation which can provide information swiftly for all levels of the security forces. Among the fundamental intelligence needs is the requirement for closer international co-operation among allied states in the exchange of information about terrorist movements and activities, about the involvement of hostile states and transnational or foreign revolutionary movements, and other relevant data for combatting political violence.

See also **Data on terrorism**

International humanitarian law and terrorism Terrorism and terrorist acts are not only a challenge, but also a twofold threat to the law of a state: a direct threat in that they jeopardise the life and physical integrity of individuals; and an indirect threat in that in combatting terrorist acts, the aggressed state runs the risk of departing from the law, possibly under the influence of public opinion. Terrorism threatens the law of each individual state and also the law of the international community.

International law cannot provide a direct answer to most questions raised by terrorism simply because it is not applicable outside armed conflicts. However, such law unconditionally prohibits terrorist acts and provides for their repression. Under the law, armed conflicts of an international character include national liberation wars, i.e. armed conflicts in which people are trying to secure self-determination. If a terrorist takes part in a genuine national liberation war he has to carry arms openly and comply with the rules of international humanitarian law, which strictly prohibits any terrorist act.

In peacetime, terrorist acts must and can generally be dealt with under the domestic law of states, for international humanitarian law is not applicable outside armed conflicts. Terrorist acts are forbidden, but to those who do not observe this prohibition, international humanitarian law grants a minimum of humane treatment, but at the same time allows, and in most cases obliges states to punish them for their acts. For the benefit of combatants, i.e. members of the armed forces, the law imposes certain restrictions on the terrorist acts which the enemy may direct at them.

In internal armed conflicts captured terrorists, whether civilians or military agents, benefit from the same fundamental guarantees as all other persons who do not or no longer take a direct part in the hostilities. In international armed conflicts, if a member of the armed forces commits terrorist acts, and if these constitute war crimes, he may and must be punished for his war crimes by the power or state on which he depends. If he has fallen into the power of the enemy, he has prisoner of war status, but may and must be punished by the detaining power for his war crimes. If he failed to comply properly with his fundamental obligation to distinguish himself from the civilian population while engaged in an attack or in a military operation preparatory to an attack, he forfeits his right to be a prisoner of war, but must be granted equivalent treatment. This means that he may be punished not only for his war crimes but also for his mere participation in the hostilities. If the armed forces of one party to the conflict commit terrorist acts, one could maintain that they do not qualify as armed forces, and consequently their members are not entitled to prisoner of war status. If the persons who have committed terrorist acts are civilians, their own party may and must punish them for their participation in the hostilities and for their terrorist acts. If they have fallen into the power of the enemy they are protected civilians, but they may be punished for participation in hostilities and for their terrorist attacks.

Terrorist acts, in so far as they are grave breaches of the conventions, become universal crimes under the jurisdiction of all parties to these instruments. Each party is under an obligation to enact the necessary legislation to extend its criminal jurisdiction to any person who has committed a grave breach, regardless of the nationality of the perpetrator, the victim or the scene of the crime.

See also **Rights of terrorists**

Iran The Islamic Republic of Iran is ruled by a Council of Revolution, consisting of (Shi'ite) Islamic spiritual leaders following the fundamentalist guidelines of Ayatollah Khomeini. In general, political parties and other organisations enjoy freedom as long as they do not 'infringe the principles of independence, freedom, national unity and the bases of the Islamic Republic'. The Ayatollah has many political enemies ranging from supporters of the late Shah, overthrown in 1979, and liberal politicians, to non-fundamentalist Muslim groups and militant members of ethnic minorities, in particular Arabs, Azerbaijanis, Baluchis, Kurds and Turkomans. Suppression is undertaken by the Revolutionary Guards (Pasdaran) who are directly responsible to the Council of the Revolution. Guerrilla activity against the government has increased in recent years, and it is estimated that nearly 10,000 executions have taken place since the Ayatollah came to power in 1979.

As a result of the large groups of regional minorities in the country there are many separatist groups. The Arab Political and Cultural Organisation is based in Khuzestan province in the south-western part of the country, and they resent the influx of Iranians attracted by the oil finds in the region. In spite of the Ayatollah's granting limited autonomy to the region, clashes with the government have occurred regularly. Many deaths and bomb explosions have occurred in Korramshahr, and throughout their dispute the Khuzestan Arabs have been supported by other Iranian opposition movements, especially the Kurds. Closely associated with the Organisation has been Black Wednesday, an Arab rebel force that has engaged in many acts of sabotage in the oil-rich province of Khuzestan.

In London, six Iranian Arabs calling themselves the Group of the Martyr seized the Iranian Embassy in April 1980, taking 26 hostages and demanding that in return for their release 91 Arabs imprisoned in Iran should be set free. After the six had killed two of the hostages, members of the British Special Air Service penetrated into the embassy, killing five of the Arabs and seizing the sixth, who was sentenced to life imprisonment in January 1981.

In another area of Iran the Azerbaijan Autonomist Movement gains members from the nearly ten million Azerbaijanis who form the largest ethnic group in Iran. They were mainly Shi'ite Muslims who acknowledge Ayatollah Shariatmadari, who rejected the leadership of Ayatollah Khomeini and the involvement of the clergy in the running of the country. The movement boycotted the referendum to approve the Constitution in 1979, and within weeks, as a result of house arrests of some of the Movement's members, a rebellion broke out in Tabriz, the chief city in Azerbaijan. Although the Ayatollah Shariatmadari reduced his violent activities in this region, he remained under close suspicion of wishing to kill the Ayatollah Khomeini.

In Iran's south-eastern province of Baluchistan the Baluchis who are Sunni Muslims form the majority of the population, while the minority Sistans who are Shi'ites enjoy a higher standard of living. Baluchi demands for limited autonomy within Iran and economic concessions have been largely ignored. Many incidents have taken place between the two groups, which are both opposed by the government. Baluchi separatists have intensified their guerrilla activities.

The two chief Kurdish movements demanding autonomy for Kurdistan on the frontier between Iran and Iraq are the Kurdish Democratic Party of Iran and the Kurdish Sunni Muslim Movement. Both believe in seeking a social revolution in Iran and stress that only armed struggle would bring about the overthrow of the Ayatollah's regime. Many believe that the current Gulf War between Iran and Iraq, and in particular the regular Iranian offensives against Iraq are, in fact, manoeuvres to encircle the Kurds.

In north-eastern Iran after the revolution in 1979 the predominantly Sunni Muslim Turkomans called for concessions involving the redistribution of land owned by supporters of the former Shah, the right to set up their own police force, the official recognition of their language and representation in the local revolutionary committees dominated by Shi'ite Muslims. None of these demands has been met and the Revolutionary Guards actively seek to suppress the autonomists.

Left-wing movements have for many years been dominated by the Tudeh, the outlawed Iranian Communist Party. Other groups do exist. The Forqan group claims responsibility for the assassination of a minor Ayatollah and an army general, in its role as a major Marxist underground organisation. The National Democratic Front, an offshoot of the Union of National Front Forces is, like the Union, an essentially secular anti-regime movement. It has consistently resented the Ayatollah's attempt to establish a religious dictatorship. The People's Sacrificers is a nationalist Marxist group on the far left whose support is drawn from young students and the radical wing of the intelligentsia.

Although the theoreticians of the fedayeen differ sharply over tactics they all condemn what they consider to be capitalist and imperialist exploitation, and seek to build a radical socialist state in Iran. Its members are intensely ideological and have a fifteen year history of guerrilla warfare. In 1980 the fedayeen splintered into three factions, including the Fedayeen guerrillas (Cherikha), the Aqaliyyat minority and the Aksariyyat majority. While the guerrilla and minority splinters have sought to pursue their radical goals independently, the majority group has revealed a willingness to compromise.

A more extreme group are the Iranian People's Strugglers, a party based on the major principle of *towhid*, a divinely integrated classless society, a society with total equity. In this ideal society there will be an end to the exploitation of man by man. Consistently, the group have attacked the rule of the religious leaders on the right whom they see as repressive, reactionary and revolutionary dilettantes. By the early 1980s they were viewed as a major armed force fighting the Ayatollah's regime. Many of their 100,000 guerrillas, out of a reputed membership of 400,000, were trained by the Palestine Liberation Organisation. The Peykar and Union of Communists are both small pro-Chinese formations which have actively opposed the Khomeini regime.

Monarchist groups have had the obvious motivations, with the country totally dominated by the Ayatollah. The government, in announcing that plots have been uncovered, have generally stated that those involved are army officers and other members of the armed forces intent upon restoring the monarchy. The Armed Movement for the Liberation of Iran is led by a niece of the late Shah. In May 1981 some members of the Pars Group were arrested in connexion with an alleged plot to restore the monarchy, with the authorities accusing the Group of having links with Dr Shapour Bakhtiar, the leader of the National Resistance Movement, then living in France, and with certain members of the late Shah's family.

Externally based movements have developed either during the latter stages of the Shah's rule or since the Ayatollah came to power. The National Front opposed both leaders. However, the National Council of Resistance for Liberty and Independence initially supported the Ayatollah, then, due to a disagreement over the powers of the government, the leader of the Council ex-President Bani-Sadr attacked the rule of the Islamic Republican Party for worsening the condition of the country. The National Resistance Movement is led by Dr Bakhtiar, the Shah's last Prime Minister, who had the task of implementing a programme of liberalisation, including the dissolution of the Shah's secret police, and the granting of a greater role to the Muslim religious leaders in drafting legislation. The Ayatollah considered Bakhtiar's government to be a betrayal, and Bakhtiar was forced to flee to France to continue his opposition.

The main religious minorities in Iran are the Bahais, Christians, Jews and Zoroastrians. The last three of these groups are officially recognised in the Constitution whereas the Bahais are not, and they have been subjected to considerable repression since the 1979 revolution, before which they had held many senior posts under the Shah.

See also **Kurdish insurgency, Shi'ites, Teheran Embassy Siege, Tudeh**

Iraq Under its 1968 Constitution Iraq is a popular democratic and sovereign state with Islam as its state religion and an economy based on socialism, dominated by the Ba'ath Arab Socialist Party. Although the Iraqis allow a Kurdish Legislative Council with limited powers to pass legislation for the Kurdish region on social, cultural and economic development as well as on health, education and labour matters, the Council has not been supported by the majority of Kurds, whose ultimate aim is full autonomy or even complete independence for Kurdistan. The Democratic Party of Kurdistan was founded in 1946 by Mullah Mustapha Barzani who for over thirty years led the struggle for autonomy of the Kurds in Iraq. The struggle came to a temporary end in 1975 after the Shah had ceased to support the Kurds and had concluded a treaty with the Iraqis. However, two years later, after Barzani's death in exile, the Party resumed the armed struggle against Iraqi government forces. An offshoot is the Kurdish Socialist Party, while the Patriotic Union of Kurdistan is in conflict with the Democratic Party over ideological issues.

The Iraqi Communist Party has had a chequered history. It was a legalised party when it entered the National Front government in 1973. With its pro-Moscow orientation, it occasionally criticised the regime on both domestic and foreign policy grounds including its handling of the Kurdish insurgency, with which some elements of the party have been associated. In May 1978, the government executed 21 communists for engaging in political activities within the armed forces, and by the early

1980s members of the Communist Party had either fled the country or moved to the Kurdish areas.

The predominantly Sunni Muslim regime has encountered strong opposition from militant elements of the Shi'ite Muslim community; Shi'ite Muslims constitute over half of Iraq's population. They are in sympathy with and supported by the regime of Iran and have formed their own Dawah party. The Ba'ath party, Arab socialists, has been actively opposed by dissident Ba'athists supported by the Syrian government. The National Democratic Patriotic Front consists of a coalition of eight opposition parties to try to bring down the current government led by Saddam Hussein. On similar lines, the Supreme Council of the Islamic Revolution, formed in 1982, aims to provide a focal point for Iraqi Shi'ite opposition to the prosecution of the war with Iran; and wishes Hussein's government to be overthrown and replaced by an Islamic republic led by a theologian on the Iranian model.

See also **Iran, Kurdish insurgency, Shi'ites**

Ireland Until the end of the sixteenth century Ulster was the centre of the most intransigent resistance to English rule. Radical change was brought by the Reformation, the defeat in 1603 of the anti-English rebellion led by the chiefs of O'Neill and O'Donnell and the union in 1605 of England and Scotland. In 1608 began the plantation of Ulster with Protestant settlers from the Scottish lowlands and England, expelling the native Catholic and Gaelic-speaking people to the poorer lands of the south and west. The old Gaelic order of Ireland had been crushed and Ulster became, in effect, a British province. Catholic emancipation and the growth of militant Irish nationalism saw religion restored in the late nineteenth century as the dominant and divisive factor in Ulster affairs. In 1914, with the passage of the third Home Rule Bill, the Orange-Unionist Protestant Ascendancy of Ulster, with the active support of many leading members of the Conservative opposition at Westminster, threatened armed rebellion. After the First World War, following the victory of the nationalist Sinn Fein Party in 1918 and the subsequent guerrilla war against the British power, the Ulster Unionists in 1920 reluctantly accepted the provisions of the Government of Ireland Act. Under this measure, which superseded the Home Rule Act of 1914, Ireland was to have two parliaments subordinate to Westminster – one in Belfast for six of Ulster's nine counties, and one in Dublin for the remaining 26 counties of Ireland. Thus the government of Northern Ireland, now a federal province of the United Kingdom, came into being against a background of civil war and sectarian disorder. This government was to last until 1972 when Stormont was suspended. The rest of Ireland – the Irish Free State – was accorded dominion status, but in 1949 it was declared a republic.

Political movements have abounded in Ireland for most of this century, and have been mostly radical and militaristic. Sinn Fein was the original Irish nationalist party which took over the effective leadership of the

Irish nationalist movement from the Irish Parliamentary Party after the death of Parnell in 1891. An open split in the movement occurred in 1921 when the republican wing led by de Valera refused to accept the Anglo-Irish Treaty of 1921 and precipitated the Civil War of 1922–23. De Valera soon returned to parliamentary politics and the label of Sinn Fein was taken over by the dissident rump of intransigents.

The Irish Republican Army (IRA) is the name of the illegal military instrument of Sinn Fein. It has the distinction of being the longest-lived organisation in history, exhibiting a remarkable continuity in both goal and method. The roots of violence in Ireland are tangled and deep, which perhaps explains the extraordinary tenacity of the IRA. It had its origins in the National Volunteer Force and became the Army in 1924. Its influence subsequently waned and it was declared illegal by the Irish government in 1939. After a period of pro-German activity during the War, calm returned. However, from 1956 to 1962, the IRA conducted a bombing campaign in Northern Ireland, but the authorities were able to confine this action to the border areas. In the mid 1960s, the Marxist wing of the IRA was recreated – and from the outset was more concerned with exploiting social issues than with taking part in the armed struggle which emerged from the communal violence of the mid and late 1960s in Northern Ireland. After the breakaway of the Provisional IRA in 1969, the rump of the IRA became known as the Official IRA, whose political wing was the Official Sinn Fein, which in Northern Ireland was known as the Republican Clubs. The Officials argued that class politics should supersede sectarian issues, and that the violence practised by the Provisionals merely entrenched reactionary attitudes. Some Officials still continued with violence, and indeed a violent clash between the two wings of the IRA occurred in 1975.

The Provisionals soon became to be seen as a direct-action organisation intent upon launching a guerrilla campaign and making Northern Ireland ungovernable by forcing the British Government to withdraw its armed forces and relinquish all responsibility for the province. Politically, the Provisionals have operated through the Provisional Sinn Fein, legal in both the north and south of Ireland, but declared a proscribed organisation in mainland Britain under the Prevention of Terrorism (Temporary Provisions) Bill enacted in 1974. The Provisionals, or Provos, are militarily organised with both a women's section involved in gathering information, planting fire-bombs and providing shelter in 'safe houses', and a youth wing who gather intelligence, act as lookouts and transport weapons. They have resorted to sniping, bombing, the use of rocket launchers, letter bombs and parcel bombs. Their action provoked Bloody Sunday in 1972, when 13 persons were killed by British soldiers; and internment without trial of suspects, which remained in force for four years in spite of a civil disobedience campaign called by Roman Catholic opposition parties in Ulster.

Over the past fifteen years the Provisional IRA has been involved in a concerted plan of bombing in mainland Britain, and despite some ceasefires, it has achieved worldwide notoriety and revulsion, notably the deaths of 18 British soldiers at Warrenpoint in 1979. It has received weapons from abroad, especially the United States. The most conspicuous operation carried out by PIRA members in the Republic was in August 1979, with the murder of Earl Mountbatten of Burma by a bomb placed on his fishing boat. In England, their most conspicuous act was the bombing of a public house in Birmingham in 1974 in which 21 persons were killed and 120 injured.

During the early 1980s it was clear that public support for the PIRA among the Roman Catholic section of Northern Ireland's population was increasing, mainly at the expense of traditional Catholic parties. Many Provisionals undertook hunger strikes in 1980–81 to try to obtain special treatment and ultimately political prisoner status. The most notable was Bobbie Sands who died in prison a month after being elected a Member of Parliament.

More extreme than the Provisionals is the Irish National Liberation Army (INLA), the political wing of the Irish Republican Socialist Party, created in 1974 with the aim of conducting armed warfare to compel the British to a military withdrawal from Northern Ireland, which would then unite with the South. This new socialist republic would then withdraw from the European Economic Community. Notable attacks have included the deaths of Airey Neave, a Conservative politician, in 1979, of 11 soldiers and six civilians at a pub near Londonderry in 1981, bombs in London parks in 1982, five persons killed at Harrods store in London in 1983, and a bomb at the Grand Hotel, Brighton, also killing five people, during the Conservative Party Conference in 1984.

On the Protestant side, radical and extreme groups have played an active role in fomenting discord. Prime among these is the Ulster Volunteer Force, a group of militant Protestant Loyalists whose origins go back to 1912. It is a military body dedicated to upholding the constitution of Ulster by force of arms if necessary. The potential membership of the UVF has always been more important than its actions. The Ulster Defence Association (UDA) has been regarded as the strongest of various extreme Protestant paramilitary organisations set up in response to the violent activities of the Provisionals. In spite of being in difficulties through the development of factions, it was the UDA which manned the Protestants' barricades of 1972. They made explosives and planted bombs in IRA hotels and meeting places. It also had strong links with Scotland. The Protestant equivalent of INLA was the Ulster Freedom Fighters, a militant paramilitary Protestant organisation loosely composed of violent elements anxious to take the law into their own hands. Members carried out assassinations on a widespread scale.

Terrorism has little effect on the domestic political structure of Great Britain or Ireland – for example, it is not an election issue in either country but it has resulted in policy changes oriented toward suppressing the IRA. Equally as important as the effects of terrorism on formal power structures and government policies is its impact on popular attitudes and on participation. Among the Protestants of the North, terrorism has only stiffened pre-existing attitudes of resistance to any compromise that hints of a drift toward Irish unity – as exemplified by the polarised reactions across the political divide to the Anglo-Irish Agreement in 1985. Among the IRA's potential Catholic constituency, there seems to be every indication that although terrorism did spark a brief Peace Movement, which expressed a strong revulsion for violence, over the past decade a residual amount of support for the IRA remains constant. Terrorism has general and diffuse consequences for the long-term prospects for democracy and stability, and in particular it affects the quality of life, patterns of political socialisation and political culture. In Northern Ireland there has been extraordinary resilience in the social order – life goes on, despite high levels of violence.

It appears that the British will stay in Northern Ireland until the British population tires of violence or until Protestants agree to a united Ireland. The lesson that violence pays has been seen by extremists, and discord has been fomented by the presence of the British army. Power sharing in the mid 1970s was achieved only in Londonderry, with a balance of Protestants and Catholics.

The Troops Out Movement of the mid 1970s was more successful. Since direct rule in 1972 the security forces have succeeded in eroding the terrorist movements by measures which have been within the existing legal framework, and the conviction of proven terrorists cannot be taken for granted in a community intimidated by terrorism. After eighteen years of trouble, no clear solutions to Ulster's political problems have been found, any more than to the problems of security.

The full recognition of Northern Ireland as an Anglo-Irish dilemma came in 1985 with the signing of the controversial Anglo-Irish Agreement between Britain and the Irish Republic. It seeks to establish a framework within which nationalists will be able to join with unionists in a devolved local executive. By encouraging the development of constitutional nationalism, both London and Dublin hope to erode support for physical force republicanism. Bitterly complaining that they were never consulted, nor even kept informed about the discussions leading up to the Agreement, unionists have rejected it as an act of treachery. Two possibilities can occur. The first is that a majority of unionists will eventually grudgingly accept the Agreement; the second, that there will be a continued and irreversible alienation of the Protestant community and the refusal of the unionist leaders to co-operate in any way with a British government which, in their eyes, has effectively destroyed the Union. The dilemma is how to handle the unionists and react constructively to their antagonism to the sharing of responsibility which is now proposed.

See also **Ewart-Biggs, Herrema, Irish Northern Aid Committee, Mountbatten and Warrenpoint murders, Supergrass system**

Irish Northern Aid Committee (NORAID) The financial broker for the Provisional IRA's transatlantic fund-raising is the Irish Northern Aid

Committee (NORAID), also known as INAC. According to its statement of registration with the US authorities under the Foreign Agents Registration Act, 1938 (FARA), NORAID was founded in New York City in April 1970 by three IRA veterans of the civil war period, Mick Flannery, Jack McCarthy and John McGowan, in response to a request from its originator, the Northern Ireland Republican Aid Committee in Belfast.

Its attitude has been consistent on a number of issues: it has boasted of the large amounts it was remitting to persons such as Joe Cahill in Northern Ireland; it insisted that while these funds were intended for 'relief', it was up to 'the people on the other side' to decide how to spend them; it agreed that part of the money was used for the purchase of arms; and repeatedly and without reservation it supported the Provisionals' campaign.

The organisational structure upon which NORAID efforts are based has been estimated at between 80 and 100 chapters or groups. There are upwards of 2,000 members who are sufficiently numerous and active to have a considerable effect on most Irish-American organisations in the United States. Of this number the largest concentration is in New York and the National Headquarters is in the Bronx. Otherwise the most important centres are Chicago, Boston, Philadelphia, San Francisco, Los Angeles, Baltimore and various towns in New Jersey and Connecticut. Among those who have spent some time observing its activities, NORAID has acquired a reputation, based on an apparently high level of visible co-ordination, as a close-knit and disciplined group.

Although it has a weekly newspaper and a considerable amount of modern technology, this has failed to advance NORAID's understanding of the issues in Northern Ireland, e.g. they have made claims that the Irish Special Branch attempted to break an IRA ceasefire by organising sectarian murders in collusion with the Northern Ireland Social Democratic and Labour Party. To further sustain the fund-raising and lobbying operations, NORAID has played host to a number of prominent Provisionals such as Billy Kelly and Ruari O'Bradaigh, but they and others were hampered by the US Immigration and Nationality Acts which exclude aliens connected with organisations advocating killing. This appears to have had little impact on the direct subscriptions as the main source of finance. Over 10 million dollars has been sent to Ulster since the present troubles started in 1968, in the form of cash, arms, pamphlets, etc. Nevertheless, NORAID have never really realised the full potential of Irish-America for their cause. In general neither the politicians nor the wealthy Irish-Americans, nor the Catholic Church have found the prospect of associating with NORAID worth the opprobrium it would have earned them. Questions of gun-running to the IRA and civil rights issues for Catholics in Ulster have become *causes célèbres* in both Irish-American and US civil rights circles. Over 12,000 guns of American manufacture have been found in Northern Ireland connected with the IRA.

Breaches have occurred, however, in relations between NORAID and their Irish supporters. In the early 1980s a rift developed between NORAID and the Irish National Caucus as a result of personality clashes and a conflict over which group was to provide the leadership for Irish-American supporters of the Provisionals.

See also **Ireland**

Islam The purpose of terrorism, whether national or international, is to murder political enemies, deter potential foes and destabilise society. Many of the more dramatic and violent incidents of recent decades have been perpetrated either in the Middle East or elsewhere by groups involved in the domestic and inter-state conflicts in that region. Groups such as the Palestine Liberation Organisation and most of its constituent factions are defined by their opponents and victims as terrorist bodies, and therefore any act of warfare or violence conducted in their name must be 'terrorist' by definition.

Sympathisers with their cause would regard Middle East groups as fighting a war of national liberation and therefore, the PLO, say, would not be regarded as a terrorist group.

Terrorism has been a prominent feature of politics of the Middle East, and large-scale atrocities have been committed in pursuit of some political, religious or other ideological goal. Both terrorism and movements for fundamentalist Islamic reform have frequently appeared in times of political, social or economic crisis. They represent no new or modern phenomenon. In any kind of man-made upheaval or natural disaster, men turned to Islam and to the mosque which served as the fortress of the most conservative, reactionary and xenophobic elements of society, and at the same time, as the custodian of the only true vision of a just society, which offered hope and guidance to the poor, the disenfranchised and the disillusioned.

The recent Islamic revival has enhanced the political significance of Islam to an extent rarely witnessed in modern times. There is strong anti-Western sentiment in many Muslim countries and various attempts have been made in countries such as Iran, Pakistan and the Sudan to reimpose strict Islamic law. Another feature has been the intensification of the traditional enmity between the various Muslim sectarian forces, and in particular between the two main groups, the Sunnis and Shias.

Islam has never been simply a spiritual community. Instead, from its rise in the seventh century it developed as a religious and political movement; the belief that Islam embraces faith and politics is rooted in its bible, the Koran, and the example or custom (Sunna) of Muhammad, its founder and prophet. This belief has been reflected in Islamic doctrine, history and politics. It was from a seventh-century revolt that the major division in Islam between Sunni and Shia emerged. The belief that participants in that revolt were martyrs to injustice has provided Shia Islam with its major theme – the battle of the forces of good (Shia) against the forces of evil (anti-Shia). Their goal is to establish righteous rule and social justice through martyrdom and protest under the political leader-

I

ship of the imam, and this is the fundamental political and legal difference between the majority Sunni stream of Islam and the minority Shia denomination. There are about 800 million Sunni Muslims in the world, who are in the majority in all Islamic countries except Iran, Iraq, Lebanon and Bahrein.

In contrast to the Sunnis, Shias believe that both the spiritual and temporal leadership of the Muslim world were vested by divine command in the descendants of Ali (a seventh-century caliph), and that successive leaders were to appoint their successors by divine inspiration. For Sunnis, success and power were signs of a faithful community and the validation of Islam, its beliefs and claims. For Shias, history was the struggle of a righteous few in protest and opposition against the forces of evil in order to realise its messianic hope and promise – the establishment of the righteous rule of the imam.

The Assassins played an invaluable role in the history, culture and ethos of Islam. They drew inspiration from a variety of sources and shared with other groups of many different religions and cultures the ancient ideal of tyrannicide and the religious obligation to rid the world of an unrighteous ruler. But they also regarded such killings as rituals with an almost sacramental quality. They were perhaps the world's first professional terrorists. The Assassins always used a dagger, even when other weapons would clearly have been safer. Their victims belonged to two main groups – princes, officers and ministers on the one hand, and religious dignitaries on the other. With only rare exceptions, the victims were all Sunni Muslims.

What are the common themes that inspire the modern 'Assassins' and fuel their resentment? They, and the Muslim fundamentalists in Iran, decry the ungodliness and corruption of most contemporary societies. For them, man's only hope of salvation lies in making society conform strictly to the word of God as revealed in the authoritative sources of faith.

The fundamentalist revolution in Iran owes its legitimacy to its secular success in overthrowing the regime of the Shah and replacing it with Khomeini's version of an Islamic theocracy. This is based upon a blend of radical Shi'ism, anti-Westernism, leftist radicalism and religious extremism.

Terrorism has its place among the means employed by extremist Muslim fundamentalist factions. For the terrorist, the enemy or target is the 'non-Muslim', the 'unbeliever', the 'infidel'.

The success of Khomeini's revolution in Iran provoked a resurgence of Islamic militancy. In various Middle Eastern countries, such as Libya, Iraq and Syria, the consolidation of power by autocratic military rulers bent on total domination at home and abroad has produced the phenomenon of state terrorism. The Islamic groups have been successful, but only where support for the existing regime was already crumbling. To date, the powerful autocratic military rulers of the Middle East have, in practice, largely been able to suppress these groups when they appeared to present a serious threat.

See also **Assassins, Egypt, Iran, Palestine Liberation Organisation, Religious terrorism, Shi'ites.**

J

Jackson, Sir Geoffrey On 8 January 1971 Sir Geoffrey Jackson, the British Ambassador to Uruguay, was kidnapped in Montevideo by 20 Tupamaros, who surrounded his car with five vehicles near the embassy. The kidnappers had trapped the car in a narrow one-way street; Jackson's driver and bodyguards were dragged from the car and beaten.

A claim was made that the attack was against British neo-colonialism, and the government was called upon to begin negotiations. This appeared to be an attempt to increase the pressure on the government which was concerned about the kidnappers of Claude Fly, an agronomist with the Food and Agricultural Organisation kidnapped in August 1970, and Dias Gomide, the Brazilian Consul in Uruguay, kidnapped in July 1970. The group demanded the release of 150 political prisoners in exchange for Jackson, and the response to this was a massive police and troops operation searching private homes without warrants and with the power to hold suspects without court hearings. In March, the Tupamaros kidnapped Uruguay's attorney-general, Guide Oribe, and questioned him on irregularities while he was a court prosecutor. Having admitted handing over political prisoners to military tribunals and detaining prisoners after their sentences expired, he was set free. Despite the kidnap of a personal friend of the President by the Tupamaros, the government remained firm in its refusal to negotiate for Jackson's release, and offered a huge reward for information regarding his location. In September 1971, 106 Tupamaros, including their leader escaped from prison by digging a tunnel. A day later Sir Geoffrey Jackson was freed, as the Tupamaros had no need to detain him. The ambassador found his captors intelligent, with certain reservations; and although they would have killed him if their hideout had been found, he agreed with the no-ransom policy. His relations with the kidnappers had been correct, stressing his dignity as the representative of a sovereign government.

See also **Tupamaros**

Japan Since the débâcle of defeat in 1945, Japan has emerged, thanks to American help, as one of the most economically strong and democratic nations in Asia. Although the Liberal Democratic Party has held power for the past three decades, there has been much opposition, and acts of politically motivated violence have been carried out by both extreme right- and left-wing groups. Although there are many right-wing organisations, membership of each of them is small, and generally they advocate totalitarian government as the best solution to overcome corruption, exploitation and unequal treaties with foreign powers. Extreme left-wing groups have extended operations to targets outside Japan, particularly in terms of hijacking to which until the late 1970s the Japanese government meekly acceded. Since then tougher approaches have been adopted to hijacking. Left-wing groups take part in violent clashes and ideological feuds with each other on regular occasions.

The most well known of the radical groups is the United Red Army (Rengo Shekigun), although in recent years its activities have decreased. This terrorist group was established among disillusioned students who saw in the Paris student riots in May 1968 their blueprint for bringing about world revolution. The group has been noted for its violent clashes, the extremism of the original female leader, Fusako Shigenobu, and the number of radical leftists who have been killed in internal clashes.

In spite of these problems, and the success of the security forces against them, the United Red Army has declared that it will continue to fight for the materialisation of a people's republic of Japan by uniting and joining forces with the oppressed people, comrades and friends in confrontation with Japanese imperialism. During early operations it stressed the need to fight against Zionism, and later affirmed the need for a revolution in Japan and its solidarity with the Japanese people in their struggle against the monarchy, and criticised Japan's economic exploitation of South Korea. Its major operations have included, for example, the hijackings of Japanese airliners over South Korea (1970), Dubai (1973) and Bombay (1977), resulting in deaths of innocents and of some of the terrorists. Oil refineries were attacked in Singapore in 1974, the French embassy in the Hague was occupied in 1974, and the US consulate and Swedish embassy seized in Malaysia in 1975. The most notorious incident was a massacre at Lod airport, Tel Aviv, Israel in May 1972, when three terrorists opened fire in the departure and arrivals lounge, killing 26 persons (mainly Roman Catholics from Puerto Rico) and wounding 78 others. Of the three gunmen, one was killed by police, one committed suicide and the other, Kozo Okamoto, was captured, tried and sentenced to life imprisonment but with the onset of insanity was released in 1985. In 1982 Shigenobu admitted that the United Red Army had abandoned terrorism because it had failed to win international support. This was perhaps surprising in view of the links (admittedly tenuous) with the Basque separatist organisation ETA, the Red Army Faction (Baader-Meinhof Group) in West Germany, and with the Popular Front for the Liberation of Palestine (PFLP).

Other extreme left-wing groups have had limited success. The East Asia Anti-Japanese Armed Front, formed in 1976, fights for the rights of the Ainu, who were the original inhabitants of the most northerly of Japan's four main islands, Hokkaido. The Front claims to fight for the rights of the Okinawan, Korean, Taiwanese Buraku (social outcasts) and other Asian peoples. They have also attacked offices of large business companies such as Mitsui and Mitsubishi, who are accused of exploiting

J

underdeveloped Asian nations. In 1974 the Front tried to assassinate Emperor Hirohito, for which two terrorists received the death penalty.

The Fourth Trotskyist International (Japanese section), along with other radical groups played a leading role from the early 1970s in actively opposing the construction and opening of a new international airport at Narita near Tokyo. Demonstrations by local farmers, left-wing student groups and environmentalists led to several years' delay in the completion of the airport. Attacks on its communications and other installations continued until well after the opening in May 1978.

The National Federation of Students' Organisations contains some Marxist breakaway groups, one of whom the Middle-Core Faction, opposed the security treaty concluded between the United States and Japan. A breakaway splinter group is the Revolutionary Marxist Faction. The Okinawa Liberation League has expressed opposition to the rule of the Imperial family over Okinawa in the Ryukyu islands and its use as a military and oil storage base.

See also **Lod Airport Massacre**

J

K

Karen revolt When Burma achieved independence from Britain in January 1948 it faced several insurgencies, mounted both by the Burmese Communist Party and a number of minority hill tribes. The most serious hill tribe insurgency was that of the two-million-strong Karens, who claimed an independent state which would have included much of southern Burma. Units of the Karen National Defence Organisation (KNDO) occupied Moulmein and several other towns in the south, and the government of Prime Minister U Nu formed local volunteer units to combat the rebels.

By 1949, the government faced some 37,000 rebels of various descriptions (including communists, Trotskyists, Muslims and army mutineers), of whom an estimated 10,000 were Karens. The KNDO achieved a number of successes in 1949 and captured several important towns, including Mandalay, but a march on Rangoon failed and a government counter-offensive deprived the Karens of most of their gains. The initiative now passed to the government, and the revolt degenerated into sporadic guerrilla fighting. The capture of the KNDO stronghold of Papun in March 1955 marked the end of the Karens as a major threat, although rebel activity continued until the acceptance of a government amnesty in May 1980. However, the amnesty was a failure and increasing ambush activity took place between the Karen rebels and Burmese troops. In late 1982 insurgents mounted the first Karen attack on the capital, Rangoon, and achieved a considerable propaganda coup. This action did result in the death of the leader Mahn Aung.

Khmer Rouge The Khmer (Cambodian) Liberation Army – dubbed the 'Khmer Rouge' by Cambodian head of state Prince Norodom Sihanouk in the late 1960s, was a peasant-based revolutionary force which established its political authority over all Cambodia in April 1975. Three years later there was a Vietnamese invasion of Kampuchea in December 1978 and a war which flickered on until the mid 1980s.

The split between Vietnamese and Cambodian revolutionaries dates back to 1954, when the new government in Hanoi, anxious to adhere to the terms of the Geneva Agreement withdrew support from the Cambodian Communist Party and left the state to pursue a neutralist policy under the autocratic Sihanouk. His widespread popularity and the relative prosperity of Cambodia, where few people starved, and many were landowners, lessened the appeal of communism, and although an irreconcilable remnant, convinced that Hanoi had betrayed the revolution,' went underground, they could achieve little on their own apart from setting up safe base areas on the Maoist pattern and organising occasional guerrilla attacks.

A turning point occurred in 1967, when Sihanouk ordered his new prime minister Lon Nol to deal with a peasant uprising in Battambang Province; his ruthless violence quickly alienated substantial elements of the population. A sudden influx of recruits enabled the communists to step up their activities and, as Sihanouk wavered, Lon Nol seized the opportunity to organise a military-backed coup in Phnom Penh (March 1970). Turning to the USA for aid, he initiated a campaign of deliberate repression and the war acquired a new and vicious intensity. By 1973, with an estimated 4,000 regular troops and up to 50,000 guerrillas available, the Khmer Rouge was strong enough to exert its control over the northern provinces of the state.

There followed a two year campaign in which Khmer Rouge guerrilla groups, armed by the North Vietnamese and Chinese, infiltrated government lines, destroyed isolated military outposts and gradually drew a noose around Pnomh Penh. The fighting was by no means one-sided – in late 1973 and early 1974, for example, Lon Nol was able to defeat a major communist offensive against the capital – but by spring 1975, with US support halted by Congress and up to 60 per cent of Cambodia already in Khmer Rouge hands, Lon Nol was isolated and communist victory assured.

By this time the Khmer Rouge had made what seemed to be a smooth transition from guerrilla force to regular army, but its new-found strength was dissipated by the bizarre actions of its leaders, particularly Pol Pot. Basing his policies on the views of Khieu Samphan, who advocated a return to the simplicity and self-sufficiency of rural life, Pol Pot forcibly removed the population of Pnomh Penh to the countryside, and introduced a campaign of terror and murder against those who would not contribute to the new utopia. By 1978 the Khmer Rouge had lost much of its military cohesion, and the Vietnamese invasion force found it surprisingly easy to advance as far as the Thai border. Sporadic guerrilla attacks continued into the 1980s, demonstrating the ability of the Khmer Rouge to survive at a basic level as an insurgent force.

Kidnapping Like assassination (the implied threat without which kidnapping would lose its power), kidnap has been used for many generations. The rise of gangsterism in the 1920s led to a massive growth of kidnapping for ransom in the United States; and there has also been a strong Italian flavour about the growth of kidnapping and gangsterism in many American cities. Italy has the highest incidence of kidnapping in Europe and there are still strong links between the American and Italian Mafia.

One of the more dramatic tactics of contemporary terrorists is that of kidnapping. The capture and detention of a prominent person has served numerous ends, including publicity, the release of colleagues being held as political prisoners, and the receipt of substantial funds in ransom payments. Many terrorist groups have relied on the prolonged detention of their kidnap victims, thus enjoying sustained media attention and inducing a state of chronic embarrassment on the part of the governments concerned.

The kidnapping of well known people – whether they be politicians, newspaper editors or the sons or daughters of eminent persons, can provide a series of major media events over a period of several weeks. Although kidnappings may be logistically cumbersome, they can provide more media attention than a single robbery, bombing or assassination. Moreover, the eventual release of a hostage can serve to minimise an adverse public reaction.

The most desirable setting for kidnappings has been the busy street in an urban area. There the prospective kidnappers are able to set up an ambush while attracting minimal attention; and following such an attack, and the immobilisation of the victim's vehicle, a capture and speedy getaway can be easily and unobtrusively accomplished. Other than the victim's totally varying his or her movements, only an armed escort or intensive patrols by police and security forces can serve as adequate preventive measures. Occasionally in the course of kidnapping, escape may be precluded. At other times, kidnappers deliberately seek to hold a hostage in public, or at least in a location known to the authorities. The siege that follows is usually the most dramatic of terrorist events. In such situations kidnappers' demands may include calls for ransom or for the release of political prisoners, and these are usually accompanied by a demand for safe passage to a friendly country as well. Sieges of this nature tend to take place in and around diplomatic missions and have occurred with considerable frequency over the past two decades.

The most dramatic form of kidnapping is that which can occur in the context of an airline hijacking. Aside from those who are motivated by personal financial considerations or those with severe personality disorders, the vast majority of skyjackers seek either to obtain the release of certain political prisoners or to express protest against a particular regime. A safe passage to a friendly country has almost always been demanded. Even after the advent of rigorous security procedures, hijackers have been able to exploit the crowded and hurried settings of urban airports to their considerable advantage.

Self-appointed avengers can seek retribution through threats or acts of violence. This is typically the case in the kidnapping of foreign businessmen by Latin American terrorists, where exorbitant ransoms are extracted as 'reparations' and murder is justified as 'execution'.

While the tactic of hijacking demands patience on the part of the operatives, and an ability to handle a duration operation, it is kidnapping which is the most demanding, rewarding and lucrative. The operation requires intricate planning, split-second timing, a large support apparatus to sustain the group holding the victim and the ability to remain secure while still communicating demands or negotiating with third parties.

Kidnapping

Ransoms paid can be of a size almost beyond comprehension – millions of dollars or pounds can change hands. Once in the terrorists' hands, the money is often spread under various names over banks in Europe and the United States, and has been and will continue to be used to finance more political terrorism. A kidnapping for ransom can be carried out by a group of any size, criminal or political, ranging from large international organisations to a single cell or even, as in the case of children, by a single criminal. The decision to kidnap centres on an assessment of the potential victim's family or firm, whether they are rich enough to find a large ransom and how willing they are likely to be to pay. Other factors are the victim's vulnerability, his life style and the publicity attached to it, the predictability of his movements, his attitude to precautions and security and his protection at home, at work and on the move. In a political kidnapping, the prospects for publicity and the potential leverage on the government will be important; and other factors, such as revenge and the extraction of information, may also apply. Professionally organised kidnap groups carry out detailed research into the background of the potential victim.

The terrorists have big advantages in kidnap situations. They have the initiative; they hold the victim and they know where everyone on both sides is based; they are willing to maim their victim, while the authorities recognise self-imposed restraints; and the terrorists know that most people will pay rather than allow a husband or child or colleague to be killed. The kidnappers' greatest weakness is that time is on the side of the police, whether measured in days or months, and every extra day brings greater chance of detection and may accumulate more evidence for eventual arrest and conviction.

The interests of those involved on the side of the law will often conflict; the victim has interests that conflict in themselves; his family will probably be less willing to sacrifice his life than he is himself; and his negotiators have a duty to balance their obligations to their client and their obligations, legal or moral, as citizens. The victim's firm may well be involved, and if the firm is a subsidiary of an overseas corporation, corporate headquarters may see the problem differently from its representatives on the spot. The police have a dual responsibility to the victim and to society; and the army can in some countries act instead of the police in terrorist operations. Security firms and advisers are often involved; the judiciary and the legislature may both be involved in serious cases, and are concerned with the provisions and operation of the laws under which the battle will be fought. The media forgo sensational news only if they are confident that all their rivals also will forgo it. Ultimately, the government stands over all these agencies and individuals, as it will want to be seen to be firm, and even overseas governments can get involved if the victim or his firm are expatriates.

With regard to the ransom, kidnappers may want this paid in hard currency in a foreign country either into a number of different bank accounts or possibly dumped in cash for collection by accomplices there.

Most kidnappers, in fact, settle for payment in local currency, but specify that it must be in well-worn notes of low denomination, not with consecutive numbers, to avoid detection. Volunteers will be needed to drop the money, and the negotiator will be in a stronger position than before because the kidnappers will be tense and wish to end the business quickly. The negotiator can thus be firm over his conditions. The better the individual or organisation is prepared, the less likely they are to be selected as targets and the greater their chances of survival.

Kurdish insurgency In September 1961, Kurdish demands for autonomy within Iraq led to the outbreak of a civil war which continued for almost fourteen years, interrupted by a number of ceasefires and an armistice negotiated in January 1970, under which the Iraqi government agreed to implement the Kurds' demands. The Kurdish rebels, whose armed forces were known as Peshmerga, controlled the mountains of north-eastern Iraq, where regular government offensives achieved little, although many Kurdish villages were destroyed by Iraqi bombing raids.

The heaviest fighting occurred after the collapse of the armistice in 1973, with the Kurds adopting a conventional static defence of the area which they controlled. Nevertheless the Iraqis advanced to within 20 miles of the Kurds' headquarters, which led the Kurds' ally, the Shah of Iran, to dispatch a contingency of Iranian troops to man the Kurds' air defences. Iranian backing was suddenly withdrawn in March 1975, however, when the Shah reached agreement with the Iraqi government over a long-standing territorial dispute. The Iranian border was closed to the Kurds and as the Iraqis moved in, the revolt collapsed.

The Iranians provided fresh support to Iraqi Kurdish guerrillas following the opening of the Gulf War with Iraq in September 1980. The Iraqi Kurds formed an alliance with anti-government Shi'ite fundamentalists and communists and by early 1985 controlled a 20-mile-deep strip of territory along the Turkish border.

The Iranians experienced their own conflict with Kurdish insurgents, however. Having fought against the Shah, the Iranian Kurds demanded autonomy after his overthrow in 1979. The Khomeini Regime sent Revolutionary Guards into the Kurdish region to suppress opposition, and serious fighting broke out, which continued into 1985, with the Kurds forming an alliance with left-wing Mujaheddin guerrillas.

See also **Iran, Iraq, Turkey**

K

L

Law and terrorism Many Western countries are attracted to the use of law to deal with terrorism and repress violence, and are committed to the use of domestic and international law to control criminal conduct and to resolve disputes. The law is regularly invoked to regulate international conduct and provide a system for bringing terrorism to justice.

The law has a poor record in dealing with international terrorism. Some terrorists are killed or captured during the course of their crimes, but few of those who evade these consequences are later found and arrested. The terrorist who is prosecuted is likely to be released far earlier than the sentence should require, often in exchange for hostages taken in a subsequent terrorist episode.

One reason for the law's ineffectiveness is that terrorism, in essence, is criminal activity. In applying law domestically, governments seek to punish and deter crime as effectively as possible. But it is recognised that law cannot eliminate crime. Governments can expect even less of law in dealing with international terrorism. The law has failed to punish and deter those who use terrorism to advance their political goals. On some issues, the law leaves political violence unregulated – on others the law is ambivalent, providing a basis for conflicting arguments. At its worst the law has actually served to legitimise international terror, and to protect terrorists from punishment as criminals. Attributing acts of terrorism to injustice and frustration inevitably tends at least to excuse, if not justify, those acts. In the international community, acts of terrorism inspired by base motives of personal gain are to be condemned; acts of political terrorism, on the other hand, are praiseworthy because they are undertaken to protect hallowed rights recognised by the United Nations.

The legitimacy of political violence is a notion that has worked its way deep into international law enforcement. Most countries have obligations on extradition, yet extradition requests are frequently refused on blatantly political grounds. Many countries are now trying to narrow the political offence exception and make it inapplicable to crimes of violence and breaches of anti-terrorist conventions.

The law against piracy shows how international law has failed adequately to control politically motivated crime. The *Achille Lauro* incident in 1985 raised the question of whether the acts of the hijackers of the ship constituted piracy under the law of nations; but the terrorists involved in the *Achille Lauro* affair would no doubt claim they were acting politically, and could not be called pirates under the conventions.

Often a legal status has been secured for terrorism which obscures or denies its fundamentally criminal nature. The laws of war mask the line between what is criminal and what is an act of combat. The law's support for political violence has been manifested recently in the efforts of some nations to establish a doctrine to justify curtailing the use of force against terrorists and their supporting states. International law regulates the use of force by a country in the territories of other states, whether this is to capture or attack terrorists, to rescue hostages located there, or is directed against the states themselves for sponsoring terrorists or conspiring with them in specific terrorist activities. In general, a nation may not enter upon another's territory without its consent. Similarly, a state may not stop, board, divert or otherwise interfere with another's vessels or aircraft without some adequate reason. The use of force against another country's territorial integrity or political independence is prohibited, except in self-defence, and any use of force must be both necessary and proportionate to the threat. If these principles were applied so as to preclude any use of force for any purpose, international law would insulate the perpetrators of international violence from any control or punishment for their crimes. States could then continue to use terrorism to accomplish their objectives with little cost or interference.

States have duties to co-operate in preventing terrorists from using their territories to perpetrate criminal acts, and many governments have explicitly undertaken to extradite or prosecute terrorists guilty of hijacking, sabotage and hostage-taking. Law can thus make clear that state-supported terrorism is illicit and in this way may deter it. Nevertheless, terrorist-supporting nations will not surrender seriously-held ambitions to expand their power and influence simply because the law is against them.

See also **Extradition, International humanitarian law and terrorism**

Lebanon Since its creation as an independent state in 1943, tensions between Lebanon's various ethnic and religious communities, especially between the Christians and Muslims, have regularly erupted into open hostilities between assorted military groups and factions. Maronite Christian and Muslim interests grew disproportionately, so that by 1975–76 the Lebanese state had collapsed in civil conflict. It had been the only place in the Middle East where a non-Muslim minority was decently tolerated in a Muslim society. However, in the early 1970s Palestinian terrorists had infiltrated into Lebanon in large numbers and almost founded a state within a state, from which they could operate freely against Israel and international targets. The delicate balance of Lebanese democracy had been established by a 'covenant', an unwritten formula that divided power among all the minorities – Christian Maronite, Greek Orthodox, Greek Catholic, Armenian Orthodox, Armenian Catholic, Sunni Muslim, Shi'ite Muslim and Druze. The president was always a Maronite Catholic, the premier a Sunni Muslim, the speaker of parlia-

L

ment a Shi'ite Muslim, the commander-in-chief of the armed forces a Maronite.

The covenant had worked since Lebanon won its freedom in 1943, although there had been a Nasser-inspired civil war in 1958, during which American troops had been landed, and another period of fighting started in 1968, caused by Palestinian terrorists.

The left in Lebanon was, and is, Muslim, while the Christians are pro-Western, including the Phalange, a group seeking to preserve the liberal democratic and Christian character of Lebanon. Palestinians became not only an independent establishment, but a state within a state ruled by the gunmen of Al-Fatah and the Popular Front for the Liberation of Palestine.

The security forces found it difficult to restore law and order, and the army was held out of action as Muslim leaders feared its largely Christian officer corps would interfere on the side of the Phalangists or other Christian groups. Initially the Palestine Liberation Organisation remained neutral and the main part of the fighting was left to local groups. Leftist forces were far more numerous and better armed, but arms were easy to buy anywhere in the Middle East and both sides had funds. Palestinians took an increasing hand on the side of the Lebanese leftists, and the Christians were slowly forced back. Fighting was especially fierce in the south, and Israeli forces clashed with Palestinian guerrillas. Within a few months the Syrians entered the northern part of the country to try to enforce some peace with their Popular Liberation Army (PLA). A series of truces broke down and fighting then occurred between the PLA and the extreme left, and fighting escalated between the Syrians and the Palestinians. The Palestinian refugee camps increased in size, and often became the scene of bitter fighting – especially at the hands of the Israelis, who suspected the camps of holding terrorists. A newly created Arab Deterrent Force managed to enforce a ceasefire; however, in the absence of real stability members of Arab countries reduced their contingents, so that it became purely a Syrian force. The United Nations established an Interim Force in Lebanon to assist the Lebanese Government in ensuring the return of its effective authority to the area. Christian forces in southern Lebanon continued to be supported by Israel. In order to eliminate the persistent threat to Israel's northern border areas posed by PLO forces in southern Lebanon, Israel launched a full scale invasion in 1982, which resulted in the occupation of most of Lebanon's southern half, and the withdrawal of Syrian forces from Beirut. Palestinian fighters were driven from the south, and then from West Beirut. Phalangist militiamen were held responsible for the massacre of Palestinian inhabitants of two Beirut refugee camps.

Central government authority proved difficult to achieve in Beirut, and Israel insisted that its troops be withdrawn from Lebanon on the basis of a withdrawal of all non-Lebanese Arab forces, coupled with the creation of a demilitarised zone in southern Lebanon. To try to maintain a fragile peace, the United Nations sent in a peace-keeping force composed of Americans, British, French and Italian troops, but after suicide car bomb attacks, with devastating effects on the American and French contingents, the force was finally withdrawn early in 1984. These attacks were instigated by Muslim fundamentalists fired by the Islamic revolution that toppled the Shah in Iran, who are fighting to establish a Shi'ite Muslim state.

Amidst increasing carnage and civil war, which has now lasted intermittently for over a decade, there has been a progressive weakening of central authority; and to avoid a total stalemate situation, cantonisation of the country has been suggested. 8,000 Druze (a pro-Syrian closed community which is an offshoot of the Shi'ites), 10,000 Shi'ites and 10,000 Phalangists and Maronites (Syrian Christians living in Lebanon) want power. Each community is maximising land ownership for its own sect, and each wants to gain control of key areas – the port of Beirut, the city itself and the airport. To the Phalange the only hope of stability is the creation of independent mini-states, yet this could lead to intervention.

In any further escalation, the situation will polarise, with each group looking for help from external supporters; for example, the Shi'ites will look to Iran and the Christians to Israel. Yet both Syria and Israel are unwilling to send in more men to add to an emotionally charged nationalistic and military situation. In Israel particularly, the war has caused inter-party bickering, a huge increase in the defence budget and also hyper-inflation.

See also **Hizbullah, Lebanese refugee camp massacres, Shi'ites**

Lebanese refugee camp massacres At the time of the Israeli advance into Beirut, following the assassination of President-elect Gemayel in September 1983, reports began to emerge from Israeli and other sources that armed men had entered the adjoining Chatila and Sabra Palestinian refugee camps in West Beirut in search of PLO guerrillas, and were engaged in wholesale killing of the civilian occupants, including women and children. Confirmation that a large-scale massacre had taken place came on the day after the departure of those responsible, when journalists and relief workers entered the camps to discover a scene of carnage and general devastation. Large numbers of bodies were found, some mutilated, of men, women and children who appeared to have been machine-gunned at close range, many of them while apparently trying to escape. Many houses had been blown up with their occupants still inside and bulldozed into rubble, and there was also a mass grave on the perimeter of one of the camps. Although uncertainty remained as to how many bodies were buried under the rubble in the camps, a commission of enquiry accepted Israeli intelligence estimates of between 700 and 800 dead in the camps as probably the most realistic figure.

As the full extent of the Chatila and Sabra atrocities became clear, a major controversy developed as to the identity of the armed men who had entered the camps and more particularly over the precise role of the Israeli forces who were in military control of the area. On the first

L

point, substantial evidence accumulated to indicate that those directly responsible were Phalangist militiamen (i.e. members of the right-wing Lebanese Christian Movement led by the Gemayel family), whereas initial reports that members of Major Saad Haddad's Christian Forces (based in southern Lebanon) had also been involved remained unsubstantiated. As regards the Israeli role, it became clear that the Israeli forces in the area had facilitated the penetration of the camps. Israeli spokesmen denied any Israeli collusion in, or responsibility for the massacre itself, and also rejected charges from PLO and other Arab sources that Israeli forces had directly participated in the operation.

Liberation theology For many years there has been an intertwining of liberation theology, politics and violence in Latin America. The theology of liberation is seen as a force for political and social reform. In South and Central America religion and politics have evolved together, taking material and symbolic support from one another. They have both embraced inter-institutional conflict and accommodation (such as 'church-state' relations) as well as more subtle exchanges whereby religious and political orders give legitimacy and moral authority to one another. In Latin America, the zeal to 'convert' the native population of the area gave liberation theology political legitimacy, but also associated it with tyranny and imperialism. Religion and politics have coalesced in meaning. Both have undergone a metamorphosis from individual to collective perspectives. This is true in Latin America where the economic and political contradictions of imperialism have had time to mature. The government's oppression of the people within the state, by selected government bodies (i.e. state terrorism) has given rise to a relatively new type of religious political motivation. To liberation theologists, communion with Christ inescapably means a life centred upon commitment of service to others; and in wider terms the uplifting (economic and socio-cultural) of individuals oppressed throughout the world. To these theologists there is a call for the liberating transformation of the history of mankind. In their view the root cause of oppression exists because of the economic, social, political and cultural dependence of some countries upon others – an expression of the domination of some classes over others. Only a radical break from the status quo and a profound transformation of the private property system, an access to power of the exploited classes and a social revolution would allow for the change to a new society.

The Western world looks upon this philosophy as provoking violence and terrorism; and the USA links such a philosophy with involvement from the USSR and Cuba. Religion, therefore, and politics are inseparable entities in Latin American history, as the theology of liberation is seen in the west as an ideology to foment revolution aided and abetted by the Soviet Union. Clerics will argue that the theology of liberation eventually grew out of the Church's involvement with the working-class poor, both urban and rural, in Latin America. Worker priests found direct involvement with the masses an unsettling experience – and they soon realised that the Church was alienated from the poor, and began to see religion and the social order through a Marxian lens. Their Church appeared as an agent of pacification and reconciliation in the absence of any effort to change or draw attention to the real situation of the poor and to the structural causes responsible for their plight. The clergy became radicalised by their experience.

The theology of liberation movement found support in Vatican II and the writings of Pope John XXIII. For example, economic growth was viewed as not synonymous with social development; efforts were required to establish conditions promoting the total growth of individuals as persons and assuring a wider distribution of income among all strata of society, especially in Latin America. Not until the 1960s did the Catholic Church ever call for direct action or even passive resistance in political movements attempting to achieve social reform or social justice. The Church has defined social justice as the fair distribution of material and non-material wealth (to include land), and of rewards among all peoples within a society. To the Western eye, these statements contradict the historical non-involvement in secular politics which the Church has traditionally followed.

Although most leaders of the liberation movement espouse a moderate and non-violent strategy for reform, there is considerable support for the use of violence. Bishop Camillo Torres's total conviction to the liberation movement and subsequent guerrilla resistance in Columbia led to widespread acceptance of violent revolution as a means to achieve social justice, and the people began to grasp at the reins of their own destiny – freedom. Yet to many in the Third World the profound basis of liberation theology is rooted in the democratic ideal, aligned with the weak and oppressed, the exploited and the poor. Unlike Guevara's strategy to use terrorist tactics such as bombings, robberies, kidnappings and assassinations to strike at the heart of the enemy, the liberation movement strives to develop a political infrastructure and mobilisation of the masses through a historical, cultural and religious ideology. Western nations use this linkage to show that liberation theology uses politics as a means to resolve community conflict and uses indiscriminate violence as a political weapon.

See also **Religious terrorism**

Lod Airport Massacre 1972 On 30 May 1972 three members of the Japanese Red Army on contract from the Popular Front for the Liberation of Palestine fired machine guns and threw hand grenades at passengers arriving in Tel Aviv from an Air France flight, killing 28 and wounding 76. Two of the attackers died in the massacre. Among the dead were 16 Puerto Rican pilgrims on a visit to the Holy Land, and one of the world's leading biophysicists. The surviving terrorist, Kozo Okamoto, was arrested.

The terrorists carried tiny paper dolls as good luck charms, and they used symbols of former Japanese Red Army 'heroes' on their false passports. The PFLP claimed credit for the attack as revenge for the failed operation at Dawson's Field which followed the arrest of Leila Khaled, and as a reprisal for the deaths of two Black September terrorists in the hijacking earlier in May of a Sabena plane flying from Vienna to Tel Aviv.

Okamoto told the jury at his trial that he and the others had left Tokyo in February and went to Montreal, New York and Beirut, Paris and Rome. At Rome they boarded a flight to Tel Aviv. He was charged with the military offence of political terrorism, and took full responsibility for his actions. Okamoto believed the revolutionary struggle was a just political struggle between the classes. It would be a long struggle in which deaths would be inevitable. The Arab world lacked spiritual fervour in the eyes of Okamoto and his followers, so the shootings took place to stir up the Arab world. The present world order had given Israel power which had been denied to the Arab refugees. This belief was the link between the Japanese Red Army and the PFLP. In interviews since his trial it was learned that Okamoto and his colleagues tore up their passports so that they could not escape, a further expression of determination to go through with the act. They had also planned to explode their last grenades in their faces to make the job of identification much harder.

Okamoto's release was demanded in a number of subsequent incidents, including the Munich Olympics massacre in September 1972 and the Entebbe affair of July 1976. Due to his proven insanity, he was eventually released without undue publicity in 1985.

The Lod Airport Massacre is one of the best examples of terrorist co-operation at an international level. By 1972 it was clear that a new international brigade had come into being, able and willing to participate in national liberation struggles all over the globe, provided the political context of these struggles happened to be to their interest and profit.

See also **Black June and Black September**

Lorenz, Peter In February 1975, three days before the West Berlin mayoral election, the Second of June Movement kidnapped Peter Lorenz, Chairman of the Berlin Christian Democratic Union and mayoral candidate of his party. Two armed men and a woman stopped his car, knocked out his chauffeur and drugged Lorenz. The group issued a communiqué demanding the release of individuals arrested during a Berlin demonstration protesting about the death in prison in November 1974 of Holger Meins, as well as the imprisonment of five others for terrorist activities. They demanded that the five be flown out of the country, with DM 120,000. The group had links with the Baader-Meinhof gang, some of whose members were mentioned in their demands, and had received its name in commemoration of the death of a student, Benno Ohnesorg, in a demonstration against a visit of the Shah of Iran to Berlin in 1967. The government agreed to the demands of the Movement within 72 hours and released the terrorists, who were flown to Aden. Lorenz was released the same day in West Berlin. A year later, four women held in West Berlin's prison for terrorist activities, including the Lorenz kidnapping, escaped, among them Inge Viett, a leader of the Second of June Movement.

L

M

Mafia and terrorism A potential development in terrorism is that terrorist groups will become more like traditional criminal organisations. There are clear parallels between Mafia-controlled kidnappings of executives for ransom in Italy, long a common form of crime in that country, and the 'politically-inspired' kidnappings of foreign executives in Latin America.

Terrorist tactics are simple but effective from the practitioner's point of view. Bombing, kidnapping, assassinations, the seizing of facilities and conveyances and maiming are not the monopoly of the terrorist. They are the trade of the criminal, the violently deranged and even the wartime saboteur. The distinctions lie not in the acts themselves, since murder, assassination and execution are all forms of homicide, but in the motivation for the deed, and in the selection of the victims. Carlos Marighella points out the distinction between guerrillas and outlaws and he cautions like Regis Debray, against a group's losing sight of its politics and becoming a mafia.

Many terrorist groups have attracted criminal elements at one time or another. Some originally bona fide politicians later turned to crime; others such as the Mafia were predominantly criminal from the beginning, but also had political interests. The dividing line between politics and crime was by no means always obvious and clear-cut: criminals were quite often good patriots or instinctive revolutionaries (or reactionaries) and they certainly had useful knowledge to pass on to the terrorists. But they would not accept discipline and their presence caused friction, corruption and eventually demoralisation. The temptation to use the loot from ransom for private gain or to settle personal accounts was overwhelming.

Malayan Races Liberation Army (MRLA) The communist-controlled MRLA came into being in 1948 as the military arm of the Malayan Communist Party (MCP) in their attempt to oust the British from Malaya and gain control of the peninsula. As a guerrilla organisation the MRLA had the great advantage of being able to recruit men who had gained valuable military experience when acting as part of the communist Malayan People's Anti-Japanese Army (MPAJA). Although disbanded in 1945, this organisation had stored away caches of arms and ammunition should the need for armed struggle ever arise.

After a period of civil unrest led by the MCP in the urban centres, the struggle was extended into the military sphere in July 1948. Able to raise and equip some 3,000 guerrilla fighters, the MRLA was organised on conventional military lines with a structure that ranged from the platoon up to units at battalion and regimental level, though the latter were more an organisation on paper, being unable to take on British forces at the level of full-scale operations. The MRLA made the initial mistake of attempting to mount relatively large military operations which played into the hands of the British who could then locate the guerrillas and destroy them in open combat.

Once the error of this strategy was realised, the MRLA adopted the traditional guerrilla approach of isolated ambushes, assassination of key figures and the carrot-stick policy of intimidation and aid to the local population. Winning over the people to the revolutionary cause proved to be difficult – the even balance of Malays and Chinese in the population was not necessarily a problem, but as the vast majority of the MRLA were of Chinese stock the ordinary Malays failed to identify with the guerrillas and consequently had little interest in the MCP's aims.

At its peak, the MRLA had a strength of around 10,000 men, but it was faced by well-organised and numerically superior government forces which amounted to some 60,000 police and auxiliary units and 30,000 regular troops. The type of war waged by the MRLA was cat-and-mouse attack and counter-attack fighting, where ambushers could easily find themselves ambushed.

The overall strategy was to terrorise the peasant population, alienate them from their masters and bring about the 'destruction of Malaya's economic wealth, based largely on its extensive rubber plantations'. The MRLA did not succeed due to the generally intelligent counter-measures adopted by the government forces in preventing the guerrillas from subverting the loyalty of both the urban and rural populations.

The MRLA soldier was a hardy fighter, often operating under the most difficult physical circumstances for long periods of time. Altogether nearly 7,000 MRLA guerrillas were killed in the conflict over the twelve years from July 1948 to July 1960, when the state of emergency was officially ended.

Marighella, Carlos After his death in Bolivia, Guevara's ideas on revolution and guerrilla warfare were the basis of discussions about the overall strategy of revolutionary activity, and the importance of the guerrilla in a strategy of insurrection. From these arguments a new revolutionary philosopher emerged, namely a Brazilian, Carlos Marighella, whose *Minimanual of the Urban Guerrilla* has become a gospel for today's urban guerrillas. According to Marighella the first duty of a revolutionary is to make a revolution, and to engage in both guerrilla and psychological warfare, especially against imperialism and capitalism. He wished all economic, political or social systems to further the objectives of guerrilla or revolutionary ideology. He provided a set of personal qualities

M

demanded of urban guerrillas; an especially important quality was the ability to live in the urban population.

The advantages of guerrillas over the enemy were surprise, better knowledge of terrain, greater mobility, and a better information network. Marighella urged that urban guerrillas should take a variety of actions against the authorities, but choose them with care. Possible actions were attacks or raids on banks, radio stations and offices; burglaries of offices and government buildings; occupation of schools, factories and radio stations; ambushing of police, businessmen and army personnel; tactical street fighting and promoting confrontation with police and the army; strike or work interruptions in factories and schools; and liberating prisoners.

Increasingly violent measures included the theft of arms and explosives; attacks against army barracks and police stations; the execution of spies, torturers and police informers; kidnapping of police, political figures and businessmen; the sabotage of factories, banks, transport and communications systems, leading to terrorism by bomb attacks and arson; armed propaganda against the media; and a war of nerves spreading false rumours among, for example, the police, embassies and international organisations.

To carry out any of these urban guerrilla actions, Marighella advised a number of methods and key factors for success – careful enquiry and analysis of information; observation and reconnaissance; study and timing of routes; mapping; transportation; selection of personnel; selection of firing ability and capacity; rehearsal of action; execution of the action; cover for those who execute the action; withdrawal; removal of the wounded; and the destruction of clues. In Uruguay, for example, the Tupamaros put into practice much of Marighella's advice and with much tactical success, such as in the kidnapping of the British Ambassador, Sir Geoffrey Jackson.

Maritime terrorism Although a number of ships have been taken over by terrorists in the past two decades, it is offshore energy terrorism which most concerns the Western nations; although there is a difference in perception between the Western European nations and the United States. The motivation for such activity against offshore energy production platforms varies – it may be to raise awareness of pollution, to gain publicity or simply destruction for its own sake, but there is a strong conviction that offshore energy will eventually become a terrorist target and that the preparations by the United States to deter and defend against this threat are woefully inadequate. The United States government and industry have tended to give a sceptical hearing to those who call for improved offshore anti-terrorist planning mechanisms and physical safeguards. Often steps are seen as unwarranted in light of the absence of a history of offshore terrorist incidents, and of evidence that an acute threat of such incidents does, in fact, exist.

The production platforms themselves consist of three principal systems:

M

the superstructure, i.e. the platform proper that holds production and utility equipment; the substructure or 'jacket' that holds the superstructure at a certain height above the sea bottom; and lastly the production wells. The harsh operating environment of wind, waves and currents, concern with pollution, and naturally the very volatility of oil- and gas-related industrial activities, place a premium on industrial safety.

Implicit in a high turnover rate in the offshore workforce is the heightened potential for penetration by terrorist 'insiders'. It is instructive that in spite of the most modern workplace safety technology, accidents due to inadvertent human intervention do occur frequently, and no physical or regulatory safeguards exist to protect against deliberate human intervention.

Certain basic elements enter into the risk-of-terrorist attack education. These are that offshore oil and gas extraction facilities are of national importance, and represent a valuable dollar investment; terrorism is, and is likely to remain, a fact of life; offshore platforms are intrinsically vulnerable to terrorist attack; and terrorists can get the means to stage an attack against a platform.

The proponents of protective measures place the weight of their evidence on the potential consequences of a terrorist incident, i.e. loss of life, property, energy, and the threat of pollution. Any legitimate risk analysis has to include a statement on the probability of a terrorist incident. To many, the terrorists' motivation is inherent in the propaganda or extortion value of attacking a platform. Sceptics argue that if terrorists are motivated to draw media publicity, a relatively remote and inaccessible target at sea is a poor choice. Much more accessible, equally lucrative and potentially spectacular targets exist on shore.

All major elements of any domestic country's energy infrastructure – oil pipelines, refineries, electrical power plants and grids, natural gas processing plants and transmission lines – are readily susceptible to malevolent interference.

The North Sea oil industry has faced more active anti-terrorist preparation; geographically, North Sea targets are easier to attack effectively than those of the Gulf of Mexico, and there are differences in the approach of Europe and the US to protection of scarce natural resources. North Sea oil and gas have made energy independence a reality for the nations skirting the area. The non-importation of oil and gas, and the net export of the oil in the case of Britain and Norway, and of gas for the Netherlands, have become vital factors in the region's balance of trade, international currency position, and economic security generally. This relative economic importance of North Sea oil and gas accounts for more active anti-terrorist precautions.

The comparative concentration of the North Sea offshore industry has significance apart from its relative economic vulnerability. The more centralised a target, the easier and cheaper it is to protect. In Europe mineral resources, whether underground or undersea, have been viewed as national assets deserving of protection and regulation by the state for the benefit of the nation as a whole. Oil is more of a scarce resource to European than to American countries. Thus there are sound economic grounds to guarantee a heightened degree of European sensitivity regarding offshore energy security. The economic and domestic political impacts of a terrorist disaster in the North Sea would be far greater than in the United States.

As regards West European countries (UK, Norway, Netherlands, West Germany) on the question of offshore assets and merchant fleets there is close co-operation between industry and government, resulting in contingency planning, training and exercising of plans and clear lines of responsibility and communications. As the value of a barrel of oil or a tanker increases, so does the threat. Thus, economic demands make some assets more attractive targets than others.

It is expensive to protect all assets to the same degree. To determine which assets should receive the greatest attention it is necessary to consider three forces that exert constant pressure on an asset. These are vulnerability, criticality and threat. Each of these forces exerts pressures in varying degrees at various times on the commercial assets of an oil corporation or shipping company; and some of the most valued assets depend on the stockholders' and public's confidence.

Marx and revolutionary violence Both Marxist-Leninists and revisionists have tended to interpret Marx for their own purposes. In general, the former have presented a Marx more prone to violence than is actually the case, while the latter have underplayed the importance of revolutionary violence in Marx's theory.

In Marxian thought, violence is never treated as a separate analytical category but integrated into a larger vision of the revolutionary process. The core of the capitalist structure is the class division between the bourgeoisie and the proletariat. The bourgeoisie, through its domination in production, exploits and oppresses the proletariat. Exploitation occurs in the form of expropriation of surplus value. Oppression results when capitalists, in order to maximise surplus value, organise production in a way which requires alienated labour. This denial of opportunity for creative labour is the basic source of revolution in capitalist societies. The economic substructure characterised by class division, exploitation and oppression provides a foundation for a capitalist superstructure which expresses bourgeois domination and sustains it. While the overthrow of the capitalist state is an indispensable condition for workers' liberation, it is not in itself sufficient for socialist transformation. The ultimate ends of revolution require universal liberation from dehumanising modes of capitalist production. If a socialist revolution is to occur, the proletariat will have to achieve a level of conscious behaviour able to maintain an effective revolutionary movement. A socialist revolution has to change the substructural economy and provide the foundation for a new way of life. Two major conditions have to be attained prior to a successful socialist revolution – a relatively highly developed capitalist economy and the existence of revolutionary consciousness and organisation within the proletariat.

Marx viewed revolutionary violence as a predetermined phenomenon which is necessarily a part of the transition from capitalism to socialism. Marx neither condemned violence as a pacifist like Gandhi did, nor did he glorify it like Sorel or, more recently, Fanon. Sorel and Fanon claimed that violence is instrumental in the psychological transformation of the oppressed into 'new men' capable of making a revolution.

Marx made distinctions between political and social revolution. The former altered only aspects of the superstructure, primarily the political institutional framework. Social revolution transformed the substructure, particularly patterns of class domination and the method of production. The essence of revolution could not occur without widespread revolutionary consciousness among proletarians. In such a context violence was inevitable and efficacious.

In Marxist theory violence is not efficacious unless it takes place in the context of developed material conditions. Throughout his life, Marx criticised revolutionaries of the Jacobin (French Revolutionary) tradition who over-emphasised the importance of political will while neglecting the necessity for advanced capitalist development in society and of revolutionary class consciousness in the working class. Marx believed terrorism to be out of step with the larger, impersonal historical process of revolution.

Marx was not opposed to violence in principle. He foresaw it as a necessary ingredient of the complex evolution of events culminating in socialist revolution.

See also **Terror in the theory of revolution**

Mau Mau The Mau Mau organisation was formed in the 1940s within the framework of the 'legal' Kenya African Union (KAU), but membership was distinguished from that of the KAU by the taking of oaths. While the oath-taking may superficially seem to be of little consequence, it was considered to be sufficiently serious to be declared illegal. All Kikuyu tribesmen discovered or suspected of taking the oath were liable to be imprisoned or detained indefinitely.

The reason for the oath-taking was that the Kikuyu were deeply superstitious, after years of attempting to defend themselves from attacks by both the warlike Masai and Arab slave-traders through the use of magic. Mau Mau leaders therefore contrived awesome oaths designed to cover all contingencies and to ensure that all members would remain both loyal to the movement and anti-white. The oath consisted of two parts, the first being a series of magic actions designed to convince the person that he was invoking a supernatural power, and the second the actual taking of the oath in which he would call upon the supernatural powers to support him. By these efforts, the Mau Mau gained some sort of hold, albeit often involuntary, over much of the Kikuyu population.

The expansion of the Kikuyu under the protection of the British administration had led to severe overcrowding within the tribal lands. Not only did this cause a great deal of tension within Kikuyu society, but it also meant that the Kikuyu looked outside at the vast acreages of land being farmed by a few white farmers.

The Mau Mau soon became divided into two groups, a militant wing and a passive wing. The passive wing was supposed to maintain forces in the field and was made up mostly of people who provided money, supplies, shelter, recruits and intelligence information. Only in the capital, Nairobi, was any real organisation and direction to be found. The militant wing lived in the Aberdare forests, and consisted of gang members. It purported to be organised into sections of up to 35 men, platoons of up to 100 men and companies of up to 250 men.

Initially orders from the passive wing were related to field operations feasibility, and the supplies of both arms and ammunition were far from abundant. Furthermore, there was little contact between individual Mau Mau groups. They were held together by an awed respect for the unit leaders, the fear of breaking oaths and the possibility of punishment.

It was not until 1951 that the Mau Mau really began to take the offensive with attacks on white farmers. By the time the state of emergency had been declared in October 1952 there were 12,000 guerrillas in the field. Despite arrests of leader figures, including Jomo Kenyatta, the organisation of Mau Mau was so loose that the effects of these arrests were hardly noticeable. Such was the nature of Mau Mau that the administration found it hard to recognise the leaders and this led to the detention of thousands of suspects.

In March 1953, Mau Mau raids took place which proved to be of profound significance. At Naivasha, insurgents stormed the police station, releasing over 170 prisoners. At Lari, insurgents killed 74 people (mostly women and children), wounded 50 more and left 50 people missing – probably dismembered. The Lari massacre did much damage to the prestige of the Mau Mau. Lari had been a settlement forced upon the Kikuyu by the government, yet despite the reluctance of the tribesmen to go, those who accepted the land were considered by the Mau Mau to be traitors and were subsequently killed. The massacre removed support for the Mau Mau both within Kenya and internationally.

Operation Anvil in 1954 and the detention of some 20,000 Kikuyu destroyed the Mau Mau hierarchy and its cells in Nairobi, severed lines of communication from the city and isolated the forest groups. As the security forces' measures began to bite, lack of organisation, loss of support and extremely limited supplies of arms and ammunition forced the Mau Mau into isolation, leaving them to fight as loosely-based armed gangs relying upon sabotage and terror as their key weapons.

Media and terrorism A free people needs a free press; but terrorism needs a propaganda platform. So in all Western countries, the news media faces a dilemma; is it possible to keep citizens informed of daily events, including the often graphic tragedy of terrorism, without becoming, to some degree, propagandists for the perpetrators?

The question of whether information is news or propaganda is very important. Even straightforward news stories about terrorism can involve agonising decisions. Do they contribute to the free marketplace of ideas helping people to understand the central issues of their day? Or do they give terrorists a megaphone through which to spread their message of fear to their ultimate target – the public at large? Do the news media provide the oxygen of publicity on which terrorism thrives, and help in the spread of sedition? Does extensive coverage by the media inflate the terrorists' ego to that of folk heroes, or does such coverage produce a sense of outrage – public revulsion against terrorist acts and demands for tougher measures by the government? Does journalism put so much pressure on the government that it acts irresponsibly, or does it provide important information to officials, since in hostile situations reporters can sometimes go where decision-makers in government dare not venture? Many people and organisations consider the media to be hooked on terrorism. To some people in the media terrorism is drama; do the media, in an effort to captivate viewers, cover terrorist incidents whenever possible? Or do they, as they themselves believe, report the facts which are verified, and with total fairness and straightforwardness?

These issues are outlined in question form because there is so much disagreement on which is the correct approach. A broad consensus exists on three points. Television is the terrorist's medium of choice. It is far preferable to print or radio as the outlet with the most immediacy and the most terrifying impact. Television is no longer simply reporting about the story, but has become part of the story. In the never-ending debate about the role of the news media in a free democracy, television is at the centre of an ongoing controversy.

One of the most noticeable developments in recent years has been the increasingly skilful use of publicity by terrorist organisations. With the growth of inexpensive videotape equipment, these groups are very often able to provide news organisations with television-ready footage: messages from terrorist leaders, interviews with captives, and even (in the case of kidnappings of subjects of western nations) visual records of executions. The Palestine Liberation Organisation now owns a share in an Arab communications satellite. At the hijacking of the American airliner in Beirut in June 1985, the terrorists were seen to be adept at organising press conferences and handling requests for interviews. This particular incident showed a very sophisticated use by hijackers and terrorists of the media.

Should a journalist be concerned with getting a one-time scoop or with saving lives? Throughout the debate on the media's role, the call for self-regulation by journalists and not censorship has been common. One of the biggest victories terrorists could ever achieve would be to force democracies to adopt the repressive press restrictions of dictatorships. With the pace of today's technology, satellite television beamed from any

M

part of the world and receivable by viewers anywhere, censorship would not work. In West Europe to a far greater extent than in North America, state-run television networks have worked out fairly high standards of editorial taste and agreements with national security forces to withhold or delay broadcasts in certain cases. In a Western society there are obvious disadvantages of the public's not being accurately informed, or being informed only by government spokesmen.

The Western media is vulnerable to misuse by international terrorists. The fact that terrorism by definition tends to be dramatic and also pictorial through the terrorist acts which take place, makes the media vulnerable.

Nevertheless, if the public are allowed access to all the information, no matter how dramatic or devastating it may be at any given point, they will eventually reach the proper conclusion. Certain standards, concepts and precepts have to be imposed on the media and obeyed. Journalists have to be aware of the role they are playing, and the risks for society if the journalist lets himself be used by the terrorists to magnify whatever are their intentions. In the West and indeed in other parts of the world an event is legitimate news and one cannot mute the media's legitimate response.

If events are repetitive enough, such as the spate of hijackings in the late 1960s and early 1970s, terrorists can be faced with diminishing returns, for there were few tangible achievements in this time and even the publicity value of hijacking decreased. The success of a terrorist operation depends almost entirely on the amount of publicity it receives. This was one of the main reasons for the shift from rural guerrilla to urban terror in the 1960s, for in the cities the terrorists could always count on the presence of journalists and TV cameras and consequently a large audience.

It is not the magnitude of the terrorist operation that counts but the publicity; and this rule applies not only to single operations but to whole campaigns. The media have always magnified terrorist exploits quite irrespective of their intrinsic importance. Terrorist groups numbering perhaps a dozen members have been described as armies, their official communiqués have been discussed in countless television shows, radio broadcasts, articles and editorials. In a few cases even non-existent groups have been given a great deal of publicity. All modern terrorist groups need publicity; the smaller they are, the more they depend on it, and this has, to a large extent, affected the choice of their targets. Even an apparently illogical or senseless attack becomes more effective if given wide coverage in the media than an operation against a seemingly obvious target which is ignored. These strategies work only in societies which have no censorship.

Mercenaries The term mercenary has become pejorative over the past two decades, primarily because of the myriad internal conflicts that have occurred on the African continent as nations attempted to gain or gained independence, and in which mercenaries were used extensively by all sides. Some of the better known of such conflicts are the wars in the Congo from 1960 to 1964, the Nigerian-Biafran War during 1967–68, and the 1975 war in Angola.

The mercenaries of those times were much like those of today – more remarkable in quantity than quality. Yet the few skilled mercenaries frequently were highly successful in battle against undisciplined, poorly-trained Third World military forces. To offset their advantage, many Third World forces hired and continue to hire their own mercenaries to train their military, provide much-needed technical assistance and highly specialised skills, such as flying modern military planes.

The mercenary issue caught worldwide attention in 1975, as three factions struggled to fill the vacuum created by Portugal's withdrawal as a colonial government in Angola. The conflict eventually swung in favour of the Soviet-backed Popular Movement for the Liberation of Angola (MPLA) with the infusion of some 4,000 Cuban troops to support the MPLA's Angolan People's Liberation Armed Forces (FAPLA). As the conflict wound down, FAPLA units captured 13 foreign-born adventurers who had been hired to fight on the side of the National Front for the Liberation of Angola (FNLA). Several Western citizens, including Americans and Britons, were captured. Four of the mercenaries were executed by firing squad.

Guerrillas' record of terrorism in any conflict far exceeds that of mercenaries in any modern conflict. Mercenaries in the Congo were responsible in part for the rescue of diplomatic personnel and other foreign civilians, including members of the clergy who were being held hostage, tortured and murdered by their Simba captors.

Currently, the greater threat to international peace and security, not only in Africa but the Americas as well is not the involvement of mercenaries but illegal intervention through insurgent and terrorist operations, in an effort to overturn lawful governments elected by popular vote.

See also **Angolan Civil War**

Messianic terror A striking development in recent years has been the use of theological concepts to justify terrorist activity – a phenomenon sometimes called 'holy terror'. The most notorious instance has occurred among the Shi'a where the revival of jihad (holy war) doctrines has produced some remarkable incidents in Lebanon and elsewhere. A major feature of the Shi'a episodes has been a striking willingness, even eagerness, to die, a disposition created by the belief that one who is killed while fighting in a jihad is guaranteed a place in paradise. This promise of personal benefit for assailants who die gives Shi'a terror an awesome dimension in the eyes of potential victims. In Israel in 1984 the government convicted Jewish terrorists who had organised the Temple Mount Plot, a conspiracy to destroy certain Muslim holy shrines. The mosques were built on the site of the Second Temple and if they were obliterated the construction of a Third Temple would at last be possible, a circum-

M

stance which some visualise as a pre-condition of the coming of the Messiah.

Prior to the French Revolution in the late eighteenth century, holy terror was the only effective form of terror. Well known examples are the Assassins and Fedayeen of Islam, and the Jewish Zealots and Sicarii. The Assassins emerged in the eleventh century, persisted for two hundred years, and are the first known example of an international conspiracy organised by a state, one which threatened the governments of several Islamic realms. The Zealots survived for a shorter period, some 60 years in the first century, but their influence was enormous. They successfully provoked a massive rebellion against Rome, which ended in disaster. The Second Temple – the ritual centre of Judaism – was destroyed and the final act was the greatest mass suicide in history at Masada in AD 70. The revolt inspired two more massive uprisings in successive generations. The results were that large Jewish centres in Cyprus and Egypt, then under Roman dominion, were decimated, Judea was depopulated, and then the final tragedy, the Second Exile or Diaspora, occurred; an exile which awakened fully the Jewish consciousness and became the central Jewish experience for the next 2,000 years, altering virtually every institution of Jewish life. No single Messianic terror group has occupied such a prominent place in Christianity as the Zealots.

A Messianic belief is one which visualises a day in which history or life on this earth will be transformed totally and irreversibly from a condition of perpetual strife which we have all experienced to one of perfect harmony.

History will end because God has promised us that it would; and at His appointed time He will intervene in our affairs, saving only those who deserve to be saved. This particular aspect of Messianism is known as millenarianism or millenialism. The significance of the doctrine depends on two conditions. The first is that believers think that the day of deliverance is near, and the second is that they think human action is necessary to consummate the process. When these conditions are fulfilled six elements of a Messianic doctrine will shape the decision to employ terror: the nature of the required human action; the cause or character of the Messianic aspiration; the proof believers think may be necessary to demonstrate sufficient faith; the moral qualities ascribed to participants in the Messianic struggle; the 'signs' or 'portents' of a Messianic intervention and finally the character of the deity's involvement.

Two factors make the possible appearance of a Messiah imminent in the minds of such believers. Firstly, the unexpected revival of religious enthusiasms, a prominent characteristic of our world since the 1950s, necessarily draws attention to a component of the revealed religions which is usually ignored. Religious enthusiasm is not Messianism; but each religious revival stimulates dormant sentiments that a Messianic delivery is imminent. Secondly, there has been the restoration of the state of Israel, a common theme in apocalyptic prophecies.

If a Messianic believer thinks he must participate in a struggle to 'force the end', the fundamental significance of the Messianic aspiration itself or of the cause will be conducive to terror. When the stakes of any struggle are perceived as being great, the conventional restraints on violence diminish accordingly. One expects wars which threaten the very existence of the belligerent parties to be much more savage than those for territory or trade. The appearance of revolutionary states in an existing international order introduces a new level of ruthlessness in world politics. Student radicals and new left and new right groups in the Western world have undertaken the bizarre activity of 'desacrilisation' – the pressing need for those who see themselves involved in the creation of a new world to profane all the sacred symbols and norms of the old.

When mankind believes that a period of inconceivable woe is a sign of deliverance and that the period has not yet occurred, there will be some eager to do their part; and both the commission and provocation of atrocities seem to be means admirably designed for that end. If the road to Paradise runs through Hell, if the fulfilment of the Promise depends upon life's becoming as unbearable as possible, violence can have no limits because it cannot be associated with a principle of reason that tells mankind when to stop because of success or failure. When even disasters do not bring redemption, the obvious remedy is to make the suffering even more profound.

Justifications for unlimited violence are strengthened when men see themselves, and not simply their causes, as wholly righteous.

Once a Messianic advent appears imminent, doctrine guides the expectations and actions of believers, doctrines which for the most part are the creation of the dominant or orthodox religious cultures, Judaism, Christianity, Islam, etc. Because the doctrines are vague and conflicting, believers must make choices and may abandon some for others more promising and equally legitimate. The power of the motivation for Messianic terror is inherent in the crusading idealism of the participation and their belief in inevitable world destruction.

See also **Islam, Religious terrorism, Shi'ites**

Mogadishu hijack On 13 October 1977 a Lufthansa aircraft carrying 86 passengers and a crew of 5 was hijacked. The hijackers were Arabs and their main demand was for the release of the same 11 Red Army Faction prisoners which the Schleyer kidnappers demanded. The leader called himself Captain Mahmoud, but he was later identified as Zuheir Youssef Okasha, who had recently slipped unnoticed out of Britain, where he was wanted for the murder in London on 9 April 1977 of the North Yemeni Prime Minister and two others.

Although the passengers described Mahmoud as unbalanced and unpredictable and his rhetoric was hysterical and concerned with world revolution, there were indications of considerable organisation.

The four hijackers boarded the plane as passengers at Palma, Majorca, where they believed security was slack. In what became the common fate of hijacked planes, it was turned away from a succession of Arab airports

(Damascus, Baghdad and Kuwait) and permitted to refuel in Rome, Cyprus, Bahrain (reluctantly) and Dubai, where it remained for 30 hours. While negotiating over the radio about deadlines, the German government concerned about Mahmoud's instability, despatched a 28-man team from its GSG9 assault force, initially to Cyprus and then to Dubai; but the aircraft took off again before they could attack. After further fruitless attempts to land at Damascus and Baghdad, it bumped down in the desert beside the blocked runway in Aden, where Mahmoud with cold callousness shot the Captain Jürgen Schumann. The plane took off again and after abortive circuits landed at Mogadishu in Somalia on 17 October.

Somalia was the base from which Wadi Haddad had organised the previous joint RAF/PFLP hijacking which had ended at Entebbe in 1976. With some persuasion from the King of Saudi Arabia and President Carter, President Barre of Somalia agreed to co-operate with Chancellor Schmidt in a rescue attempt by the GSG9 team. The team was then back in Germany, but its leader Ulrich Wegener had been waiting in Dubai with two members of Britain's SAS regiment. They flew to Mogadishu and made plans for the assault.

The hijackers had given Schmidt a deadline and an hour before they prepared to blow up the aircraft with plastic explosive, sprinkling the passengers with kerosene and spirits from the bar. Negotiations from the control tower were handled with great skill by the psychiatrist, Dr Salewski, who kept the hijackers talking. In a further play for time, a false message was sent that the German government had given in and had put the release of the prisoners in motion. The deadline was postponed until 2.30 a.m. The GSG9 team landed just after dark at 7.30 p.m. and put in their assault at 2 a.m. The technique, as used by the Dutch against the South Moluccans in March 1978 at Assen, was to stun everyone with noise and the hijackers, believing themselves to be on the verge of victory, were taken completely by surprise. Though Mahmoud managed to throw two grenades, none of the hostages or the GSG9 troops received more than slight injuries. Three of the four hijackers (including Mahmoud) were killed and the fourth, a girl, was severely wounded.

When Ensslin and Baader heard the news on the radio in Stammheim Prison, they committed suicide, along with another of the original RAF gang, Jan-Carl Raspe. A fourth, Irmgard Möller, tried to kill herself but failed.

See also **Red Army Faction**

Moluccans, South After a bitter war of liberation the Netherlands East Indies achieved independence and became the United States of Indonesia in 1949. Initially a confederal republic, Indonesia included within its territory the Republic of the South Moluccas, whose inhabitants were converted to Christianity by the Dutch, in whose Royal Netherlands Indies Army (KNIL) many of them served.

Immediately after independence the Indonesian government made moves towards the establishment of a unitary state; this alarmed the

Moluccans, who responded by proclaiming an independent Republic of the South Moluccas in April 1950. Indonesia did not recognise the RMS and proceeded to incorporate the South Moluccas into a unitary Republic of Indonesia.

On the island of Sulawesi, Moluccan troops of the KNIL – which had not yet been disbanded – participated in an armed rebellion against the Indonesian government. The rebellion was suppressed, but the Moluccan troops who had participated in the rising then refused to be demobilised by the Dutch in Indonesia. As a result in 1951 they were transported with their families to the Netherlands, where they were demobilised and housed in temporary camps. The community of some 15,000 experienced enormous problems of assimilation, and dreamed of a return to an independent South Moluccas.

Resistance to Indonesia in the South Moluccas effectively ended with the capture in 1963 of the President of the independent Republic, Dr Sumotel, but the growing militancy of young South Moluccans in the exiled community was revealed by the series of attacks upon Indonesian targets in the Netherlands which followed the execution of Dr Sumotel in 1966. In 1975, the Free South Moluccan Youth Organisation decided upon a strategy of violent action, and broke away from the moderate RMS 'government-in-exile' headed by Dr Manusama. Following an unsuccessful attempt to kidnap Queen Juliana of the Netherlands, the organisation mounted two attacks in the Netherlands in December 1975 which brought it worldwide attention.

On 2 December, seven armed Moluccans hijacked a train near the village of Beilen, killing the driver. They took the passengers hostage, and demanded to be flown to where they could join the Fretilin movement on East Timor. They also called for the release of all Moluccan prisoners in the Netherlands and for talks on the independence of the South Moluccas to be held under UN auspices. Two days later, another group of six Moluccans occupied the Indonesian consulate-general in Amsterdam, taking a number of Dutch and Indonesians hostage. After tense negotiations, and the death of a hostage, the hijackers gradually released all of their hostages, surrendering on 14 December, to be followed five days later by the surrender of the group in the Indonesian consulate.

A second train hijack, this time co-ordinated with the occupation of a primary school, took place on 23 May 1977. The Rotterdam-Groningen express was halted near the village of Onnan by a group of nine armed Moluccans, who released about half of the 100 passengers, holding the rest as hostages. At the same time four Moluccans entered the primary school at nearby Bovensmilde, taking about 100 children and five teachers prisoner. Police and troops sealed off the area, while the Moluccans made known their demands, which included the release of all South Moluccans imprisoned for earlier incidents.

The terrorists threatened to kill their hostages but the Dutch government ruled out any negotiations until all the children had been released. Although the schoolchildren were released, the Dutch government

M

decided that it must end the sieges by force, and at dawn on 11 June 1977, Marines stormed the school and train simultaneously. The troops released the remaining schoolteacher hostages without casualties, but at the train six South Moluccans and two hostages were killed.

In March 1978, three Moluccans took 71 hostages in government offices near Assen, and demanded the release of 21 Moluccans who had been imprisoned for previous attacks. Five passers-by were wounded and one hostage shot dead. Specially trained Dutch Marines ended the siege next day.

The Dutch government acted decisively during each of these incidents, and subsequent prison sentences were heavy. The Netherlands have shown some sympathy for the underlying causes of Moluccan terrorism, and the government has acted to improve housing conditions, employment opportunities and education facilities. The Dutch also established an agreement with Indonesia whereby Moluccans are encouraged to develop links with relations remaining in the Moluccas and given financial assistance to return there to live.

Morality and terrorism The problem of the limits of the permissible is the central issue in any discussion of both revolutionary and counter-revolutionary violence, or of terror and counter-terror. Someone who embarks on terrorism, like one who clings to power, knows where he begins but never knows how or where to finish. The terrorist dream of a final, redemptive blow, the dream of both state and individual terror, is a false dream. Terror flourishes in a step-by-step struggle, whether it is embarked upon as a stage in some overall, long-term strategy, or perceived from the outset as a sole and total weapon.

Terror movements rise and fall in a wavelike curve. The terrorist wave is the work of a generation trapped in despair as a result of some historical shock, feeling it has no way out. The generation of the terror destroys itself, has no direct continuation, yet the tradition renews itself in later waves of violence. Historically revolution has paved the way for a terror far more powerful – the counter-terror of the totalitarian state. Terrorist strategy has sought to make use of the latest in technological advances ever since the advent of dynamite.

Another lesson learned from the history of individual terror is the decisive role played by society in its prevention and eradication. Society has to live up to its responsibilities, even when this involves abandoning its tranquil ways and its illusions of safety. The danger of terror has and should continue to alert and awaken society to just this degree of responsibility. However, the prevention of such a horror cannot be left to the technicians. There can be no substitute for society's own critique, for its own treatment of its ills. It is a moral struggle which has been and will continue to be waged fearlessly.

The means and their realisation must be determined by humble and critical attitudes toward the aims. Aims cannot justify the means. One cannot abandon the balancing of means against ends, but it must be kept free of religious fanaticism and rigid dogmatism. Terror is a fact of life to which one must respond somehow or other. Terror tempts society to violent reprisal because it strikes one as irrationally violent. On the other hand, a violent response caters to the propaganda of terror. Society's violence supports the terrorist's otherwise weak case, or seems to do so for many. Therefore accommodation is sought, which may appear as a sign of the success of the terrorist methods.

Ultimately, democratic society has to admit that the terrorist's uncompromising position makes it impossible to treat him or her as other than the enemy – as an outlaw.

Guilt transfer is a very old technique of propaganda more widely used today than ever before. It involves a switch of public attention away from the embarrassing acts of its originator toward the embarrassing acts of the adversary, so that the former may be forgotten or forgiven, while the latter may erode the confidence and legitimacy of the other side. In the campaign to discourage and contain international terrorism, as well as in the East-West struggle, the liberal democracies cannot afford to operate under the handicap of the guilty mind. Contemporary society seems particularly vulnerable on account of its confused attitudes and lack of moral reference points. Part of the answer lies in political leadership and part in a better-informed and more responsible news media. The public have to understand the technique and reject fraudulent appeals directed at their consciences.

Motivation for terrorism The scope and complexity of the enigma of terrorism is a real problem for the world community. The terrorist is dedicated to the political goal which he sees as one of transcendent merit. He seeks attention and publicity for his cause. Terrorists aim to erode support for the established leadership or undermine the authority of the state by destroying normality, creating uncertainty and polarising the country. They aim to liberate colleagues in foreign jails and desire money to buy arms and finance the organisation. Their action is a measure of deep frustration when there is no legitimate way to redress grievances.

Frustration escalates in its expression, developing from protest, violent demonstrations, disruption, sabotage, robbery, burning, bombing and casual killing, to selective killing and kidnapping. When one level of the escalation fails, terrorists try the next level. Many drop out at each stage of the escalation. Frustration may arise from the success of the society – in a democratic form which is perhaps too successful for the extremists, and the process of escalation may take up to seven years, as in West Germany.

See also **Beliefs of terrorists**

Mountbatten and Warrenpoint murders In August 1979 Earl Louis Mountbatten of Burma, second cousin of the Queen, was killed when a bomb exploded on his fishing boat in County Sligo in the Republic of Ireland. His grandson and his friend were killed and the dowager Lady Brabourne died from her injuries. Others were injured. The Irish

National Liberation Army and the Irish Republican Army claimed credit, the execution being part of a struggle to drive the British 'intruders' out of Ireland. The bomb may have been planted in Mountbatten's boat, which was left at an unguarded mooring, and then set off either by remote control from the nearby hills or by a timing device.

Two individuals were arrested the same day and later sentenced to life imprisonment for the murder and for belonging to the IRA. Irish police believe seven other men were involved in the murder. Shortly after the Mountbatten murder, the IRA claimed credit for two bombs that killed 18 British soldiers and wounded 8 others in an ambush at Warrenpoint on the border with the Irish Republic. Troops travelling between the two army bases were injured when a bomb hidden in a civilian truck loaded with straw exploded as they passed. An army truck and jeep were demolished by the explosion of what the IRA claimed was 1,200 pounds of dynamite. Gunmen then opened fire from inside Ireland, which pinned down troops and prevented ambulances rescuing the wounded. When an army helicopter arrived to pick up the casualties a second bomb hidden nearby and containing 500 pounds of explosives went off, damaging the helicopter and injuring two more soldiers. The pilot managed to take the wounded back to his base. There were reports that the gunmen used automatic rifles and that local residents were hurt. The IRA Provisionals in South Down claimed credit, although they denied that they had fired guns. Among the dead was one of the most senior army officers to be killed in direct guerrilla violence in Northern Ireland.

Mozambique war of independence 1964–74 Frente de Libertação de Moçambique (FRELIMO) began its military campaign against Portuguese control in September 1964. Its operations were initially confined to the north–eastern province of Cabo Delgado and it encountered resistance to southward infiltration from Muslim tribes, but in 1967 it extended its activities to Niassa Province. In 1968, FRELIMO guerrillas became active in Tete Province, forcing the Portuguese to fortify heavily the area around the Cabora Bassa dam project.

In February 1969, the FRELIMO leader, Eduardo Mondlane, was assassinated by a book-bomb, and was succeeded by Samora Machel, who later became President from 1975 to 1986, when he was killed in a plane crash. In spite of a vigorous counter-insurgency campaign against FRELIMO in the north during 1970, in Tete the Portuguese became increasingly passive, allowing FRELIMO to use the province as a jumping-off point for raids into neighbouring Rhodesia in co-operation with ZANU (Zimbabwe African National Union) guerrillas, and for infiltration south and east into central Mozambique. By 1973, FRELIMO forces were active in Vila Pery and the Beira region, and the strategic Beira railway was increasingly coming under attack.

Fighting continued in spite of the April 1974 Portuguese revolution, but guerrillas, armed with Soviet weapons, had penetrated Zambezia

Province by July, and in September 1974 a negotiated settlement was reached which led to full independence in June 1975.

Mukti Bahini The Mukti Bahini emerged in 1971 as an Indian-backed partisan group, dedicated to the elimination of West Pakistani rule over East Pakistan and to the creation of an independent state (Bangladesh). India's invasion of East Pakistan in December 1971 was clearly the key factor in eventual success, but rather like the French resistance in 1944, the Mukti Bahini contributed to the liberation of their country, tying down the enemy and loosening his military grip through a policy of escalating guerrilla violence.

Armed opposition to West Pakistani rule was an inevitable outcome of General Yahya Khan's decision to crack down on the National Awami Party after its landslide victory at elections in late 1970.

In March 1971 the martial law administrator in East Pakistan initiated a programme of deliberate repression, which swiftly degenerated into genocide, and although he tried to pre-empt organised opposition by interning the bulk of the locally-raised East Bengal Regiment (EBR) and East Pakistan Rifles (EPR) sufficient numbers of officers and men escaped to act as a focus for spontaneous guerrilla action. Roads and railways were hit and Pakistani military outposts attacked, but the groups (known collectively as the Mukti Fawj) lacked co-ordination and were easily contained. What was needed was foreign backing, safe bases, effective central leadership and a supply of arms – all the attributes of successful modern guerrilla warfare.

These were provided by India. As the remnants of the EBR, EPR and East Pakistan Police (up to 10,000 men) withdrew across the border into eastern India in April, they were kept together in special camps, and allowed to recruit from refugees fleeing from the repression of the martial law administrator in the East. Many of the latter were members of the educated middle classes and proved relatively easy to train in the rudiments of military skill. Backed by EBR and EPR regulars, they were organised into guerrilla groups for action in East Pakistan. Renamed the Mukti Bahini, they grew in size – but despite 2,000 recruits emerging from training camps every six weeks, it took time for them to be prepared for a sustained campaign. Initially they concentrated on small-scale actions, designed to make continued West Pakistani rule inoperable.

Guerrilla groups exploiting their local knowledge and support infiltrated the border but rarely penetrated deep into the country. The West Pakistanis found little difficulty in absorbing such attacks, generally leaving the process of counter-insurgency to specially-raised and exceptionally brutal Razakars, recruited from the Bihari minority, which opposed the creation of an independent state. By October 1970 the Mukti Bahini had a potential strength of over 100,000 men, backed by Indian Army units. This enabled larger and deeper penetrations to be organised, concentrated against road and rail networks, power plants and shipping

M

off the East Pakistan coast. As confidence grew, liberated zones were created.

The growing intensity of the guerrilla war proved a significant advantage to the Indian Army when it invaded East Pakistan in December 1971. The Mukti Bahini continued to aid their ally as the campaign progressed, providing intelligence, disrupting enemy communications and attacking rear-area targets.

Once Bangladesh had been created, the bulk of the guerrilla force was disbanded, although a hard core was retained to form the nucleus of the new state's army.

Munich Olympics Massacre, 1972 On 5 September 1972, eight members of Black September led by Abu Iyad broke into the Israeli quarters at the Olympic Games village in Munich, killing two Israeli athletes and taking nine others hostage. They demanded the release of 236 guerrillas in Israeli jails including Kozo Okamoto (captured during the Lod Airport Massacre), the release of Andreas Baader and Ulrike Meinhof of the Red Army Faction, and safe passage to a foreign country. After a shootout with police, the hostages were killed as were five of the terrorists and a German policeman. The three surviving terrorists, two of whom were wounded, were released after the hijacking of a Lufthansa jet in October 1972.

Initially, two weightlifters were killed – members of the Israeli Olympic team, and their colleagues were taken hostage pending agreement to the terrorists' demands. They threatened to kill hostages every half-hour. The Germans offered an amount of money to be specified by the terrorists and the German interior minister offered himself and his colleagues as substitute hostages. These suggestions were turned down.

The police were unsuccessful in plans to trick the terrorists, which included a suggestion to poison food sent to them. The terrorists further demanded to be flown to Cairo with their hostages and called for a swap of hostages for the prisoners in Israel when the plane touched down. The West German Chancellor was urged by the Israelis not to meet the demands of the terrorists, although the Israelis were willing to give the group safe passage if their athletes were released.

The terrorists then agreed to leave the building with their hostages and were taken by helicopter to a nearby military airport to board a Lufthansa jet; police had initially been on board the jet disguised as the plane's crew, but had been ordered off at the last minute. Three terrorists were then killed, themselves killing a policeman during the exchange of shots, and a further two terrorists threw a grenade into the helicopter before they were shot. The grenade exploded, killing all the hostages. Some terrorists were captured.

In the aftermath, the Games which had been allowed to continue during the negotiations were postponed for one day while a remembrance service was held for the Israeli athletes. The dead terrorists were flown to Libya and a heroes' funeral. Three Israeli government officials were fired as a result of poor security arrangements; and Germany later toughened immigration and registration restrictions on Palestinian students and workers. The Palestine Liberation Organisation stated that it was not responsible for the attack and that their own objective was only to pressure Israel to release detained guerrillas from Israeli jails.

In February 1973 a Palestinian, Abu Daoud, who later figured prominently in a 1977 extradition squabble between Israel, West Germany and France, was arrested by Jordanian police and questioned. Despite Daoud's protestations of innocence, many observers believed Daoud was a major organiser of the attack – and certainly his passport contained a valid German visa. No German national or Arab resident in Germany took part in the operation. The terrorists themselves were based in Beirut, Damascus, Tripoli and Tunis, received tacit support from these governments, and made use of terrorist training facilities.

In late October, Black September hijacked a Lufthansa flight flying from Damascus to Frankfurt and successfully obtained the release of the three remaining terrorists. The Israelis retaliated by raiding refugee camps in Lebanon in February 1973, killing 31 people. They later shot down a Libyan airliner that had overflown Israeli air space, killing all 107 on board. Israeli officials blamed Egypt, Syria and Lebanon for being behind the Olympic attack, and the Egyptians in particular were the prime party blamed. Israel believed Egypt had the power and influence to stop these groups instead of actively encouraging them. Many Black September group members were to die at Israeli hands in subsequent years.

Black September reportedly received the equivalent of seven million dollars from Libya for the Munich murder of the Israeli athletes.

See also **Black June and Black September**

M

 **N**

Narco-terrorism Narco-terrorism is a new and sinister aspect of the international terrorist phenomenon because its effects are insidious, persistent and more difficult to identify than are the sporadic, violent outbursts of the armed assailant.

The manufacture and delivery of narcotics is part of the terrorist portfolio for various reasons. The most obvious is that drugs are a source of revenue to support the general activities of terrorist organisations. Another reason is that the use of drugs in target countries, such as the USA, is part of the terrorists' programme to undermine the integrity of their enemies. This is achieved by weakening the moral fibre of society, by encouraging widespread addiction and by nurturing the socially enervating criminal activities that flourish around the drug trade. There is no lack of evidence of connections between the international narcotics trade and terrorist organisations. For example, the Palestine Liberation Organisation has been involved in over a hundred operations in the last decade involving drugs, and linking that organisation through Syria, Bulgaria and Cuba to drug traffic to the United States. Many of these examples include organised crime networks as the effective distribution mechanisms, and also involve drugs-for-arms transactions.

Narco-terrorism in the USA has been uncovered during investigations of illegal immigration, organised crime, political corruption and Japan's penetration of the American car market. For some years the Sandinista guerrillas were involved in the international drug trade both before and after achieving power in Nicaragua.

The narco-terrorist, connected to drug traffic and employing the method of random killing of innocent bystanders, is a very special hybrid and the latest in a long line of terrorist groups. The Federal Government of the USA has known for quite some time about the narco-terrorist threat to the integrity of the state, but generally has been unable to control the spread of the problem.

The links between terrorist and insurgent groups and traffickers are most substantial in drug source countries, including Colombia, Peru, Burma and Thailand. In Colombia, four major insurgent organisations work in collaboration with cocaine traffickers. In 1982 the Revolutionary Armed Force of Colombia (FARC) reportedly obtained over 3.8 million dollars per month by collecting protection tax. Such taxes are used to buy weapons and supplies which are often shipped into Colombia on return drug flights.

Both the terrorist problem and drug problem are international and domestic issues; but governments and the media in many Western countries, notably the United States, treat the drug issue and terrorist problem on separate agendas. Information gathering and dissemination and policy formulation about narco-terrorism and how to confront it are subject to overlapping and competing jurisdictions, especially on the American continent.

National Liberation Movement
See **Tupamaros**

Neo-Nazi terrorism German right-wing terrorism has two roots. One is the National Democratic Party (NPD) which is still the strongest force in German right-wing extremism, at least in its numbers. The NPD is experiencing a continuing decline. In the last twenty years it has lost 25,000 members. Today it has only 4,000 members. This process of decay fed some small neo-Nazi groups which are the second root for the now existing German right-wing terrorism. Young members of the NPD went into ranks of these neo-Nazi groups and brought into their organisations more militancy. Neo-Nazi groups which became a hotbed for terrorism are the Aktion-gemeinschaft Nationaler Sozialisten and the Deutsche Aktionsgruppen. Two other organisations of German right-wing extremism which went into terrorism later were the Wehrsportgruppe Hoffmann, and the Volkssozialistische Bewegung Deutschland/Partei der Arbeit (VSBD/PdA).

Right-wing terrorists are much more ready to use violence than it was believed in the past. Killings happened for the first time in 1980 – the most spectacular being the killing of 12 visitors to the Munich Oktoberfest, and the suicide of the perpetrator. Another killer committed suicide after murdering two Swiss customs officials. Others have blown up American cars, attacked Jewish cemeteries, Jewish restaurants and daubed paint on synagogues. Many Neo-Nazis have been captured and are currently in jail.

The Neo-Nazis failed to obtain support from potential criminals and disaffected young people outside the political arena. The links between the German Neo-Nazis and Middle Eastern terrorists have collapsed. The worldwide publicity given to their links with the PLO and their training in the Al-Fatah camps, has deterred even terrorists like Abu Iyad, responsible for the 1972 Munich massacre. Neo-Nazi organisations in Denmark, Belgium, France and the USA have had their communications severed by the success of the German security services. Extreme Right terrorism has lost its motivation and no longer represents any real danger in the near future. It has lost its leaders and ideologists for some time to come, and consequently there is no sign of any significant political comeback, as opposed to straightforward crime.

New Left The late 1960s and early 1970s witnessed the rise and decline of the New Left, which became the leading force on the university

N

campuses; since there were millions of students, and since they were among the most politically active members of society, their radicalisation was bound to have political consequences.

The New Left was of mixed parentage: there was a genuine idealism, anti-militarism, revulsion against the inequities of modern industrial society, of poverty, hunger and exploitation in the Third World. However, politically it was not a very innovative movement – its gurus, such as Marcuse, were men of an older generation. The ideas they advocated had been floating around for many years – Gramsci, Lukács, the unorthodox German Marxists of the 1920s, and Reich. Perhaps the only new admixture of any significance was Frantz Fanon's concept of the liberating influence of violence. He avowed that violence not only unified the people but that it was a cleansing force, freeing the native from his inferiority complex and from his despair and inaction.

The New Left lasted for three or four years, after which some of its proponents converted to orthodox (Soviet-style) communism, while others continued to read the works of the Frankfurt School of Korsch, Block and Benjamin; a few turned to anarchism, others to Maoism, situationism and a variety of small sects. In the USA the great majority opted out of politics while retaining a vaguely liberal (American-style) orientation. In Western Europe, on the other hand, the process of depoliticisation did not go so far. When the rapid decline in the fortunes of the New Left set in, a few of its members opted for terrorism. Thus, more or less simultaneously, the United Red Army developed in Japan out of Zengakuren; the extreme student organisation, the American group Students for a Democratic Society (SDS) gave birth to the Weathermen; and some of the German students of the far Left founded the Rote Armee Fraktion (Baader-Meinhof) and the Second of June Movement. There were smaller groups in Italy (Brigate Rosse) and in England (Angry Brigade).

Non-violence The Indian attitude to violence has been characterised by ambiguity. Firstly, living beings are qualitatively different from the non-living. They represent the divine and feel pain. As such 'all life is one' and is sacred. Violence is therefore evil and must be avoided. Secondly, every living being lives on or forms the livelihood of some other living being. To live is to kill and destroy. Violence is thus inherent in existence and inescapable.

A small body of Hindu opinion condemned violence in all its forms. It not only disapproved of war and political violence but was also uneasy about the human need to destroy non-human life. From its ranks grew two powerful dissident movements, namely Buddhism and Jainism which set out to provide an alternative view of violence. They condemned all forms of physical punishment, including imprisonment, and proposed a wholly non-violent state. The Jains went even further and advocated an intensively ascetic way of life from which even the minimal necessary violence to non-human life was eliminated. Buddhism and Jainism included *karuna* (compassion) and *ahimsa* (non-violence) among the cardinal virtues and sought to found personal and political life on them.

The Indian tradition of moral and political thought thus contained two different strands of opinion. Most Hindus regarded violence as an inescapable fact of life and approved of its use in certain situations. Some Hindu and most Buddhist and Jain writers disapproved of violence in principle, and thought that it was possible and desirable considerably to minimise and even eliminate it altogether. The conflict between the two strands of thought came to a head during India's struggle for independence.

Although India's struggle for independence was largely non-violent, it was shadowed and periodically vitalised by a small but vocal terrorist movement. Yet by international standards this movement was fairly sober and restrained. It saw violence primarily as a means to achieve India's independence and justified it on three grounds. First, that the British were contemptuous of Indian public opinion. Popular petitions and appeals had proved futile and hence violence was the only course of action left to Indians. Second, British rule was based on terror and ruthless suppression of dissent, and terror could only be met with counter-terror. Third, under British rule, the Indians had become 'lifeless', 'cowardly' and 'passive', and incapable of organised action.

Gandhi was familiar with the terrorist movement. He even met many of its prominent members in London and had long discussions with them. He was convinced that they had a great appeal for his countrymen and were likely to receive wider support unless their advocacy of violence was effectively countered.

Gandhi agreed with the 'school of violence' in their belief that the liberal methods of rational discussion, parliamentary opposition and electoral pressure were either unavailable or ineffective in India. He was convinced that violence was not the answer; his objections were at two levels – violence was in principle unacceptable, and it was inappropriate and undesirable in the specific context of India's struggle for independence. Gandhi disapproved of violence on four grounds, ontological, epistemological, moral and prudential. Ontologically Gandhi contended that since all men are one, their relations can only be based on love and goodwill, not hatred and ill will. Unlike many other critics of violence, Gandhi advanced a novel epistemological argument against it. In his view the use of violence implies a belief in absolute and infallible knowledge.

For Gandhi, morality consists not merely in doing what is right, but doing it because one believes it to be right. Finally Gandhi rejects violence on the ground that it can never achieve lasting results, and because an act of violence can be considered 'successful' only when it has achieved a specific objective.

For Gandhi independence was necessary for the regeneration of the Indian character and civilisation. He argued that the terrorists were obsessed with independence and failed to ask why it was desirable and what India should do with it. He went on to argue that even as terrorist

N

violence was doing nothing to end Britain's economic, moral and cultural hold over India, it perpetuated the unmanly condition of its people. In his view violence is confined to a few and does not actively involve the vast masses of men.

No government can last a day without the co-operation of its subjects. Indeed, its power and authority have no other basis than their support. Now to support a government is to co-operate with it and to co-operate with it is to be morally responsible for its actions. If a citizen is convinced that the government is unjust, he has therefore a moral duty not to co-operate with it. To non-cooperation, Gandhi later added the powerful weapon of civil disobedience, which was an open, principled and courteous violation of laws believed to be unjust. Gandhi's adoption of fasting was to some highly dubious, and made his followers uneasy. It had a twofold purpose: it was an expression of his sense of outrage at an evil practice and his consequent refusal to live in a world where this kind of evil was being practised. It was his last desperate attempt to stir the 'sluggish conscience' of his opponents.

Gandhi wondered whether the enormous increase in the quantity and intensity of violence during the last two centuries might not owe its origin to the modern bourgeois industrial civilisation itself, especially its ruthless exploitation of nature, endless multiplication of wants, search for instant gratification, individualism, greed, the centralised economy and the decline of moral and spiritual depth. Gandhi was perhaps also right to question the widespread view that persuasion and violence are the only available methods for securing social change.

There were limitations to his theory, however – he was wrong to regard all violence without exception as carnal, and non-violence as spiritual in nature. He exaggerated the difference between non-violence and violence. He failed fully to appreciate the nature and role of violence in human affairs and when he did, did not know quite how to come to terms with it. He was wrong to argue that non-violence only exercised moral and not indirect political pressure, and although he did not intend it, his theory of non-violence tended to glorify suffering.

By Gandhi's definition, violence always harms people or destroys property. Non-violence does not always harm, and is at any rate not intended to cause harm. As long as Gandhi defined non-violence narrowly to mean no more than a moral appeal to another's conscience on the basis of innocent and uncomplaining suffering, it made sense in his mind to draw a rigid distinction between non-violence and violence.

See also **Political disobedience**

NORAID
See **Irish Northern Aid Committee**

Nuclear terrorism The possibility that terrorists might test fissionable material or nuclear weapons, attack nuclear facilities, use radioactive material to contaminate or create alarming nuclear hoaxes, has drawn increasing attention from government, the news media and the public.

N

The rapid growth of the civilian nuclear industry, increasing traffic in plutonium-enriched uranium and radioactive waste material, the spread of nuclear technology both in the United States and other Western nations, have all increased the opportunities for terrorists to engage in some type of nuclear action. To many observers the increased public concern with the potential terrorist threat to nuclear programmes and the virtual guarantee of widespread publicity may increase the possibilities that terrorists will attempt such actions.

The possibilities for action by nuclear terrorists can encompass the creation of potentially alarming hoaxes, acts of low-level symbolic sabotage, the occupation or seizure of nuclear facilities, acts of serious sabotage aimed at causing widespread casualties and damage, thefts of nuclear material or weapons, armed attacks on nuclear weapons storage sites, the dispersal of radioactive contaminants, the manufacture of home-made nuclear weapons and the detonation or threatened detonation of such devices.

Potential perpetrators are diverse, ranging from common criminals, disgruntled guerrillas, employees, ex-guerrillas and political extremists among whom there may be anarchists, leftists, racists, rightists, separatists, or simply authentic lunatics. Motives may be personal or collective. Objectives may include, but are not limited to, publicity, sabotage, extortion, causing widespread damage and casualties or possibly discrediting the nuclear industry by demonstrating that current security measures are inadequate. To date a few nuclear hoaxes and a handful of incidents involving contamination with radioactive material or sabotage of nuclear facilities represent the range of practical experience in nuclear terrorism.

The primary attraction for terrorists in 'going nuclear' is not necessarily the fact that nuclear weapons would enable terrorists to cause mass casualties, but rather the fact that almost any terrorist action associated with the words 'atomic' or 'nuclear' automatically generates fear in the mind of the public. Terror is violence for effect and is theatre; nuclear power, whether in the form of peaceful energy or weapons, is the most potent and to many people the most sinister force known to mankind.

Terrorists may try to take advantage of the fear that the word 'nuclear' generates without taking risks or making the investment necessary to steal plutonium and build a working atom bomb. A well publicised hoax could be as alarming as actual possession of a real weapon, provided people have no way of knowing that it is a hoax. A well publicised terrorist attack on a civilian nuclear facility, even if the terrorists failed in their intended mission, could be almost as alarming to the world as a terrorist success. Thus anything nuclear could, in the terrorists' plan, be little more than a dramatic backdrop or prop that guarantees them worldwide attention. The public may be comforted to know that nuclear terrorism is the least likely threat of all.

Among the possible employers of nuclear terrorism are anti-nuclear extremists whose primary objective would be to halt all nuclear programmes. The spread of nuclear technology and growth in numbers of nuclear facilities throughout the world will increase the opportunities for some type of nuclear action by terrorists. Terrorists do not have to build a nuclear bomb and indeed may not be interested in or capable of doing so. Within their resources and technical proficiency, they may carry out actions on nuclear targets that will give them almost as much publicity and leverage at less risk to themselves and with less risk of alienation or retaliation. Any incidents involving nuclear material or facilities are certain to receive extensive media coverage.

At some time in the future, the number of low-level nuclear incidents might then decline, possibly because alarm generated by these incidents conceivably might suffice to bring about the abandonment of nuclear power as a safe source of energy. The nuclear terrorism of the future can be seen, from a political and psychological viewpoint in the same light, as dynamite terrorism in the last century. Superexplosives were useful for attracting attention to demands whilst simultaneously publicising the identity and ideals of the perpetrators. They were deployed to avenge unjust acts, and were justified as an instrument for self-defence whereby the weak could prevent further exploitation and oppression by the state.

Nuclear power may appeal to terrorists who crave attention for their demands, or who wish to wreak vengeful punishment against specific targets. It is hard to imagine nuclear devices being advocated for defence of the interests of the workers.

Nuclear terror constitutes the greatest threat to democracy in the future because, more than any other extant form of struggle, it represents a serious attempt to establish a political system by which a tiny minority can rule a vast majority. The principal object in obtaining a nuclear weapon would be to blackmail the leaders of a society into meeting demands and to threaten the lives and effectiveness of the principal authorities concerned in dealing with terrorist activity, e.g. the government and the police.

There have been very few actions directed against nuclear facilities and no nuclear installations have been attacked, seized or sabotaged in a way that caused the release of radioactivity. No nuclear weapons have been stolen. No special nuclear materials have been diverted or taken by force from installations or while in transit; and no radioactive matter has been maliciously dispersed so that public safety was endangered.

Nuclear terror seems more attractive as a threat than as an action. If once in possession of a nuclear device, it seems terrorists could demand anything. But the idea of nuclear blackmail has some weaknesses – notably the ability to turn the capacity for destruction into commensurate political gains.

Even with a nuclear device, terrorists could not make impossible demands. They probably could not permanently alter national policy or compel other changes in national behaviour; to do so would require at least that they maintained the threat and it is unclear how long this could be done without discovery or betrayal.

The probability of nuclear terrorism remains in the final analysis a matter of speculation; and many people believe that when the next nuclear bomb is used, it will be by terrorists and not by a national government. Terrorists emulate states. If a nuclear device becomes a widely perceived symbol of state power, terrorists may be more inclined to go nuclear, or at least to try to attack or seize nuclear reactors. Terrorists could also try to obtain nuclear material for the clandestine fabrication of a nuclear explosive or to spread radioactivity, or they could try to steal a nuclear weapon which they could threaten to detonate if demands were not met. Alternatively they could fabricate alarming nuclear hoaxes intended to cause public panic.

In recent years the possibility of nuclear terrorism has become both a source of dread and an ally for the supporters of nuclear disarmament and the opponents of nuclear energy. To possess nuclear weapons illegally would be to possess a potential for great wealth, through extortion, ransom or sale to a competitive market. Recourse by terrorists to nuclear terrorism would depend on their access to nuclear weapons, inclinations to nuclear violence, insensitivity to conventional weapons and a degree of co-operation between terrorist groups.

The long-term results of nuclear terrorism might well be a strengthening of opposition to the use of nuclear energy and a serious loss of confidence in the government. The threat exists due to the growth of the nuclear power industry and its vulnerability to theft or attack by small groups. Moreover, it could become a reality because of the increasing international flow of information about high technology. From current international relations theory, it is impossible to predict the likely threat in the future from nuclear terrorism.

See also **Counter-nuclear terrorist strategy, Dynamite terrorism, Technological change**

O

O

Offender states Eight states around the world can be considered as practitioners of state-sponsored terrorism. Indeed, international terrorism comes from groups sent by various state sponsors to attack third-party interests on foreign soil. State-sponsored terrorism has been increasing in the last five years.

Iran is the world's leading supporter of terrorism, which it openly espouses as a tool for spreading Islamic fundamentalism and reducing Western influence. Iran is heavily involved in Lebanon and supported, for example, Shi'ite terrorist bombings of American targets there. Iran reportedly trained the gunmen involved in the Rome and Vienna airport massacres in December 1985.

Syria supports some of the most extreme Palestinian terrorist groups, such as that of Abu Nidal, to further the secular goals of President Assad. Syria directs terrorism against Western targets and Israel, Egypt, Jordan and the moderate Gulf States to thwart the Middle East peace process. It maintains training camps in Lebanon and is a major source of arms for terrorists.

Libya openly encourages terrorist groups to strike at Western and Israeli targets to further Colonel Gadaffi's presumed plan for a new pan-Arabic order with himself as head. Libya supplies money and arms to European and Middle East terrorist organisations. It maintains training camps and networks of support systems through its embassies.

South Yemen is a deeply anti-Western ally of the Soviet Union and for the past twenty years it has supplied training and safe haven for Palestinian groups. The coup of January 1986 has only slightly hindered their involvement.

North Korea provides training, funds and weapons to foreign terrorist groups. It sells large quantities of arms to Iran and maintains links with Japanese terrorist groups. In 1983 its agents set off a bomb in Burma that killed 17 South Korean government officials on a visit to that country.

Nicaragua maintains strong links with the Soviet Union and Cuba and provides facilities for training terrorists, especially Latin American groups. Nicaragua is a haven for members of Palestinian organisations, the Montoneros, the Tupamaros, ETA and the Red Brigades.

Cuba trains guerrillas and insurgents fighting in El Salvador and Honduras, as well as terrorists. Cuba is a main channel of supply for groups, offering funds, asylum and training to terrorists, with Soviet backing.

172

The Soviet Union provides intelligence, weapons, funds and terrorist training at facilities in the USSR and Eastern Europe. It also provides generally safe passage through Eastern bloc countries for terrorists moving into Western Europe. The Soviet Union also supplies arms to terrorists via the state trading companies of Bulgaria (Kintex) and Czechoslovakia (Omnipol).

See also **Cuba, Hindawi, Soviet Union, 'Terrorist states'**

O

OPEC Siege, Vienna 1975 In December 1975, six members of the Arm of the Arab Revolution, believed to be a cover term for the PFLP, attacked a ministerial meeting of the Organisation of Petroleum Exporting Countries (OPEC) in Vienna, seizing 70 hostages, including 11 oil ministers. In the attack and subsequent shoot-out with police, three people were killed and eight injured, including one of the terrorists. The group was led by the notorious Venezuelan terrorist Ilyich Ramirez Sanchez (known as Carlos).

According to various popular accounts, although the PFLP-Habash Wing denied being a party to the attack, planning was initially engaged in by Carlos and Wadi Haddad of the PFLP. Participants included a Second of June Group member, a German terrorist who had been released as a result of the Lorenz kidnapping, and some Palestinians. The group was armed with Beretta model 12 machine pistols, Chinese grenades, plastic explosives, fuse wires, batteries and detonators and also carried Vitamin C tablets and amphetamines to aid them in a siege operation.

In an initial attack, the group members ran up the stairs toward the meeting hall where the OPEC conference was in session – killing an Austrian security guard, a security officer with the Iraqi delegation and a Libyan economist.

The terrorists rounded up their hostages and barricaded themselves in the conference roof, where they discovered that they held 11 ministers – from Algeria, Ecuador, Gabon, Indonesia, Iran, Iraq, Kuwait, Libya, Nigeria, Saudi Arabia and Venezuela. At the start of the siege the hostages were separated into four groups. Libyans, Algerians, Iraqis, Kuwaitis and Palestinian OPEC employees were considered friends. Neutrals included citizens of Gabon, Nigeria, Indonesia, Venezuela and Ecuador. Austrians were placed by themselves and the rest were considered to be enemies. The terrorists demanded the broadcasting of their political manifesto by Austrian radio and television, and a bus to take them to the airport.

Despite surrounding the building with troops, the Austrian government soon gave in to the terrorists' demands for a flight out of the country. The plane flew to Tripoli, where hostages from Saudi Arabia, Iran, the United Arab Emirates, Qatar, Algeria and Libya were released.

An especially large ransom was demanded from Saudi Arabia and Iran for the release of their oil ministers. These countries had been two of the most important participants in the OPEC meeting, and were in disagreement with the Rejection Front of the Palestinian movement. The ransom sum was estimated at five million dollars, of which Carlos, Habash and Haddad recouped two million dollars. The remaining hostages were finally released in Algiers.

See also **Carlos**

Organisation Armée Secrète (OAS) OAS had its origins in the bitter feelings of resentment against President Charles de Gaulle's policy of self-determination for Algeria, announced in September 1959. The Colons (European settlers in Algeria) found this unacceptable, but a substantial group of them within the army blamed the President for betraying a cause which had already cost a lot of French blood, and formed the OAS.

The abortive generals' coup of April 1961 was one symptom of the army's anger, coming only three months after the creation of the OAS. In March 1961, the OAS mounted its first, and rather unsuccessful, attacks on prominent politicians. The OAS added immensely to the atmosphere of political instability that surrounded the Fifth Republic during the period of negotiations for an independent Algeria.

After the failure of the generals' coup in April 1961 the OAS was strengthened by the addition of many of the officers involved in the plot, and it soon assumed a structure familiar to those who had read the works of the theorists of *guerre revolutionnaire*.

The OAS was far less centralised than many other underground groups. This made it difficult for government agents to penetrate the OAS, but on the other hand, led to tactical errors that often had counter-productive results. Throughout the summer of 1961 it carried on its campaign of terror with sub-machine guns, grenades, stabbings and plastic explosives. Despite the growing number of outrages committed by the OAS, serving officers remained well disposed towards it.

As the campaign went on, the leadership of the OAS became increasingly divided. Salan (one of the leaders of the abortive generals' camp in 1961) and his supporters in Algiers believed that OAS activities within Algeria would force de Gaulle to reconsider self-determination, while the Madrid group, which included Colonels Antoine Argoud and Charles Lacheroy, were in favour of applying vigorous pressure in France as well.

There was also disagreement over tactics. When in September 1961 OAS agents narrowly missed killing de Gaulle at Pont-sur-Seine, General Salan publicly disavowed their actions in a letter to *Le Monde*. There was popular fury against attacks which in their course led to the deaths of women and children. Matters were made worse when the police overreacted in their attempt to control a left-wing protest in outrage against the disfigurement of a four-year-old girl. This protest led to eight deaths and 200 injuries.

Only a month later, in March 1962, the Evian Agreement was signed, under the terms of which Algeria was eventually to become independent. The OAS carried out a wave of attacks in an effort to disrupt the referendum on Algerian independence. Meanwhile the government was increasingly effective in tracking down the OAS leaders: Jouhaud was captured in March and Salan in April. At his lengthy trial, distinguished by the brilliance of his defence lawyers, Salan acknowledged his 'total responsibility' for the OAS, and was eventually sentenced to life imprisonment rather than to death.

With the capture of Salan, the OAS fell into the hands of the Colonels in Madrid, and the struggle went on until shortly before the Algerian independence which they had so resolutely opposed became an established fact in August 1962.

The OAS failed in its aim of keeping Algeria French, and had pursued a bloody campaign of terror. It attracted many criminals and misfits, but also contained a large number of men who embarked on terrorism reluctantly, and who believed that only by taking up arms against their own government could they preserve their personal honour. For them, intractable moral problems were at stake.

See also **Algeria**

O

P

Pakistan The Islamic Republic of Pakistan is ruled by a national law administration set up under the country's leader, General Zia ul Haq, in 1977. The eighty political parties in the country were declared dissolved in 1979, but many remain active, and are expected to register with the Election Commissioner. However, the country's two most influential parties have refused to register – namely the democratic socialist Pakistan People's Party of the late Zulfiqar Ali Bhutto, and the Islamic Pakistan National Alliance, with the exception of the Jamaat-i-Islami, one of its six constituent parties. The president is empowered to dissolve any party operating in a manner prejudicial to Islamic ideology or the sovereignty, integrity or security of Pakistan.

There are numerous left-wing movements. One of the more powerful is Al Zulfiqar, established by the son of the former Prime Minister Bhutto, hanged in 1979. It has a political and a military wing – the latter is composed largely of students and trained by dissident Pakistan Army officers, and has claimed responsibility for numerous acts of terrorism and sabotage. Although many of its members have been arrested, the movement is still active in Sind province.

The National Awami Party formed in 1970 has been opposed to the idea of a single Muslim nation in Pakistan, and has promoted the concept that Punjabis, Pathans, Baluchis and Sindhis constitute separate nations, each with a right to self-determination. It is generally a left-wing party with pro-Chinese and pro-Soviet wings (it supported the invasion of Afghanistan), and it represents the interests of workers and peasants. Similarly, the Pakistan National Party stands for increased decentralisation, with complete autonomy for Pakistan's four provinces and the federal government retaining responsibility only for defence, foreign affairs and communications.

The party likely to take over power in the future is the Pakistan People's Party, led by the wife and the Oxford-educated daughter of the former Prime Minister Bhutto, Begum Nusrat and Benazir Bhutto. After house arrest and intermittent detention, Benazir Bhutto returned to Pakistan in 1986 after a long period of exile in London. The current ruler General Zia ul Haq has for a long time viewed her party as a threat to the stability of Pakistan. Its principal demands are for an end to terror and bloodshed, the signing of a new constitution providing for a federal and parliamentary form of government, and the release from imprisonment of all opponents of the Zia regime.

Islamic fundamentalist parties are growing in influence. The Islamic Democratic Revolution Party hope that their threat of an Islamic revolution in Pakistan on the pattern of the Iranian revolution will force the government to effect peaceful constitutional changes. Many of its leaders have been detained under house arrest. The Jamiat-i-Jalaba is a rigidly orthodox right-wing Islamic fundamentalist organisation strongly opposed to the emancipation of women and to liberal and Western influences in education. A similar party, the Jamiat-i-Ulema-i-Islam, is a fundamentalist party which advocates a constitution in accordance with Islamic teachings.

Separatist and minority movements are common. In Baluchistan, a tribal area in south-west Pakistan, there has been an intermittent guerrilla war over the last two decades – with as many as 25,000 guerrillas under arms. Even the ending of the Sadari system, i.e. the rule of tribal chiefs with private armies and the power to administer justice and raise taxes, has not curbed the hostility felt by Baluchis to the strong controls imposed by the Pakistan government. Both the Baluchistan Liberation Front and the Baluchi Students' Organisation stand for the creation of an independent state of Baluchistan.

There is also a claim for an independent Pathanistan – a claim for separate nationhood which was first made in 1946 by political leaders of what was then the Indian North-West Frontier province, who strongly objected to a British proposal to group the province with the Punjab. Pathans number over three million and have their own distinctive culture, language, legal code, traditions and calendar, and distinctive natural skills and ambitions. For many years the Afghan and Pakistani governments have disputed the control of Pathanistan. The issue of statehood appears no nearer solution.

See also **Mukti Bahini**

Palestine Liberation Organisation (PLO) The PLO is a 'government-in-exile', dedicated to the aim of establishing an independent Palestinian state in territory now under Israeli control. Formed in 1964 after a sixteen-year period in which resistance to Israel had been fragmented and largely ineffective, the PLO was designed to co-ordinate and command the nationalist movement.

Politically the organisation has achieved much – since 1964 over a hundred states have recognised the PLO as the official voice of the Palestine people, and since 1974 it has enjoyed observer status at the UN – but in military terms the PLO has failed to have a decisive impact.

There has been a lack of consensus about the most effective use of military force. The first chairman of the PLO, Ahmed Shugairy, favoured the creation of an 'army-in-exile', organised along conventional lines and allied to the armies of the other Arab states intent on physical destruction of Israel. As the 1948–9 war had already shown, this was a questionable approach, implying a dependence upon ineffective non-Palestinian forces and an acceptance of PLO subordination in military terms. As early as

1965, Yassir Arafat's Al-Fatah group mounted selective 'hit and run' raids into Israel, indicating the potential for guerrilla warfare, and after the crushing failure of the conventional war approach in June 1967 (the Six Day War) this became the favoured strategy. Arafat was elected chairman of the PLO in February 1969, but he could not unite the movement behind a single approach. Already Georges Habash had declared his preference for terrorism, founding the Popular Front for the Liberation of Palestine (PFLP) in 1968, and this triggered the creation of a number of splinter groups, each one progressively more extreme. When it is added that the conventional units of the earlier period – notably the Palestine Liberation Army (PLA), and the Syrian-controlled Saiqa – continued to exist, the degree of confusion may be fully appreciated.

But even if coherence had been achieved, success would probably have remained elusive, for despite the existence of a large, predominantly pro-PLO refugee population, within which guerrillas could be raised, trained and supported, the Palestinians have lacked the benefits of unassailable 'safe bases'. In the early 1960s this may not have been an acute problem, since refugee camps in the Gaza Strip, the West Bank and the Golan Heights forced the PLO to withdraw deeper into Egypt, Jordan and Syria. This lessened the impact of the guerrillas as they had to travel so much further through hostile terrain to reach their targets in Israel (a factor which contributed to the growing preference for international terrorism), but more importantly it created intolerable strains between the Palestinians and their host nations. As 'front line' Arab states suffered the effects of Israeli retaliatory raids in response to guerrilla attacks and faced the emergence of PLO controlled enclaves inside their own territory, the Palestinians lost significant support. In 1970 King Hussein of Jordan forcibly ousted the PLO from its bases east of the Jordan river, while both Egypt and Syria imposed close controls upon the Palestinians within their boundaries. A PLO move to bases in South Lebanon enabled the guerrillas to regain a degree of effectiveness, but the subsequent civil war there (1975–76), followed by an Israeli invasion in 1982 and its continuing repercussions weakened them still further.

The result was an undermining of PLO independence, particularly in the aftermath of Arafat's enforced withdrawal from Beirut in 1982; the humiliation of defeat, coupled with the effects of both Israeli and international counters to guerrilla and terrorist activity, drove a deep wedge into the Palestinian movement. A virtual civil war between Arafat's supporters and a Syrian-controlled faction led by Abu Musa in Northern Lebanon in late 1983 reinforced this division, leaving the PLO militarily a spent force. Arafat survived, exploiting the political strengths of the PLO, but the Syrians assumed the power to dictate Palestinian strategy, destroying the military initiative of the PLO and subordinating its aspirations to those of a wider Arab world.

As a result of initiatives towards peace proposed by President Reagan and the Arab League in 1982–83, serious differences were generated within the PLO itself. For example, five PLO groups, Syria claimed, specifically rejected the proposal for a Palestinian-Jordanian federation on the grounds that it ran counter to the PLO's commitment to a fully indepen-dent Palestinian state and derived from 'American schemes aimed at the liquidation of our national cause'. The five PLO factions were the Popular Front for the Liberation of Palestine (PFLP) led by Dr Georges Habash; the Popular Front for the Liberation of Palestine – General Command (PFLP-GC) led by Mr Ahmed Jabril; the Democratic Front for the Liber-ation of Palestine (DFLP), formerly known as the Popular Democratic Front for the Liberation of Palestine, led by Mr Nayef Hawatmeh; the Popular Struggle Front (PSF) led by Mr Bahjat Abu Gharbuyya and Dr Samir Ghosheh; and the Palestine Liberation Front (PLF) led by Mr Abul Abbas. However, the PFLP, the DFLP and the PLF all denied Syria's claim and reaffirmed their commitment to the unity of the Palestinian cause. Moreover the chairman of the Palestine National Council (the Palestinian parliament-in-exile), Mr Khaled Fahoun, said that although differences existed within the PLO on the federation proposal, these did not amount to a split and in no way represented a challenge to Mr Arafat's leadership.

Following the December 1983 evacuation from Tripoli (Lebanon) by Fatah forces loyal to Mr Yassir Arafat, the leader of Al-Fatah and chairman of the PLO, the existing split within the PLO was widened when Mr Arafat met President Mubarak of Egypt (this constituted the first official high-level contact between the PLO and the Egyptian regime since the conclusion of Egypt's peace treaty with Israel in March 1979).

An agreement between Al-Fatah and the Democratic Alliance (a grouping of four smaller PLO factions which had expressed varying degrees of sympathy for the anti-Arafat rebels) was concluded in June 1984 after a series of meetings in Aden and Algiers. This agreement was denounced by the National Alliance (composed of rebel Fatah members and three other PLO factions based in Damascus).

The four organisations grouped together by the mid 1980s, and known as the Democratic Alliance, were the Popular Front for the Liberation of Palestine (PFLP), the Democratic Front for the Liberation of Palestine (DFLP), the Palestine Liberation Front (PLF), and also the Palestine Communist Party. Those grouped within the National Alliance were the Popular Front for the Liberation of Palestine – General Command (PFLP-GC); Al-Saiqa; the Palestinian Popular Struggle Front (PSF), and the Fatah rebels.

Peaceful end to terrorism – the Basque theory Peaceful methods might be used to stop some types of terrorism. The Commission to the Basque Government on the Basque Problem reported in 1986 that Basque terrorism can be beaten through greater regional autonomy, and through negotiations with the violent separatist group, Euskadi and Freedom (ETA).

Basque separatism, as an indigenous struggle, is easier to solve than international terrorism. Basque demands can be reconciled in today's Spain, as Basques share Spanish ethnicity and the Roman Catholic religion. The Basque problem, an indigenous nationalist struggle, goes back four centuries. Ever since Philip II made Madrid the capital of Spain in 1561, the Basques have felt stifled and exploited by Madrid. Frustration became terrorism when Franco, who ruled Spain from 1939 to 1975, outlawed the Basque language, banned Basque public meetings, and brutally enforced his policies on the region.

Basque terrorism continued after Franco's death. Since 1975, ETA has been responsible for about 500 deaths. ETA has political muscle too; United People – a Basque political party that is linked to ETA's political wing and supports ETA's demand for an independent state – draws about 10 per cent of the region's ballots.

However, the violence has diminished in recent years, as Spain's democratic government has moved to satisfy Basque aspirations. Polls show that 75 per cent of Basques oppose ETA's terrorist tactics. A majority of Basques believe that an independent Basque state is not a workable possibility but that increased Basque self-determination is.

The 1986 Commission advocates firmness to show that violence has no chance of succeeding. This means the continued use of a method that has proved successful in Italy – pardoning terrorists who inform against other terrorists. Such tactics, it is argued, have helped reduce the number of ETA terrorists to fewer than 200.

Nevertheless, ETA remains a political problem and negotiations cannot be ruled out. Instead of denying suspected terrorists habeas corpus under a recently adopted Spanish law, the experts argue that people arrested for ETA membership or activity should be tried in Basque courts. If negotiations take place they should centre on trying to remove frustrations inherited from Franco's regime. Allowing the Basques more powers to police themselves is the most vital recommendation. Many Basques mistrust the Spanish government's Civil Guard.

The region's political parties are also expected to have a hand in stopping terrorism. In 1984 the Socialists joined the moderate Basque Nationalist Party in a ruling coalition in the regional parliament. The Commission believe the pact should be broadened to include other parties so that all groups could work together for more Basque self-determination. Such a coalition would isolate the United People party and further erode support for ETA.

The Basque region's struggle with terrorism has some relevance for the wider struggle against terrorism. To end the violence, the political causes sparking it must also be addressed. Indigenous nationalist struggles elsewhere in Western Europe are declining, e.g. in Corsica since 1982, when President Mitterrand of France granted the island a significant amount of autonomy.

See also **Basque nationalism**

Permanent revolution Permanent revolution is a concept derived from the ideas developed by Trotsky in 1906, stipulating the interdependence both between Russia's own bourgeois and proletarian revolution, and between the Russian and the European revolution. In Russia, according to Trotsky, only the proletarian minority could bring about a successful revolution. This revolution, Trotsky argued, could and would pass in an uninterrupted process from its bourgeois-democratic to its proletarian stage initially with the willing support of the peasantry. But in order to maintain and consolidate its power and to overcome the anticipated peasant resistance to its policies of collectivism and internationalism, the Russian proletarian minority would have to rely on the support of the victorious proletarian revolutions in Europe which would be set in motion by its own example. These concepts which envisaged both the Russian and the European revolutions as a single continuous process, anticipated the strategy which Lenin adopted at a much later stage for the Bolshevik seizure of power in 1917 and the subsequent foundation of the Communist International. On the other hand, they were irreconcilable with the later attempt to build 'socialism in one country' once it became evident that European and world revolution could not happen. The theory of permanent revolution subsequently served Stalin as ammunition in his struggle for Trotsky's liquidation.

See also **Terror in the theory of revolution**

Personalities of revolutionaries Three theoretical approaches to the study of revolutionary élites can be identified: the psychoanalytic, the psycho-historical and the sociological.

The psychoanalytic approach focuses on the inner dynamics of human personality, and seeks to locate the impulse to revolution in the early psychological experiences of individuals. The psycho-historical approach seeks to move beyond the purely psychoanalytic theories by placing personality dynamics in the wider context of society and history; it attempts to combine psychological motivation with life experiences of an individual through time. The sociological approach – which is prominently associated with the concept of charisma – stresses certain exceptional or supernatural qualities of individual leaders that sharply distinguish them from the masses, while at the same time eliciting the latter's commitment and devotion. Since group behaviour is characterised by irrationality and emotionality, leadership is the key to understanding collective phenomena. A group is as intolerant of authority as it is obedient to it. The mutual ties binding together group members are based upon their common emotional ties to the leader. The political personality compensates for his feelings of inadequacy and low self-esteem by a relentless pursuit of power. A stoic, austere, puritanical life style is widely adopted by revolutionary leaders. Situations of economic deprivation, social stress, political crisis and psychic stress can crystallise into a collective call by the people for a leader to come to their rescue. Crisis can lead to the emergence of charisma, and charisma in turn provides strong leadership which produces stability and order. However, from a study of revolutions in the twentieth century it is quite clear that not all revolutionary leaders are charismatic and neither are all charismatic leaders revolutionary.

Revolutionary leadership is primarily dependent on situation or context. A situation of crisis – whether political, military, social, economic or psychological – catapults the leaders into prominence and provides them with ready and willing followers. Political crises may consist of inter-élite rivalries or coups d'état, riots or rebellions, nationalist movements set in motion by imperialist penetration and control, or widespread governmental corruption and ineptitude. Military crises are represented by defeat in war or army mutiny. Social crises include the disintegration of the prevailing ideology, normal order and social institutions. Economic crises are represented by severe inflation or depression. Psychological crises consist of widespread frustration, alienation and relative deprivation. The greater the intensity and coalescence of various crises, the greater the likelihood and the more rapid the emergence of revolutionary leaders. Situations of uncertainty, unpredictability, anxiety and stress rally the people and mobilise them in a common search for safety and security.

Revolutionary leaders are motivated by varieties of nationalism and patriotism, and are drawn by a sense of justice and a corresponding mission to set things right. As an earnest of good faith in their mission of justice revolutionary élites adopt a posture of virtue and purity. Many leaders adopt a simple, spartan life style.

In their attempt to right the wrongs they perceive, some revolutionaries begin as reformers, and try to bring about change by working within the system. Relative deprivation and status inconsistency may serve as other sources of revolutionary motivation. Revolutionaries may articulate an alternative vision of society embodying themselves as a superior order or élite. The revolution can be undertaken by highlighting grievances and injustices, undermining the legitimacy and morale of the ruling regime, mobilising the masses to the cause and subtle propaganda for the justice of revolutionary action. Not all revolutionary situations give rise to revolutionary leaders and not all persons with the appropriate psychology and skills emerge as leaders of revolution.

Revolutionary élites are broadly middle-class in origin with substantial representation from the lower class, and have extensive histories of involvement in clandestine or open radical activity. They have a positive attitude towards the nature of man and towards their own countries. Their attitudes towards international society are dualistic, seeing it as divided into unmistakable friends and foes.

Anti-West national revolutionary movements have mushroomed since the 1960s throughout Africa, Asia and Latin America and they were led, ironically enough, by men who had been educated in Western countries. The genesis of many post-war revolutions can be traced to student and émigré groups from various colonies who met, planned and organised in London, Paris and other European cities and then 'transported' the revolution to their native countries. Revolutionary leaders of divergent cultures and backgrounds have shared wide knowledge and experience.

Revolutionary élites are typically formed legitimately, and the leaders tend to be drawn from mainstream ethnic and religious groups. The jobs performed by members of élites are inconsistent with their expectations, and despite being well-educated, many leave their vocation and become professional revolutionaries. Members of revolutionary élites are cosmo-politan in many senses, and they travel widely, spending long periods of time in other countries, developing foreign contacts and learning foreign languages. From an early age, members of élites are heavily involved in illegal organisation and agitation. Contrary to expectations, revolutionary leaders tend to have normal family lives.

Because of the low level of economic and social development and the firm grip of the imperialist powers, it takes longer for revolutionary élites in colonial countries to develop a radical consciousness, spread consciousness among their peoples and cultivate sufficient military strength openly to challenge the imperialist powers in revolutionary warfare.

Revolutionary leaders with divergent ideologies do not vary signific-antly in their attitudes toward human nature, but do vary in attitudes toward their own countries and toward international society. Formative years are relatively unimportant as sources of radicalisation – the tranquil or stormy nature of early life is not strongly associated with an individual's emergence as a revolutionary.

Education has in some cases been a source of radicalisation for post-war leaders with stormy beginnings from colonial or neo-colonial coun-tries with nationalist, communist or nationalist/communist ideologies. Foreign travel can have a radicalising influence in many ways; the traveller may witness oppression, exploitation and brutality of unimaginable proportions. He or she may see privation, misery, hunger, disease and death and observe or even personally experience cruelty, torture, impris-onment and exile.

Revolutions all occur under identifiable conditions, whether political, military, economic, social or psychological. Distinctions have to be drawn between revolutions that are systematically thought out, planned, organ-ised and executed by élite groups over relatively long periods of time, and revolutions that explode upon the scene as a consequence of sharp escalation of insoluble conflicts between major social groups, taking rela-tively short periods of time. Political, social, economic and religious issues coalesce to produce revolutionary explosions. The sluggish and frequently ill-conceived responses of the established regimes serve only to aggravate the situation and mobilise the masses.

Relative deprivation and status inconsistency have been instrumental in shaping the motivation of a number of revolutionaries. Relative depri-vation refers to one's perception of discrepancy between one's 'value expectations', or aspirations, and one's 'value capabilities', or achieve-ment. Status inconsistency denotes a perceived discrepancy between one's economic status and one's political power. Relative deprivation and status inconsistency characterise most if not all lower-class revolutionaries, and tend to be inherent in the very nature of colonial contexts and hence of colonial revolutionaries.

Regional variations are found when revolutionary leaders are set apart by their ethnic backgrounds from the populations of their homelands. Asian and Latin American leaders tend to be from the main ethnic groups: African and European and North American revolutionaries represent a variety of minorities, large and small.

Latin American and Asian revolutionaries belong to the main religions of their respective regions, whereas significant proportions of African, European, and North American leaders represent minority religions. These variations are associated with the more pluralistic character of Africa, Europe and North America. European, North American and Latin American leaders are likely to have been educated in institutions in their home country.

African and Asian revolutionaries are more likely to have travelled to foreign lands than their Latin American, European and North American counterparts. The type of ideology to which revolutionary élites subscribe varies by region. Asian and Latin American leaders are least varied in their political orientations, combining as they do shades of Marxist and nationalist ideologies. African revolutionaries are only slightly more varied, since their pan-Africanism is nothing more than nationalism on a regional basis. European and North American élites are most diverse, subscribing to a spectrum of radical ideologies; these people, and to a lesser extent the African élites, are more likely to incorporate both indigenous and foreign doctrines. Asians and Latin Americans tend to adapt foreign ideologies to local needs.

Much of the ideological radicalism of élites is rooted in their proclaimed belief in various shades of Marxism. The relative diversity of ideologies and attitudes among European and North American élites in contrast to their relative conformity among African, Asian and Latin American leaders is most likely a result of history – revolutions in the Western world span four centuries; revolutions in the other three regions are post-war phenomena.

See also **Terrorist mindset, Terrorist roles**

Peru The Republic of Peru has alternated between military and democratic rule throughout its 150-year history. Military regimes have generally predominated, increasing the numbers of political prisoners, expropriating newspapers considered to be dangerously destabilising, and dismissing workers at random. In 1981 the civilian government elected in 1980 passed an anti-terrorist law, largely in response to the terrorist activities of the Maoist Sendero Luminoso guerrilla movement, which provided for prison sentences of up to twenty years for those convicted of terrorism. Since then, the government has frequently declared states of emergency in areas of guerrilla activity (notably Ayacucho department in the south), and the Peruvian army is now deployed in the struggle against the insurgents.

Outside Peru the group which is often in the news is the Sendero Luminoso or Shining Path, which is a Maoist movement founded during a period of student unrest in the 1970s. It broke away from other leftist groups and went underground with plans to organise the peasantry. The founders themselves were the sons of peasants and small traders who met as a group while at university. The movement started with Robin Hood-like actions but in a later stage these became more severe and more bloody, with bombings and bank robberies becoming a regular occurrence in the early 1980s. Thousands of attacks have been carried out in the course of waging a 'people's war' from the countryside in order to carry it eventually into the cities. The group aims to pursue total war until the government is overthrown. There are four stages of activity – acts of sabotage designed to draw attention to the existence of the Shining Path; attacks on business premises and banks to obtain funds; actions against police posts in remote areas with the aim of seizing weapons; and ultimately the seizure of power.

A group which has had generally less success than the Shining Path has been the National Liberation Army, which has been in existence since 1962. It has proclaimed that for the liberation of the country's workers and peasants, it would pursue both armed struggle and a policy of unity. The Peruvian Army has effectively managed to infiltrate this group. A group with strong Indian support is the Tawantinsuyo Liberation Front, created in 1981 by Indians from Bolivia, Ecuador and Peru. Named after the region of the former Inca empire centred on Peru, the Front aims to regain sovereignty over the old Tawantinsuyo region which it regarded as having been 'artificially fragmented' by the frontiers of Peru, Bolivia and Ecuador. So far, it has achieved little success.

Philippines In August 1946, peasant rebels, many of whom were former members of the wartime communist-led anti-Japanese guerrilla movement, were fighting against landowners supported by the Philippine security forces and their own private armies. They were joined by a group of communists opposed to the newly independent regime of President Manuel Roxas, and by 1950 the Hukbong Managpalaya ng Bayan (People's Liberation Army – known simply as the Huks) led by Luis Taruc, was engaged in battalion-sized operations against government forces.

Huk successes were countered increasingly successfully after the appointment of Ramon Magsaysay in September 1950 as secretary for national defence. Magsaysay reorganised the armed forces and promoted a number of reforms in order to undermine peasant support for the Huks. The rebels were isolated and ruthlessly hunted down, and by 1954 the back of the rebellion had been broken.

A succession of presidents, under the control of American economic interests and the Filipino landowning class, did little to help the peasant majority or to curb disorder and political violence. In 1965, President Macapagal (Liberal Party) was defeated by President Ferdinand Marcos of the Nationalist Party.

For two decades until 1986 the Philippines were ruled by Marcos, who wielded ever-increasing and wide-ranging executive powers. The growing authoritarianism of the regime provoked widespread opposition, particularly after the introduction of martial law in 1972. Legal opposition by moderate liberal groups became ineffective. The two main guerrilla groups which, though not constituting an immediate threat to the regime, have in recent years engaged almost the full strength of the country's armed forces, have been the Moro National Liberation Front (MNLF), which is Muslim autonomist or secessionist, and the New People's Army, which is Maoist. In 1986 President Marcos was forced to leave office after a fraudulent election (which he claimed he had won) and was replaced by the genuine winner Mrs Cory Aquino, who had avenged the death of her husband, the Opposition leader Benigno Aquino, allegedly at the hands of Marcos, on his return from exile in the USA in 1983. It is considered that the change of leadership will not placate the guerrilla groups, although Cory Aquino's accession has led to an uneasy calm, with one attempted coup in November 1986.

The Moro National Liberation Front is an Islamic nationalist movement in rebellion against the government, with the particular objective of achieving independence or autonomy for the Muslim population of the Philippines within the area of Mindanao island in the southern part of the country. It has a factionalised political wing with separate groups allegedly supported by Libya, Saudi Arabia and Egypt, while the military branch is the Bangsa Moro Army. The guerrilla war has already resulted in the deaths of more than 60,000 people. By February 1974 the Moros were strong enough to capture a city for several days, but by 1975 Moro guerrilla activity had begun to decline and Marcos opened negotiations with the MNLF in order to end the war. Although Marcos's diplomatic offensive resulted in the withdrawal of Libyan support for the rebels, the Moros fought on, though their chances of gaining a separate Muslim state continued to decline as Christian settlers began to form a majority in many areas of the south. The MNLF split into several factions and many Moro guerrillas took advantage of government amnesty offers in order to surrender.

The front stopped establishing control over territory after it realised that the army's tactic of burning down a whole village or destroying a whole island dominated by the Front was causing the people too much hardship. The guerrillas now attack the enemy in isolated incidents, and the army maintains that this is a result of reduced firepower. The chain of command has weakened, and quite often local commanders act on their own initiative. Because supply lines can no longer be maintained as a result of the government patrols, a cottage industry of weapon manufacture has developed. The Moros continue to demand an end to the reported repression and mass extermination of Muslims in the southern

Philippines and to take prompt measures to provide protection and security for the Muslim minority and to resettle the thousands of refugees in their homes. Basically, the Front is in a state of stalemate because it has never established a military capability.

Since 1969 the military branch of the Maoist Communist party has been the New People's Army (NPA), formerly the People's Liberation Army. It is particularly active in Luzon province, with several thousand guerrillas and a large support base among the population. By 1971 the NPA had some 2,000 men under arms, but as the Philippines security forces became more professional during the mid 1970s the NPA suffered a series of reverses, and was forced to reorganise.

By the early 1980s, the NPA was operating in alliance with the MNLF as far south as Mindanao, where it became firmly entrenched by 1985, remaining seemingly unbowed by the political changes. The struggle is organised into at least 30 strategic guerrilla fronts, each with its own party structure, militia and political machinery.

Among the smaller opposition groups is the Rock Christ Sect, which is a religiously fanatic movement responsible for brutal murders. It consists of members of the Tingol clan and claims a membership of several hundred of which a few are reported to be armed. It is an animistic sect with a thin overlay of Christianity. They believe that the chiefs have healing power and that incantation of their special prayer, Orasyon, shields them from danger. The sect's high priests are rich landlords and farmers – and it is widely believed that the army has infiltrated the sect to form small groups and to train them.

Phraseology of terrorists The statements of terrorists characterise their philosophies and ideologies, which are a frontal attack on liberal values and principles. Terrorism is an instrument or political weapon developed by revolutionaries, and they believe that because states commit acts of terror and violence, it is permissible for terrorists to do the same.

Gorillas (Marighella) – the military in Latin America, in the opinion of guerrillas such as Marighella.

Guerrilheiros (Marighella) – the revolutionaries.

Latifundio (Marighella) – large estate worked by peasants and generally under-exploited.

Mass front (Marighella) – a combat front, an action front going as far as armed action.

Urban guerrilla (Marighella) – an armed man who uses other than conventional means for fighting against the military dictatorship, capitalists and imperialists.

Outlaw (Marighella) – concerned with his personal advantage and indiscriminately attacks exploiters and exploited.

Armed struggle (Marighella) – includes civilian elements and can develop into a peasant struggle.

Military struggle (Marighella) – conflict within the armed forces which must be combined with working-class and peasant struggle in line with the tactics and strategy of the proletariat.

Guerrilla warfare (Marighella) – a technique of mass resistance – a type of complementary struggle, which will not by itself bring final victory. In ordinary warfare and in revolutionary struggle, guerrilla warfare is a supplementary form of combat.

Yin-yang (Mao) – a unity of opposites in Maoist theory. Concealed within strength there is weakness and within weakness, strength. It is a weakness of guerrillas that they operate in small groups that can be wiped out in a matter of minutes. But because they do operate in small groups they can move rapidly and secretly into the vulnerable rear of the enemy.

Resistance (Mao) – is characterised by the quality of spontaneity; it begins of its own accord and then is organised.

Revolutionary guerrilla movement (Mao) – is organised and then begins.

Revolutionary army (Guevara) – an army which is welded to the people – the peasants and workers from whom it sprang. An army which is conversant with strategy and ideologically secure. It is invincible.

Terrorism (Marighella) – a form of mass action without factionalism and without dishonour, which ennobles the spirit.

Armed struggle (German terror groups) – a legally justified campaign against the power of the state.

Every terrorist group in a liberal democratic society tries to make maximum use of the freedom of speech and of the press which prevails. Only when terrorists have a solid constituency of public support can they hope to become a more effective political force.

PLO
See **Palestine Liberation Organisation**

Police response in Europe Terrorist acts have and always will be regarded first and foremost within the context of criminal law. Whether one deals with a transnational or international group of perpetrators or with small-scale 'home group' terrorists, countering the effects and dealing with the offenders falls within the framework of internal security and is therefore a case for the department of justice and the police forces. The question of how a society counters terrorism touches the fundamental principles of democracy. There is strong evidence of the fate of governments which decide to drop legal restrictions, step outside the borders set by the democratic system and deal with terrorism at its own level, fighting fire by fire, employing the military to the full extent. In general, the West's peacetime armies cannot afford to provide year-round internal security without their training and overall defensive capabilities beginning to suffer.

Unlike the Anglo-American community-operated police, the European police forces were always government-orientated structures which emerged from the military. This is not only evident in a term such as '*gendarmerie*', which dates back to a military rural unit of the eighteenth century, but also in uniforms, armament and training. Many European police officers were discharged army veterans and this left its mark on the tactical and structural development of the police.

Police response to terrorism is twofold – terrorism has to be dealt with at the tactical level, both preventive and reactive, and it demands an investigative and intelligence approach. In both the patrol and the criminal investigation departments, hierarchical bureaucracies exist which have an inbred reluctance towards change and reforms.

Specialised tactical police response teams have been developed in Germany (GSG9, Grenzschutzgruppe 9); the USA (SWAT, Special Weapons and Tactics, and CIRT, Critical Incident Response Team); France (GIGN, Groupe d'Intervention Gendarmerie Nationale); Austria (the Cobra); and Spain (the GEO). These have some basic tactics in common – the men are police officers with training and prior experience as officers of the law, coming from regular patrol or investigation work. Their missions, their use of force, and their employment of firearms are subject to the same legal safeguards as normal police actions. Trained specialists always function as a team where tasks and responsibilities are divided, making it easier for a member of the team to concentrate on and fulfil his appointed task.

Speed, not haste, which is essential to any counter-terrorist operation, results from this team approach. The key to success is a system of mutual 'overwatch', in which every team member is covered by one or two of his partners so that a real need to use one's guns in self-defence seldom arises. Over the years many incidents have proven that even hard-core criminals and terrorists are likely to give up when faced by a swift-moving police response team barring all exits. Experience in the West has shown that the use of such teams has lowered a department's use of deadly force in arrest situations.

In 1971 West Germany provided a turning point in the history of criminal investigation. The Bundeskriminalamt, the federal investigative office, was remodelled to become a central agency to guide, control and co-ordinate the work of the various state investigative offices, the Landerkriminalamter. It had quickly emerged that an effective counter-terrorist campaign cannot be run without a centralised intelligence-gathering and evaluation network. To many people the build-up of any such computer network will be on a confrontation course with the restraints and safeguards embodied in the constitution of any democratic society. Despite this, there has been a tendency to neglect conventional detective work in favour of the highly technicalised systems such as databases and computer terminals.

Terrorists generally choose their targets with great care to detail, and an awareness of their symbolic value. Few victims are chosen at random. Schleyer and Moro were kidnapped although they were both guarded by a detail of policemen; the terrorists took possible resistance into account and used more firepower. Similar threat of resistance was the reason for the 'stand-off' or remote control attacks directed against the American Generals Haig and Kroesen. Throughout recent years, airport security has been considerably increased, but this has not deterred attackers willing to pay the price, as witnessed at Rome and Vienna airports in 1985.

Special units do have a deterrent effect to some degree, and most of the groups currently existing worldwide have a healthy respect for such units as the GSG 9, the SAS, Delta Force, the Israeli Jamam or the French GIGN – but these teams cannot guard every airport, every embassy or politician. The terrorists recognise the reactive character of the tactical response units and plan accordingly – to create the damage before the police can rush in the specialised counter-terrorist teams. Conversely, many people in the democratic countries are aware that much time is lost every year in highly visible 'deterrent' guard duties, at road-blocks and similar routine police jobs – these have been described as pseudo-responses to terrorism.

Although international terrorism has demonstrated repeatedly that there is no neutral ground anywhere and that in the long run no country is immune, there has been very little effective international co-operation between the democratic nations apart from political pronouncements, the establishment of isolated measures and international declarations. Tactical response groups have been in the forefront of informal co-operation, but they are restricted by certain directives of their respective agencies and governments.

Interpol has been reluctant to accept the role as central exchange for information about politically-motivated crime. Interpol is greatly restricted by the problem of defining what constitutes terrorism, and its own statutes forbid any activities linked to 'political, military, religious or racist cases'. Though the organisation has grown rapidly in post-war years, and there are now more than 125 member states, it is doubtful which of the 70 members from Asian and African countries would actively support counter-terrorist intelligence measures they had to implement against Middle Eastern groups with whom they might be in sympathy. Nevertheless, Interpol can and has furthered the exchange of information referring to stolen material, i.e. guns, documents, vehicles, licence plates, explosives and other ordnance, which belong to the 'life support system' of terrorist groups.

The international exchange of information needs to be improved and a pool created among democratic states, concentrating on documented information to simplify the prevention of terrorist acts and limit the free travelling of perpetrators. The intelligence pool could then be enlarged to become a source for real co-operation. The Western democracies should now make it easier to establish a trial ground for police co-operation at tactical level, which would be less politically sensitive than economic or political sanctions.

See also **Law and terrorism, Trevi group**

Polisario Polisario (Popular Front for the Liberation of the Saquiet el Hamra and Rio de Oro) is made up of guerrillas armed, trained and indoctrinated and given sanctuary by Algeria and Libya. It is a vigorous guerrilla movement for regional liberation, which came to prominence when Spain formally withdrew from the Spanish Sahara on 26 February 1976, resulting in the immediate partitioning of the territory by Morocco and Mauritania. During a battle in October 1981, Polisario guerrillas using Soviet missiles brought down Moroccan aircraft.

Military activity is generally matched by diplomatic efforts. In November 1980 the UN General Assembly adopted a resolution reaffirming the right to self-determination and independence and more than half the 50 members of the Organisation of African Unity (OAU) had recognised the Sahraoui 'state' formed by Polisario.

The main leadership of Polisario is Mauritanian and the future of the movement will affect some important and tenacious Mauritanian dissidents. The withdrawal of Mauritania from the conflict meant that Polisario only had to fight on one front. Recognition of Polisario is mainly confined to African and Arab nations, in spite of the OAU rebuff for some of their policies.

Political crimes Political offence as a legal concept plays a special role in extradition law and the granting of political asylum, which has developed over a century. Most states make no distinction between common and political crimes for their own citizens, but they often do for foreign citizens. A political act is directed at the furthering of changes in current laws or existing government policy, whereas a criminal act is contrary to penal law in a particular country. The concept of political crime is not recognised on a global scale. Anglo-American law, for example, does not recognise political crime as a distinguishable class of crime.

Political crimes are linked with acts of corruption by politicians, acts of treason and espionage, acts of disinformation that cause havoc, acts that incite riot, mayhem or disorder and acts of torture. Political criminals are ideologically motivated offenders – there is consistent opposition of the values of another society, real or imaginary, to those of the society in which the offence is committed. The political criminal acts in unison with like-minded people and the criminal acts are carefully planned and organised. Often the organisation he works for enjoys some foreign government support. To the political criminal, repressive laws protect the particular privileges of the ruling classes rather than the fundamental necessities of life of the community as a whole. Certain activities are viewed as repressive crimes – these include on a global scale electoral fraud; illegal transgressions by the police; acts of terror by organisations close to the police force; governmental crime and colonial crimes.

The question of when violence is legitimate to support political beliefs is an emotional one. It can be legitimate when it is used by the government with public support and when society accepts it as right. Many democrats hold violence to be legitimate when peaceful means have failed; when government fails or ceases to rule in the perceived interests of citizens and when the government removes basic rights and liberties accepted as inalienable by the constitution or by individual tradition; and when no other means of political expression exist. Political crimes and political violence are part of a contest for legitimacy and are based on value judgments.

See also **Political violence**

Political disobedience Political disobedience is the refusal to abide by laws or commands of the established political authorities; laws may be objected to either in themselves or for what they represent or permit. In a broader sense, political disobedience embraces the performance of any act prohibited by the law or the state, or the non-performance of any act required by the law or the state, with the purpose of securing changes in the actions, policies, laws, government or constitution of the state, or of the social and political system underlying it. Political dissenters and protesters are typically minorities, in conflict not only with their rulers but with wide sections of the ordinary populace.

The great difference between past advocates of political disobedience, like Tolstoy and Gandhi on the one hand and the Marxists on the other, is that the former were moral revolutionaries who preached non-violence as the only way to bring about the improvement of each individual, which alone would make possible a new and better social order; the latter saw men as the creatures of society who would change only when society was changed. Disobedience directed against the government or the political or social system is an open declaration of war on the government or the system supporting it, which can be settled only by capitulation or suppression. Political authorities will exhibit different attitudes to what appears to be the same form of political activity. One can distinguish between liberal states which regard the questioning of authority as a political right, authoritarian states which forbid the public manifestation of dissent as dangerous to their existence, and totalitarian states for whom the absence of positive identification by dissidents with the purposes of the state indicates the need for ideological re-education.

The importance of any cause to those who support it can be seen in their conception of the consequences of their failure to fight for what they believe in. It is only when temporal causes have something of the urgency of religious causes, driven by the prospects of divine wrath or spiritual salvation, that deep-seated resistance to authority is likely to be pressed.

In Western states, not all those who exhort others to disregard or break the law are prosecuted for incitement. Much depends on the circumstances and manner in which the call is made, and on how far it succeeds. The form of disobedience practised by a group can change under the impact of its own experience. Where men have been concerned to gain public support for their policy under democratic conditions, political disobedience has normally been adopted as a shock tactic to supplement the normal constitutional means of protest. Where political disobedience has failed to secure its objectives, there is pressure to adopt more militant tactics.

In modern societies there is widespread disagreement on even the most fundamental principles of political and social behaviour. Political disobedience needs to be justified in non-legal terms and grounded on something firmer than the sincere convictions and sense of rightness of those involved. It has to be justified in terms of the cause; if the cause is acceptable, it must then be shown why it requires the rejection of one's obligation to the state and its laws. The political weapon of civil disobedience must be shown to further the immediate objective of the cause.

The strongest case which can be made out in support of a direct challenge to authority which threatens the peace of the community, is that that peace has been bought at the expense of neglecting urgent issues and needs. Widespread disobedience usually arises from the release of pent-up and bitter resentments against severe discrimination or deprivation by a significant proportion of the sufferers, often with support or leadership from sympathetic outsiders; or from acts of repression or aggression by the authorities that are felt to be morally indefensible. In over a third of the countries of the world, there is no channel for action by those who want to bring about major changes in the structure of society by constitutional means. Many will become apathetic as a result, but some will draw the lesson that the only way to transform their society is to join those concerned to smash its institutions.

See also **Law and terrorism, Morality and terrorism, Non-violence**

Political sub-state violence Sub-state violence is directed against a state (whether or not that state practises terror) from within the state.

Violence at sub-state level has a particular relevance to those groups which have definable political objectives and can be called 'rational rebels'. The problem facing political leaders and contemporary states is that one man's terrorist is another man's freedom fighter. Sub-state violence and its particular problems are inseparable from the operation of the state and the international system generally, and raise questions about the nature and morality of government as well as of those who take violent actions against established governments. There must be a good prospect of an end in view and a chance for the cause to succeed before blood will be shed.

Newly formed small terrorist groups usually find it easier with each passing year to obtain at least minimal means for taking life. Well-established terrorist groups find it easier to obtain supplies of conventional weaponry, often of a sophisticated level. A terrorist group may well decide that concentration on the ownership of a nuclear bomb is not the most expeditious means of inflicting mass destruction. Advanced democracies are much more vulnerable than in the nineteenth century. With or without terrorists, some communities may become ungovernable because of largely non-violent conflicts of interests. Those states with

193

democratic constitutional frameworks are greatly at risk from both terrorism and non-violent conflict, and some may decide on authoritarian solutions. Even advanced states without ballot-box democracy face strains due to the delicate balance of the inter-relationship between different parts of a modern advanced economy. With advances in modern communication, small groups can internationalise their activities with ease. There is a strong relationship between improvements in technology and the growth of international terrorism. Many observers believe it is only a matter of time before a terrorist group obtains weapons of mass destruction, if they have the wish and strong determination to do so. However, terrorists are often more interested in drawing attention to their cause than in the mass destruction of life for its own sake, without reference to geography or nationality. Some terrorists can be driven to radical innovation by continuing failure to achieve success by previous methods.

Restraint by terrorists in their use of violence can be broken down as a result of a cumulative series of random events, or by a deep yearning by terrorist leaders to pursue uncontrolled escalation of the struggle. In the post-colonial era, it has proved impossible for states to pursue policies that can remove many of the conditions and the grievances, real or imagined, that motivate terrorists. It is inevitable that terrorism will grow in conditions in which many governments face increasing difficulty in governing effectively with broad consent.

States have many options open to them in combatting terrorism, but most individual sovereign states show no signs of being able to put an end to the growth of terrorism in its present form. This is because they are fighting in varying degrees a losing battle against the disenchantment of their exceedingly restless citizens.

The line separating wars between states and conflicts between sub-national actors is hard to determine. State-sponsored terrorism can increase without becoming widespread. State-sponsored groups are unlikely to wish to threaten the use of weapons of mass destruction at any early date, and most non-sponsored groups have difficulties in doing so. Most sovereign states do not feel sufficiently threatened to sacrifice their narrow interests for the collective good. Ad hoc deals in international agreements to cover events such as hijacking may be attainable. Some sovereign states will sponsor terrorist groups, but there are limits beyond which states find it imprudent to allow their friends to go. Sponsorship, in this context, will mainly originate in Third World countries. Ingenuity and sophistication are the hallmarks of future political sub-state violence.

Political terrorism Political terrorism is generally defined as the systematic use or threat of violence to secure political goals. It is a sustained policy involving the waging of organised terror either on the part of the state, a movement or faction, or by a small group of individuals. It is different from political terror, which occurs in isolated acts and also in the form of extreme, indiscriminate and arbitrary mass violence. Such terror is neither systematic nor organised and is often difficult to control.

Political terrorism can be divided into three types: revolutionary terror, sub-revolutionary terror and repressive terror.

Revolutionary terror can be defined as the use of systematic tactics of terrorist violence with the objective of bringing about political revolution. It has four main attributes: firstly, it is always conducted by a group, and is not an individual phenomenon, even though groups may be very small; secondly, both the revolution and the use of terror to promote it are always justified by some revolutionary ideology or programme; thirdly, there exist leaders capable of mobilising people for terrorism; fourthly, alternative institutional structures are created because a revolutionary movement must change the political system and therefore must develop its own policy-making bodies and codification of behaviour.

Revolutionary terror's four other essential properties are that it is part of a revolutionary strategy, it is manifested in acts of socially and politically unacceptable violence, there is a pattern of symbolic or representative selection of the victims or objects of acts of terrorism, and the revolutionary movement deliberately intends these actions to create a psychological effect on specific groups and thereby to change their political behaviour and attitudes.

Seven sub-types of revolutionary terror exist – organisations of pure terror, in which terror is the exclusive weapon; revolutionary and national liberationist parties and movements in which terror is employed as an auxiliary weapon; guerrilla terrorism – rural and urban; insurrectionary terrorism – short-term terrorism in the course of a revolutionary rising; the revolutionary Reign of Terror; propaganda of the deed, when this form of terror is motivated by long-term revolutionary objectives; and international terrorism motivated by revolutionary objectives.

Sub-revolutionary terrorism is terror used for political motives other than revolution or government repression. Whereas revolutionary terrorism seeks total change, sub-revolutionary terrorism is aimed at more limited goals such as forcing the government to change its policy on some issue, warning or punishing specific public officials, or retaliating against government actions seen as reprehensible by the terrorists.

Repressive terrorism is the systematic use of terroristic acts of violence for the purpose of suppressing, putting down, quelling or restraining certain groups, individuals, or forms of behaviour deemed to be undesirable by the oppressor. Repressive terror relies heavily on the services of specialised agencies whose members are trained to torture, murder, deceive, etc. The terror apparatus is deployed against specific opposition groups. However, it frequently is later directed against much wider groups, for example ethnic or religious minorities.

Political terrorism is thus the systematic use of murder and destruction, and the threat of murder and destruction, in order to terrorise individuals, groups, communities or governments into conceding to the terrorists' political demands. Terror is often employed within the political context and this makes it different from some other violent acts.

See also **Terror in the theory of revolution, Terrorism and terror**

Political violence Political violence is either the deliberate infliction or threat of infliction of physical injury or damage for political ends, or it is violence which occurs unintentionally in the course of severe political conflicts. Political violence is particularly difficult to classify and analyse because it frequently involves the interaction and effects of the actions of many persons and collectives, with widely different motivations and attitudes. Most political violence serves both instrumental and expressive functions simultaneously. Almost invariably, the 'price' of relaying a message of terror to a 'target audience' is the death, injury or dispossession of victims whose rights and liberties have been arbitrarily curtailed by the perpetrators of violence.

Two general characteristics of violence render it a peculiarly dangerous disease for a political community and one which is especially difficult to cure. It is difficult for its promoters and perpetrators to control. Many of the immediate physical effects of political violence – death, maiming, destruction – are irreversible and cannot be atoned for. Compromise or reconciliation, the cement of normal politics, become less and less attainable the longer political violence continues.

Political violence is often measured by its scale and intensity. By scale is meant the total numbers of persons involved, the physical extent of their area of operation, the political stakes involved in the conflict and the significance of the level of violence in the international system. Major indicators of its intensity would be the duration of the violence, the number of casualties caused and the amount of firepower and weaponry employed. Most violent states, movements or groups employ violence simultaneously at several different levels for their political ends. For example, terrorist violence is a thread running through modern war, revolution and internal political struggles in the contemporary history of many countries. And in many regimes concurrent traditions of *intercommunal* (defence or furtherance of alleged group interests in conflicts with rival ethnic or religious groups); *remonstrative* (expression of anger and protest which can be used to persuade government to remedy grievances); *praetorian* (used to coerce changes in government leadership and policy), and *repressive* (quelling actual or potential opposition and dissent) violence have wrought endemic instability. The most serious threats of violence facing liberal states internally are those which directly endanger the survival and stability of the liberal constitution itself, and those which indirectly and cumulatively undermine the state's authority and support through major defiance of law and order, and by endangering the lives of citizens to the point where confidence in the authorities is eroded. In reasonably secure and well-established liberal democracies these really dangerous levels of internal political violence are likely to occur only if there is mass disaffection among large sectors of the population, combined with large-scale popular support for a resort to violence in defiance of the state.

Some of the most frequent contributory causes of internal political violence constantly recurring in the recorded history of political conflict include ethnic conflicts, hatreds, discrimination and oppression; religious and ideological conflicts, hatreds, discrimination and oppression; perceived political inequalities, infringements of rights, injustice or oppression; lack of adequate channels for peaceful communication of protests or grievances and demands; the existence of a tradition of violence, disaffection, or popular turbulence; the availability of revolutionary leadership equipped with a potentially attractive ideology; weakness and ineptness of the government, police and judicial groups; erosion of confidence in the regime, its values and institutions afflicting all levels of the population including the government, and deep divisions within governing élites and leadership groups.

In strict terms, where a majority is subjected to tyrannical or despotic rule by a minority, the minority is imposing its sovereignty by violence and therefore can be legitimately opposed by force of just rebellion or resistance by the majority. By definition such a purely coercive regime cannot be a lawful democratic state and therefore majority opposition to it cannot be regarded as seditious or violent according to liberal democratic principles. In two situations a prima-facie case can be made for a morally justifiable resort to political violence by a minority within a liberal democratic state. There is the situation of the minority whose basic rights and liberties are denied or taken away by arbitrary action of the government or its agencies. The second situation arises when one minority is attacked by another minority and does not receive adequate protection from the state and its forces of law and order. In such circumstances the attacked minority community may have little alternative but to resort to violence in order to defend itself. If violence becomes the accepted or normal means for groups to gain political objectives within a state, one can say goodbye to liberal democracy.

Many variables exist in the study of political violence. Scale is of primary consideration – at first sight this may not appear to be a variable in itself, but any particular set of events being studied will need to be placed on a scale relative to previous acts of political violence. The number of people and the size of the group behind the violence is important whether it be an individual, small group, members of a social class, an institution, domestic state, foreign state, or group of states. The power and legitimacy of the individual or group have to be borne in mind. Targets of violence can vary from a person, object or symbol, to a foreign state or a group of states. A variety of means can be used; the threat or use of loud noise, fists, sticks, molotov cocktails, rifles, bombs, the deprivation of freedom of movement, direct injury or killing. Intentions can be wide-ranging – to gain publicity, deter attack, prevent an action, physically destroy a symbol (either person or object), change the policy of the institution or government, replace government personnel, change the social, economic or political system, or destroy the state and cause international war. The effect can be on spectators, targets, opponents, the domestic and international system. Time scale can vary; incidents may be single, sporadic, frequent or continuous. Political violence can reflect precedents which are historical or contemporary, or it can take a new direction. The cost depends on the economics of damage – this is not central to typologising but is an important measurement of scale from the point of view of perpetration and target. The state and security forces can often respond by illegal or legal means, changes in law, detention, death penalties and genocide. Nevertheless, the respondent to violence may be another group in society, especially if they are the target, or feel threatened. Similarly, if the perpetrator of political violence is the state, the respondents may be various groups within society, who can emigrate, riot, or plant bombs.

Types of scenarios can be 'group against group', i.e. usually a right-wing group trying to destroy a left-wing group which is threatening to become successful, e.g. anti-ETA groups and the death squads of South America. Groups can be opposed to a social category. If that category is ethnic or religious then opposition will usually be from a right-wing ideological minority group: as in the case of FANE, or the Horst Wessel Sporting Commando. If the social category is specified as 'the rich' or 'foreign imperialists' the source is likely to be a left-wing ideological minority group, although right-wing groups have attacked such categories. If both the group and the social category are primarily religious in affiliation, then often a fanatical level of violence can arise. A group can be opposed to the establishment and usually violence by pressure groups can get an institution to change its policies. This is often the early stage of a pattern that develops into a challenge to governments, e.g. Italian Marxists in Milan and Turin demanding a better hearing for their grievances, soon developed their arguments into violent attacks against the Fiat car company and its executives. A group can be opposed to the city environment. The test is which of the opposing groups can survive longest. If violence is sporadic, an ideological minority will eventually concentrate its efforts on an institution, as have the Montoneros, ERP and Tupamaros. Lastly, groups can be against a foreign state, e.g. exiles and exiles' auxiliaries, or the Angry Brigade in England; or against a group of states, such as internationalists in their attacks on NATO.

There are numerous scenarios for the origin of violent groups, which have developed over the past fifteen years. Violent groups can emerge from a previously unopposed campaign of government violence, or violence by another organised group or community. The USA government in the 1960s responded to civil rights marches with violence; from this developed the black city riots of the 1960s, and the 1968 Democratic Convention violence from which emerged the Black Panthers and Weathermen. At the same period in Northern Ireland, from the NICRA marches and Protestant violence, the Ulster Defence Association, Ulster Defence Force and Provisional IRA emerged. There are also scenarios where small, violent groups, such as the Animal Liberation Front, have emerged from a single-issue campaign without being provoked by a violent response by anybody.

Secondly, there can be the appearance or reappearance of a group attracted to a cultural, religious or ethnic minority, demanding independence, autonomy, respect for religious practices or simply to be allowed to indulge in activities declared illegal by the state, e.g. ETA, the Corsicans and the Shi'ites. New patterns of behaviour have emerged with Islamic fundamentalism.

Auxiliary groups have been created by exile movements such as the Palestinians.

The appearance of the urban guerrilla has led to a new set of tactics being adopted by already existing groups, who wish to change the nature of various regimes in Latin America or in response to a takeover of a regime by military coup. This is a genuinely revolutionary scenario and involves professional revolutionaries, e.g. the Montoneros and Tupamaros. Some groups are facing military regimes and responding to violence by those regimes, and others are facing regimes which are democratic but corrupt.

Groups have appeared in response to immigration of new ethnic groups, usually with anti-Semitic overtones, e.g. FANE and Column 88 in France.

Both right- and left-wing organisations have appeared to counter changes of government seen as resulting in a revolutionary path, or to challenge a government imposed by conquest, e.g. the Mujaheddin in Afghanistan.

More recently groups have been formed to settle scores with the opponents of particular regimes, particularly within the Palestinian movement, or at the behest of the Iranian and Libyan regimes.

Traditional anti-colonial scenarios are numerous; because of the defeat of the occupying power or examples of liberation close at hand, a population would often take to violence after years of subservience.

Finally, groups may be formed in attempts to create continent-wide insurrection, like Action Directe.

Once a group exists, possible scenarios of development can occur.

Firstly, splitting is the most frequent cause of development in a group, arising from the perception by some of its members that violence has become counter-productive. Violence has successfully publicised the cause, but it is now time to adopt peaceful tactics. Foreign sponsors may make unreasonable demands – the Sino-Soviet split led to the appearance of Maoists. Similar splits among state supporters of the Palestinian cause have produced similar effects in the movement. There can be genuine ideological differences of emphasis, e.g. among the IRA, Basques and Palestinians. Right-wing groups can split around individuals, new factions can take members away with them, and regional splitting can develop.

A second means of development is amalgamation – where groups may begin operating in restricted geographical areas, as in Italy, and later amalgamate, even with groups on other continents. Some groups may dwindle numerically to the point where they have to join other groups to continue operating.

Thirdly, there is the 'generational' change. Many European groups began with symbolic attacks on property, and the first generation leadership was older and more idealistic than its successors. It was more sophisticated about its use of violence and when this could be counterproductive. The arrest of the first generation results in the leadership passing to a more hard-nosed group that favours hijacking and kidnapping. In turn, a third generation arises that is much more cold-blooded, and engaged in more killing – this can result from a perception by activists, as in Italy, that the government responds more to kidnapping and killing than to symbolic bombing.

Turning to exile as a source of violent action, the Jews were themselves the first exiles who used violence to try to return home. In the process they in turn have exiled the Palestinians. Exile groups have frequently become mercenaries – either for other groups or for governments who wish to cause problems for other groups. As a result, they frequently split.

Where there is a double minority, the demands made by one group or social category threaten the position of another group – especially where religion or race are the root of their disagreement. Violence can frequently be used by one minority to pre-empt or discredit a relatively peaceful campaign of protest. It then produces counter-violence from small groups that emerge from the peaceful campaign, who may also use violence against the government and security forces.

With reference to the development of urban guerrilla groups, many groups have taken this route, but without the success that their rural or colonial counterparts have achieved. None has moved successfully from pinprick attacks to the use of large units. Towns and provinces have been overrun for short periods, but only in Nicaragua has there been any lasting success.

There are five main scenarios of group collapse. There may be total victory, in which the terrorists become the government and the armed forces – as in rural anti-colonial sectors; partial victory, where the government makes sufficient concessions to split the insurgents; partial defeat: the government makes sufficient concessions to satisfy the insurgents' constituency, but not the insurgents themselves, and the insurgency collapses as the insurgents are killed or captured one by one. In a situation of total defeat, there are no concessions and potential support can be alienated by the violence. Finally, the government may respond with state terror – arbitrary violence, which terrorises the population into submission. Loss of foreign sponsorship can mean that with no easy source of money or weapons the group will move back to logistical operations and lose the initiative. Scenarios also occur where the state sets out to wear down the insurgents and new issues arise to arouse the popular imagination. Most of the campaigns of political violence that began twenty years ago continue today. The US Weathermen, Tupamaros and Montoneros are the most notable casualties. European, African, Asian and Central American campaigns have proved more durable.

Popular Front for the Liberation of Oman (PFLO) The PFLO had its origins in the Popular Front for the Liberation of the Occupied Arabian Gulf, formed with the object of overthrowing the Sultan of Oman and also other 'conservative' regimes in the Gulf area.

In 1972 it merged with the National Democratic Front for the Liberation of the Occupied Arabian Gulf to form the Popular Front for the Liberation of Oman and the Arab Gulf (PFLOAG). In its activities it had the support of the People's Democratic Republic of Yemen (South Yemen), from whose territory it conducted most of its operations, and also of China and later of the Soviet Union.

In 1974 it changed its name to the Popular Front for the Liberation of Oman, thus indicating that it was to be a national liberation movement fighting against British and Iranian 'occupation armies' in Oman, and not a revolutionary organisation trying to overthrow governments in the Gulf area. A ceasefire between Oman and South Yemen negotiated by Saudi Arabia came into force in March 1976, when the Sultan offered an amnesty to all Omani rebels. Although a number surrendered, a hard core of PFLO members continued their fighting inside Dhofar province (Western Oman), but there were only sporadic clashes until 1979, when new PFLO attacks were reported. Surrenders of leading PFLO members to the Omani authorities continued to be announced from time to time.

A delegation of the PFLO was present at a summit meeting in Aden in 1981 attended by the leaders of Ethiopia, Libya and South Yemen, who agreed to conclude a trilateral treaty of friendship and co-operation providing for closer political and economic co-ordination between their governments. In 1982, Oman and South Yemen agreed to normalise relations, and in early 1983 the Omani government proclaimed a further amnesty for all Omani citizens still in South Yemen.

Process of terrorism A comprehensive awareness of the process of terrorism can be obtained by consideration of the following:
- the types of participants engaged in the terroristic process as precipitators, instrumental targets, primary targets and spillover victims;
- the objectives of the participants and other relevant identifications, demands, and expectations;
- the situations of actual interaction;
- the types of resources at the disposal of each type of participant, including analysis of their value positions;
- the particular tactics or strategies of terror utilised;
- the outcomes of the terroristic process;
- the effects of the terrorism process upon the effectiveness of all relevant legal policies;
- such policies can be overtly generalised in terms of world public

order values and those of human dignity, as has been recognised in the UN Charter and elsewhere.

Terrorism is viewed as a form of violent strategy, a form of coercion used to alter the freedom of choice of others.

There must be a terror outcome, or the process could hardly be labelled as terrorism. There are fine lines for judicial distinction to be made between fear and intense fear outcomes, although in many cases the type of strategy could well be prohibited under different normative provisions of the law of war. Terrorism can be precipitated by governments, groups or individuals. The law of war already makes no distinction between single or systematic terrorist processes, governmental or non-governmental whether or not these are precipitated by the government, and whether government or non-government targets are chosen.

See also **Law and terrorism**

Propaganda Propaganda can be defined as any information, ideas, doctrines or special appeals disseminated to influence the opinion, emotions, attitudes or behaviour of any specified group in order to benefit the sponsor either directly or indirectly.

Propaganda and terrorism are identical insofar as they both seek to influence a mass audience in a way that is intended to benefit the sponsor. Terror's aim is to induce fear and uncertainty, while propaganda can and does serve every imaginable purpose from religion to politics and commerce. Terror might be seen as a sub-species of propaganda. The political objectives of propaganda can only be reached by a complex psychological-military process in which propaganda and violence play a key role. Successful terrorism depends on effective propaganda about terrorist operations. The true revolutionary believes that crimes committed for the cause are just and argues that he or she is answerable only to the revolutionary leadership, or to some higher authority such as God or history. The dissemination of revolutionary propaganda requires a circle of true believers with the object being one of total, unquestioning loyalty. This creates a need for totalitarian state propaganda, which can only exist within a tightly disciplined organisation.

Although terrorists regard the regime, its institutions, and its agents as evil enemies to be destroyed without mercy, they see the general public as an audience whose allegiance is required. The purpose of all revolutionary activity is conversion. Elimination is reserved for symbolic or vengeance targets, those who threaten the movement, and those who refuse conversion. True believers, who are in fact dedicated to extreme objectives are seen and heard by the public arguing for reasonable objectives within the existing norms. Their real agenda is hidden behind tactical reasonableness. Over many terrorists' campaigns this century, some consistent attitudes to the public have emerged.

Terrorists blame the consequences of all violence on the regime they are opposing. All that the police and military do is presented in the worst possible light, and casualties are made into martyrs. Terrorist violence is often blamed on the authorities too, as in El Salvador. Terrorists also use the ploy that the violence they use is a reluctant but inevitable response to violence by the state.

The term 'long war' is used frequently, as a terror campaign is often seen as a full-scale revolution with victory ultimately assured. For the regime to win, the authorities have to eliminate every last terrorist and extinguish the cultural and spiritual inspiration. This is often an impossible demand. The IRA and Latin American terrorists, particularly the Shining Path in Peru, have used this technique.

Spurious arguments are used to protect terrorists from the full force of public wrath. Murder is justified by reference to injustices, e.g. the Iranians speak of a war by the impoverished and deprived against the United States, Israel and all enemies of Islam. Television appearances by terrorist leaders and spokesmen provide occasions for justification; and Yassir Arafat justified the role of Palestinians in the terrorist field when he addressed the United Nations in 1974.

Terrorists can also aim to discredit and destroy any method, individual, police or military unit, weapon or policy that, because of its potential effectiveness, threatens the terrorist's integrity and freedom of action. The case for disarmament is argued in terms of conventional morality, and, for example, terrorists can infiltrate innocent pressure groups and bury demands of operational importance within a programme of reforms assembled in good faith by concerned citizens.

Whether terror is itself a theme in propaganda is hard to measure, because propaganda is slow and unacknowledged. Journalists who decide to report from direct contact with terrorist groups have no alternative in this dangerous situation but to bias their reporting, e.g. Western journalists in the Lebanon. Terror isolates the police and other security force members because the judiciary, bureaucracy and general public fear to commit themselves to the fight. Violent campaigns hope to deflect government responses until it is too late to reverse the shift of popular allegiance from regime to terrorist. Terrorist campaigns never seem to fail – for their whole reason for existing seems not to be for the solution of a social problem to be bound up in the struggle, which becomes an end in itself.

If terrorists promote a 'just cause', this can help in the recruitment of alienated youth, the creation of networks of survival in urban environments and opportunities for exploiting the weaknesses, divisions and confusions already present in NATO. Anti-NATO terrorists could tempt mainstream peace movements into a supportive or at least ambivalent position in relation to terrorism.

With regard to counter-propaganda against the terrorists and the possible infusion of a psychological component – this can fail under the weight of public opinion being uneasy at any form of propaganda. If the subject were handled effectively, then an informed public might agree that in a choice of evils terrorism was worse than government publicity to help control it. Counter-propaganda has to work within the accepted norms of publicity or public relations. To a large extent government contact with the public on terrorism issues is through the media. Media coverage of terrorism can be closely linked to propaganda. Terrorism directed at the democracies is a direct attack on democracy itself, because by its very nature it proclaims that elected governments and their laws are subordinate to demands backed by violence or the threat of violence. The West perhaps has an ambivalent attitude towards terrorism. Moulded by Soviet propaganda, the West now seems generally to believe that the use of force and of deliberate counter-propaganda to defend democracy is illegitimate in the wake of the inevitable victory by 'progressive' forces.

See also **Media and terrorism**

Psychological theories Many theories regard the terrorist as a peculiar personality with clearly identifiable character traits. A cross-section of rural and urban terrorist guerrilla groups shows that they are composed largely of single men aged 22 to 24 who have some university education. The women terrorists, except for those in the Baader Meinhof and Red Army Faction in West Germany, and an occasional leading figure in the Irish Republican Army, Japanese Red Army and Popular Front for the Liberation of Palestine, are preoccupied with support rather than operational roles. Terrorists come in general from affluent, urban, middle-class families, many of whom enjoy considerable social prestige. Like their fathers, many of the older terrorists have been trained for the professions and may have practised these occupations before their commitment to a terrorist life. Whether they turned to terrorism as university students or later, most were provided with an anarchistic or Marxist world view and recruited into terrorist operations while at university.

A terrorist is a person engaged in politics who makes little distinction or differentiation between tactics and strategy on the one hand and principles on the other. Terrorists possess a self-fulfilling image of their own role in life, and plan with varying degrees of success their actions involving murder, destruction and other activities against society. They are always 'death-seekers', and generally take part in killing from patricidal impulses, directed against anyone in authority. Terrorists believe that the act of violence will encourage the uncommitted public to withdraw support from a regime or institution and make wider revolutionary acts possible by weakening the resolve of the opposition. Terrorists can direct their activities against the leadership of the opposition or against the symbols and agencies of the establishment.

Many terrorists are zealots who seek aggressive confrontations with authority in the name of the social justice. Over the last two decades three character traits have become apparent: terrorists' handling of their own emotions is disturbed, which shows itself in fear to engage in real commitments. Fear of love leads them to choose violence. Attitude towards authority is disturbed and ambivalent, in the sense that a principally negative attitude to traditional authorities is combined with an uncritical subjection under the new counter-authorities. Most importantly, they have a disturbed relationship with their own identity; and having failed to develop an identity of their own they try to achieve this by the use of violence.

They are unable to be part of the community, lose the capacity to understand reality and experience an aimlessness due to lack of felt authority. To be effective they have to pursue absolute ends, which coalesce into violence.

Driving forces behind terrorism include the assertion of masculinity, or femininity in the case of women; the desire for depersonalisation, that is to get outside or away from oneself, as a result of a chronic lack of self-esteem; the desire for intimacy, and belief in the magic of violence and blood. Terrorists tend to resemble each other, regardless of their cause. Most are individuals for whom terrorism provides profound personal satisfaction, a sense of fulfilment through total dedication to the point of self sacrifice; and a sense of power through inflicting pain and death upon other humans. Insecurity, risk-seeking behaviour and its associated suicidal intentions are present in varying mixtures in the terrorist. Out of this insecurity, the need for self-realisation and ego inflation arises.

The use of the term 'identification' in terrorism is generally confined to the identification with the aggressor which manifests itself in the positive attitude some hostages show to their captors (as in 'Stockholm syndrome'). The tremendous public interest in acts of hostage-taking seems to be because most members of the audience identify with the fate of the victim, sharing his suffering in an act of empathy. Not all members of an audience will automatically show compassion for the victim. Some will identify with the terrorist because he represents the awesome power of one who can destroy life at his whim. If the victim is guilty in the eyes of the spectator he may derive pleasure from humiliation and suffering. Depending on the identification, with victim or terrorist, the spectator's attitude may be either empathy or cruelty. The direction of the identification can be determined by factors like class, race, nationality and party. The process of taking sides whenever a polarising act occurs stirs some members of the passive audience so deeply that they emerge as actors of their own, engaging in new polarising acts.

The switch from love for mankind to destruction of human beings is easier for young people, who may find it hard to identify with the older generation or with their nation. Identification, which enables one to empathise with others, is capable of leading to wide-ranging emotions – to anger and aggressiveness towards the source of the misery of the person or group for whom one has love and compassion. The strategy of terrorism of an insurgent nature is to bring about identification processes. In many cases terrorists attack the targets with which people consciously identify. The terrorist in this context uses the identification mechanism to bring home the terror to a target group by stimulating the identification between the instrumental victim and the victims' reference group.

See also **Personalities of revolutionaries, Targets, Terrorist beliefs, Terrorist mindset**

Q

Quebec separatists French-Canadians clinging to their language and way of life have long resented what they see as English-speaking dominance, including that of the Anglo-Scottish business community. French pressures for independence led in the late 1960s to a campaign of violence and the use of troops to try to maintain law and order.

The Québécois have strong economic grievances. Canada has a record of high unemployment, particularly in Quebec – which has never enjoyed full employment. The average income of the French speaking worker in Quebec is 40 per cent lower than that of his English-speaking counterpart. Resentment at the high stake of American investment in Canada is felt because of linguistic reasons. The Canadian civil service is also predominantly English-speaking. A further source of contention, always endemic in a federal system, is the relationship of the provincial assemblies to the central body, again accentuated by the language problem. Rather like the Scottish nationalists, the Québécois feel that they contribute more to the central government than they receive in benefits.

After the war, separatist movements grew. A royal commission on bilingualism and bi-culturalism was set up in 1964; a year later the Communist Party of Quebec was formed; and in 1967 Rene Levesque left the Liberal Party and formed the Mouvement Souveraineté Association (MSA), which allied itself with the Ralliement Nationale (RN) in a common objective – the creation of a separate sovereign state, corporate in structure, with the recognition of equal rights for all minority groups. The two parties merged in 1967 to form the Parti Québécois (PQ) under the presidency of Levesque. General de Gaulle added fuel to the fires of separatism by proclaiming in 1967 in Quebec province, 'Vive le Québec, Vive le Québec Libre! Vive le Canada Français!'. The PQ held high popularity with the electorate and this was in evidence at the provincial elections in 1970, where they took a quarter of the vote.

The Front de Libération du Québec (FLQ) formed in 1963, came to prominence in 1973. They believed that the limits of open struggle were to be pushed as far as possible if necessary in massive militant demonstrations that would help to develop a crisis atmosphere. This was to be reinforced by forcing governments into unpopular repressive measures, thus pushing Quebec into increasing conflict with the Federal Government. Once this framework had been established, some grave crisis was to act as a catalyst to begin the power-struggle, such as a serious problem with the economy. The FLQ leaders were disparate in origin and background and this was reflected in the character of the FLQ and its allied organisations – loosely organised, cellular and clandestine. While the leaders were at one in their desire to create maximum disorder, their methods differed and they seem to have exercised little control over their own followers, in contrast with many other terrorist organisations. Infiltration was a principal tactic, and the group indulged in systematic violence, and robbery. The revolution moved into the streets and the bombing continued. Disorder, riots and constant protests were organised – the latter not helped by the Montreal police strike in October 1969.

In October 1970, the British Trade Commissioner James Cross was kidnapped. A communiqué from the kidnappers demanded the release of 23 FLQ prisoners, and their passage to Cuba or Algeria, a large sum in ransom, identification of the informer who led the police to another cell in the organisation, publication of their manifesto and the cessation of police activity relating to the kidnapping. The Federal Government decided to meet one of the kidnappers' demands and broadcast the manifesto. A few days later the government agreed to provide safe passage for the kidnappers to a foreign country and clemency for the 23 prisoners if the victim were released. The other demands were refused.

A separate cell of the FLQ acting on its own initiative then kidnapped Pierre Laporte, the Quebec Transport Minister, and reiterated the original demands in full. Political confusion developed – some denounced the deeds, and others believed the kidnappers should be dealt with by the Quebec administration and accused the Federal Government of nullifying provincial authority. The Federal Government then invoked the War Measures Act, outlawing the FLQ and similar organisations and providing the police with powers to search without warrant – over 200 arrests were made. As a result Pierre Laporte was murdered by the FLQ. Later, with Cuban help, an aircraft was made available for the kidnappers in return for the release of Cross. The terrorists duly left for Cuba, but were liable to arrest if they ever returned to Canada.

The separatist groups were not eliminated. Unpopular and repressive measures initiated by both the Federal and provincial governments exacerbated rather than healed the situation.

In the 1970s, thanks to the success of the reformed PQ and the suppression of the FLQ, nationalism took priority in Québécois politics, but social radicals remained a strong and influential minority in Quebec's ruling party.

In November 1976 a separatist Parti Québécois government was elected in Quebec, which provoked a flurry of world interest and speculation. In a way this was the culmination of the 'Quiet Revolution' which had stimulated a steady change in the social, economic and political aspirations of Francophone Quebec, a change which had found radical expression not only in the terrorist campaign of the FLQ but also in a variety of political movements devoted to national and social revolution.

Nevertheless, a downturn in fortunes did occur. The PQ's commitment to a referendum on the constitutional future of the province was fulfilled in May 1980. Levesque asked for a mandate to negotiate his own proposals for sovereignty for Quebec – political separation from, but economic association with, the rest of Canada. The mandate was refused by a sizeable majority.

Québécois are having doubts about independence – voters are concerned with jobs and economic issues and they need much persuading to see if an independent Quebec can offer them a secure future. The need for new investment capital has obliged the PQ government to take a more conciliatory attitude towards foreign and especially United States businesses. The position of the Québécois has improved – no longer is there Anglophone domination and the striking gap between the two linguistic groups has narrowed. The overall trend in Quebec in the mid 1980s seems to be away from separatism.

R

Rebellion Rebellion can be considered as open resistance to the authority and commands of a ruler or government. It can take the form of civil war or revolution if it persists or grows. There is violent opposition by a substantial body of persons against the lawfully constituted authority of a state, in the attempt to overthrow it. A rebellion can succeed in installing in power members of the same class as those whom they replace.

Red Army Faction (RAF) German terrorism consisted of two main centres of activity: the Second of June Movement, and Revolutionary Cells (RZ). At the beginning of 1980 the Second of June Movement abandoned the 'armed struggle', and the RAF took over its remaining cells later that year.

The RAF, also known as the Baader-Meinhof Gang, is the oldest and most brutal of the terrorist organisations in Germany. It was born with the violent release of Andreas Baader from prison on 14 May 1970 by a gang led by Ulrike Meinhof and Horst Mahler.

Immediately a strategy of armed anti-imperialistic struggle was developed, aiming at destroying the 'imperialistic feudal' system, politically, economically and militarily. International action is being taken against NATO forces and at a national level the struggle is conducted against the armed forces of the state apparatus which represents the monopoly of power of the ruling class, that is the police, the Federal frontier police and the security services. The group is also opposed to the power structure of the multinational organisations, e.g. state and non-state bureaucracies, the parties, trades unions and the media. There is an overriding element of 'anti-US imperialism'.

In 1974 and 1975 follow-up groups were formed to obtain the release of their prisoners. In April 1975 the German embassy in Stockholm was attacked, during which two officials, the military attaché and the commercial attaché were shot dead. By way of these murders the terrorists were pressing for the release of the Red Army Faction prisoners. A further follow-up group was formed in 1976, and at the end of the year two lawyers, including the leader of this group, Siegfried Haag, were arrested. 1977 saw the zenith of their activity to date, which included the murder of the Attorney-General Siegfried Buback and his guards, and of police officers and customs officials; the kidnapping of Hans Martin Schleyer and the murder of his three guards and driver, and later of Schleyer himself; and the events at Majorca and Mogadishu, namely the hijacking by Palestinian terrorists of the Lufthansa plane with 91 hostages, and the murder of the pilot Jürgen Schumann. 19 terrorists, ten of them women, were sought in connection with these crimes.

The RAF was able to carry out its armed struggle even after the arrest of its most important members. They could rely on a circle of supporters who kept up the link between the arrested terrorists and the 'operational' ones. Several lawyers had an essential function for these links. They also succeeded in recruiting new, young lawyers for their cause. The RAF, with the help of supporting groups, succeeded in developing propaganda actions designed to portray West Germany as a fascist state and to justify the aims of the terrorists. In the view of the RAF terrorist, violence is always 'propaganda of the deed'. This propaganda by terrorist activities was and still is aimed above all at German students.

Currently, the RAF consists of a hard core of 'commandos', a 'legitimate' fringe and 36 terrorists in custody. The fringe amounts, as in the past, to about 200 people, and the hard core is a 'commando' of about 15 people. Inge Viett and Henning Beer are the only remnants of the RAF of the 1970s. Other members joined the 'commando' recently, coming from the 'legitimate fringe' of the supporters. Four women have left the RAF and joined Middle Eastern terrorist organisations. Setbacks for the RAF have not hamstrung it, and after failing to create a 'revolutionary situation' they have limited themselves to for example, operations against key NATO establishments, and to killing key military personnel, such as Herr Zimmerman and the head of Siemens, both of whom were involved in close economic links with the West German military.

On 15 January 1985 the RAF and the French Action Directe issued a joint statement announcing the formation of a united front to combat NATO imperialism.

See also **Action Directe, Mogadishu hijack, Schleyer, Western Europe**

Red Brigades (Brigate Rosse) This organisation of Marxist-Leninist urban guerrillas was established in 1969, initially to attack industrialists, the 'enemy of the working class'. It was particularly active in the industrial centres of Northern Italy, where kidnapping operations were a regular occurrence, in order to achieve large-scale ransom payments. For the past decade the group has operated in most parts of the country, intimidating, wounding or murdering. The Brigades have always hoped to create a situation in which a fascist coup could be provoked, leading to a return of the Communist Party of Italy to a revolutionary role which the Party had abandoned by co-operation with the government.

The Brigades compare their activity to the work of the Provisional IRA; the Red Army Faction (Baader Meinhof Group) in West Germany and the Palestine Liberation Organisation. In 1981 these links were borne out in the call for a creation of a terrorist international in which the central role would be played by the Brigades and the Red Army Faction, and the support roles could be undertaken by the European revolutionary forces of ETA in Spain and of the IRA, once they had abandoned nationalism.

After two or three years of increasingly violent acts, police arrested Renato Curcio and Alberto Franceschini, the chief ideologues of the Brigades. Both were given prison sentences; Curcio was then sprung from jail, rearrested and returned to jail, despite threats of further activity by the terrorists if Curcio was put in jail. The trial was suspended.

The greatest success for the Red Brigades was in March 1978, when members seized Aldo Moro, the President of the Christian Democratic Party, who had been Prime Minister on a number of occasions between 1963 and 1976. He was threatened with trial by a people's court, and the release of certain detainees was demanded as the price of freeing their hostage. No concessions were made by the Government, and in April the Brigades declared that Moro had been found guilty, and the death sentence passed on him at the 'people's court'. In May he was shot dead and his body dumped in the boot of a car in the centre of Rome. Within weeks nine terrorists were arrested and charged with complicity in the murder.

Meanwhile, the trial of Curcio continued and in June he was sentenced to 15 years in prison for forming an armed group to subvert the state and for carrying out political kidnappings. In February 1979 he was given a further 12-year prison sentence for attempted murder and possession of arms, and a six-year sentence in November for his escape from prison in 1975, while nine other Brigades members were also sentenced to up to six years in prison for 'terrorist activities'. Finally, in October 1979 Curcio received a further ten-year sentence, and 13 other Brigades members were given up to ten years for insulting the judges and inciting Brigades followers to insurrection during the 1978 trial.

The killings and kidnappings continued, ranging from police, magistrates and directors to civil servants, councillors, journalists and armed services personnel. In this latter category was Brigadier-General James Dozier, a US Army staff officer and deputy commander of NATO land forces Southern Europe, who was abducted in Verona in December 1981. He was tried by a people's court, found guilty and threatened with death. However, in late January 1982 police acting on information received from a suspect, freed Dozier unhurt and arrested five Brigades members who were holding him in an apartment in Padua. The police action was the first occasion on which Italian police had succeeded in freeing a hostage seized by the Brigades. Later, the court passed prison sentences totalling over 300 years on the defendants. The aftermath of the Dozier kidnap produced considerable success for the security forces and many persons were arrested on terrorism charges from the Brigades and affiliated organisations. Many arms caches and safe houses also were found. Most of these terrorists realised that they had failed to attain their political aims. Indeed, some of the Dozier abductors issued an appeal to fellow members of the Brigades to give up the armed struggle, which they claimed had proved a failure over the previous decade. A bloodstained struggle could produce no change in the political programme.

By January 1983 the last of the Moro kidnappers was sentenced, and out of 63 defendants, life sentences were passed on 32 of them for 17 murders (including that of Moro), 11 attempted murders and four kidnappings during the years 1977 to 1980. Although the Brigades had in 1980 an estimated membership of about 500 activists, with a further 10,000 supporters, thereafter the active membership declined, principally because of the success of the security authorities in penetrating and neutralising the organisation's cells in different parts of the country.

Religious terrorism Some of today's terrorist groups can no longer specifically be considered as secular Marxist organisations with specific nationalist and socialist goals. While calling for socio-economic betterment for their people, their motivation is religious. Although their demands have a political content this is distinctly secondary. Violence in the name of religion has been used since Herod, but there has been a recent re-emergence of religious terrorism. The Inquisition and Protector (Oliver) Cromwell practised terror in the name of religion. In the West where religious faith has been diluted with materialism, the absolutionist sanction has largely been lost. This is not the case with certain third-world movements, for instance the radical Shi'ites. Specific historical events have led to the emergence of the new terrorists.

Iran's fundamentalist Shi'ite revolution is primary among these. Besides Iran, the Ayatollah's message inspires Shi'ite communities in Lebanon, Iraq and elsewhere in the Persian Gulf to lash out against the Western influences that permeate the regimes they perceive as corrupt and oppressive. Syria's quasi-Shi'ite Alawite rulers share a number of values, goals and tactical objectives with Iran.

The main goal of the radical Shi'ite factions in Lebanon is to undermine the relatively pragmatic leaders of Lebanon's Shi'ite community and pave the way for more radical, fundamentalist influence. Displaying the impotence of moderate policies, as compared with effective extremist activism is a means of accomplishing this. The position of Nabih Berri, as the moderate head of Lebanon's largest Shi'ite organisation remains uncertain.

Similar motivations lay behind the seizure of the US embassy in Teheran in 1979 by radical Shi'ites. In February they had toppled the relatively moderate Shah government which was then engaged in close political and economic contacts with the US.

Indian Sikh terrorism is also based on religion. The Sikhs are acting in reaction to Hindu repression of their aspirations for autonomy. The assassination of Indira Gandhi, subsequent Sikh-Hindu bloodshed, and threatened international terrorism, share some of the more extreme qualities associated with Shi'ite violence.

Violence motivated by religious beliefs is more difficult to cope with than its secular predecessors for several reasons. Threats to kill hostages are credible. For Islamic fundamentalists, killing of 'non-believers' is not perceived as murder. Threats of self-sacrifice are also believable for the same reason. Religious ideologies are also extremely tough for any intelligence organisation to penetrate. Powerful, absolutist convictions are a barrier to the recruiting of agents, even when access can be arranged, and the rudimentary forms of communication used by such groups are often among the most impregnable.

Retaliation to acts of religious terrorism is extremely difficult. A Libyan or Palestinian guerrilla base may be considered an easy and 'acceptable' target, but a Mosque complex or holy shrine would not. And as is the case in Beirut, virtually the entire community can be used to disperse and hide hostages.

Being based on community-wide conviction as opposed to that of a small, clandestine group, terrorists will be supported. If an event is played out on territory they control, as in Beirut, and earlier in Teheran, replacements and logistical support from local governments will not be forthcoming.

The more pragmatic a terrorist, the easier it is to negotiate a solution. At one extreme lie money-motivated kidnappings of businessmen in Latin America. A group of professionals has come into being, whose business it is to settle the level of nearly automatic ransoms in such cases. Most are now resolved in this manner. In the middle lie the politically-based demands of classic secular organisations that use violence as a tool. The new breed of extremists represents the opposite pole. Their demands are absolute, their hidden motivations obscure, their threshold of violence low.

In considering religious terrorism one has to ask whether the problems of the dark ages reappearing in the twentieth century can be dealt with by enlightened methods, or whether the West itself must revert to the toughest of measures in dealing with the phenomena.

See also **Islam, Messianic terror, Shi'ites, Sikh extremism**

Responses to terrorism When one speaks of the 'policy response' to terrorism, then one is thinking of a complex and broad set of challenges for the policymaker and for the country. Terrorism is but one feature of a much larger and more threatening pattern of low-level conflict. There are a number of measures which can be taken in response to terrorism: detecting, capturing and prosecuting terrorists; and avoiding terrorist acts by counter-measures such as physical security of facilities, personal security of targetted officials, and behaving in ways that make the person or place difficult to target. The costs of committing terrorism have to be seen to be high, and direct retaliation against the terrorist or terrorists must be undertaken, assuming one knows precisely who and where they are. Terrorists and would-be terrorists have to be persuaded to seek non-violent means to achieve their goals or redress their grievances; this is a tough aspect of terrorist incident management.

Working to mitigate the underlying causes of terrorism is hard. Where the issues concern social justice, lack of participation, lack of social or economic opportunity, or grievances of this type, the need and the opportunity exist to do something constructive about the complaints of people who would resort to terrorism. Much terrorist activity stems from actual or perceived problems of social justice. The practice of terrorism by states raises questions about when, where and how to use force, which are not necessarily raised by terrorist acts of small non-state groups or individuals.

Gaps exist in the laws of many Western nations – criminal statutes need updating; the law needs to influence activities like training and equipping terrorists abroad. Authority has to be used to pay rewards for information about international terrorist acts that might result in saving lives or obtaining release of hostages. Changes of national laws are needed in order to implement fully international agreements such as the Montreal Convention against aircraft sabotage, and the UN Convention against taking hostages.

In changing laws and practices to deal with terrorism, the West has to be seen not to damage institutions and must protect the rights of citizens. Response to the problem must not destroy the fabric of society.

International co-operation is good in some respects and poor in others. The Western democracies work well together, particularly within the framework of NATO or the Summit Seven, the so-called Bonn Declaration Group. Despite the growing pattern of terrorism which affects almost all countries, many have not seen the need actively to enter into either bilateral discussion of the issues or to take decisive stands in international forums. There is need with respect to the laws of many countries for greater concordance of laws on the prosecution, extradition and punishment of terrorist acts. The Western community is concerned that differences of law do not provide unintended safe haven.

Differences of views among states as to what is an act of terrorism can cause obvious problems. Some states want to exclude terrorism of the left. Some wish to make a specific exemption respecting wars of national liberation, which gives problems in contexts such as enforcement of the Helsinki Declaration. The West has always had a problem with the ambivalent terms of terrorism, and perhaps a lack of clarity as democrats as to what terrorism is and what its dangers are for the West. The public have a need of a better understanding of how serious is the new challenge posed by state sponsored terrorism.

The number of active terrorist groups, their target range, their capabilities, their causes and world events all change on a daily basis. World events very much influence terrorist activities. Through the media the coverage of terrorism is more extensive now than ever before in human history – more pervasive, more vivid, more emotional and more massively powerful in its impact on people and events. Mass communications have accelerated the post-war revolutionary tide by rapidly transferring information from one society to another. Total media silence will not stop the terrorist.

From the economic and business point of view there are some preventive measures to reduce the risks of terrorist attacks. Prevention can result from trying to prevent loss or injury to employees and other assets;

terrorist success can be limited by prior planning, and there needs to be communication with employees in the event of a serious problem. Multinational businesses have to find out about a country, its people and problems, whether it is already established there or is considering investment.

Any successful response for combatting terrorism requires the West to study intelligence capabilities, the conditions and limitations under which force will be employed in response to terrorism, and public attitudes to the problem.

See also **Western Europe**

Restraint Prevention and perspective are two keys to dealing with terrorism, including political kidnappings. A substantial degree of physical security ought to be provided for those who are at particular risk. Western nations have to build up security for their government officials overseas.

Meeting the legitimate aspirations of the world's downtrodden is an important means of long-range prevention, so that small groups do not become sufficiently frustrated to seek satisfaction through unacceptable levels of violence. Nations should also decide on broad guidelines within which media and government should respond to terrorist acts.

When incidents arise, media, government, victims, and their relatives become unwitting participants in the drama. Restraint is required of all parties. The media have to cover news developments, but without excesses. For terrorists, media exposure constitutes leverage. Terrorists seek to increase their importance to pressure governments to meet their demands.

Government officials should also show restraint, refraining from a public refusal to negotiate, which puts the government in a diplomatic corner. Negotiations generally occur, regardless; they ought to be conducted out of the public view and at a lower level than by top members of the government. It is generally counter-productive for any democratic country to confer status and importance on kidnappers who seek these through their appalling actions. The correct approach in kidnap situations is patient, behind-the-scenes negotiations.

See also **Media and terrorism, Responses to terrorism**

Revolution Revolution is a relatively sudden violent and illegal attempt to change the regime of a state or other political organisation, in which large sections of the population are involved as participants. During the French Revolution of 1789, the word revolution became identified with the seizure of key political decision-making positions by some coercive force and the introduction of structural changes in society. These can include changes in the political and social system (the French and Russian Revolutions); changes in the mode of production (the Industrial Revolution, and technological revolution), or in some aspect of social, intellectual or cultural life (scientific and cultural revolutions).

Theories of revolution are concerned not with mere changes of rulers (as in palace revolutions), but with changes of ruling classes, of the methods of rule, and of social institutions, and with the revolutionary passions and actions which lead to these changes and with their consequences. Revolutionary theories like Marxism or Leninism not only advocate revolution, but also try to explain how it comes about – Marx concentrating on the relationship between revolution and economic development; Lenin on the relationship between revolution and under-development, and the New Left on the links between revolution and over-development.

Modern theorists recognise that the important modern events called revolutions have involved the seizure of political power, usually by soldiers or intellectuals. The most successful revolutions have been those which have achieved their ends while avoiding the violence and social upheaval of later revolutions, and which have concentrated on transformation at the political level, while retaining sufficient social continuity to guarantee stability.

See also **Terror in the theory of revolution**

Rights of terrorists Any terrorist explores the outer limits of wrong-doing. Terrorists not only violate the rights of others by violence, but they do so with the purpose of making everyone's rights insecure. Terrorists seek to destroy the community of understanding and mutual self-restraint upon which the existence of rights depends.

A terrorist group sets out systematically to alienate a population from its government. The group does succeed in creating a general sense of insecurity among the populace and provoking repressive measures, including the roundup and detention of those suspected of complicity with the terrorists. The terrorists argue that their rights as citizens and human beings are being violated. They argue, in fact, that this way of dealing with them in disregard of established legal standards is a denial of all rights.

Having a right consists precisely in having the title to command respect for demands that others act or refrain from acting in a particular way towards us, and for our complaints when they fail to do so. Terrorists have undoubtedly through their conduct jeopardised their claims to human rights – as they have murdered, tortured, and in every respect, violated the human dignity of their victims.

Rights are important as they give to each person the capacity to decide how and to what extent that person wants to defend his or her interests. To some people even a terrorist has a right to protest the destruction of that capacity which is at the core of humanity – the capacity for autonomous choice. However, if a terrorist is seen not merely as a common criminal, but as an enemy of rights in general, an argument can be made that he has forfeited his rights. A terrorist can respond that he is not the enemy of rights at all, but the only effective proponent of them against a corrupt and illegitimate regime.

There is a tight connection between the idea of having rights and the idea of being allowed to assert them. A human can be respected not simply by refraining from interfering with his interests; rights can be respected by attending to their holder's assertion of them. Both torture and detention violate the rights of those subjected to them. If the conditions of fear created by an effective terrorist campaign require a repressive government to be established it must be regarded as a violation of rights.

The arguments for denying rights to terrorists rest upon the perception that claims of rights are grounded in a relationship; the relationship between people who have a shared understanding of what they owe to one another as people. Terrorists have forfeited the right to have rights, because they have by word and action made clear their complete rejection of that shared understanding, destroying the relationship of which they now wish to take advantage by making claims of right.

Whilst the terrorist, by his acts and words, has damaged that relationship and has lost the capacity to make some claims he could otherwise have made, he has not and could not destroy the relationship entirely. Because he retains the distinctively human capacity to preserve life or seek death through his unique actions, we continue to have a relationship with him, characterised by a duty to respect him as one who has that capacity.

See also **International humanitarian law and terrorism**

Riot A riot occurs when people in large numbers, and over a prolonged period, break a variety of laws, attack the police trying to restore order, loot and damage property. This is a qualitatively different situation from a demonstration which is generally peaceable but which may produce a short term violent clash with the police.

Risk management The task of risk management is to identify precisely the risks and the probable effects of risks on the personnel and organisation to be protected. The threat of terrorism is a serious risk, and only a thorough programme of risk management ensures that security planning is adequate and properly directed. The price for not having a risk management programme is the uncertainty that can breed fear or over-confidence if the threat is under- or overestimated. The methodology of systems analysis is a format that is useful in implementing risk management. Generally a programme of risk identification, evaluation and reduction, that is a comprehensive systems risk analysis, is undertaken.

In any analysis the original problem has to be kept in mind, as it will determine the scope and structure for recommendations. Defining the problem will determine the current situation. Information has to be gained from discussions with key executives who are potential victims of kidnapping. Whatever the specific objectives of the analysis it has to define and evaluate all threats and risks relevant to the problem; assess the criticality of all threats and risks; and assess the vulnerability to all threats and risks. All resources internal to the company, such as the security programme and personnel, have to be identified and their present and potential effect on the risk evaluated. External resources, both public and private, such as government agencies, police departments, consultants, private security companies and the media have to be examined to determine if the risk can be controlled by recognisable sources.

The definition and assessment of objectives will provide data that can be structured into an outline of the approach to be taken, based on fact-finding, data analysis, development of a new system, cost analysis, testing of new ideas.

Since risks are inherent in nearly every situation, types of risk have to be classified according to relevance. The important categories are *property* (reduction in value, or loss); *liability* (responsibility for loss by others); *personnel* (disability, death, reduced efficiency); *physical* (destruction or damage); *social* (individual or group conduct); *market* (price changes and competition); *pure* (chance of loss but no chance of gain), or *speculative* (chance of gain or loss); *static* (caused by irregular condition always possible); *dynamic* (caused by changing trends); and lastly, *fundamental* (group losses) or *particular* risk (individual loss).

In the case of the risk of terrorism, one is confronting potential pure economic, social and physical risks to property, of liability or to personnel. Present security strength and policy have to be fully detailed, so that the ability to meet threats and reduce risk can be evaluated. The complete spectrum of risks has to be determined so that they can be evaluated in terms of the degree of exposure and level of current protective systems.

Each risk has to be measured by a number of criteria to determine its impact on the organisation – the probability of occurrence, impact of occurrence, and the ability to predict its occurrence. The results of the measurement determine how the risk is to be handled. The impact of the occurrence is determined by measuring the severity of the possible loss (the effect each risk could have on each activity) in terms of maximum possible loss, maximum probable loss and actual expected loss. The most subjective category of measurement is how far it will be possible to predict the occurrence.

When risks are identified and measured, they must be reduced. In risk management there are a number of risk reduction types.

Risk avoidance can be accomplished by permanently neutralising the hazard, or eliminating the activity which exposes personnel to risk; or simply by occurrence reduction and risk acceptance, which allows the risk to exist because it cannot be cost-effectively reduced. The last types of risk reduction are of risks spreading over a greater part of the organisation, and the transferral of risk, that is the use of insurance or other means to transfer the liability for the loss to other parties.

The assessment of risks allows for priorities of reduction to be created. In the case of acts of terrorism, which frequently involve the loss of life, risk avoidance, occurrence reduction and risk acceptance as means of risk management, are the most important.

See also **Crisis management, Extortion and product pollution, Threats to persons and property**

Rote Armee Fraktion
  See **Red Army Faction**

S

Sandinist National Liberation Front (SNLF) The Front was named after a Nicaraguan patriot, General Augusto Cesur Sandino, who having opposed American rule for six years, was murdered in 1934 by supporters of the Somoza family. He was the great example for Che Guevara and Castro. The liberation movement was formed in 1961 as a pro-Havana group by Carlos Fonseca Amador, who with other leaders was killed by government forces in 1976. The year before their deaths, the Sandinists split into three factions, the smallest of which was the Marxist-Leninist GPP. The largest was the extreme Third Party, or Terreristas, which waived its ideological bias to allow the bourgeoisie to join their common front against the Somoza regime. In this way it succeeded in winning a broad spectrum of support from peasants to upper-class intellectuals. The Front displayed a great capacity for survival despite numerous 'eradication' attempts during the later years of the Somoza regime. Despite some setbacks, the groups began to co-ordinate activities and establish operational unity by 1978. Subsequently unity waned to some extent and two Marxist groups entered an anti-Third Party coalition, while a fourth faction, the authentic Sandinist, emerged.

The 'junta of national reconstruction' which headed a provisional government installed in July 1979 was dominated by the Third Party, although the three principal tendencies were equally represented in the SNLF's Joint National Directorate. Elections were held in 1985, which brought success for the Sandinists led by Daniel Ortega. His government has faced difficulties because its policies (revealing a growing pro-Soviet and pro-Cuban trend) not only led to strained relations with the United States but also alienated those sections of the Nicaraguan people who wanted even greater democracy. There has been a threat from armed 'Somocist' groups (i.e. those identified with the former Somoza regime), operating from bases across Nicaragua's northern border with Honduras and including many former National Guards who had fled the country in 1979. The Ortega government claims that such groups receive support from the United States and from neighbouring right-wing regimes.

See also **Contra insurgency in Nicaragua**

Schleyer, Hans-Martin President of the West German Employers and Industrial Associations, kidnapped by the Red Army Faction on 5 September 1977.

The kidnap was undertaken by a new, ruthless and more professional generation of terrorists which had emerged in April 1977 as a self-contained unit, scorning the support of the idealistic students who had sympathised with their predecessors. Prior to Schleyer's kidnap and to show their hatred and contempt for the state, they chose as their victims well-guarded public figures such as the public prosecutor Siegfried Buback and the Chairman of the Dresdner Bank, Jürgen Ponto. Schleyer's name was one of sixty on the coded RAF list found by German police in November 1976. He himself had no doubts about the threat. At the memorial service for Jürgen Ponto, he remarked to a friend that 'the next victim of terrorism is almost certainly standing in this room now'. Despite being provided with three police guards and an escort car, he was kidnapped in a one-way street near his home in Cologne, by five terrorists who had emerged from a minibus, killed the driver and his bodyguards but avoided hurting Schleyer. He was held in several flats before being taken from the country. There was a report that Schleyer was held for a time in a boat in a canal or an inland sea in Holland, and even a (false) conjecture that he might have been taken to England. His body was, in the event, found in France. His own behaviour was staunch and courageous; he left a letter with a friend saying that he wished the government to make no concessions to obtain his release. The RAF terrorists demanded the release of 11 terrorists serving sentences in prison, to be flown to a country of their choice, each with $45,000, and that their communications should be read out in full on television. The government ignored all deadlines, warned the terrorists that they were fighting a losing battle and imposed a news blackout. They played for time, which probably encouraged the terrorists not to kill Schleyer immediately. However, the government did maintain an uncompromising line in its negotiations and public pronouncements.

Continuing firmness, this time over the Mogadishu hijack in October 1977, persuaded the kidnappers that there would be no giving way either over the kidnapping or the hijacking. Schleyer's family's attempts to deal directly with the hijackers failed. Schleyer died, but the result was both humiliating and damaging for the RAF. There was world-wide disgust at the murder. The German people closed ranks behind their government, whose strength and authority was reinforced both at home and over the world.

Scottish and Welsh nationalism For a brief period in the 1970s Celtic separatism in Wales and Scotland bred the prospects of violence, but the separatists were weakened by the long-running debate on devolution and the subsequent referendum in 1981, when by quite sizeable majorities the Scottish and Welsh people voted against devolution.

The most well-known of the nationalist movements in Scotland is the Army of the Provisional Government of Scotland – the Tartan Army. It is an extreme nationalist organisation which describes its aim as being to free Scotland of its British yoke, by revolutionary means. Oil pipelines have been bombed, and there have been conspiracies to rob banks and to break into explosives magazines and military establishments. Many of the original members have been sent to jail.

The Scottish National Liberation Army, with a few active and ardent members, claimed responsibility in 1982 for the manufacture of ten incendiary bombs. One of these was sent to the Queen and another to the Defence Secretary. Less well-known groups include the Army for Freeing Scotland and the Army of the Gael.

The most active of the movements in Wales has been the Welsh Language Society, established in 1962 to protect the Welsh language by extending its use in the media. However, some members of the Society gradually began to use violence, destroying cottages owned as second homes by English people and removing English language road signs. The arson attacks were undertaken to show that the sale of such houses resulted in inflated prices and put housing beyond the means of most Welsh people. Two other groups, the Remembrancer and the Sons of Glyndwr, have also committed arson attacks against holiday cottages. The Welsh Socialist Republican Movement gives close support to Sinn Fein and the Irish Republican Socialist Party.

Selous Scouts Formed in December 1973 and disbanded less than seven years later in March 1980, the Rhodesian Selous Scouts had a short operational history, but during their existence they gained a reputation as the best bush soldiers on the African continent. Named after the Victorian explorer Courtney Selous, the Scouts were organised as a combat reconnaissance force, their chief function being to locate the elusive nationalist guerrillas in the bush and relay information back to the main body of the Rhodesian security forces.

They were strictly a volunteer force, and near the end 80 per cent of the Scouts were black. They were responsible for the deaths of 68 per cent of all nationalist guerrillas killed in Rhodesia during the course of the war. By comparison only a small number of Scouts were killed in action. They attained a maximum strength of over 500 men. Their basic tactical formation was the troop, each made up of three sections of eight men. Once in the bush the section was divided into two 'sticks' or groups small enough to remain undetected from enemy eyes and yet sufficient to be operationally effective.

Apart from their function as intelligence officers, the Selous Scouts had a second, clandestine role to play. Selected black Scouts would infiltrate the nationalist areas, both in and outside Rhodesia, to gain a true picture of guerrilla activities and intentions. A key Selous Scout strategy was the elimination of the nationalist leaders, either by capturing them so that they could be interrogated, or simply assassinating them. Most undercover operations were small-scale affairs but occasionally full-scale cross-border raids would be launched. The most successful was the audacious attack against the Zimbabwe African National Liberation Army's (ZANLA) Nyadzonya camp in Mozambique on 9 August 1976. Disguised as Frelimo troops from Mozambique, a small force of Selous

Scouts surrounded the camp, some 5,000-strong, and in a quick attack destroyed it, killing more than 600 of the enemy, most of them guerrillas.

That such a small force could cause such destruction was clearly proof of the tactical superiority of the Scouts over the nationalists. Although a disciplined force, they affected a deliberately casual approach to uniform and general appearance – but this apparent contradiction only helped them to increase their effectiveness.

Shi'ites Shi'ites have always felt alienated from more moderate Arab groups, and in the Arab world, even where they make up the majority of the population as in Iraq and Bahrain, the Shi'ites are usually treated and often feared as a lower-class minority. Persecution is at the root of the faith. A thirteenth-century parable explains why the Shi'ites believe in martyrdom, or purification through death. The biggest schism in Islam emerged within forty years of its founding by the Prophet Muhammad, whose revelations are recorded in the Islamic holy book, the Koran. The schism began as a dispute over leadership of the Islamic empire.

The group that became the Shi'ites felt that the line of leadership should descend through the family of the Prophet's cousin and son-in-law, Ali, who eventually became the Caliph, or God's representative on earth. The single strain of Islam formally split after Ali was murdered in AD 661, and a new leader was selected from outside the family. Those who broke with the mainstream Sunni sect became known as the Shiat Ali, or followers of Ali – today's Shi'ites.

It was Hussein, Ali's son, who set the tone for the Shi'ite faith. Hussein and a small band of followers set out to defend the rights of the Prophet's family to hold the title of Caliph. To Hussein it was more honourable to die for belief than live with injustice. At the Iraqi town of Karbala, Hussein and his followers were massacred by the Caliph's army. It was a precedent for a tradition that grew in importance with time. Hussein left a legacy of the dignity of ultimate protest, and sowed the seeds of a movement centred around revolt against tyranny and oppression as a duty to, and in the name of, God.

Today the world's largest concentration of Shi'ites is in the Gulf, where they form nearly 75 per cent of the population, mostly in Iran and Iraq. Just over 10 per cent of the world's 832 million Muslims are Shi'ites.

Their sense of persecution is fuelled by the fact that Shi'ites live in oil-rich nations. The eight major Gulf states – Saudi Arabia, Kuwait, Iran, Iraq, Bahrain, Oman, Qatar and the United Arab Emirates – have 60 per cent of the world's known oil reserves. The Shi'ites, who make up the largest work force on the oilfields, feel they have not reaped adequate benefits from petrodollars. Most of these dollars have been used to develop other parts of their home countries under Sunni domination. All the Arab Gulf states have experienced growing threats from Shi'ite extremists, resulting in part from Shi'ite resentment over feelings of exploitation and discrimination by the Sunnis.

Shi'ite hostility towards the West dates back two centuries to Napo-

S

leon's conquest of Egypt, when France became the first Western power to control a Muslim territory. Western colonisation further entrenched Sunni rule, even in countries where Shi'ites were the majority. In the wave of independence in the Arab world after World War II, Shi'ites have been allowed very few positions of political or military power.

The only major nation to be ruled by Shi'ites since 1502 is Iran. But as witnessed during the protests of 1979, many Shi'ites felt Shah Muhammad Reza Pahlavi had sold Iran's soul to the West, particularly the USA. The Shah and US influence were banished from Iran.

Iran's experience since its 1979 Islamic revolution has inspired not only the minority extremists, but also the general population of Shi'ites and some Sunnis. Iran has survived the challenges of its seven-year war with Iraq, economic sanctions and political ostracisation by most of the world. Those who have seen themselves as underdogs and victims at the hands of other Muslims and foreign ideologies finally have a base and an advocate – and as in the case of the 1985 Beirut hijack, an example to follow in challenging a superpower.

See also **Hizbullah, Iran, Iraq, Islam, Lebanon**

Sikh extremism The current campaign of violence by Sikh extremists illustrates the challenge India faces in maintaining national unity in the face of efforts at sectionalisation. The pull of ethnic and religious factions has strained the Indian nation since its independence in 1947. The Indian Prime Minister, Rajiv Gandhi, is trying to end the strife which existed between his late mother Indira Gandhi, and the Sikhs. In June 1984 she ordered the Indian Army to invade the holy shrine of the Sikh religion in Amritsar to flush out armed resistance, generating deep resentment and outrage among Sikhs. As a result she was assassinated by her two Sikh bodyguards in New Delhi in October 1984, which led to 2,000 revenge killings of Sikhs by Hindus.

Sikhs have always wanted a greater role in a predominantly Hindu India; in addition some seek greater autonomy for Sikhs, especially in the state of Punjab where many live. Some Sikhs demand an independent state of Khalistan.

Before the formation of the National Council of Khalistan in 1972, a demand for an independent Sikh state (Khalistan) had first been put forward by Dr Jagjit Singh, the general secretary of the Akali Dal (the Sikh political party). Dr Singh stated in London in December 1971 (a day before war broke out between India and Pakistan) that President Yahya Khan of Pakistan had promised his support for the secession of Punjab from India and the establishment of an independent Sikh state, and had allowed the Sikhs to open a broadcasting station in West Pakistan. The Akali Dal's working committee expelled Dr Singh from the party at the very end of 1971 for his anti-national activities, and he did not return to India. His followers formed the National Council of Khalistan, which from its headquarters in the Golden Temple in Amritsar (the central Sikh shrine) issued Khalistan passports, postage stamps and currency notes. Critics of the Khalistan movement were in some cases shot; and fundamentalist sects clashed with those who they considered to be heretical. A youth organisation – the Dal Khalsa – was founded in 1979 under the leadership of Gajendra Singh, and two years later took part in the unsuccessful hijacking of an Indian airliner.

The problems in Amritsar started in April 1982 when fighting broke out between Hindus and Sikhs after several cows' heads had been discovered outside two Hindu temples. Responsibility for the desecration was claimed by the Dal Khalsa, which declared that it would be repeated until its demand for a total ban on smoking and cigarette sales in Amritsar was conceded (the use of tobacco being forbidden to Sikhs). A bomb also exploded in the Temple of the Sikh religious leader, Sant Jarnail Singh Bhindranwale. Sikhs burned down cigarette shops and slaughtered cattle in front of Hindu temples, while in Chandigarh, Hindus invaded a Sikh temple and tore up a copy of the Sikh scriptures. About six hundred people were arrested and as a result of the disturbances the National Council of Khalistan and the Dal Khalsa were banned by the Indian government.

Akali Dal leaders, undeterred, launched a new campaign for an autonomous state of Punjab (similar in status to Kashmir), enlarged to include adjacent Sikh-populated areas, and also in support of various religious demands. Although these demands stopped short of the full independence demanded by the Khalistan movement, secessionists participated in widespread agitation and demonstrations, to which the authorities responded by arresting thousands of Sikh activists. Talks between the Government and Sikh leaders towards the end of 1982 failed to produce any agreement on the Sikhs' political demands, although the Prime Minister, Mrs Gandhi, made concessions to their religious demands by announcing that Amritsar would be declared a holy city, and that the sale of tobacco and liquor would be banned within its walls. Tensions have run high since that time, reaching a pitch at the Golden Temple siege in Amritsar.

Few steps can be taken to meet Sikh demands other than slight modifications in government policies, without setting a precedent that would threaten national unity. If Sikhs were offered a substantial degree of autonomy within the Punjab, other minorities could be expected to demand similar autonomy in other regions. Sikh demands are the thin end of the wedge, and India realises its national unity has to be paramount.

Most Indians oppose the Sikhs' demand for greater influence, believing they already have sufficient power. Sikhs are only two per cent of the population, but they have an influence in government, military and economic spheres far beyond their numbers. Rajiv Gandhi's task is to convince Sikhs that India's present system already provides substantial protection of Sikh rights. Organised Sikh terrorism against random targets is thought to be an effort by extremists to prevent Rajiv Gandhi from reaching accommodation with Sikh moderates. An estimated thousand Sikhs have been detained for questioning; and new anti-terrorism proposals will seek broad powers for police and government. The government also does not wish to drive moderate Sikhs into the extremist camp.

See also **India**

Simulation Through the use of simulations, individuals and groups can be trained to respond effectively to terrorist attacks. An act of terrorism is like a theatrical performance. The terrorists write the scenario, from which they, the hostages and the responding forces improvise the action. The members of the media prepare the reviews and the public is the audience. Today terrorists use a global stage to dramatise their causes, and with mass communications they play to a mass audience. They can strike anywhere at any time. Acts of terrorism are characterised by high drama and uncertainty. However, common behaviour patterns assist the authorities in responding to terrorist acts. Careful planning can produce a highly realistic exercise in crisis management and effective procedures for evaluation. The resulting simulations integrate the skills and considerations of the military and the law with social-science and improvisational-theatre techniques. Participants learn under pressure how to resolve the crises and acts of violence surrounding an act of terrorism.

Society often chooses to insulate itself from acts of violence it witnesses. Even when individuals grudgingly recognise that they may be potential targets, the temptation remains to avoid thinking the unthinkable. If individuals accept the possibility that they are vulnerable, the realisation can provoke anxiety in an already pressured society. The concern over the threat has come to influence policy-making and its implementation.

There needs to be a set of integrated programmes in which specialists can combine their different skills to respond effectively to the alliances formed by the new terrorists. Simulation has partly met this need. It is an approach that not only provides training, but also can be used to evaluate fully the forces designated to deal with a threat. Programmes that emphasise formal procedural checklists often break down under the stress of actual events. Simulation avoids that danger. At the same time it provides means by which police and policy-makers can test existing plans, revise them, or develop new measures based on training that generates the pressures occurring in actual incidents.

The development of a simulation combines the analysis and application of terrorist tactics and strategies with an exercise in imagination. In the formulation and execution of the exercises – from the development of the plot (the scenario) to the writing of the script (the operations order), and the subsequent reviews (the evaluation) – a mixture of different approaches are used. The line between the terrorist 'play' and the actual terrorist event is deliberately blurred in a successful exercise.

In building a scenario, several elements have to be considered: the selection of the type of incident and target, the selection of hostages, the motivation and ideological factors behind the incident, the selection or recruitment of the terrorists and the organisational framework. The operational phase includes the means of infiltration and breaching security;

securing the hostages; the communications function and the development of potential alternative conclusions.

In writing scripts or operations orders for the simulations, adjustments have to be made to meet the various requirements created by the imaginary local conditions under which the simulation exercises are carried out.

Operations orders adhere to the format employed by the military in planning for small-unit exercises. The writing of operations orders by the would-be terrorists assists them in physically preparing for the assault. It prepares them for a simulation by helping them to assume their individual and collective roles. The recruitment of the terrorists takes place without the knowledge or co-operation of those representing the law.

In initiating a simulation care has to be taken to reconcile the need for surprise and realism with adequate safety measures. The likely emotional and intellectual responses of the participants have to be assessed.

In simulations, while the victims await their uncertain fate, the responding police forces and military units attempt to override a reactive, emotive response with administrative techniques and related tactical measures to manage the siege. The initial shock and disorientation created by an assault are replaced by attempts by the responding forces to develop a series of counter-measures at the start of a protracted siege. The responses of the individual hostages differ as a result of their different personalities; but a simulation experience enables the victims not only to evaluate responses under stress, but also to appreciate how others feel when they face the barrel of a terrorist's gun. Some simulations end in stalemate and many are 'resolved' by the resort to force. Routines to deal with each of these situations have to be established by the responding units.

Command posts in simulations are microcosms of critical tension areas. The patterns observed in them are experienced by policy-makers who have to prepare for a potential crisis, and by those who may have to deal with an actual incident in the execution of everyday responsibilities. Confronted with changing threats, simulations are one means by which authorities can learn to deal with terrorism.

See also **Terrorist roles**

Sociology of terrorism Sociologists define terrorism as the use of covert violence by a group, for political ends. Terrorist movements have mainly consisted of members of the educated middle classes, but there has been terrorism by the desperate and refugees, trade unions and working classes (for example in the United States 1880–1910 and Spain 1890–1936). In some cases there has been a link with social dislocation and economic crisis, at other times there has been no such connection. Movements of national liberation and social revolution (or reaction) have turned to terrorism after political action failed. Sociologists have been able to account for mass movements, but for small movements this has proved difficult – thus it is hard to generalise about terrorism. For many terrorists, their perceived historical 'mission' ended with the destruction of the system (or of foreign oppression). Yet terrorist campaigns have continued, and inevitably, some terrorists have become concerned with the seizure of power and more distant perspectives.

Urban terrorists have on the whole been aware of the difficulties facing them and, in theory, urban terrorism and rural guerrilla warfare make parallel attempts to win over sections of the army or start a general insurrection or a people's war. But in practice the emphasis is usually on urban terror, either because the countries concerned are predominantly urbanised, or because the masses do not respond, or because the army is not inclined to co-operate with the terrorists.

All major terrorist movements have had a central command, sometimes professional and at other times rudimentary. The central command of the terrorist movement has sometimes been located abroad – Switzerland, the USA and Lebanon have been centres for movements operating elsewhere. Terrorists can move around freely, but the more remote the headquarters from the scene of action, the less complete its knowledge of current events. The larger a terrorist movement, the greater the danger of detection. Urban terrorist campaigns have seldom lasted longer than three to four years.

The success of terrorist operations depends on reliable information about the targets to be attacked and the movements of the victim to be killed or abducted (for example, the Irish Republican Army have built up strong sources of information). The dagger and the pistol were the traditional weapons up to the dawning of the age of dynamite. The bomb clearly was not the all-destroying weapon it had been thought to be, but it had become a symbol, replacing the barricade. Terrorists have the great advantage that, unlike the security forces in a democratic society, they are not compelled to act within the law. The police cannot in theory use illegal means to repress terrorism, and so it becomes more necessary for the police to collect information via informers, and perhaps financially tempting for terrorists to act as informers – for instance, by 1912 the Okhrana (the Russian secret police) had some 26,000 paid agents, most of them part-time informers, and in addition a permanent staff of some 50,000. The most dangerous threat to terrorists is the promise of a reward for information leading to their capture. This weapon has been widely used. Many captured terrorists have behaved with dignity and heroism, but quite a few terrorists have broken down during interrogation.

Many terrorist groups have attracted criminal elements at one time or another. Criminal elements have joined the ranks of terrorist groups in times of general unrest when there were sound excuses for looting, as in the Russian revolution of 1905.

Internal dissension has dominated the threats faced by terrorist groups. Most groups came into being as a result of a split between the moderate and the more extreme wing of an organisation, and almost all of them later underwent further fission – such as the Narodnaya Volya in Tsarist Russia, and the Irish Fenians. The assassination of leading representatives of the 'system' is the oldest method of terrorist tactic and has been the one most frequently adopted by terrorists – it was first practised in Persia and much later in nineteenth-century Ireland. Expropriation, for example bank robbery or, less frequently, robbery of trains carrying large sums of money, has also been popular. Kidnapping for political purposes and the extortion of ransoms has been practised for generations.

Agrarian terror took place in the nineteenth century in Andalusia in southern Spain, in Ireland, in eastern Poland and in north Germany against big landowners, tax collectors or government representatives.

With regard to the media, it is not the magnitude of the terrorist operation that counts, but the publicity, and this rule applies to single operations and whole campaigns. Terrorist groups usually hope for a measure of public support. Extreme nationalists operating against foreigners can always count on some sympathy from fellow countrymen and at the very least do not expect to be betrayed by their compatriots. In Latin America, as in pre-revolutionary Russia, there has been much goodwill for what terrorists have done – and in an emergency they have been able to count on the support of intellectuals, churchmen and sections of the middle class to defend them against the harsher forms of government repression.

Since the early nineteenth century conspiratorial links have existed between revolutionary groups in Europe. The Russian terrorists of the 1880s found imitators in many parts of the world, and neighbouring countries have often provided sanctuary for terrorists. Historically, the terrorist groups that have been more successful in attaining their aims have been those with narrow, clearly defined objectives, and those with powerful outside protectors; for example, terrorist groups facing imperial powers no longer able or willing to hold on to their colonies or protectorates. Seen in historical terms, terrorism has been effective only occasionally. It has not succeeded against effective dictatorships, let alone modern totalitarian regimes. In democratic societies or against ineffective authoritarian regimes, it has on occasion been more successful. However, terrorists are driven by thirst for action rather than rational consideration of the consequences, and past failures have not acted as a deterrent.

Apart from the fact that most terrorists belong to the early twenties age group, there are few other features they hold in common. Nationalist-separatist groups consist of young people of lower social background than the socialist-revolutionary groups. Political issues in nineteenth-century Russia were clear-cut – there were no constitutional or elementary rights, and no legal redress against the abuse of power. The less clear-cut the nature of the political purpose of terrorism, the greater its appeal to unbalanced persons. Men fighting a cruel tyranny have quite different motives from those rebelling against a democratically elected government.

See also **History of terrorism**

Solidarity Solidarity is an independent labour union outside the official union structure in Poland. It arose out of the formation of various independent workers' committees, strike committees and finally trade unions.

During 1980–81, for the first time in any country of the Soviet bloc, a workers' movement was created which succeeded in forming a strong independent trade union federation. Solidarity effectively replaced the existing official trade union organisation controlled by the state and confronted the government with demands of an increasingly political nature, which were eventually seen as a threat to the regime. The movement was supported by other groups which were anti-communist. The Roman Catholic Church, of which the vast majority of the population of Poland are practising members, also supported the free trade union movement, and acted as a mediator in negotiations between the Solidarity leaders on the one hand and government representatives on the other.

As a result of a strike in the Lenin shipyards in Gdansk in 1980 as part of a campaign for the reinstatement of 25 sacked workers, the government began to negotiate with the inter-factory committees organised by strikers led by Lech Walesa (who had been an organiser of a previous demonstration in 1970 over workers' rights). The shipyard workers were supported by miners and agricultural workers. The government, as a result of the talks, expressed a willingness to legalise new unions which could be based on strike committees, while the committees themselves recognised the undisputed leading force represented by the main Polish United Workers Party.

However, the demands of Solidarity became increasingly hard for the Government to accept – for example, they asked for greater access to the media, greater wage increases and a five-day working week. In early 1981 the new Prime Minister General Jaruzelski warned Solidarity members to resist anti-Communist propaganda and agitation, and that the Government would resist Solidarity's 'counter-revolutionary' measures.

Rural Solidarity grew increasingly vociferous and called for a reduction in excess spending power and a progressive system of income tax. It also demanded greater social egalitarianism and the observance of civil liberties. Increased food prices in mid 1981 were followed by violent protest demonstrations and strikes; and while Solidarity was willing to let the government run the country, they were determined to run the factories. They continued to remain in dispute with the Government on issues of self-management, censorship and government proposals for economic reform. A Solidarity congress called for the creation of a life free from poverty, exploitation, fear and lies in a society organised on the principles of democracy and the rule of law. Increased Solidarity activity coincided with a deepening in the economic crisis in Poland with the decline in labour productivity, industrial production, coal production, construction and exports. The only increases appear to have been in wages.

In December 1981, Solidarity laid down conditions for achieving a national reconciliation with the government, including the cessation of anti-union repression, and the passage of a law on trade unions in a version approved by Solidarity. Within days the Polish authorities claimed to have conclusive evidence that Solidarity leaders were planning a deliberate confrontation with the government, with the ultimate aim of overthrowing it. As a result, martial law was introduced, a Military Council of Salvation was created and virtually the whole of the Solidarity leadership was detained by the army. The right to strike was abolished, trade union and other organised non-government activities were banned, and only the official news media were tolerated. Whilst Solidarity was not officially banned, all gatherings were prohibited.

Over the subsequent four years a number of Solidarity members were arrested for illegal trade union activities, and the last remaining Solidarity presidium member still at large, Zbigniew Bujak, was betrayed to the secret police in May 1986. In late 1982 the Polish parliament, the Sejm, effectively dissolved all existing unions and created the framework for new and more closely controlled unions to replace them. Although martial law was suspended at the end of 1982, the government retained the right to reimpose martial law at any time. Lech Walsea has been repeatedly called for questioning by the police and his influence has been forcibly curbed. Nevertheless the spirit of Solidarity remains alive and its members still believe that ultimate victory can be achieved.

Solidarnosc
See **Solidarity**

South Africa In recent decades violence has become endemic in African political life; there are many examples of this in existing political regimes – black, white, coloured and Arab – throughout the African continent. In South Africa, violence has become a fact of life, and the use of terror is part of the apparent norm of political action. The possibility that under certain conditions the original aim of the end of apartheid may become lost sight of and violence unleashed, is not confined to any one race, group or community within the Republic. Terrorism as part of the overall attack on the existing government and social system may also be seen as an outcome of a lack of inhibitions regarding the use both of violence and of the established tactics now known as revolutionary warfare. Terrorism is included among the tactics being used to force the surrender of the current government and the installation of a 'progressive', radical, political group. Whether the aim of terrorism in South Africa is perceived as liberation, capitulation, or both, is not necessarily dependent upon the observer's racial origin.

The terror campaign in South Africa is carried out, by its own claim, by the African National Congress (ANC), through its military wing, Umkhonto We Sizwe (MK), or 'Spear of the Nation'. Its stated strategy is to destroy the existing political, economic and social structure of South Africa by means of political subversion and propaganda, and sabotage and terrorism. Such tactics, in effect, amount to a revolutionary war strategy. The term 'revolutionary war' has been widely interpreted as the forcible attempt by politically organised groups to gain control of a country's decision-making structure through unconventional warfare and terrorism, which is integrated with general political and social mobilisation to win over the sympathy of the nation.

1976 is generally regarded as the time when the ANC managed to put into effect its 'second Umkhonto Campaign' of armed action against South Africa. The independence of Mozambique provided a continuous area for infiltration into South Africa and also opened up Swaziland as an infiltration conduit. Widespread domestic troubles throughout South Africa, epitomised by the unrest in Soweto, succeeded in radicalising many blacks. A large number of radicalised and comparatively well-educated young blacks fled from South Africa – many joining the ANC. By the late 1970s, several thousand fugitives were undergoing insurgency training in Angola, Libya and Tanzania. Increasing ANC operations caused South Africa to deploy police and military forces in increased strength along South Africa's landward borders.

Over the last ten years ten main categories of terrorist activity have developed. The main areas of activity are the sabotage of railroad communications, mainly in urban areas, and of links between black residential areas and the city centre; assassination and attempted assassination aimed at perceived opponents; attacks on industrial installations such as electricity sub-stations and oil refineries; contacts between insurgents and security forces; attacks on administration offices, and pamphlet bombs; attacks on police stations; bomb explosions in city centres or public areas; attacks on military targets, and attacks on the diplomatic offices of Homeland states.

The main attacks have occurred in African townships, in central business districts and in the countryside. Most incidents cluster around the urban industrial complexes of Johannesburg and Durban and in other areas of the Transvaal and Natal.

Sabotage has included a number of spectacular incidents designed to achieve wide national and international media coverage in order to fulfil the aim of a strategy of armed propaganda – sabotage of oil tanks; rocket attacks on military complexes and a nuclear power station; bombs outside and inside government administration buildings, and car bomb attacks on the South African Air Force HQ and on the Department of Internal Affairs. Attacks on police stations have increased, along with the use of more advanced weapons.

The ANC's armed activity has escalated, although its scope and intensity are limited. Unable by its nature to challenge the state's control of power, the campaign is characterised by armed propaganda, as one step in a multi-dimensional, multi-phased, protracted 'people's war'.

While the ANC has attempted to increase its participation in mass-based local action and to extend its insurrection-type tactics, it has also developed a stronger inclination towards terrorism, as proclaimed at the Kabwe Conference and Lusaka Press Conference in 1985, and as manifested in incidents of rural and urban terrorism. Kabwe consciously included South Africa's white farmers as legitimate targets of ANC insurgency. As a result many bomb incidents took place on roads near the borders of Zimbabwe and Botswana.

The mobilisation of the masses in South Africa has been a major function of front organisations for the banned African National Congress and the South African Communist Party since 1970, when the explosive power of youth groups was realised. This has developed into the politicisation of black and coloured schools and other educational centres. A direct result have been school boycotts, and also the burning of classrooms, books and, occasionally, teachers. 'Black consciousness' has also been fostered, and groups adopting this philosophy or psychological attitude are playing a large part in politicising that majority group of the population, especially students at tertiary establishments. The South African Student Organisation (SASO) was formed as a result of the efforts of Steve Biko and others at the University of the North Turfloop, in 1969, and was a conscious effort to break away from the all-white National Union of South African Students (NUSAS). Most of the followers of SASO were supporters of the Pan-African Congress. Indians and coloureds were also admitted, giving a new dimension to the concept of 'Black African'.

On the question of township unrest, the current wave of rioting sweeping across South Africa, the often harsh, repressive response by the state, the severe economic recession and unemployment have provided the ANC with a firm basis for action in this field. While the ANC has been partly responsible for the unrest, it would appear that it, like the government, has reacted to rather than initiating the situation. The state itself has acknowledged this. The five main causes of the unrest in the townships are the crisis of legitimacy and credibility of local authorities, which are unable to live up to black moderates' expectations; grievances over influx control; atrocious physical conditions in many of the townships, and unpopular resettlement policies; a lack of say in political decision-making processes; and real and perceived inequalities in education and facilities.

The ANC attempts not only to exploit and take credit for the unrest, but also, if possible, to control the situation. Indeed, the widespread violence has forced the ANC to reformulate its strategy to encompass a more detailed perspective on how insurrection can be put to use in the specific conditions of the South African situation. Because of the power of the South African state, unrest and revolt alone will not overthrow the system, but the ANC contends that such tactics can certainly be used as part of a protracted strategy of revolutionary warfare. Insurrection (mass unrest and revolt) can weaken the state and serve as a radicalising and recruiting agent for the ANC's people's army.

Fuelled by local grievances and popular enmity towards the administration, insurrection and armed action have been used in attempts to render the urban black areas ungovernable by destroying local government. To this end there have been numerous petrol-bomb, hand-grenade and rifle attacks on policemen and town councillors and their property. The ANC has ordered cadres to eliminate all blacks who assist the white

233

government in administering black townships. The Congress has recently called on township residents to move from the stage of ungovernability to one where independent people's political committees are set up.

The aim of the banned ANC, in informal alliance with the South African Communist Party, is a closely organised seizure of state power. To this end they visualise a protracted struggle against the present incumbents of state power, embracing all forms of struggle, violent and non-violent, in a complete revolutionary warfare strategy. Once state power has been captured, the aim of any future ANC/SACP alliance may be defined as the radical restructuring of South African society on the political basis of majority rule, in a military state, within an economic framework of Marxist socialism. A 'nationalist liberation struggle' is defined by the ANCS as its primary strategic objective. Limited reform, such as President Botha is trying to undertake at present, which falls short of a complete transfer of power to the ANC will fail to satisfy the revolutionary who is seeking state power.

The continuing schism between the South African government and the ANC is illustrated by the recent conditions laid down by the ANC as basic prerequisites before negotiations can begin: the lifting of the ban on political organisations in South Africa; the regime's acceptance of, and commitment to, universal adult suffrage in a united and non-fragmented South Africa; unconditional release of Nelson Mandela and all other political detainees; and abolition of all 'homelands'.

ANC insurgency since 1960 falls into distinct phases with varied repercussions: the early period between 1960 and 1964 proved conclusively that the particular conditions existing in contemporary South Africa make any internal organisation highly vulnerable to state counter-action. Indeed, the experiences of this period and later point to the manifest and intractable problems of attempting to establish 'base areas' or 'liberated zones' inside South Africa, in the face of the state's overwhelming coercive apparatus (administrative, legal, social, police and military). The period between 1964 and 1975 served to demonstrate the problems contained in any attempt to develop insurgency against South Africa from external base areas that were not contiguous with South Africa's northern borders. There were almost insurmountable obstacles posed by the geographically intervening zones of buffer states which were actively hostile to the aims and intentions of the ANC. Conversely, the period between 1970 and 1984 showed that given access to facilities in neighbouring states, infiltration and insurgency could begin to develop actively. This development was attenuated by the conditional, restricted nature of the access provided by black states unwilling to allow the development of large guerrilla bases.

Within the Republic, the important factor of information and misinformation is largely controlled by government regulations, which considerably limits what can be reported for public consumption. Within this situation the English language media is accused of left-wing bias, the Afrikaans press of complicity with the government, the black and Indian press with much of the misinformation and speculation regarding the origins and motives of terror acts – a position which is exploited quite naturally by cadres of the ANC and SACP and by UDF, AZAPO and other front organisations engaged in subversion in South Africa. This state of affairs is not helped by the banning of publications and people. The state's response, most other countries believe, should be to make all information freely available, or at least not to impede its propagation. Outside South Africa, the ANC seems to be regarded in many quarters as worthy of assistance in its fight against the evils of apartheid.

South West Africa People's Organisation
See SWAPO

Soviet Union There is still considerable dispute among experts about whether and to what extent terrorism is sponsored and controlled by the Soviet Union. Many observers believe that Moscow's strategic thinking calls for the manipulation of terrorism as a suitable substitute for traditional warfare, which has become too expensive and is too hazardous to be waged on the battlefield except in special circumstances in close proximity to Soviet borders, as in Afghanistan. By overt and covert use of non-military techniques, and by exploiting low-intensity operations around the world, the Soviet Union is able to continue its revolutionary efforts against democratic pluralism in a free world, and expand its own influence into a wider target area.

On the other hand, there are those who are sceptical about direct and indirect Soviet control of terrorist groups. While admitting that Moscow approves of and gives some assistance to what it considers legitimate 'liberation movements', or struggles of people for their independence, proponents of this view argue that the dynamics of modern terrorism are so uncontrollable that the Soviet leaders must be ambivalent about the usefulness of this form of warfare.

Whether or not Moscow controls terrorist and guerrilla warfare operations, the Soviet Union does continue to supply massive amounts of arms and money to the revolutionary forces involved. The scope and nature of Soviet involvement in terrorist activity is still obscure in the minds of many observers because it is fundamentally secret or covert, ranging from the sanctioning of violence by propaganda to the supply of funds, training, arms and other operational assistance.

The Soviet role in these activities has fluctuated over the years in accordance with Moscow's changing appreciation of its vital interests in different parts of the world. Specific terrorist operations have sometimes seemed to be no more than militant behaviour or the coincidental by-product of Soviet propaganda.

It is not always easy to determine whether a particular terrorist action or series of actions in any targetted country is home-grown or Moscow-inspired. However, the pattern of Soviet sponsorship of violence in many different regional conflicts is becoming clearer. The Soviet Union's position as an undisputed superpower has permitted it to control or

S

strongly influence the foreign policy and international conduct of other socialist countries that subscribe to the Soviet ideological line. In this context, Bulgaria, Cuba, Czechoslovakia, East Germany and North Korea, indirectly supported by Syria, South Yemen and Nicaragua, act as Soviet surrogates in exporting violence.

The broad goals the Soviet Union hopes to achieve from terrorism include:

(1) Influencing developments in neighbouring countries.

(2) Regaining irredentist territories in the Soviet orbit.

(3) Helping to create new states in which it will have considerable influence as a result of its support of those nations' claims for self-determination.

(4) Weakening the political, economic and military infrastructure of the anti-Soviet alliances such as NATO.

(5) Initiating proxy operations in distant geographic locations where direct organised conventional military activities are logistically impracticable.

(6) Stirring up trouble for the United States in the highly visible regions of Central America, particularly where such a policy entails no serious financial burden and is politically low-risk because of the use of surrogate supporting nations like Cuba and Nicaragua.

(7) Waging a 'secret war' against individuals considered by the Kremlin as 'mortal enemies' of Communism and the Soviet Union.

See also **Agca, Mehmet Ali, Dissidents in the Soviet Union, 'Terrorist states'**

Spaghetti House Siege, 1975 Criminals, with the obvious exception of kidnappers, take hostages as a last resort. While criminals are rational when committing a crime, they obviously do not want to be arrested, and may display somewhat less than their usual reason when the police corner them. In many cases it is possible to suggest to them the fact that their original crime will not be so seriously viewed as kidnapping or murder.

Some criminals try to convince the police that they are political terrorists rather than robbers. In September 1975, three men armed with a sawn-off shotgun and two pistols burst into the Spaghetti House in Knightsbridge, London, with the intention of committing a robbery. Two of the men were black militants who were fringe members of a black extremist group, and the leader was a convicted armed robber who also supported black militancy. However, in spite of their connections with an extremist organisation, it was apparent that the three were there as armed robbers, not terrorists. After the police arrived, the robbers took hostages and it took them a week to decide that the only way out was to surrender. Initially they claimed they were members of the Black Liberal Army, and hoped to bluff their way out by forcing concessions. Eventually six hostages were released and the gunmen surrendered, although the leader attempted to kill himself.

The Spaghetti House Siege was important for two reasons. It was one of two incidents (the other being the siege of IRA members at Balcombe Street, London, in December 1975), in which Britain perfected its approach to hostage negotiations, which have been used successfully on many subsequent occasions. It also showed the overlap between political and criminal hostage-takers, and showed why security authorities needed to have a detailed knowledge of all types of hostage-takers if they were to assess properly the threat posed by any particular incident.

Spasm terrorism Terrorism's challenge to public order arises when terrorists act not in response to domestic problems but as part of a campaign to affect events in another country. Campaigns and incidents so far experienced in Britain, can be described as 'spasm terrorism', that is a series of attacks of relatively low intensity and brief duration. The police response to these incidents or campaigns has to include intelligence-gathering, the prevention of, and protection against, terrorist acts, and the ability to carry out counter-terrorist operations.

State-sponsored terrorism State terrorism can be viewed as taking the forms of oppression, repression and terrorism. Oppression is a situation where social and economic privileges are denied to whole classes of people, regardless of whether they oppose the authorities. Repression can be viewed as the use or threat of coercion against opponents or potential opponents in order to prevent or weaken their opposition to the authorities and their policies. Terrorism, in this context, is the use of a deliberate act or threat of violence to create fear or compliant behaviour in the victim or audience of the violence.

Every government in the world utilises some form of political repression. Many use repression extensively, for it has proved to be an effective tool to shape the media interest groups, political parties and, through them, the ideas and attitudes of citizens. The tactics and strategies of terrorism have become integral to the foreign policy instruments of the modern state. States and their supporters shrink from labelling their own actions as terrorism, preferring more neutral designations such as 'coercive diplomacy', 'nuclear deterrence' and 'assistance to a friendly state in its pursuit of internal security'.

Repression is a coercive and frequently a secretive style of governing. The more it is used by a government the more that government is revealed as insecure and threatened. Repressive governments cannot induce voluntary compliance and support. Enforcement terrorism is the most extreme form of government repression. Whereas activities such as arbitrary arrests, press censorship and the outlawing of demonstrations, unions and strikes may be defined as some of the techniques of repression, assassinations and secret arrests, followed by torture, mutilation and perhaps death, can be interpreted as enforcement terrorism. Acts of enforcement terrorism are more severe than acts of repression, and more likely to be deliberately lethal and cruel. However, both are designed to force compliance through a climate of fear; both can be employed for

237

reactive or pre-emptive purposes; and both are indicators of illegitimate authority.

All political systems face conflicts over who is to rule and what public policies are to be pursued. Because many Latin American nations did not achieve political stability in the nineteenth century, they are now confronted with problems of illegitimate governments trying to promote economic growth and distributive justice, and to handle successfully the challenge of increasing political participation. In South Africa, both state and anti-state terror emanate from the unique condition of apartheid, and not simply from the disgruntled masses and political extremists.

It is hard to measure the extent to which state violence works to destroy or strengthen people's visions of their community, their future or their deeply held values; and the extent to which some people perceive that they live in a nation of citizens against the government.

See also **Offender states, 'Terrorist states'**

Stockholm syndrome Transference, the development of a sense of closeness and attachment between hostage and captor, was first noticed during a bank robbery in Stockholm. The attempted robbery developed into a barricade and hostage situation. During the episode, a young woman hostage allegedly initiated sexual relations with her captor. The motivation was not a response to fear or coercion, but an intimacy that developed from sharing a common fate in a situation of mutual crisis and the protracted dependence of the woman captive on her captor. The relationship persisted after the bank robber's incarceration.

In the United States FBI agents have noted that had observers been attuned to the problem of transference earlier, the syndrome would have been called Shade Gap syndrome rather than Stockholm syndrome. Their reference is to a kidnapping that took place in Shade Gap, Pennsylvania, in 1967. When law enforcement officials came upon the kidnapper in a wooded area, he was hurriedly walking to escape pursuit and encirclement. A considerable distance behind him was the kidnap victim, straining to keep up. The victim had only to turn round and walk off to freedom.

The most publicised episode of transference by a hostage to captors was in the case of newspaper heiress Patricia Hearst, who not only took a lover from among her captors but also provided them with covering gunfire when they were about to be seized for shoplifting. Patricia Hearst's behaviour was different only in degree from what is commonly observed in hostages under long-term stress. If Patricia Hearst's responses were more extreme, it is also true that the conditions of her captivity were severe, in terms both of deprivation and duration. These factors were probably exacerbated by her age and lack of experience.

See also **Psychological theories**

Supergrass system In November 1981 Christopher Black was arrested in Belfast after having participated in an IRA roadblock staged for publicity purposes. After two days of silence in police custody he began to make the first of a large number of statements implicating himself and others in a catalogue of IRA-related offences. Within days he was granted immunity from prosecution and subsequently, in a trial which began in December 1982 and ended in August 1983, he gave evidence against 38 accused, 35 of whom were convicted. Although there were at least four paramilitary supergrasses in Northern Ireland in the ten years before Black's arrest, his willingness to give evidence is generally taken as the beginning of the 'supergrass system', because it was so rapidly followed by a flood of similar cases. Some of the accomplices retracted their evidence before their names became public, but in the two years between November 1981 and November 1983 seven Loyalist and 18 Republican supergrasses were responsible for the arrest and charge of over 590 people for offences connected with paramilitary activities in Northern Ireland. Fifteen supergrasses retracted their evidence either before the trials in which they were involved began or before these could be concluded.

The word supergrass was originally coined by journalists for a succession of London bank robbers who, in the early 1970s, not only informed on a large number of suspects but took the next step and entered the witness box to testify against them. 'Supergrasses' from terrorist organisations have also recently been used by the authorities in Italy.

Supergrasses in Northern Ireland have a number of interesting features to witness; they have been products of deliberate law enforcement initiatives directed specifically at organised acquisitive crime. They have been deeply involved in these crimes, which are serious and violent, rather than any in other type of offence. Ultimately, they have been motivated by a highly developed sense of self-interest. The prosecuting authorities in Northern Ireland maintain that the closed and secretive nature of paramilitary organisations precludes normal investigative policing, and that if those who have been active in such organisations are prepared to testify it would be wrong for charges not to be preferred on their evidence.

The use of accomplice evidence as a method of controlling violent political unrest is not a new departure in Ireland. In both the United Irishmen and Fenian uprisings, in the eighteenth and nineteenth centuries respectively, the authorities relied heavily for convictions on those prepared to betray their comrades-in-arms. But the routine use in the 1980s of supergrasses to deal with large numbers of terrorist suspects developed out of the unique succession of counter-insurgency initiatives introduced since the early 1970s to control the violence of Loyalist and Republican paramilitary organisations. The 1978 Bennett Report on the treatment of terrorists in custody appears to have made the extraction of confessions much more difficult, and consequently the policy of securing convictions on confession alone became no longer viable. This seems to have prompted the prosecuting authorities to concentrate on enlisting the services of informers. Whilst the quest for informers is an old practice throughout the world, the objective in Northern Ireland in the early 1980s seems to have been not only to garner low-grade intelligence, but also to cultivate a batch of high-powered accomplice witnesses who would be prepared to testify in court against those suspected of being leaders in the Republican and Loyalist paramilitary organisations. It seems illogical that the financial and manpower resources which this has required were not authorised at the executive level in advance, rather than, as the authorities maintain, agreed case by case as each 'converted terrorist' came forward.

In recent months there appears to have been a decline in the use of the supergrass system, because of its unsatisfactory conviction rates.

Northern Ireland's supergrass system is the latest in a series of controversial law enforcement initiatives introduced in the attempt to deal with the violence of Loyalist and Republican paramilitary organisations. The same objective of conviction maximisation has been the dominant theme in nearly all of these strategies, although the supergrass policy has had other spin-off advantages from the authorities' point of view; e.g. the provision for holding suspects on remand for long periods, and the sowing of fear and mistrust in Loyalist and Republican communities.

The attempt to convict virtually everyone whom the supergrasses implicated has come unstuck, and the claim that the role of the courts is to apply politically neutral rules to proven facts, in complete independence from the executive, has been undermined.

At its inception, the system was claimed to save lives because the 'godfathers of terrorism' where at last being taken into custody and prosecuted. This is now in dispute – the nature of the conflict has changed as a result of a complex interplay between anti-terrorist policies and self-initiated changes by the various paramilitary organisations.

Suppression of terrorism, 1977 European Convention This measure was adopted in Strasbourg in November 1976 and signed in January 1977. It greatly restricts the notion of 'political' crimes in the eyes of liberal democracies which were the main signatories. EEC member governments must in part have been motivated to explore the adoption of common principles in the area of fighting terrorism by the inadequacy of existing international provisions and by the desire to intensify co-operation among themselves on the matter. Realisation of the convention's limitations encouraged members of the EEC to examine what steps could be taken, at least within the Community, to orchestrate measures against terrorism.

The internationalisation of terrorism was seen as the main reason why measures complementing or modifying existing extradition and mutual assistance arrangements among the Council of Europe's member states would be an effective and appropriate way of combatting terrorism in Western Europe. For extradition purposes, the Convention provides that the following specified offences shall be regarded as political:

(a) an offence within the scope of the 1970 Hague Convention on hijacking;

(b) an offence within the scope of the 1971 Montreal Convention against acts prejudicial to civil aviation;

(c) a serious offence involving attack on the life, physical integrity or liberty of internationally protected persons;

(d) an offence involving kidnapping or taking of hostages;

(e) an offence involving the use of a bomb, grenade, rocket or parcel bomb;

(f) an attempt to commit any of the foregoing offences or participation as an accomplice of a person who commits or attempts to commit such an offence.

Under Article 2, other specified offences may not be considered as political, regardless of their political content or motivation, which provides an escape clause for member states anxious to avoid obligations to extradite.

The overall intended effect of the Convention on the Suppression of Terrorism is obvious: the plea that a terrorist act is politically-inspired, justifiable and defensible is no longer to be regarded as a legitimate reason for non-prosecution of a terrorist. The problems with the Convention remain not simply in its limited regional applicability and caveats, but in the fact that terrorists may still escape prosecution or extradition if they land or seek refuge either in a country not party to the Convention or to the various UN provisions, or in one that does not have reciprocal arrangements with members of the Council of Europe regarding the prosecution and extradition of terrorists committing offences within the Council of Europe's member states. The Convention does not define a terrorist offence. It excludes certain 'terrorist' offences from claiming the advantages of the political defence, and it imposes strict obligations upon contracting states to extradite all fugitives who have committed such offences, or failing that, to submit them to the jurisdiction of their own courts. It imposes a further obligation upon contracting states to extend their jurisdictional claims over criminal offenders in order to tighten the European jurisdictional net.

Despite its grandiose name, the Convention has limited objectives. It aims to secure the extradition or trial of all persons convicted of, or charged with, offences of violence, loosely classified as 'terrorist' offences. It certainly does not seek to meet, nor to solve any of the problems that give rise to terrorism. The number of persons affected by the Convention will not be large. Nevertheless, the decision of the contracting states to abolish between themselves the availability of the 'political defence' does represent an important change in policy. It is open to signature only by states that are members of the Council of Europe, all of whom are, in fact, parties to the European Convention on Human Rights.

See also **Responses to terrorism, United Nations and international terrorism, Western Europe**

SWAPO: South West Africa People's Organisation SWAPO was founded in June 1960, probably in Namibia, by Hermann Toivo ja Toivo (who in 1968 received a twenty-year prison sentence for offences under the South African 'Terrorism Act' of 1967). It replaced the earlier Ovamboland

People's Organisation, created in 1957 with the object of gaining support from ethnic groups other than the Ovambos. SWAPO absorbed smaller parties from various parts of the territory, among them the Caprivi African National Union. The executive contained members from all the main groups within South-West Africa.

In its early years SWAPO sent petitions to the UN in order to gain that organisation's support. These petitions asked the UN to terminate immediately the League of Nations mandate, to entrust the temporary administration of the territory to a UN commission composed of African states, to arrange for free general elections to enable South-West Africa to accede to self-government immediately through the establishment of a democratic African government based on the principle of 'one man one vote', and for independence from South Africa not later than 1963. The UN General Assembly and various UN committees passed successive resolutions condemning South Africa's policies in Namibia.

SWAPO's guerrilla operations started in 1965, supported from the outset by the liberation committee of the Organisation of African Unity (OAU) as a means of furthering the eventual independence of South-West Africa.

Sam Nujoma, the President of SWAPO, specifically opposed the implementation of the Odendaal Report, a South African plan to divide the territory into distinct ethnic areas. Before the UN Council for Namibia, Nujoma declared in 1973 that the people of Namibia rejected further diplomatic contacts and that 'an intensification of the armed liberation struggle' was the 'only language' which the South Africans understood.

However, in January 1975 Nujoma offered to negotiate with the South African Government on six preconditions, failing acceptance of which SWAPO would renew its guerrilla warfare. The conditions were that South Africa publicly recognised the right of the Namibian people to independence and national sovereignty; that Namibia's territorial integrity was inviolate and respected; that SWAPO was recognised and accepted as the only authentic representative of the Namibian people; that all political prisoners in Namibia and South Africa were released; that all Namibians in exile be allowed to return without fear of arrest or victimisation; and that South Africa undertook, before talks began, to withdraw all troops and police from Namibia.

In 1974 the South African Prime Minister, B. J. Vorster, said SWAPO was not the representative of South-West Africa and that its so-called leaders outside the territory were 'neither the natural nor the elected leaders of any of the peoples', and would not be imposed on them by any outside organisation.

At the end of 1975, SWAPO formed a Namibian National Convention which later in the year boycotted a constitutional conference called by the South African administration and held at the Turnhalle in Windhoek. SWAPO insisted on holding elections on the basis of 'one man one vote' for political parties rather than ethnic groups, and only after withdrawal of South Africa's 'occupying forces'. SWAPO held talks on the future of Namibia with Soviet leaders in mid 1976, and later in the year it was granted observer status by the UN and invited to participate in the Assembly's sessions and in the work of all international conferences convened under the Assembly's auspices. Nujoma proudly claimed that his party was a believer in neutrality and non-alignment.

However, guerrilla warfare between the South African forces and SWAPO increased significantly and conflicting claims were made on both sides regarding the number of casualties inflicted. SWAPO made it clear that it would not accept any settlement plan which did not include as a precondition a total withdrawal of South Africa's troops, and the retention of Walvis Bay as part of Namibia. SWAPO reiterated its wish to establish in Namibia a democratic secular government founded on the will and particpation of all the Namibian people; and that it was prepared to test its strength in free and fair elections. With continuing procrastination by the South African authorities, SWAPO called for a UN Security Council meeting to improve 'comprehensive mandatory economic sanctions' on South Africa.

In the absence of any agreement between the UN, the five Western members of the UN Security Council, the South African government and SWAPO on the modalities of transition to independence for Namibia, the armed struggle between SWAPO units and South African forces continued during 1980. South Africa continued its 'limited operations' into Angola, which it had commenced in 1978 to snuff out SWAPO units – yet this had not prevented greater SWAPO incursions by the early 1980s, with stronger weapons and more attacks. Church circles in South Africa believed SWAPO enjoyed wide support among the people of Namibia. Ultimately the UN Council for Namibia set up in Lusaka a UN Institute for Namibia, to train officials for a future SWAPO government there.

Sykes, Sir Richard In March 1979 Sir Richard Sykes, the British Ambassador to the Netherlands, was killed by two gunmen as he was entering his official car to go to the embassy. His Dutch valet was also killed, but a visiting Foreign Office official who was sitting next to Sykes was unharmed in what police characterised as a very professional operation.

The IRA claimed responsibility according to one source, while another source stated that the Red Brigade, a previously unknown Dutch group, had carried out the killing on behalf of the IRA. According to press reports, Sykes' embassy had been fighting gun-running to Irish guerrillas by left-wing sympathisers in the Netherlands.

Sykes was a leading security authority among British diplomats. As deputy under-Secretary of State at the Foreign Office, he had been sent to Dublin to investigate the murder in 1976 by the IRA of the British Ambassador, Christopher Ewart-Biggs. Sykes wrote a government report recommending increased security precautions for UK diplomats abroad, particularly at their residences. Dutch police said there were no policemen on duty outside his home at the time of the attack because the embassy had not requested any guards.

A few hours after the Sykes murder, two gunmen shot and killed a Belgian banker, André Michaux, in Brussels. Police and British investigators believed the attackers might have killed the wrong man and had hoped instead to kill his British neighbour Paul Holmer, assistant to the UK permanent representative to NATO, Sir John Killick. Although some police sources initially suggested that the same men could have been responsible for the Sykes and Michaux murders, ballistic tests established that different weapons had been used.

Syria This Arab Republic is a 'socialist popular democracy'; its President is head of the predominant Ba'ath party. The government, the left-wing Arab Socialist Ba'ath party and the armed forces are dominated by members of the minority Alawite sect of the Shi'ite Muslim community, yet most of the population are Sunnis. Sunnis demand the recognition of Islam as the state religion. The principal opposition to the regime has come from Muslim extremists within the Sunni community, their strongest organisation being the Muslim Brotherhood. Violent actions against the regime have also been carried out by dissident Ba'athists supported by the right-wing historic Ba'ath party of Iraq.

The Muslim Brotherhood in Syria shares many objectives with the Shi'ite revolutionaries who came to power in Iran in 1979. The Brotherhood propagates Islamic fundamentalist tenets, and demands free elections, a more liberal economy and an end to Alawite dominance. Christians and other non-Muslims are promised the maintenance of their religious rights. A government satisfactory to the people is promised, but full political rights will be given only to ideologies not contradictory to Islam.

The Brotherhood is well organised, not only in Syria where it is said to have cells in the armed forces and publishes an underground journal, but also in many other countries, including Austria, West Germany, the UK and the USA, where there are Syrian émigrés and where funds are collected on its behalf.

After the assassination of a number of Soviet military advisers and an attempt to kill the President, the Syrian army moved against the Brotherhood in 1979–80. There were violent clashes in many parts of the country, and in 1981–82 it was estimated that 25,000 Syrians had been killed, with Aleppo and Hama the worst affected towns. In addition, in Hama an armed Brotherhood insurrection in early 1982 resulted in the deaths of thousands more civilians. There are rumours of some Israeli support for the Brotherhood.

The National Alliance for the Liberation of Syria is an amalgam of 20 political and religious groups with the aim of consolidating opposition to the Assad regime from within Syria and abroad, and creating a constitutional elective system in which freedom of faith, expression and association would be guaranteed. The Alliance also works for the liberation of Palestine and for the long-term objectives of Arab unity. An Arab

Communist Organisation has been outlawed for acts of sabotage on foreign buildings in Damascus.

See also **Hindawi, Offender states, Shi'ites, 'Terrorist states'**

T

Tamil Tigers Sri Lanka achieved independence from Britain in 1948. The 1948 constitution was modelled upon the Westminster Parliament, and was thought to provide guarantees of the civil rights and cultural identity of the predominantly Hindu Tamil minority community. As in Northern Ireland, the dominant majority community, in this case made up of the largely Buddhist Sinhalese, was able to manipulate what was formally a model parliamentary democracy by gerrymandering of elections and by its inbuilt parliamentary majority, in order to deprive the minority of effective political representation.

Although Tamils and Sinhalese had both inhabited the island of Sri Lanka for over two thousand years, the status of Tamils remained uncertain after 1948. An act in that year deprived one million Tamils of Indian origin of Sri Lankan citizenship, and a further act in 1949 excluded them from participation in elections. Sinhalese gradually became the single official language, and anti-Tamil riots became more frequent.

The assassination of Prime Minister Solomon Bandaranaike in September 1959 led to the dissolution of parliament, and in the subsequent general election his wife became head of government. Official policy continued to favour the Sinhalese language, leading to discrimination against Tamils in higher education and the civil service, the main channels of economic advancement. A severe crisis developed in the economy with a fall in the world market price of tea and rubber.

An insurgency waged in 1971 by the Sinhalese Janatha Vimukti Peramuna (JVP) led to the introduction of a nation-wide state of emergency, which lasted until 1977.

Sri Lanka became a Republic in 1972 and this coincided with the uniting of Tamil opposition groups to establish the Tamil United Front (TUF), which called for linguistic and religious equality. A year later they proposed the creation of an independent Tamil state, as they were angered by mounting government attempts to impose Sinhalese cultural and political domination.

The change from non-violent to violent tactics came when young Tamil militants, calling themselves 'Tigers', spearheaded a radicalisation of the TUF, transformed to the Tamil United Liberation Front (TULF). The election of 1977 brought a new Prime Minister to power, Junius Jayawardene, and established the TULF as the largest single opposition party. This strengthening of Tamil separatism provoked violent anti-Tamil riots in which many were killed, and over 40,000 Tamils (mostly tea plantation workers) were forced from their homes and fled to safety of refugee camps. The government insisted on the unity of the state of Sri Lanka. The appointment of Jayawardene as President gave greater control to central authority, but while the TULF leadership was prepared to compromise with the government, the younger Tamil militants became more radical.

After the deaths of police in 1978, armed forces were sent to maintain order in the mainly Tamil north and east of Sri Lanka in what virtually amounted to a military occupation of a hostile country. Although the Tigers were banned, they became increasingly active, blowing up the country's only airliner at the time, and killing more police. A Prevention of Terrorism Act passed by Parliament in 1979, which increased penalties for terrorist offences, only appeared to bring further attacks by separatist guerrillas on police stations and patrols, which provided the rebels with a source of arms and ammunition.

The Sinhalese population reacted violently to the increase in Tamil terrorist activity during local elections in 1981. Anti-Tamil disturbances became communal riots and led to a hardening of the ethnic divide as large numbers of Tamils living in predominantly Sinhalese areas fled to the largely Tamil provinces of the north and east.

The capital, Colombo, suffered particularly badly, and massacres here and elsewhere led to nearly 400 deaths. Support for the Tamil cause grew among large Tamil communities in southern India and Malaysia. The overseas Tamils were an important source of financial support for the separatist insurgents operating in large areas of the Tamil provinces, well armed with modern automatic weapons. The tacit support of the Indian central government under both Indira Gandhi and Rajiv Gandhi (although denied), and of the state government of Tamil Nadu in southern India was an important factor in sustaining the Tamil separatist movement. From 1984 boatloads of Tamil guerrillas came to Sri Lanka from the Indian mainland, but had mixed degrees of success.

Currently the Sri Lankan government appears to be losing control of many areas of the country and the continued existence of Sri Lanka as a unitary state is threatened. There are now 23 anti-government Tamil groups, and two in particular – the Liberation Tigers of Tamil Ealam (LTTE) and the Tamil Ealam Liberation Organisation (TELO) – have had pitched battles which have left over a hundred members of both groups dead, including the assassinated TELO leader, Sri Savaratenam. A bomb aboard an Air Lanka Tristar at Colombo airport in May 1986 killed 15 people, mostly foreign tourists. This was followed by a bomb in Colombo's main telegraph office, which killed 11 people. A group calling itself the Ealam Revolutionary Organisation of Students (EROS) claimed credit for the second explosion.

Targets Four targets of terrorism can be distinguished – the target of violence, the target of terror, the target of demands and the target of attention. The targetting of terrorist organisations, both state and non-state, left and right, ethnic and vigilante, shows some similarities as well as dissimilarities. The targets of violence are alleged lawbreakers, people with deviating habits, aliens and others considered to be subordinate races and classes or any other representatives of forces of change who threaten the status of the group whose interests are defended by the vigilantes. The targets of vigilante terrorism are members of the same group or class as the victim. It is for their benefit that the example has been made. In vigilante terrorism there is often no target for demands. The warning to the target of terror is the message and the demand is implicit: know your subordinate place. Sometimes there is a target of demands, namely a government which is considered to be too efficient, forcing vigilantes to take the law in their own hands. The link between targetting and objectives is visible in vigilante terrorism. Terrorism is a cost-effective method of freezing the challenging group into its place. Everyone who challenges the *status quo* is likely to become a possible target of vigilante violence.

The targets of violence of authoritarian state terrorists are the representatives of democratic and socialist parties, intellectuals, liberals, trade unionists and other dissidents. The targets of terror are all the other non-members of the ruling élite, the populace and in particular the actual and potential opponents. There are generally no targets of demands and attention.

The targets of violence of right-wing terrorism are often non-specific, with bombs being exploded randomly in public places. Specific targets can include left-wing leaders, intellectuals and traitors. The targets of terror are regime opponents and more generally society as a whole. Where there is a target of demands in right-wing terrorism it is often the military which is invited to stage a coup d'état. A target of attention is sometimes the government, sometimes the population as a whole, and sometimes other ultra-right groups abroad. The media and potential sympathisers among the populace also figure as targets of attention. Right-wing targetting is highly random. By making the populace rather than the regime in power the major target, it is unlikely that it can seize power by itself.

Ethnic and nationalist terrorist targets of violence are members of the dominant or alien political authorities, especially the security forces and other tools of the ruling regime. Sometimes members of the dominant ethnic population are targetted; sometimes multinational enterprise personnel are selected. Other foreigners, including tourists, have also been targets. Still other targets of violence are members of the terrorists' own ethnic group, especially leaders who are either considered to be collaborators with the dominant regime or moderates. The targets of terror can be even broader, to include whoever denies the nationalist or ethnic goals.

The targets of violence of Communist state terrorism targetting are dissidents, mainly at home but also abroad. Potential as well as actual regime opponents have been targetted, independent of class background of the victims. In fact, frequent targets of violence and terror have been state workers and rival groups challenging the legitimacy of the regime on ideological class grounds. The targets of terror are the domestic public and the émigré communities abroad. People in the camps can be said to be targets of violence with the remaining population figuring as targets of terror. Since the victimisation of the target of terror can be avoided by compliance and obedience, an important element of terrorism, the arbitrariness and unexpectedness of victimisation, is absent.

For left-wing terrorists the targets of violence are representatives of the state apparatus from ministers to policemen, government employees and military men, diplomats, judges, businessmen (from large multinational corporations), and managers (from firms manufacturing military equipment). Targets of terror are all those who share the victim's characteristics or who strongly identify with the victim. The target of demands for left-wing terrorism can be the media, which are expected to report certain statements, wealthy people and the government. The main targets of demands are the government or foreign governments. Targets of attention are groups or classes for which the terrorists purport to fight – the international proletariat, the poor, and the imprisoned. Sometimes the targets of attention are legal left-wing parties who are considered to be too passive and are invited to follow the path paved by the terrorists. For the left, it is not so much the creation of terror in one specific target group as the use of the act of violence for political blackmail and propaganda that matters. Depending on the way the actual victims of terrorist violence are linked to the target of terror, the target of demands or the target of attention, different objectives can be aimed at. By activating the interplay between the four target groups, terrorism can create multiple secondary effects which serve a variety of purposes.

Since the international terrorist can be a government, a left- or right-wing non-state actor, or a combination of the two, the targetting is largely the same as for the national terrorist. The hegemonic powers, especially the US government and American citizens abroad have become targets. Diplomats, embassies and airlines are prime targets of violence and terror. NATO officials, soldiers and installations have also become favourite targets. Foreign governments which are seen as supporters of local oppressors, and journalists and media seen as conduits to foreign public opinion are major targets for demands and attention.

Terrorists see strong links between targetting and objectives and goals. The target of Abu Nidal's 'Fatah Movement – Revolutionary Council', who are relatively small in number, include Jewish schoolchildren, restaurants and synagogues and diplomats. However, the majority of the Nidal group's victims are Arabs whom he considers traitors to the Arab cause, since they have made contacts with Zionists and have shown a willingness to come to terms with the Jewish state. A third group of declared targets are those Nidal says support Israel – namely the USA and the American President.

Most non-state left-wing terrorism is aimed at tactical objectives such as the liberation of imprisoned colleagues through coercive bargaining following acts of kidnapping or hostage-taking, mere advertising of the movement's existence, targetted at foreign terrorist movements, sympathisers who have not yet joined the movement and the terrorists themselves who need reassurance of their activities by seeing their projected image mirrored in an uncritical press. Acts of terrorism such as kidnappings have also been useful in raising funds for terrorists, in extorting concessions from the target of demands.

See also **Terrorism and terror, Victims of terrorism**

Technological change There have been significant changes both in the philosophy and tactics of terror and in the social and political environment in which it operates. Many of the differences are directly or indirectly a consequence of technological change. The most relevant developments have been in the fields of transport, communications (particularly as applied to news gathering and distribution) and weaponry. The emergence of transnational terrorism, involving terrorists of different nationalities planning, training for, and executing acts of political terrorism has been greatly facilitated by air travel.

The organisation, orientation and technical sophistication (particularly in the field of satellite technology) of the news media have significant implications for the style and range of terrorist activities to which modern society may be prey. Media coverage of a terrorist operation is often the major objective of the perpetrators. The insistence of many news directors that they have a social obligation to present the news 'as it happens', without restriction or censorship, while ignoring its potential consequences, makes it very easy for the terrorists to stage events with guaranteed worldwide audiences. One of the possible social consequences of concentrated populations and technological innovations is that the small bands of extremists and irreconcilables that have always existed may become an increasingly potent force.

Because of technological advances, society now also faces threats of a different order to those that have existed in the past. The most obvious example is the possibility that a terrorist group may gain access to nuclear, biological or biochemical materials. The possession of a very crude nuclear device would give such a group unheard-of publicity and negotiating power, with unknown effects on public confidence. If only for its dramatic publicity value it is likely that a terrorist group in the future will attempt to penetrate a nuclear facility or divert radioactive material.

The consideration which weighs against the likelihood of a threat to detonate a nuclear device or release a biological agent is the realisation that such an action would almost certainly harm the terrorists' cause. In particular for biological and biochemical materials, the possibility has existed for some time that these could be used in a blackmail situation. But they have not been used, probably because terrorists want a lot of frightened people watching rather than a lot of people dead. In 1975, German terrorists stole 54 litre bottles of mustard gas from a military store and threatened to release it in several cities. There may be future situations in which a terrorist group perhaps needing to escalate violence to be taken notice of in a world used to killing and maiming, feels compelled to employ extreme measures. Another possibility is that the so-called 'lunatic fringe' of the terrorist movement will employ these special weapons. Whatever the cause, it is clear that the potential for the use of special weapons is present and needs to be considered in national and international policy planning.

Probably the greatest threats posed by technological advances, however, are in the field of conventional weaponry. Until recently, most significant advances in military technology have involved relatively large weapons and weapons guidance systems. Because of the ability to miniaturise weapons and guidance systems, a completely new range of small, portable, cheap, highly accurate and relatively easy-to-operate weapons has been created. Because they are mass-produced, they stand a much greater chance of falling into the hands of terrorists. Furthermore, since advances in weaponry are so rapid, large numbers of these new weapons will quickly become obsolete and be disposed of via arms dealers and other routes, increasing still further the chances of distribution outside the armed forces. Already earlier generation weapons of this type have found their way into terrorist hands, e.g. the IRA have used the RPG-7 rocket launcher in Belfast.

In addition to delivery systems, there have also been advances in propellants and explosives. Non-military developments such as digital clocks, day-date watches and long-lasting power cells have further increased the flexibility available to the amateur bomb-makers. There is greater scope for terrorist activities from increased accuracy, destructive power, distance from target (and hence greater chance of escape), and most of all a greater dramatic impact. This suggests that there should be more concern for the side-effects of military technology policy, and certainly steps should be taken to increase security precautions for weaponry. Thus, although the authorities have access to equally sophisticated technology to combat terrorism, its application could be costly in terms of human liberty.

See also **Nuclear terrorism**

Teheran Embassy Siege 1979–81 In November 1979, about 500 radical Muslim students attacked the US embassy in Teheran, seizing 100 hostages after a two-hour battle in which 14 marine guards lobbed tear gas canisters. The students demanded the extradition of the exiled Shah of Iran, who two weeks previously had left Mexico for hospital treatment in the USA for cancer. The students claimed they were armed with only ten pistols, although they later said they had mined the embassy grounds and had placed explosive charges throughout the buildings. They threatened to kill the hostages and blow up the embassy compound if the US attempted a military rescue.

Two days after the siege the Iranian Cabinet resigned, leaving all formal authority in the hands of the Khomeini-led Revolutionary Council. There were up to five different groups of students holding the embassy – members of the fundamentalist Phalange, theological students from Qom (Iran's holy city), students from the University of Teheran, leftists and Communists. Some of these students may have been trained by the Popular Front for the Liberation of Palestine. Although the students said they were loyal only to Khomeini, many observers suggested that they were leading the handling of the negotiations themselves. Even though the Shah left the US for Panama after successful surgery, the students said this would not affect the freedom of the hostages, whom they threatened to try as spies.

While the takeover appeared initially to be student-led, the government quickly moved to back the demands of the students. A former foreign minister, Bani-Sadr, stated that Iran demanded American recognition that the Shah was a criminal and must be extradited, the return to Iran of the Shah's fortune, and an end to American meddling in Iranian domestic affairs. He announced an oil embargo on the United States at the same time President Carter was announcing that the US would no longer buy Iranian oil.

The American response placed incrementally increasing pressures on Iran, as well as the diplomatic isolation of Teheran. Numerous anti-Iranian protests in the United States underscored widespread support for the President's action – for example, Iranian students in the United States were told that they would face deportation unless they proved that they were enrolled as full-time students and had committed no crimes. Pilot training for the Iranians was cancelled, and the USA ordered all but 35 of 218 Iranian diplomats in the USA to leave within five days. Internationally the US focused on obtaining condemnations of Iran's actions by governments and international organisations. Scores of governments agreed that Iran had violated fundamental international legal norms. The United Nations proved impotent, and the UN Secretary-General was refused permission to meet the hostages when he visited Iran.

The Iranian government claimed that the issue was not its holding hostages, but rather the crimes of the Shah and alleged American intelligence collusion with the former regime. Numerous demonstrations in Teheran showed the solidarity of the people behind their government's action. The Iranians subsequently released several hostages, holding only those they claimed were spies. Visits by outsiders to the hostages were also carefully orchestrated as media events by the students. Visitors were not allowed to see all the hostages, leading observers to suggest that some of the hostages had been removed from the embassy grounds. Iran refused to state how many hostages were being held. Envoys from Syria, France, Sweden and Algeria were the first outsiders permitted to visit the hostages.

In January 1980, the Canadian government helped smuggle out of Iran six Americans who had escaped from the embassy during the initial attack. Letters from several hostages, including some who had been accused of being spies, trickled out of the embassy to the hostages' families. In February the Greek Catholic Archbishop Hilarion Capucci (who had been held in an Israeli prison for smuggling arms to Palestinian terrorists in the mid 1970s) visited the hostages. In a flurry of behind-the-scenes negotiations, the US agreed to the sending of a UN panel to Teheran to investigate Iranian complaints against the Shah. This coincided with the Shah's flight from Panama to final asylum in Egypt.

In early April the United States broke off diplomatic relations with Iran, imposed an economic embargo banning all exports to Iran except food and medicine, ordered a formal inventory of Iranian financial assets in the US and cancelled all future visas for Iranian travel in the USA. Three weeks after this action, an attempt by US military forces to rescue the hostages failed when three of the eight helicopters assigned to the mission became unavailable due to various mishaps in the desert.

The US Secretary of State Cyrus Vance resigned in protest over the mission. The Iranian students claimed that they would prevent future rescue attempts by moving the hostages out of the embassy to other locations throughout Iran.

In mid 1980 the International Court of Justice unanimously ordered Iran to release the hostages. The situation continued in stalemate for the rest of 1980; it became President Carter's aim to achieve the hostages' release before his term as President ended in January 1981. This was in fact achieved in the same week that he handed over the Presidency to Ronald Reagan. The 444-day ordeal of the hostages was over; and the release was the result of a complex financial deal involving Iranian assets in the UK and USA, with Algeria acting as the honest broker.

Terror in the theory of revolution War and revolution are intimately related. In ancient Greek mythology, terror (Phobos) and dread (Deimos) were the names given to the twin horses that drew the chariot of Aries (Mars), the god of war.

Revolution is like war in that it involves the convincing use of force. Terror, however, must be distinguished from dread, or fear. Fear is a physical and psychological reaction to the strange, the unexpected, or the hazardous. Fear is a normal reaction to major political changes if they are seen as so significant as to threaten the physical safety of individual citizens.

Terror, on the other hand, is the systematic use of fear in revolutionary circumstances to aid the establishment of a new government. It may be directed towards members of the former élite, other likely power seekers or even towards the mass of population to ensure their compliance. It is not a new phenomenon, being referred to by Thucydides in ancient Greece. In the Roman Empire, governments rose and fell by violence, ultimately with significant political and social consequences.

The term revolution designates such periods of fundamental social change. What makes them possible is the change of governments by force, so that new groups rise to power, and it is the successful use of

253

force that marks out revolution as a concept from all other related concepts, such as revolt, insurgency and insurrection.

The modern use of the concept of terror in revolutionary circumstances derives from the French Revolution of 1789. The Terror is the name given to the period after the most extreme faction, the Jacobins, had obtained power, in which physical violence was used in order to create the basis of a new social order. The most spectacular feature of the Terror was the execution of members of the aristocracy, and terror was seen as a method of rooting out opponents of the regime and eliminating them. The Terror was, in fact, a method of legitimising a minority government and justifying its continued maintenance of its position.

The French Revolution was viewed as the type example of a great social revolution by later theorists of the revolution and above all by Karl Marx. Marx and Engels ridiculed those who believed in terror as a means to initiate revolution. In Western Europe revolution would, Marx thought, be the product of the prrgressive development of class consciousness among the proletariat. As a Marxist, Lenin did not see terrorism as having a role in the promotion of revolution, but as a Russian he did see it as having a role in its actual execution once open resistance had begun. He believed the purpose of fighting guerrilla operations must be to destroy the government, police and military machinery. Lenin was merely carrying out the view held centuries earlier by Machiavelli that terror is after all merely a development of fear, and fear is the instrument of government.

In sixteenth-century Russia, Ivan the Terrible employed terror simply to instil fear into the majority of the population regardless of their beliefs or intent. Tsar Nicholas I adapted to Russian conditions the secret police, the classic government instrument of terror in the twentieth century.

The role of the secret police is derived from, though by no means identical with, the role of the police in general. The secret police differ from the regular police, not in their secrecy, but in the use of their powers to keep the government secure. All police forces have a certain latitude in the interpretation and application of the laws they nominally apply with rigorous impartiality. The secret police, however, make use of this area of uncertainty to focus pressure on individuals believed to be politically unsympathetic to the regime. The use of informants, a normal part of police work, is extended in these circumstances into the systematic compilation of all information likely to lead to the disclosure of political dissent, and the arrest of suspects is conducted in such a way that if the 'right' people have not been arrested, they will be in any event intimidated into conformity.

Terror used to instil fear can be of two kinds: discriminating, i.e. directed towards target groups and capable of being regulated in intensity according to the perceived needs of the situation, as was practised in the nineteenth century; and indiscriminate terror, as has become common in this century as the last resort of the extremist. After the abortive Russian Revolution of 1905, the lesson for revolutionaries was that good intentions were not enough, the seizure of political power was something that could not be achieved simply by instilling fear into an incumbent government; if anything, that was likely to strengthen it in its resolve. What was needed was the precise direction of force towards specific political targets and here, as in any other military operation, surprise and careful planning were crucial. This lesson was the main one which made the Bolshevik seizure of power in Petrograd in 1917 possible, and even then this would not have been possible without the impact of war on the social fabric and the corresponding weakness in all respects of the provisional government.

The Bolshevik ideology gave the use of terror additional dimensions – it was a strategy in the class war, seen as an armed conflict, in which the use of force was as natural as it would be in any other circumstances of belligerency. Since the basis of class lay in the relation of individual social groups to the forces of production, the achievement of working-class domination could only be attained by the economic restructuring of society.

Up to the Second World War terror remained a feature primarily of the consolidation phase of great social revolutions. It was once again a feature of consolidation both of the Chinese and of the Cuban revolutions, as well as in the consolidation of the power of the Islamic regime in Iran after 1979. On each occasion terror was employed not only against the military as supporters of the old regime, but against prominent members of the former oligarchy.

The development of a technique of guerrilla warfare as a path to revolution was to create an important additional role for terror in the theory of revolution. Mao's theory of the three stages of guerrilla warfare envisages a preliminary stage of preparation, followed by a stage in which a guerrilla movement is established and expands its control over a wider and wider area, and finally, a period in which the guerrilla force tranforms itself into a regular army capable of defeating the forces of the government in a series of pitched battles.

Violence is a mere tool in the process of psychological warfare, with victims being random victims, not individuals selected on the grounds of justice, revolutionary or otherwise. Thus, though one must always distinguish between 'terror' as a technique and 'terrorism' as a belief in the value of terror, the two are closely related. Indeed, the historical myths of the efficacy of terror in earlier times and other situations have led to the association of the techniques of terror with several varieties of political thought. Both Marxist and militant Islamic groups have used terrorist methods, and links have developed between revolutionary movements of very different backgrounds, including the Japanese Red Army, the Italian Red Brigades (Brigate Rosse), the PLO, the Basque nationalist movement ETA and the IRA.

In the period since 1945 terror has ceased merely to be a feature of the consolidation stage of revolutions, and even then something which may be invoked only when the challenges appear to be otherwise insuperable. It has become instead a feature of the actual achievement of power itself. Just as the stages of guerrilla warfare itself overlap, so the use of terror has moved backwards into the earlier stages of the revolution. It continues to be used in the actual processes of government. It has been assumed in many circles that its use by governments faced with revolutionary challenges is not only normal but natural, and critics have identified and criticised what has often been called 'the national security state', which typically is a Latin American military dictatorship. The use of terror originates in a decision by the armed forces that the political situation is becoming unmanageable as a result of challenges by either rural or urban guerrillas. It forms an excellent excuse for the military to assume supreme power. For this purpose they create a large but unmanageable security apparatus – unmanageable partly because of the secrecy which surrounds all military operations, but also because of the impact on such circumstances of traditional inter-service rivalry. Each individual, isolated in themselves, is left to stand alone before the ruthless and uncontrolled power of the state. Today even a relatively weak government has a huge potential for violence and destruction, not only if it chooses to exercise it, but also if it fails to restrain those whose professional duty it is to use it.

Once a government agrees to bind itself, and particularly if it agrees to limit its own term of office, the impetus to violence is much reduced. Che Guevara consistently maintained that a revolution could not succeed until the possibilities for peaceful change were seen to be exhausted.

Both in theory and in practice the factor most conducive to the use of terror by the political opposition is its use by government; and conversely if terror is to be avoided, repressive measures on the part of government should be eliminated and a tolerable level of government repression established as soon as possible.

See also **Marx and revolutionary violence, Targets, Terrorism and terror**

Terrorism and terror No consensus exists on the relationship between terrorism and terror. Observers often see terror in a historical context such as in France under Robespierre or Russia under Stalin. Some see terrorism as the more organised form of terror, and yet others stress that terror is a state of mind while terrorism refers to organised social activity. The most polarised views are that terror can occur without terrorism, and that terror is the key to terrorism.

The suffix '-ism' that is added to terror is sometimes held to denote its systematic character, either on the theoretical level, where the suffix refers to a political philosophy, or on a practical level, where it refers to a manner of acting or an attitude. Some attribute a doctrinal quality to terrorism, but it is more common to see it as a deliberate manner of acting.

Terror originally referred to a period characterised by political executions, as during the French Revolution from May 1793 to July 1794.

Originally conceived as an instrument against monarchist traitors, the Terror of the Committee of Public Safety (of which Robespierre was the most prominent member), soon began to kill Republicans as well. The revolutionary allies on the right of the Jacobins (the Indulgents, under Danton) and on the left (the Hébartists), became victims of the unleashed Terror. Altogether at least 300,000 people were arrested during the Reign of Terror and 17,000 were officially tried and executed, while many died in prison or without a trial. Those who had originally supported the draconian measures of Robespierre began to fear for their lives and conspired to overthrow him. They could not accuse him of the Terror since they had declared it to be the legitimate form of government, so they accused him of Terrorism, which had an illegal and repulsive flavour. For this Robespierre and his associates were sent to the guillotine on the 9th and 10th Thermidor of the year II (27 and 28 July 1794).

Under the reaction to Robespierre the agents and partisans of the revolutionary tribunals were termed 'terrorists', and this name spread over Europe, appearing in England in 1795. The Jacobin terrorists were labelled anarchists under the directorate; while for the émigrés and their monarchist followers the term 'terrorist' was sometimes used synonymously with 'patriots', or used for all republicans and even for the soldiers who defended the liberty of the republic. By the end of the nineteenth century the term 'terrorist', originally used to describe violence in the name of the revolutionary state and then the reactionary state of the Restoration, became associated with anti-state violence under the impact of the Russian terrorists of the 1880s and the anarchists of the 1890s. The twentieth-century experience of state terror notwithstanding, the anti-state sense of the term has become paramount again in the late twentieth century, under the impact of wars of national liberation and the revolutionary aspirations of students and ethnic minorities in the industrialised countries.

Terrorism does not only produce terror; and terror is perhaps not even the main result for the majority of the audience of an act or campaign of terrorism. Psychologists define the psychological condition of terror as extreme fear or anxiety. Though terrorism is a real, not an imaginary danger, it is a vague, incomprehensible, unpredictable and unexpected menace. Terrorism affects the social structure as well as the individual, and may upset the framework of precepts and images that members of society depend on and trust. Uncertainty about what sort of behaviour to expect from others results in disorientation.

Terror is a constituent of many ordinary crimes. An act of terrorism has a purpose similar to general deterrence; the instant victim is less important than the overall effect on a particular group to whom the exemplary act is really addressed. Terrorism, although it has individual victims, is an onslaught upon society itself. Terror is a natural phenomenon, and terrorism is the conscious exploitation of it. Terrorism is coercive, designed to manipulate the will of its victims and its larger audience. The degree of fear is generated by the crime's very nature, by

T

the manner of its perpetration or by its senselessness, wantonness or callous indifference to human life. This terrible fear is the source of the terrorist's power and communicates his challenge to society. Intimidation is based on threat and threats have occasionally to be enforced to remain credible.

An implicit assumption is that the product of terrorism is terror. But who exactly is terrorised? The immediate victim of a terrorist bomb explosion may be dead before he gets a chance to be filled with terror. The potential fellow victims, in a hostage situation where one hostage has been killed to show that the terrorists mean business in their demands, are those most likely to be terror-stricken.

Four levels of response can be induced by terror. Firstly, there is enthusiasm among the adherents of the insurgent movement. Secondly, the lowest level of negative reaction is fright. Thirdly, the middle level of response is anxiety called forth by fear of the unknown and the unknowable. Lastly, the most extreme level of response is despair, an intensified form of anxiety. The response to an act of terror can vary greatly, depending on the danger of repetition and the degree of identification with the victim.

See also **Fear, Targets, Victims of terrorism**

Terrorism: future sources There will be no shortage of potential causes for terrorism: rising population; increased poverty and scarcity of resources; racial tension; inflation and unemployment; increased tension between the 'have' and 'have-not' nations; waves of refugees shoved about by wars and repression; immigrants moving from poorer states to wealthier ones, often bringing with them the conflicts of their home countries, sometimes causing resentment among native citizens; rapid urbanisation; the disintegration of traditional authority structures; the emergence of single issue groups; the rise of aggressive fundamentalist religious groups or religious cults. Yet there is no demonstrable connection between poverty, scarcity, inflation or any other socio-economic indicators and terrorism. Indeed, countries experiencing the highest levels of terrorism are often among the economically and socially most advanced nations in their region or in the world, and often the least authoritarian. Contemporary terrorism seems to come with modern society. Traditional authority structures have collapsed with ensuing violence throughout history and the present time is no exception.

Ideology and ethnic nationalism have been the two major engines of modern terrorism. Ideology drove the urban guerrillas in Latin America and their terrorist imitators in Western Europe and the USA. Most of these groups adhered to some variation of Marxism. Dreams of independent homelands have inspired groups from the IRA to the Armenians, and more recently religious fanaticism, although directed toward secular ends, and secret wars waged by states have accounted for a growing share of the world's terrorist violence.

Authorities on terrorism have identified state sponsorship, ethnic conflict and religious fanaticism as the most likely sources of future terrorist violence. Ideology, never a major factor in the United States, has always been a more serious business in Europe. However, over the last decade, the public have grown tired of violence which until then had been fashionable, at least in some circles. Discredited by their actions, groups on the far left lost ground as the political centre of gravity moved right on both sides of the Atlantic in the late 1970s. The resurgence of Euroterrorism in 1984 and 1985 demonstrated that the left-wing extremists did not abandon the field. They did abandon visions of revolution and instead concentrated on more concrete issues that offered them a potential constituency, such as disarmament, opposition to NATO and the deployment of further nuclear weapons. Meanwhile, the shift to the right seems to have brought about an increase in right-wing violence in the 1980s.

Ideology may remain a powerful force in the Third World, where left-wing guerrillas fight governments in Latin America, Africa and the Philippines, while anti-Marxist guerrillas wage war on Marxist governments in Central America, Africa, Afghanistan and Indochina. All of these guerrilla groups, left and right, have their terrorist branches to intimidate foes, enforce obedience, extort funds or gain publicity. This traditional use of terrorism will no doubt continue. The use of terrorism by insurgent groups could increase as some of the movements are defeated or stalemated.

Possibly some Third World groups will find common cause and launch terrorist campaigns directed against targets in the developed world on behalf of Third World causes. Terrorist groups have obliged corporations to pay them revolutionary 'taxes', provide free food and medical supplies to the poor or finance philanthropic enterprises. A consortium of terrorist groups could carry out campaigns of violence aimed at coercing the world into a new international economic order or to extort concessions to relieve the Third World's massive debt burden. Terrorists have retaliated against corporate managers for industrial accidents that harmed workers and chemical spills. It is not inconceivable that Third World terrorists might retaliate for pollution or industrial disasters in the Third World. On the other hand, terrorist groups have not had much success to date in making common cause.

See also **Uncontrollable international terrorism, Western Europe**

Terrorism in the 1960s By the late 1960s the signs in the global community were that violence was gaining ground. Broad historical changes, ideological changes and technological changes were occurring. The world was living under a nuclear stalemate created by the superpowers and it was becoming more attractive for groups to use low-risk, potentially high-yield and very effective methods of struggle such as terrorism. European colonialism had ended, leaving a host of newly independent nations to grapple with unfamiliar problems. Restless minorities in many of these countries were no longer restrained by European-style police and military forces. Disputes arose with neighbouring states over boundaries that had often been established arbitrarily by colonial administrations. Guerrilla uprisings and low-intensity warfare often included terrorist activity. A growing emphasis on human rights led Western democracies to place high value on the life of a single citizen. Democracies proved to be susceptible to hostage-taking threats. Terrorists found kidnapping could bring concessions unattainable by other means.

Several key religious and political changes also occurred during the late 1960s. Guerrilla warfare became increasingly urbanised, and indeed urban terrorism came into its own mainly as a result of the defeat of the rural guerrillas in Latin America. Islamic fundamentalism growing out of the reaction against Westernisation and modernity provided a breeding ground for Shi'ite terrorism. The Vietnam War radicalised large numbers of young people in developed nations throughout the world, and taking up the cause of inequality between first and third world nations, they became more committed to Marxist-Leninist ideals, created underground cells and took up terrorism.

The growth of mass communications, especially television, was seized upon by terrorists as a propaganda tool. By 1970 air travel had come of age, and this helped to provide rapid movement for terrorists between target nations and countries that provided safe havens. The number of hijackings also increased; in 1969 alone there were 33 successful hijackings of American planes bound for Cuba. Weapons also improved and by the start of the 1970s it was clear that, for example, modern rapid-fire submachine guns fitting easily into briefcases could be a major weapon in the armoury of the terrorist.

1968 was the year which witnessed the big upsurge in terrorism with a number of events uniting in that year in its favour. Members of the Popular Front for the Liberation of Palestine (PFLP) seized an El Al airliner and forced it to fly to Algeria – launching a campaign of air piracy that has been the hallmark of terrorism ever since. In West Germany the Baader-Meinhof gang began to gain prominence through a series of arson attacks. In Egypt, Yassir Arafat was appointed leader of the Palestine Liberation Organisation. Across the world in the Americas, two important events occurred. In the United States Martin Luther King was assassinated, unleashing a spate of domestic violence by groups such as the Black Panthers and Weathermen. In Mexico City marches culminated in protests at the Olympic Games, aiding growth of a terrorist movement with Cuban and Soviet connections. Cubans gave more or less indiscriminate support to Latin American guerrilla movements and terrorist movements. Doctrinally, the Cubans should have assisted only rural guerrillas but they also supported urban terrorism, especially after the collapse of most Latin American rural guerrilla movements. The first widespread terrorist training centres were established in North Korea in 1968–69; since then former trainees have been traced to and in some cases apprehended in Latin America (Mexico, Brazil, Bolivia, Colombia and other countries), to the Middle East (in the PFLP), Asia (Sri Lanka, Malaya, Indonesia) and Africa.

Most of the terrorist groups of the 1960s were left-wing in orientation or used left-wing phraseology in their appeals and manifestos. Right-wing terrorist groups operated in Turkey, Italy and Guatemala, in Argentina and Brazil, but their impact was felt on the domestic scene only. Foreign powers began to intervene directly or discreetly, and provide help to terrorist movements. It was only in the 1960s that this new form of warfare by proxy really came into its own, thus opening entirely new possibilities for terrorism. Operations in third countries became far more frequent; in past ages it had been the rule that Russian terrorists would limit their attacks to Russia, and the Irish to Ireland or the United Kingdom. In the 1960s, on the other hand, Palestinians operated in Paraguay or France, Japanese terrorists in Kuwait, Israel and the Netherlands, and Germans in Sweden or Uganda. This new multinational terrorism was bound to create confusion about the identity of the attackers and the purpose of their actions.

While political violence became intellectually respectable in the 1960s in some circles, the ability of the authorities to counteract terrorism was more restricted than in the past. Up to the Second World War, terrorists who had been apprehended by the authorities faced in many cases long prison terms. With the dawning of the permissive age, it became far less risky to engage in terrorism, except in a few less enlightened countries. Where terrorism would have been dangerous, it was rare. If the judiciary was reluctant to impose draconian penalties on its own citizens, the foreign terrorist could expect to get away with light sentences if his case reached trial at all, for his imprisonment would have exposed the host country to retaliation, to fresh terrorist attacks, to the seizing of hostages and to blackmail.

Like the Palestinians, the Latin Americans realised that the mass media, domestic and foreign, were of paramount importance; on various occasions they seized radio and television stations and broadcast their propaganda. They were the first to engage in the systematic kidnapping of foreign diplomats and businessmen, correctly assuming that such operations would both embarrass the local government and attract worldwide publicity.

In 1968 the most recent and still current wave of Irish terrorism started, distinguished from all previous outbreaks by its greater efficiency and even greater cruelty. Terrorism was indiscriminate; it was not directed against the leaders of the enemy camp – bars, stores and public transport were among the favourite aims of bomb attacks both in Ulster and England. It was perhaps because terrorist operations were so easy that the IRA did not engage in some of the terrorist techniques such as the hijacking of planes, that were so popular among terrorist movements elsewhere.

Manifestations of urban terrorism were reported from many parts of the globe, excepting always the Communist countries and other effective dictatorships. By the late 1960s the achievements of the small terrorist groups which had evolved from the much broader New Left Movement in Europe, Japan and the United States were few and far between. The small New Left groups withered away or were absorbed in the new international terrorism. This was also to expand at a far greater rate than the Latin American and the nationalist-separatist movements. Wide publicity for terrorist acts contributed to the growing international status of the Palestine Liberation Organisation. Democratic societies were compelled to divert some resources to defence against terrorist attacks but these were minute measured by any standards. It was not until the 1970s that there was the internationalisation of terrorist violence, which in the 1960s had been centred on mainly domestic problems within Latin America, Europe and the Middle East.

Terrorist mindset Given the typical age of a terrorist (22 to 24), it is unsurprising that certain characteristics of a terrorist's mind are often attributed to adolescence.

Terrorists often over-simplify complex issues to black and white. The groups are intensely intellectualised, inward-looking and politically naïve in their theorising. The terrorist lives out a fantasy war convinced that he has broad support from numerous like-minded followers.

Terrorists have many pent-up concerns about an individual's inability to change society. Apart from frustration there is also self-righteousness, as the terrorists believe implicitly in their own rectitude. Intolerance, dogmatism, authoritarianism and a ruthless treatment of their own people who deviate from the set view are common to terrorist mentality.

Many terrorists seem to feel that a reasonable, if not near-perfect future lies just around the corner, once the present order has been destroyed. This utopianism, coupled with frustration at the slow pace of social change, frequently produces left- and right-wing political extremism. Terrorists are often lonely people who use religious or political ideals to interest political recruits. For many of them, the terrorist group has been their first family.

To assert their own existence terrorist actions are laden with symbolic overtones, involving the choice of captives, locations, weapons and timing.

Many terrorist murders are coldblooded, but captors who hold hostages for protracted periods tend to develop a kind of bond with them that makes coldblooded murder less likely.

See also **Beliefs of terrorists**

Terrorist roles Counter-terrorist organisations all over the world have to try to understand something of the dynamics of the terrorist personality as it functions within certain roles in the group. Three distinct roles are discernible and frequently emerge in terrorist groups found in democratic nations.

The *leader* is a person of total dedication, a trained theoretician with a strong personality; the *activist-operator* is a person with an anti-social personality, frequently an ex-convict, an opportunist; and the *idealist* is usually the university drop-out, the minor functionary, with a life pattern of searching for the truth. The leader of leftist groups is often a female, e.g. Nancy Perry of the Symbionese Liberation Army (SLA) in the USA; Ulrike Meinhof of the Baader-Meinhof in West Germany; Fusako Shigenobu of the Rengo Shekigun (Japanese Red Army), and Norma Aristoto of the Montoneros in Argentina. They are cynical but dedicated and show few signs of self-interest. The leaders see themselves as unique with superior ability and knowledge.

Whilst the leader is dedicated, he or she is not nearly as dedicated as paranoid personalities within the group. The paranoid individual refuses to be confused by the facts, unlike the leader, and only his interpretation of events is correct; he is right, and others, unless they totally agree with the leader, are not right. The leader is more single-minded, intelligent and theoretically oriented than most people; is more suspicious and inclined to interpret events selectively, but not to the degree found in true mental illness.

The leader reads people well and appeals to their needs, and uses followers in comfortable, fulfilling roles. Allowance is made for the followers' needs for recognition, achievement and self-fulfilment. Each follower is able to be a self-appointed general.

Police involvement with the leader is infrequent, since the leader is behind the scenes as a policy-developer. Occasionally the leader may venture out with the group to show it how to accomplish a particular task. If apprehended, the leader is bright enough to maintain silence. Should he or she begin to talk, a generally superior attitude and an assured discussion of the 'conspiracy theory of history' will begin to emerge. This is true if the leader thinks the interrogator is a possible convert.

The role of opportunist operator is generally a male role, held by one whose criminal activity predates his political involvement. He has similarities to the anti-social personality, also known as the sociopath or psychopath. Terrorist groups that operate against democracies appear to embrace this person, the muscle of the organisation. Some of the more infamous include Donald Defreeze of the Symbionese Liberation Army; Greg Adornedo of the Emiliano Zapata Unit (EZU); Andreas Baader and Hans Joachim Klein of the Baader-Meinhof gang, and Akira Niehei of the Japanese Red Army. The opportunist generally is oblivious to the needs of others and unencumbered by the capacity to feel guilt or sympathy. He is usually recruited from the prison population by the leader or the third functionary in the organisation, the idealist. The intelligence of the opportunist varies; the brighter he is, the more of a threat he could pose to the leader. The opportunist could take over the group, therefore, to maintain control if the leader became paranoid. Relationships between leader and opportunist are extremely sensitive – and internecine war is a threat. Given his penchant for aggressive behaviour, his criminal experience and his anti-social orientation, the opportunist is well-suited for the responsibilities of a terrorist group field commander. Without the opportunist a group is radical only in rhetoric – and he provides the terror element of the terrorist group. The opportunist is familiar to the police officer. Even the officer who has limited experience has met someone with this personality disorder many times – the vicious con artist or the good informant, the individual who is meek as a kitten when cornered yet vicious when he has the upper hand. The leader of the group can lure the opportunist into the organisation by making him a compellingly attractive offer. This process can be and has been used by the police to develop the opportunist as an informant defector or informant in place.

The idealist role in the group is the soldier; the idealistic follower who reconnoitres buildings prior to bombings, follows the opportunist into the bank, carries the messages and is generally the cannon fodder for the revolution. His rhetoric is heavy with statements calling for protracted wars of national liberation; but generally there is lack of depth in his rhetoric, and he merely parrots pet phrases. He is the group member most likely to become committed to new ideologies, but is unlikely to become an informant. The extreme idealist or 'true believer' is not a successful person, and his self-concept is poor, for he views his life only as a member of the group.

Terrorist groups are fluid, task-oriented gatherings of individuals. Individuals change; roles remain. When two leaders appear in a group, one must go. The displaced leader may become an idealist or start his own group. These three roles are seen in many terrorist groups that operate in democratic nations throughout the world. The hostage (particularly in a kidnap and imprisonment situation) is likely to encounter all three types of terrorists. The activist operator (opportunist) seizes him; he is interrogated by the leader or person responsible for propaganda, and finally encounters the idealists who guard and feed him.

See also **Personalities of revolutionaries, Terrorist mindset**

'Terrorist states' With increasing frequency, acts of terrorism are being labelled the direct or indirect products of state policies.

A number of governments do assist terrorist organisations, although they do not usually plan or direct specific operations. If efficiently employed, the technological resources and knowledge of a state could dramatically increase the sophistication and effect of terrorist actions against the peculiar vulnerabilities of advanced societies. What to date has been only an irritant to modern society could become a true danger.

It is true that a number of third world states now unashamedly sponsor terrorist activity with only the flimsiest attempts at denial: Iran and Islamic Jihad; Syria and various groups in Lebanon: Libya and several 'rejectionist' Palestinian and Egyptian groups. But the true extent of the increase in state-backed terrorism is obscured by propaganda charges and counter-charges. Furthermore several other factors can deceptively magnify the image of burgeoning state terrorism. Many of these are intellectual or semantic in nature.

Firstly, a body of research implying Soviet complicity has accumulated about the attempted assassination of Pope John Paul II. Whether or not a Bulgarian-Soviet connection is ultimately proven, the very existence of this work encourages those inclined to charge frequent Soviet involvement in such activity.

Secondly, violent retaliation by a state against enemies ensconced in the midst of a civilian population inevitably takes a toll of those civilians. Israeli attacks against Palestinian guerrillas in refugee camps, for instance, become 'state terrorism' in the eyes of Palestinian supporters. In the past, such actions would have been called 'police actions' or 'pre-emption' – not terrorism.

Thirdly, conspicuous support to insurgents who periodically practise internal terrorist activity as a part of their overall programme has also come to be considered state terrorism.

Many Europeans consider the USA responsible for fostering sporadic terrorism, because of its support for the Nicaraguan guerrilla movement. Soviet support of various Palestinian factions, while ostensibly similar, is greatly complicated by a Palestinian propensity to operate internationally.

There is also a political imperative that tends to inflate the intensity of accusations of state terrorism. The desire to 'retaliate' or 'pre-empt' terrorists is unfulfilled if no accessible target can be found. Most terrorists cannot be identified and removed without causing unacceptable civilian casualties.

But if a state sponsor of the terrorist group is identified, it can be targeted by a range of diplomatic, economic or military reprisals. As a result, policy-makers bent on combatting terrorism follow the human urge to grope for evidence of state complicity. To do nothing would be politically unacceptable. A guilty state provides one other advantage not normally found among terrorists: it responds more or less rationally to outside pressure to change behaviour; terrorists and their organisations do not. A Shi'ite extremist in Lebanon has personal reasons for martyrdom in an act of terrorism against the West. But the Iranian leaders who have backed him must heed the litany of responsibilities that accompanies state power. These responsibilities induce caution when a credible challenge is given.

The crescendo of voices accusing states of engaging in or supporting terrorism is grounded only partly in truth. It is also partly based on a desire to render the problem more susceptible to resolution by rational means – even military ones.

Unless a link is incontestably uncovered, reprisals against a state for a terrorist event could serve to escalate a relatively minor act into a far more serious confrontation. Ironically, the escalation of such an event to state conflict serves the purposes of most terrorists well.

See also **Hindawi, Offender states**

Therapy terrorism In anarchist doctrine, atrocities serve two purposes. They were a means of producing politically favourable reactions in others, and they were ends in themselves, enabling the terrorist to gain self-respect. Different terrorist movements subsequently emphasised one purpose at the expense of the other. The more successful political movements have always stressed terror as a means; most groups which see terror as expedient have functioned in colonial areas where the limited goal of the enemy's withdrawal was feasible. Arguments about the effectiveness of atrocities are common within a terrorist movement, causing an original nucleus to split into a proliferation of organisations like Irgun and the Stern Gang in Israel, Al-Fatah, PLP, IRA Officials and IRA Provisionals. Proliferation usually results from arguments about how far terrorists can expand the scope of atrocities without making the target's will to resist inflexible.

Some terrorist movements have stressed terror as an end in itself. They are less interesting as political forces, but like the psychotic who reflects in an exaggerated way tendencies not usually noticed in ordinary persons, these terrorist movements should be studied because each teaches something about the necessary foundations of terrorist movements everywhere.

Terrorism is a form of conflict, and most people enjoy conflict for its own sake. One can gain therapeutic value from conflict, especially if a cause seems worthy.

Serious conflict embraces a variety of concerns. Most people have good reason to feel ashamed of joy they feel when conflict seems unfair, irrelevant to any achievable social object and in which the participants are being consumed by their own hate. The difference between a normal person who enjoys a good fight, and a sadist or masochist, is that the sadist inflicts violence on another person solely as an instrument for pleasure and the masochist uses himself for that purpose.

The satisfaction most people get from fighting is related to feelings of respect they feel for the other party, for themselves, and for a cause; these feelings are usually embodied in conventions which are supposed to regulate the conflict even after victory.

The anarchist terrorist assumes that society is corrupt, and as a member of it, the terrorist is corrupt at least to the extent that one limits oneself by society's conventions. To grasp one's true self, one must break through the boundaries of 'normal' actions, thoughts and feelings. In anarchist terms the greatest atrocity a terrorist could commit would be to murder a colleague for the sole purpose of proving himself free of guilt.

One does not know how deep the belief in terror as personal therapy is in contemporary groups, and what new levels of atrocities against themselves are conceivable even to terrorists. It may be impossible simply to pay lip-service to a set of ideas; people will keep trying to raise the commitment of group members to violence.

Threats to persons and property The likeliest sources from which threats of violence may come include criminals; disgruntled or dissident groups or individuals attempting arson or sabotage; demonstrators or rioters motivated by political dissent, industrial conflict or social unrest; ideologically motivated terrorists, indigenous or international left-wing, right-wing, environmentalist, nationalist or religious groups; domestic state terrorists, overtly or secretly sponsored or condoned by their own governments in their own countries; international state terrorists operating outside their own countries and sponsored by their own or foreign governments; and warring factions, whose scale of fighting may range from guerrilla terrorist actions to civil war, and with whose conflicts expatriate organisations and individuals may get involved quite incidentally.

Personal attack and intimidation, especially of diplomats and expatriate executives, are likely to increase. The aims will be to force changes in government policy (as was achieved by Shi'a terrorists in Lebanon 1983–84) or to drive out foreign-based companies (as was achieved by left-wing terrorists in Argentina in the 1970s and in Central America in the 1980s). Methods of intimidation other than killing or wounding are sometimes used, such as harassment of families or malicious damage to cars and homes. The tactic may be extended to intimidate locally recruited staff, to deter them from working for foreign organisations, or to suborn them into sabotage, betrayal of confidential information or collaboration with intruders or kidnappers.

Kidnapping is a growing form of crime, generally for the extortion of a ransom, although there is sometimes an element of political blackmail, for example for the release of prisoners or publication of a political manifesto. The two forms of kidnapping – short-term and long-term – require rather different responses. Short-term abduction has been prevalent in European countries and is usually carried out by criminals rather than political terrorists. A short-term kidnap can become a long-term kidnap in which the hostage is taken to an unknown location for days, weeks or months while a ransom is negotiated, usually by a series of short, sharp telephone calls. A long-term kidnap will more usually begin with the abduction of the hostage, often between home and work or home and school.

There are a number of reasons why kidnap for ransom and other forms of extortion are likely to increase. Security of banks is constantly improving. The rapid supplanting of cash transactions by computerised credit transfers, and the payment of wages and salaries by bank credit will result in a massive decline in the circulation, holding and transport of cash.

Hostage seizure in a known location presents a problem totally different from that of a secret hideout because from the start it becomes a siege in which the police can deploy whatever force is necessary, and they hold the initiative. The hostage-takers' aim is almost always to gain publicity, so they will pick a newsworthy target such as an embassy, a computer centre, an oil refinery or a power station. Secondary aims may be to extort political concessions or simply to disrupt a key facility.

Hijacking is just another form of hostage seizure in which the aircraft, ship train or coach are treated as 'mobile premises' of a government or corporation. Success against aircraft is likely to encourage more hijacking but it should also have the effect of goading airport authorities to tighten security. As with hostage seizure, the level of hijackings will rise and fall. Extortion by threat to kill, maim or kidnap people can be even more effective than threats against property. Multinational corporations have paid ransoms in the face of threats to their executives to try to save lives at the time, prevent future extortions by threats, and ultimately to protect their own property. The long-term motivation of political terrorists is the furtherance of political and religious objectives. To achieve long-term aims there are often short-term tactics such as publicity, political blackmail, extortion of money, humiliating or discrediting a government or corporation, or coercing it to change its policies. Attacks on property can therefore be both a short- and long-term objective.

Arson and sabotage can be carried out clandestinely by people who have penetrated or bypassed the processes of staff selection, vetting, identification, control of access or control of visitors, including labour employed by contractors doing work in the building, i.e. by people who are inside, and whose malice is unsuspected.

The growing scale and interdependence of data processing systems, including computers and communications, make manufacturing and service industries and public service establishments more vulnerable to sabotage.

Bombing has for many years been the most prevalent of all kinds of terrorist attack. There has been rapid growth over the years, including the use in recent times of huge explosive charges in trucks and cars, occasionally driven by suicide drivers and directed against embassies, government buildings and multinational corporations. Bombs have been used less by the far left than the far right – religious fanatics, racialists or nationalists such as neo-fascists in Germany and Italy, Islamic fundamentalists, the IRA, and ETA. This type of activity will increase because religious and racialist fundamentalism seems to have a growing appeal, especially to those who believe or are persuaded that they are unfairly deprived, and because growing public familiarity with mass killings by terrorists means that still more outrageous shocks are needed to capture attention on television. The development of smaller, slimmer bombs with more sophisticated remote control for activation and detonation makes letter and parcel bombs more effective and harder to detect.

Hoax bomb calls are highly disruptive, and aim to disrupt a commercial organisation at minimal risk. Telephone warnings, hoax or real, are usually at very short notice.

Blocking access to sites by demonstrations is increasingly attractive to anti-NATO or environmentalist movements in Europe against government and corporate targets. This tactic is used especially against installations connected with defence or the processing and storage of data.

Demonstrations can be used as cover by saboteurs, armed raiders or bombers to gain access to sensitive installations, with or without the connivance of the organisers of the demonstrations. This has been alleged in relation to demonstrations in France and West Germany.

Contamination and disruption of utilities (water, electric power, fuel, drainage, ventilation, heating and cooling) can be an attractive tactic to the more ruthless terrorists who now appear to be emerging, particularly those with the religious or racial convictions which engender a disregard for human life and public opinion – such as terrorists sponsored by Libya and Iran. Many such systems are very vulnerable and access to them is often less effectively protected than access to other more obvious key points.

Long-range weapons, with their improving accuracy and power of penetration of steel and concrete, may well become more fashionable for use by terrorists firing from the windows of buildings overlooking factories and office blocks, especially if they can locate key facilities which are close to outside walls.

Product extortion by threat to pollute food, drink or pharmaceutical products has increased substantially in recent years, largely due to the power of the media. The most lethal case on record, which cost at least seven lives, was the injection of cyanide into Tylanol tablets in the USA in 1982.

See also **Extortion and product pollution, Hostage-taking, Kidnapping, Nuclear terrorism, Risk management**

Trevi group A number of meetings of interior and justice ministers to discuss measures against terrorism resulted from a suggestion by the then British Prime Minister, Harold Wilson, at a meeting of the European Council at Trevi in Rome in December 1975. The first meeting was held in Luxemburg in June 1976 when a six-point programme was designed, principally to help prevent future terrorist attacks in the European Community. It included the provision for the exchange of technical information on the operation of terrorists, and the exchange of police personnel between Community members to acquire greater knowledge of operating methods in different countries. Information on past acts of terrorism was to be pooled and mutual assistance was to be provided in the event of future terrorist action. Agreement was also reached on the desirability of closer collaboration on such matters as nuclear safety and air security. The Community programme would complement the anti-terrorist co-operation which already takes place within other international organisations such as Interpol.

All these issues have been discussed at various times over the subsequent decade. In September 1976 the twelve member states of the Community agreed to an unprecedented sharing of information by their police forces as part of a major new campaign against international terrorism. A new hotline was set up for the instant sharing of intelligence on terrorists' movements, supplies of money, arms and equipment. The ministers agreed to examine more effective extradition measures and to consider the present visa arrangements to make more effective use of exclusion and expulsion procedures. A review of the current security checks at airports and in particular the scanning of diplomatic baggage was ordered.

Most important was the achievement of a belated recognition of the problem by all the members of the Community, and the acceptance that terrorism should be treated as a crime and not, selectively, as the pursuit of international politics. Neither had been especially evident at an EEC forum before. The Trevi Group has yet to solve the problem of imposing uniformly strict airport security, visa requirements and border controls.

See also **Suppression of terrorism, 1977 European Convention**

Tudeh The Iranian People's Party (Tudeh) had its origins as a Communist party in the Iranian Social Democratic Party (Adalat), which had arisen out of a social democratic group founded in 1904. Established in 1920 as the Communist Party of Iran, it was banned in 1931 and forced to continue its work illegally. In 1941 it was reorganised as the Tudeh Party of Iran, which was itself repressed and officially declared illegal in 1949. In 1965 the party was divided into three factions – respectively of pro-Soviet, Maoist and Castroite orientation – but the first of these remained the official Tudeh Party. In 1973 it adopted a new programme with the object of uniting all democratic forces by means of flexibility, initiative and consistency.

From its base in exile in East Germany, the party welcomed the Islamic revolution of 1979 and pledged full support for its 'anti-imperialist and democratic' aims. Allowed to operate once again under the new Islamic revolutionary regime, it called in particular for an alliance of all socialist forces, which would enjoy the support of the USSR. Relations between the Party and the Khomeini regime became critical, as the regime became more committed to clerical fundamentalism. Tudeh also opposed the Iran-Iraq war. In 1982 the ruling Islamic Republican Party published a strong critique of the policy of Tudeh and of the dominant pro-Tudeh faction of the Fedayeen el-Khalq (People's Fighters), attacking in particular their opposition to the war.

The Tudeh party opposed Iran's participation in the Gulf War because it had the effect of strengthening Iraq's relations with conservative Gulf regimes; it involved the Iranian government in heavy expenditure on arms to the detriment of the masses and increasing popular discontent with the war could lead to counter-revolution.

As an alternative to the pro-Soviet posture of Tudeh, the Communist Party of Iran, an extremely small group, was organised in early 1979. On the ultra-left the Tudeh was overtaken by the violence-prone Fedayeen and the establishment of the Trotskyist Socialist Workers' Party.

See also **Iran**

Tupamaros The name Tupamaros, describing members of the National Liberation Movement in Uruguay, was derived from Tupac Amaru, a Peruvian Indian leader who claimed Inca descent and led an anti-Spanish revolt at the end of the eighteenth century, but was eventually captured and executed. The Movement was founded at a time when Uruguay was experiencing a deepening economic crisis with growing inflation and unemployment. Following the establishment of the Movement in 1962, Tupamaros leaders were active among sugar workers. From 1963, they extended guerrilla warfare to urban areas on the basis of theories developed by Abraham Guilten, a Spanish ideologist of urban terrorism, who had recommended a strategy of small guerrilla action to compel the security forces to surrender terrain, and also the establishment of small cells which could act without reference to high command – this strategy to be reinforced by political work in order to gain mass support.

By mid 1972 the Tupamaros was said to number about 6,000, recruited mainly from among left-wing students and teachers. Their early actions included robberies, the spoils of which they distributed among the poor, and later they engaged in kidnappings, assassinations, shootings and bombings with the aim of weakening the country's political leadership, which they held responsible for the economic crisis. By 1971 it appeared possible that they might seize power, but the Government of President Bordaberry succeeded in crushing the movement by November 1972 after proclaiming in April of that year a 'state of internal war' which was repeatedly extended. Victims of the Tupamaros included Dan Mitrione, a US adviser to the Uruguayan police force, who was kidnapped and murdered in 1970, the Uruguayan government having refused to accede to a Tupamaros demand for the release of all political prisoners; and Sir Geoffrey Jackson, British Ambassador in Montevideo, seized in January 1971 and released in September 1971, although the Uruguayan Government had refused to negotiate with his captors.

After the murder of a Uruguayan military attaché in Paris in 1974, the Uruguayan government killed five former Tupamaros (apparently as an act of reprisal), arrested numerous persons, rearrested hundreds of provisionally released political prisoners as well as dismissing many university staff and imposing sanctions against the press. Thus the movement lost much of its initial popular appeal and largely fell into a state of dormancy.

See also **Jackson**

Turkey From 1980 the Republic of Turkey was under a period of military rule until democratic elections were held in 1985, which led to a Centre Right administration coming to power. The object of the military was to stop the anarchy caused by terrorist groups of both the right and the left, and to develop the new democratic system. To cleanse the political arena, the military rulers dissolved all political parties, confiscated their property, and it was only prior to the 1985 elections that they gave permission for a few parties to be created. After the military takeover in

1980, the military regime of General Evren sought to dismantle militant organisations of the extreme left, and also brought many right-wingers to trial in connection with violent attacks on the left committed before the military takeover. Even though over 45,000 persons were in detention for suspected terrorist activities, many of them belonging to left-wing groups, by the end of 1982 over 7,000 alleged terrorists were still at large. The Turkish government claimed that 662 organisations were operating against Turkey from abroad, of which 286 were described as extreme left-wing, 17 as separatist and 280 as religious extremists. Millions of rounds of ammunition and about a million pistols were seized in the early 1980s.

There are about thirty left-wing movements, but only a handful play a significant role. The Revolutionary Left (Dev-Sol) was the first extreme left-wing group to pledge opposition to the military regime, describing it as fascist and anti-working class. Many people have been assassinated by the Revolutionary Left, most notably Dr Nihat Erim, Prime Minister from 1971 to 1972. Hundreds of its members were arrested by the military and charged with breaches of the Constitution, including murders, bombings and robberies, with the object of setting up a Marxist-Leninist social order. They co-operated closely with the Popular Front for the Liberation of Palestine (PFLP), a group led by Dr Georges Habash, which has provided substantial quantities of weapons, and training facilities.

Another movement, the Revolutionary Way (Dev-Yol) is led by a woman and is based in Paris. Before 1980 this organisation held a dominant position in several small towns and had engaged in numerous acts of violence, in particular against political opponents. Under the military regime large numbers of the organisation's members were arrested and tried.

The Communist Party, which took part in the Turkish national movement between 1918 and 1922, was also purged by the military in the 1980s. The Party was blamed for dividing Turkey by calling for the establishment of a Turkish state in eastern Anatolia, of an independent socialist state without military bases in Cyprus, and by setting up a national democratic front as an umbrella organisation for all anti-fascist elements.

Various movements of the extreme right were engaged in violent action against the left in the period before the military takeover in 1980. Afterwards, these movements backed the Evren regime in its offensive against the extreme left, but were themselves frequently the subject of trials brought by the authorities for illegal activities carried out before 1980. The National Action Party is an ultra-nationalist party known until 1969 as the Republican Peasant National Party. It stands for the defence of freedom and of the interests of the peasantry, and has promoted the formation of various militant right-wing organisations outside its own party framework, such as the Federation of Turkish Democratic Idealist Associations, the Great Ideal Society and the Grey Wolves. The latter is a militant youth wing of the Action Party and has been involved in killing immigrant workers in European countries. One of the Grey Wolves members was Mehmet Ali Agca, who killed a newspaper editor in 1979, and received life imprisonment for his attempt to kill the Pope in 1981.

Islamic fundamentalism has assumed greater importance in Turkey in the last decade. After the Sunni and the Shi'ite Alevi Muslim sects in Turkey had lived for several centuries in relative peace with each other, a polarisation began in 1970, with the Sunnis favouring conservative policies and the generally under-privileged Alevis left-wing ones. A large amount of mutual destruction has been undertaken. The principal Islamic fundamentalist party opposed to the institutionalisation of the secular state in Turkey has been the National Salvation Party. Islamic fundamentalism has also been propagated by the relatively small Turkish section of the Muslim Brotherhood. These groups wish for the establishment of a state based on the rule of Koranic law.

There are numerous Armenian and Kurdish movements, which have each maintained their own culture and associations. The organisations formed to conduct 'warfare' against the Turkish authorities represent only a minority of Armenians as a whole, and many Armenian organisations condemn those of their fellow countrymen engaged in acts of violence. The Turkish Government consistently refuses to give in to demands made by militant Armenians; the Government also never recognises the existence of a Kurdish minority. A number of Kurdish groups adhere to Marxist-Leninist principles.

See also **Agca, Armenian Secret Army for the Liberation of Armenia, Armenian terrorism, Islam, Kurdish insurgency**

T

U

Uganda This East African country has been beset by political violence and instability almost since its independence in 1962. The regimes of Amin and Obote have both been charged with violations of human rights, arising to some extent from undisciplined actions of the country's army. There are thousands of political detainees, of whom many may have been killed, and illegal executions, torture and abductions are commonplace.

The National Resistance Army under the leadership of Yoweri Museveni, a former Minister of Defence, was created in 1980 largely with help from arms suppliers in Europe and the Middle East. It has concentrated on guerrilla attacks on the capital, Kampala, and both the official Ugandan Army and the guerrillas have claimed considerable successes against each other.

The political wing of the National Resistance Army is the National Resistance Movement, led by Professor Yusufu Lule, based in London. The Movement and the Army are composed of Baganda and Bantu tribes and were opposed to Obote's rule. Although Obote was overthrown for a second time in 1985 (the first in 1971), the struggle continues.

The Uganda Freedom Movement was formed by various opponents of President Obote, including several prominent politicians who had served under him since 1980. They supported an armed struggle and a year after their inception in 1981 merged with the Resistance Movement, the Resistance Army and the National Rescue Front (formed in 1981 by a former Finance Minister in the Amin regime to oppose Obote and try to restore Amin to power), to co-operate within the Uganda Popular Front. The aim of these groups was to overthrow Obote, by force if necessary, as no negotiable handover appeared possible.

Obote's replacement in 1984 was Colonel Tito Okello of the National Liberation Army, which had been able to consolidate its hold among the Acholi and Langi tribes in the north, and then built up a base in the west of the country.

Opposing all these groups during the early 1980s was the Uganda People's Congress under the leadership of Obote. It was a party based on support by the Langi tribe, with a programme founded on pragmatic socialism. At the time of the elections in 1984 it was accused of killing Democratic Party candidates and establishing an army of northern tribes with the help of Tanzania, in order to take over power violently in case Obote lost the elections.

See also **Entebbe raid**

Uncontrollable international terrorism Terrorism raises a number of issues of international concern that escape the effective control of individual states. There is increasing international contact and co-operation among terrorist groups, including the flow of arms and co-ordination of actions. Methods of international communication and travel have proved to be both useful and vulnerable to terrorism. In the absence of common agreement on international crimes, states may become sanctuaries for terrorism committed in other states. In some cases terrorism becomes an instrument in the hands of small groups to aggravate or disrupt the resolution of major international tensions and conflicts. The potential impact of terrorism on world order is increasing, because of the proliferation of weapons capable of mass destruction and because of the erosion of state authority in recent years. The latter often provides fertile ground for insurgent activity. Finally, terrorism has been tried and proved to be a frequently successful tactic for extorting money and for gaining a substantial amount of worldwide publicity. Prime responsibility for the apprehension and punishment of terrorists lies with individual states and their law enforcement authorities, and these have proved to be very weak, both by private and public sectors within democratic nations.

See also **Terrorism: future sources**

United Nations and international terrorism The performance of the UN in combatting international terrorism is a controversial subject. Some observers claim that far from combatting terrorism, the UN has been actively promoting it through its support of wars of national liberation and its formal recognition of the Palestine Liberation Organisation. The UN, like so many bodies, organisations and individuals has for most of its existence been unable to agree on a definition of terrorism.

Some modicum of agreement is sustained, but the countries within the UN do not agree on the following issues. State terrorism comprises the use of terror by governments, including torture, genocide and assassination of political enemies abroad by the use of diplomats and other persons enjoying special status by virtue of their governmental functions. Within the definition of terrorism are included acts inflicting terror during 'armed conflict' covered by the law of war, e.g. the massacre of defenceless prisoners of war. In the context of international terrorism by private individuals, the UN defines this as the threat or use of violence by private persons for political ends, where the conduct itself or its political objectives or both are international in scope.

In the wake of the Munich Olympics tragedy in 1972 and at the USA's behest, a draft convention on international terrorism was agreed. The convention was purposely drawn to be narrow in its coverage. It did not seek to define terrorism or to deal with all acts that might fall within the definition of terrorism. Only unlawful killing, serious bodily harm or kidnapping fell within the scope of the convention. Four conditions had to apply before the convention could come into force. The act had to be committed or take effect outside the territory of the state of which the alleged offender was a national. The act had to be committed or take effect outside the state against which the act was directed, unless such acts were knowingly directed against a non-national of that state, e.g. the attack on Israel's Lod Airport. Acts committed either by or against a member of the armed forces of a state in the course of military hostilities were excluded from coverage. The act had to be intended to damage the interest of or to obtain concessions from a state or an international organisation.

The US purpose in drafting such a convention was to meet the concern of third world countries that the US initiative was directed against wars of national liberation, and thereby by allaying this concern to gain as wide an acceptance of the convention as possible. In December 1972 the UN adopted a resolution which, while expressing deep concern over terrorism and inviting states to become parties to existing conventions on international terrorism, focused its primary attention on finding just and peaceful solutions to the underlying causes which give rise to such acts of violence.

A dramatic increase in plane hijacking during the 1960s led to the conclusion of the 1963 Tokyo Convention which, in effect, requires state parties to return a plane and passengers if they have been hijacked; the 1970 Hague Convention provides that state parties must either extradite or prosecute the hijackers, and the 1971 Montreal Convention contains the same requirement with respect to those who engage in any kind of sabotage of aviation such as blowing up planes on the ground. These conventions, especially the latter two, were not widely ratified, especially by certain Arab states that provide sanctuary for the hijackers. An International Conference on Air Law and an Extraordinary Assembly of the International Civil Aviation Organisation (ICAO) in 1973 failed to agree on any other proposals to enhance the security of civil aviation.

During the 1970s and early 1980s, General Assembly resolutions as well as negotiations in the Assembly have helped to induce more states, including some Arab states, to ratify the three ICAO conventions against aircraft hijacking and sabotage. In 1974 the General Assembly adopted by consensus the Convention on the Prevention and Punishment of Crimes against Internationally Protected Persons, including Diplomatic Agents. The convention provides for international co-operation in preventing and punishing attacks against diplomats and other persons enjoying a special status under international law.

In 1979, an International Convention against the Taking of Hostages was adopted by the General Assembly. The Convention requires international co-operation toward the prevention, prosecution and punishment of all acts involving the taking of hostages, except where the act is purely domestic in nature. The Convention seeks to ensure that international acts of hostage-taking will be covered either by the Convention itself or by one of the applicable conventions on the laws of war.

In the same year, a resolution was adopted which contains a number of useful provisions regarding possible future measures toward combatting

276

international terrorism, in particular the request to the Secretary-General to build up a body of national legislation regarding international terrorism. This information would be useful to states wishing to structure their law and policy so as to combat terrorism effectively while safeguarding fundamental human rights.

Measures adopted to date by the United Nations to combat international terrorism have had a narrow focus. They have covered only a particular type of target or victim – civil aviation and diplomats – or a particular manifestation of international terrorism, such as hostage-taking. There is now a need for the UN to come to grips with other facets of international terrorism. The so-called war of assassination by states against their enemies abroad is particularly disturbing, threatening international peace and security. The UN has to move more effectively against gross violations of human rights, such as torture, that create an environment in which terrorism may flourish. The justness of one cause does not excuse the use of terrorist methods. Whatever the end, the means cannot legitimately include the exploding of bombs in towns, the taking of hostages, the killing of diplomats, the hijacking of planes or the sending of letter bombs. Ultimately all states have an interest in suppressing such actions. The future stability and peace of the world may depend upon recognition of this fact.

United States The United States is, and has long been, the primary target of a variety of foreign terrorist organisations. The country itself (as has also long been the case) has remained relatively insulated from these escalations of terrorist violence. Although the USA is the country most frequently targetted by terrorists abroad, it is near the bottom of the list in terms of the number of terrorist attacks within its own borders. Despite the fact that the USA has the highest crime and homicide rates in the industrialised Western world (as well as the greatest number of both legal and illegal weapons in the possession of its citizens), politically motivated crimes are relatively infrequent. The country is not a politically polarised country. Unlike France, Italy or Germany, where a variety of political parties represent the extremes of the ideological spectrum in national politics, the USA has traditionally been a two-party country. The two parties differ little in actual substance from one another. Terrorism is also inhibited because of the country's unparalleled upward economic and social mobility which provides opportunities for social and economic advancement.

In addition, the USA is a politically absorptive society. American politics have been ethnic politics, and immigrants have been readily absorbed by the major political parties and integrated into the American political system. While other Western nations have violent irredentist groups, there are none in the USA except for a Puerto Rican faction.

Three types of terrorist organisation do exist in the USA: ethnic separatist and émigré groups; left-wing radical organisations; and right-wing racist, anti-authority, and extreme survivalist-type groups. Two-thirds of all terrorism in the USA is carried out by ethnic separatist or émigré terrorists. Their causes and grievances often have little or nothing to do with domestic American politics. Of the three types of terrorist organisation in the USA, the ethnic émigré groups have generally shown themselves to be the most persistent and violent. These groups also give rise to 'successor' generations of younger terrorists. Despite the potentially wide appeal of these organisations within their own communities, the narrow focus of their parochial, ethnically centred causes means they have a far smaller political constituency than ideological terrorist groups have. Support comes only from other ethnic émigré groups in scattered, tightly-knit communities around the country.

Left-wing radicals and other issue-oriented groups have a much wider constituency because of the broader political nature of their causes. They are more moderate than the ethnic groups, and engage in symbolic bombings to call attention to themselves and their causes, but they are generally careful not to undertake actions that might alienate potential supporters in their perceived constituency.

Radical leftist groups have existed in one form or another since the late 1960s. They originated in student movements that were organised to protest against United States involvement in the Vietnam War. When the War ended, their influence declined. In recent years, US involvement in Central America, and South Africa's apartheid policy have given new life to left-wing groups such as the Weather Underground, or Weathermen, and the Black Liberation Army (BLA). These issues have led to the foundation of new, more narrowly focused, leftist-leaning groups, including the Revolutionary Armed Task Force, the United Freedom Front and the Armed Resistance Unit.

Right-wing terrorists embrace traits of both ethnic separatist and left-wing terrorists. They are violent and concentrate on specific political issues. Such groups can be divided into specific issue-oriented terrorists and traditional vengeance or 'date' groups. In recent years, several racist and reactionary groups have surfaced in the West. These include anti-federalists, anti-Semites, racists, extremists and Christian fundamentalists – such as the Aryan Nations, the Order, the Covenant, the Sword and the Arm of the Lord.

American-based terrorists concentrate on bombing, which provides a dramatic way of drawing attention to the terrorists and their causes. Members of these groups are more skilled with weapons than other terrorists in the United States, and are well trained in survival techniques and living rough.

The groups are in decline due to the continuing success achieved by the FBI as well as state and local law enforcement agencies in tracking down and arresting wanted and suspected terrorists. Widespread arrests of members of ethnic terrorist organisations such as those in the large Armenian and Cuban exile communities have similarly undermined these two movements. An additional factor is disillusionment and exhaustion among old members and the waning enthusiasm of potential recruits.

Friction in relations between the United States and Libya has been cited as increasing the likelihood of Libyan 'hit-squads' being deployed to the USA. Libyan actions so far have been restricted to attacks on Libyan nationals in America and not directed against American targets. Libyan student activity is closely monitored.

Domestic left-wing radicals always have had trouble recruiting new members to their organisations. The only recent increase in domestic terrorist activity has come from Jewish extremists associated with the Jewish Defence League (JDL). Initially the group used terrorism to draw attention to itself and its causes, to maintain momentum and perpetuate its image as an 'action-oriented', non-traditional Jewish pressure group. The recent increase of militant Jewish terrorism represents not only an escalation of violence but a significant change in patterns of targetting, and a dramatic shift in tactics. Middle East targets in the USA have been hit, and assassinations as well as bombings carried out. By expanding targets the Jewish extremists are trying to appeal to a larger and more diverse constituency. In the future, terrorist incidents that occur abroad, and which specifically target or indirectly involve Jews from the United States or elsewhere, may provoke deliberately retaliatory or revenge-minded strikes and create a cycle of international terrorism and domestic, vigilante responses.

Right-wing terrorists embody many of the traits typical of both ethnic émigré and left-wing terrorists. The rightists, like the ethnic émigré groups, are more violent than their leftist counterparts, have been able to replenish their ranks with new recruits and, like left-wing terrorists, are motivated in some cases to enlarge their power base by ostensibly taking action against controversial, popular political issues (such as abortion).

See also **Teheran Embassy Siege**

Urban guerrillas in Latin America The importance of urban guerrilla theories has often been exaggerated. Regis Debray placed greater emphasis on developing guerrilla warfare than on building a revolutionary party. The appeal of the urban guerrilla was eminently anti-intellectual. In the early 1970s a cult of action emerged in the course of a revolt against the traditional left . The guerrillas were impatient with the pace of developments. The emphasis was upon action, in Uruguay as a means of uniting the left and in Argentina as a way of overcoming a stalemate in the post-war conflict between Peronist and anti-Peronist forces. In Brazil, Marighella at times seemed to advocate action for action's sake. Some practitioners of the new variant of the armed struggle claimed that 'objective' revolutionary conditions already existed and presented themselves as a fuse to trigger the explosion.

Urban guerrilla warfare, it was argued, would act as a catalyst to accelerate social and political processes leading to revolution; it would expose the corrupt and oppressive nature of the regimes being challenged while winning mass support through demonstrating the vulnerability of state forces. Under no circumstances did the theory envisage the guerrillas themselves inflicting a military defeat on their enemy; rather, success depended on the guerrilla nuclei developing into people's armies. Originally the Brazilian and Uruguayan guerrillas looked to a rural campaign, but soon realised that what support there was for armed struggle lay in the major cities. The lack of rural potential obliged the insurgents to initiate their struggle in the cities, but in turn rendered the latter suicidal; once urban repression became overpowering, the rebels lacked the option of a secure retreat into the countryside.

Why did they fail? While it is true that the political context in which a guerrilla organisation attempts to develop is an important determinant of the degree of success, general principles as to the optimal conditions for the launching of urban guerrilla campaigns are elusive.

Where possibilities exist for legal mass activity by the population, the initiation or continuation of warfare is likely to engender extreme guerrilla isolation. However, urban guerrillas have yet to prosper against well-equipped authoritarian regimes prepared and able to use draconian methods against them.

The most propitious conditions for the implementation of urban guerrilla strategies are either against a quasi-democratic regime inhibited by legal restrictions and electoral considerations from all-out repression, but sufficiently intolerant of democratic opposition for guerrillas to be able to pose credibly as the only viable popular alternative; or under an authoritarian military regime lacking political legitimacy, already weakened by mass opposition or crisis of some kind, and preparing to return authority to politicians.

Political conditions can and do change during the course of urban guerrilla campaigns. When their enemy is on the defensive, guerrillas can be flexible and modify tactics and strategies to meet new political circumstances; but they cannot retreat when their enemy is on the offensive.

In a war of infiltration and counter-infiltration, forces drawing upon state resources have an overwhelming advantage, and little can be done by their opponents to overturn the situation.

Urban guerrillas can be effective through time only if they establish a significant mass base as a source of recruits, auxiliaries, resources and intelligence data. A high degree of isolation is guaranteed by their adopted strategy for a number of reasons. Firstly, urban guerrilla warfare is, at least in its origins, a highly elitist form of struggle, embarked upon by would-be vanguards of the masses. It also reflects contempt for the collective struggles of labour. Isolation is very much a question of class. Worker antipathy to the urban guerrilla is an expression of strong economic sentiment and a reformist rather than revolutionary political stance. Urban guerrilla warfare is a physically isolated form of struggle. Since the urban guerrilla operates in the centre of the enemy territory, he cannot establish liberated zones, unlike his rural counterpart. In South America, there was thus no possibility of organising a substantial social, economic and political support base while fighting a guerrilla war in the cities. With regard to guerrilla actions themselves, there was everywhere a marked tendency for military operations that were in some way related to popular demands to constitute a declining aspect of urban guerrilla repertoires as campaigns developed.

When the urban guerrillas reached levels of development where open confrontations with the armed forces became technically feasible, their operations became totally divorced from popular activity.

Though many urban guerrillas started out as political activists who regarded armed struggle as an extension of politics by other means, those guerrilla organisations which grew soon became dominated by military rather than political criteria. As the urban guerrillas developed militarily, and moved on to higher planes of warfare through a series of leaps, the political wisdom of specific guerrilla actions tended to take second place to considerations of what was technically feasible.

In many campaigns the urban guerrillas would have been more circumspect over promoting armed confrontation had they appraised the strength and capacities of their opponents more accurately. In South America, militarism, in part a product of the weakness of revolutionary parties in the countries concerned, was inherent in the logic of urban guerrilla strategy.

Urban guerrilla theory was a defective guide for action, for it failed to explain clearly how guerrilla action would impel the masses to revolutionary deeds. It merely assumed that efficient military operations would galvanise them. Most of the urban guerrilla formations were weak on revolutionary theory and ideologically vague. The commitment of the urban guerrilla was not the only cement holding the groups together but it was considered the most decisive factor in defining who was a revolutionary.

See also **Argentina, Debray, Marighella, Tupamaros**

V

Victims of terrorism Terrorism purposely uses fear as a means to attain particular ends. It is by nature coercive, dehumanising, a theatre of the absurd, and designed to manipulate its victims and, through them, a larger audience. The effects of terrorism on society centre around a democracy's peculiar vulnerability to terrorism.

Looking at the impact of terrorism on individual citizens in countries that have consistently borne the brunt of terrorism, such as Italy, Ulster, Spain, Egypt, Israel, Lebanon, Turkey, Argentina, El Salvador, and Nicaragua, one notes a serious erosion in the quality of life. Terrorism is exacting a heavy toll on international diplomacy and on the life styles and work habits of political leaders, diplomats and business executives the world over. Concerns for personal safety are affecting a widening circle of people, e.g. air travel is now encumbered by the scanning and frisking procedures for travellers who must endure a serious invasion of privacy. Airports, banks, industrial complexes, private and public institutions and even prisons have been affected by terroristic actions. The fear generated by terrorism and by the possibility of victimisation in an ever widening arena are raising the social costs of the problem, in addition to the economic costs. It does so by weakening the social and political fabric of affected countries and by diverting scarce economic and criminal justice resources from other vital areas.

There are varied circumstances under which individuals may become victims of terrorist acts and these are as varied as the causes of terrorism. Victims can be chosen selectively or at random. In selective terrorism specific groups, such as police, judges, soldiers or prison personnel are targetted. In randomised terrorism, victims are chosen indiscriminately, a method guaranteed to instil maximum fear among the public.

Regardless of the objectives and format of terrorisation, it involves an unpredictable, powerful force, which threatens the victim with annihilation. The experience is immensely stressful and generates in the victim feelings of anomie, total helplessness and powerlessness. Terrorisation denies the victim's ability to control his behaviour. The psychological and physical shock characteristics of any severe trauma follow. Since the choice of victim in many terrorist attacks is determined by chance, victims can neither anticipate nor control the event. The multiple threats, to security, bodily integrity and self-esteem, precipitate in most victims a crisis reaction in which the emotions and behaviour of the threatened person are significantly disrupted. A victim faced with the very real possibility of imminent death finds himself unable to muster the necessary physical and mental resources to rise against the assault on his person.

The first phase of the victim's response to terrorisation is concerned with the immediate situation and its experience. The response is one of shock, disbelief, denial and delusion. It is characterised by a paralysis of action and the denial of sensory impressions. Secondly, there is paralysis of effect, or 'frozen fright', and, unrealistically, victims expect authorities will rapidly rescue them. If victims are not rescued during this period of initial adaptation, the pressures of the situation and terror combine to overwhelm most victims and produce a state of traumatic psychological infantilism. Individuals lose their ability to function as adults and begin to respond instead with adaptive behaviour first learned in early child-hood. The identification of the victim with the aggressor becomes a central theme, which has been termed Stockholm syndrome.

Victims of terrorism suffer serious and long-lasting damage to their physical, mental and emotional health. Strategies of successful adaptation to the terrorist experience can bring the crisis situation to quick resolution with a minimum of loss of life or injury: keeping one's anxiety level within tolerable limits to remain alert and functional; maintaining one's self-esteem in spite of dehumanising and degrading experiences; preservation of one's relationships with fellow victims and establishing some link with the terrorists without ingratiation. Once caught up in the crisis situation, one's experiences have to be adjusted to the reality of the situation; one has to learn from the coping behaviour of fellow victims and accept constructive criticism without losing one's sense of self-worth and self-esteem.

Pathological transference is found in individuals held hostage by criminal terrorists. Hostage victims become instrumental victims. They are used and exploited by their captors as leverage to force a third party (the family, police or government) to accede to captors' demands. The behaviour of a terrorist victim during captivity cannot be judged or criticised.

Terrorists often assert in their struggle that there are no innocent victims. Nevertheless, human life has value; commitment to this value binds together terrorist, victim and audience in the three-way relationship that characterises modern terrorism and makes activities like hostage negotiation possible. Where the terrorist's aim is to kill, one has assassination; where the terrorist does not value his own life we have suicide; where he values it less than something else, martyrdom; where he sees himself as a soldier who accepts risks of combat, we have a prisoner of war – but not a hostage. Ultimately, where the target of terrorist blackmail does not value individual human life, there is nothing to negotiate. Thus terrorism is not a problem in totalitarian states, but a country like Lebanon, which is conspicuous for the value placed on life and individual rights, has figured disproportionately in the history of modern terrorism.

Terrorism can exist only when and where retributive violence is limited in scope or space. Whereas revenge is limited in space, it is limitless in time. The endurance of revenge and of movements based on vengeance is a major source of discouragement for those who must plan responses to the phenomenon of terrorism.

Grief is the psychological reaction to the loss of a close relative, of a cherished goal, or of a cherished aspect of one's life. Grief and mourning may be very much a part of the experience for victims of terrorists. Hostage victims are isolated by their own feelings of guilt and shame: guilt over whether they perhaps should have resisted at the cost of their lives, and shame at having been taken and used. This makes it harder for victims to share experiences with others.

In terrorist incidents, guilt is most likely to become a problem when some hostages have been released before others, or when persons with military or law-enforcement backgrounds have not resisted the hostage-takers with force. Terrorist leaders fight hard to maintain absolute control over the information given to their members and hostages. There has hardly been any real human relationship between the terrorist and his victim before the act that brought them together – and in the case of random bombings, even during the act. A source of strength for the victim of terrorism lies not merely in the possibilities of escape and of coping with stress, but in the possibility of finding the best in the midst of the worst, in the presence of fear and with the memory and possibility of failure.

Terrorisation is very much related to the effect of stress, particularly trauma-induced stress. Children brought up in conditions of constant violence soon become drawn into the terrorist world; although not all children growing up in turmoil and violence become terrorists. Terrorism appears in waves about once every two decades, or about once in every generation. Over time, the ameliorating and exacerbating conditions for a social group are a product of the social system in which they exist.

People who are badly treated and unjustly punished will seek revenge. Even some whose punishment is appropriate will struggle to wreak vengeance on those who imposed that punishment. Once a terrorist incident has occurred, helping efforts must concentrate on reducing the harm it causes. The situation has to be resolved as quickly as possible with a minimum loss of life. Concern for the victims plays a big role in the planning of these interventions and many other political and situational factors also influence decision-makers.

The victim of terrorism holds a special position among victims of premeditated human violence. He or she often represents the government that the terrorist is challenging when he takes his victim hostage. The value of human life is pre-eminent over all other issues in considering responses to human cruelty. Victimisation by terrorists results from groups perceiving conflicts of vital interests, differences in status or differences in beliefs.

See also **Fear, Stockholm syndrome, Terrorism and terror**

Vigilante terrorism Terrorist actions taken by one group of terrorists or their sympathisers to protect other terrorists by working as a smoke-screen for them.

W

Western Europe Middle East terrorist activity, in particular, has been and continues to be a major security and political problem for most countries in Western Europe. Many of these countries (West Germany, Spain, the UK, France, Italy, Greece, Portugal and Belgium) are also confronted with a serious indigenous terrorist threat from various separatist and Marxist revolutionary groups. The most active and dangerous of these groups are the Red Army Faction and the Revolutionary Cells in West Germany; the Red Brigades in Italy; Action Directe, and the Corsican National Liberation Front in France; the Popular Forces of April 25 in Portugal; the Popular Revolutionary Struggle and the November 17 Group in Greece; the Basque Euskadi and Freedom Movement (ETA-m) in Spain; the Fighting Communist Cells in Belgium and the Irish Republican Army in the UK. On 15 January 1985 the RAF and Action Directe issued a joint statement announcing the formation of a united front to combat NATO imperialism. While the short-term threat posed by these groups varies, the long-term threat remains high.

The activities of Middle Eastern terrorist groups only compound the problems posed by the groups listed above. More attacks by Middle Eastern terrorist groups take place in Western Europe than in any other region, excluding, of course, the Middle East. Moreover, there are certain Middle Eastern terrorist elements that prefer operating in Western Europe rather than in the Middle East.

The continent is attractive for a number of reasons. It provides these groups with a pool of potential manpower which facilitates the building and maintenance of a logistical infrastructure. Large communities of Palestinians and Arabs, especially students, live in West European countries. Businessmen and tourists frequently travel to Western Europe. This makes it easy for Middle Eastern terrorist groups to send in operators who can not only blend into the environment but also receive logistical aid from sympathisers and in-country supporters.

The area offers these groups geographical proximity and compactness, excellent transport and relatively easy cross-border movement. It is easy to get to Western Europe and move around between countries. Groups can be offered abundant, easy and attractive targets. Middle East terrorists carry out attacks against three targeted sectors: Israeli or Jewish, Western, and Arab or Palestinian. There are many of these targets in Western Europe. Western Europe offers these groups immediate worldwide publicity when they carry out an attack in the region. The publicity spotlight is broader and brighter in Western Europe than in most other regions. Middle Eastern groups can be provided with a 'substitute battle-ground' in which to carry out their inter-Palestinian and inter-Arab feuds. The majority of the attacks carried out by Middle Eastern terrorist groups are aimed at other Arab and Palestinian targets; the authoritarian nature of the Arab regimes at home and tight Israeli security measures make it difficult for these groups to operate within Israel. It is less risky and operationally easier to attack Libyan, Syrian, Iranian, Iraqi and Israeli targets in Western Europe.

The types of target have ranged from ambassadors, embassies, consular buildings, airline offices and restaurants, to American military bases, mosques, synagogues, railways, buses and multinational corporations. In some cases the attacks are direct retaliations for terrorist events in the Middle East and aim to secure the release of Arabs imprisoned in Euro-pean jails for terrorist crimes in various Western European countries. The attacks by Middle Eastern groups against 'Western' targets in 1985 signalled the beginning of a terrorist campaign by certain groups to focus on the perceived 'Achilles Heel' of West European governments – the economic importance to them of tourism.

The time is perhaps near when a Middle Eastern terrorist group and a European terrorist group will carry out a joint operation. The radical Palestinian groups under the protection of Syria and Libya will continue to focus on indiscriminate bombings designed to cause mass casualties. Proportionately, more attacks will be directed at 'Western' targets.

See also **Responses to terrorism, Suppression of terrorism, Terrorism: future sources, Trevi group**

Women and terrorism In certain guerrilla and terrorist groups such as the Tupamaros in Uruguay, the Montoneros in Argentina, and some of the Japanese groups, women act as collectors of intelligence, taking part in operations as couriers, nurses and medical personnel, and maintaining safe houses for weapons, funds and supplies.

Leftist groups tend to be an exception, sometimes having female leaders; Leila Khaled and Fusako Shigenobu were leaders of the Popular Front for the Liberation of Palestine and the Japanese Red Army respect-ively; Norma Aristoto was co-founder of the Montoneros in Argentina; Genoveve Tarat played a key role in ETA-v and Margharita Cagol in the Italian Red Brigades.

However, most female terrorists act in a supportive capacity. They play a useful role because several women living together is perceived as more usual than a group of men. Posing as wives and mothers, female terrorists can enter areas where males cannot go. In the early 1970s women formed a third of the operational personnel of the Baader-Meinhof group in West Germany, and have taken part in robberies, burglaries and kidnappings.

Unmarried women terrorists are the rule except in the Tupamaros. Women usually work in a familiar or specific area, with many having an urban background. There is a general lowering of the entry age into operational activity, and some women have been operationally trained and undertake operational leadership roles. Many women have the nomadic lifestyle of the groups and have a desire for action and money.

Z

Zimbabwe African People's Union (ZAPU) This organisation was founded in 1961 by Joshua Nkomo, whose later attempts to negotiate with the Rhodesian government failed in 1976. Based in Zambia, ZAPU built up a disciplined guerrilla force but never engaged its full military strength inside Rhodesia. The more militant nationalists had already broken away from ZAPU in August 1963 to form the Zimbabwe African National Union (ZANU) under Sithole and Mugabe. At this time fierce factional fighting broke out in most towns. ZAPU survived only to be torn apart by tribal animosities in 1969–70 when the Zambian President Kaunda was compelled to intervene.

After the failure of talks in 1976 between Smith and Nkomo, ZAPU guerrillas re-entered the war, infiltrating Rhodesia from the south-west through Botswana. ZAPU activity was increasingly prevalent in Matabeleland – its guerrillas were said to be better trained than ZANU cadres operating from Mozambique in the east. In 1979, the final year of the conflict, ZAPU men were fighting for territory in the south in areas of ZANU influence, where guerrilla met guerrilla in combat.

ZAPU contested the February 1980 elections as the Patriotic Front. By early 1981, however, 42 battalions had been trained, each with more than a thousand men and consisting of mixed ZAPU-ZANU ex-guerrillas, known as the Zimbabwe People's Revolutionary Army (ZIPRA).

Z

REFERENCES AND SELECT BIBLIOGRAPHY

Alexander, Y. (ed.) (1976), *Terrorism. International, National, Regional and Global Perspectives*, New York, Praeger.

Alexander, Y., Carlton, D. and Wilkinson, P. (eds) (1978), *Terrorism Theory and Practice*, New York, Praeger, Westview Special Studies in National and International Terrorism.

Alexander, Y. and Finger, S. M. (eds) (1977), *Terrorism: Interdisciplinary Perspectives*, New York, John Jay Press.

Alexander, Y. and Gleason, J. M. (eds) (1981), *Behavioral and Quantitative Perspectives on Terrorism*, New York, Pergamon Press.

Alexander, Y. and Myers, K. (eds) (1982), *Terrorism in Europe*, New York, St Martin's Press.

Alexander, Y. and O'Day, A. (eds) (1984), *Terrorism in Ireland*, New York, St Martin's Press.

Arendt, H. (1951), *The Origins of Totalitarianism*, New York, Harcourt, Brace, Jovanovich Inc.

Aron, R. (1966), *Peace and War*, London, Weidenfeld & Nicolson.

Bassiouni, M. Ch. (1981), 'Terrorism, Law Enforcement and the Mass Media: Perspectives, Problems, Proposals', *The Journal of Criminal Law and Criminology*, Vol. 72, No. 1, New York.

Bite, V. (1975), 'International Terrorism', *Foreign Affairs Division, Library of Congress*. Appendix of US Congress, Senate Committee on the Judiciary. Subcommittee to Investigate the Administration of the Internal Security Act and Other Internal Security Laws. Part IV, May 14, Washington DC, GPO.

Bonanate, L. (ed.) (1979), *Dimensioni del Terrorismo Politico*, Milan, Franco Angeli Editore.

Carlton, D. and Schaerf, C. (eds) (1981), *Contemporary Terror Studies in Sub-State Violence*, London, Macmillan.

Chisholm, A. J. (1948), *The Function of Terror and Violence in Revolution*, Washington DC, Georgetown University (MA Thesis).

Cline, R. S. and Alexander, Y. (eds) (1986), *Terrorism as State-Sponsored Covert Warfare*, USA Virginia, Hero Books.

Clutterbuck, R. (ed.) (1986), *The Future of Political Violence*, London, Macmillan, RUSI.

Clutterbuck, R. (1978), *Kidnap and Ransom, the Response*, London, Faber & Faber.

Clutterbuck, R. (1977), *Guerrillas and Terrorists*, London, Faber & Faber.

Clutterbuck, R. (1975), *Living with Terrorism*, London, Faber & Faber.

Crelinsten, R. D. (ed.) (1977), *Research Strategies for the Study of International Political Terrorism*, Montreal, International Centre for Comparative Criminology.

Crenshaw Hutchinson, M. (1981), 'The Causes of Terrorism', *Comparative Politics*, Chicago.

Crenshaw Hutchinson, M. (1978), *Revolutionary Terrorism: the FLN in Algeria 1945–1962*, Stanford, Hoover Institution.

Crenshaw Hutchinson, M. (1972), 'The Concept of Revolutionary Terrorism', *Journal of Conflict Resolution*, Vol. 16, No. 3.

Crozier, B. (1974), 'Aid for Terrorism', *Annual of Power and Conflict, 1973–74. A Survey of Political Violence and International Influence*, London, Institute for the Study of Conflict.

Dallin, A. and Breslauer, G. W. (eds) (1970), *Political Terror in Communist Systems*, Stanford, Cal., Stanford University Press.

Day, A. J. (ed.) (1983), *Political Dissent: An International Guide to Extra-Parliamentary Guerrilla and Illegal Political Movements*, London, Longman.

Dobson, C. and Payne, R. (1982), *Terror! The West Fights Back*, London, Macmillan.

Dobson, C. and Payne, R. (1982), *The Terrorists, their Weapons, Leaders and Tactics*, New York, Facts on File.

Evans, A. E. and Murphy, J. F. (eds) (1978), *Legal Aspects of International Terrorism*, Lexington, Heath.

Fairbairn, G. (1974), *Revolutionary Guerrilla Warfare: The Countryside Version*, London, Penguin.

Fanon, F. (1983), *The Wretched of the Earth*, London, Pelican Books.

Feary, R. A. (1976), remarks made 19 February 1976 as US Coordinator for Combatting Terrorism, quoted in Wolf (1981).

Francis, S. T. (1981), *The Soviet Strategy of Terror*, Washington DC, Heritage Foundation.

Freedman, L., Hill, C., Roberts, A., Vincent, R. J., Wilkinson, P. and Windsor, P. (1986), *Terrorism and International Order*, London, Routledge & Kegan Paul.

Fromkin, D. (1975), 'The Strategy of Terrorism', *Foreign Affairs*, Vol. 53, No. 4, Washington DC.

Goren, R. (1984), *The Soviet Union and Terrorism*, London, Allen & Unwin.

Guevara, C. (1968), *Episodes of the Revolutionary War*, New York, International Publishers.

Hacker, F. J. (1981), 'Contagion and Attraction of Terror and Terrorism', in Alexander and Gleason (eds) (1981).

Hamilton, L. C. (1978), *Ecology of Terrorism: A Historical and Statistical Study*, Boulder, Colorado, University of Colorado.

Hardman, J. B. S. (1936), 'Terrorism' in *Encyclopedia of the Social Sciences*, Vol. 14, New York, Macmillan.

Herman, V. and van der Laan Bouma, R. (1981), 'Nationalists without a Nation: South Moluccan Terrorism in the Netherlands', in Lodge (ed.) (1981).

Hess, H. (1981), 'Terrorismus und Terrorismus – Diskurs', *Tijdschrift voor Criminologie*, No. 4, Amsterdam.

Heyman, E. S. (1980), *Monitoring the Diffusion of Transnational Terrorism*, Gaithersburg, Maryland, USA, IACP.

Heyman, E. S. and Mickolus, E. (1980), 'Responding to Terrorism: Basic and Applied Research', in Sloan and Shultz (eds) (1980).

Horowitz, I. L. (1977), 'Transnational Terrorism, Civil Liberties, and Social Science', in Alexander and Finger (eds) (1977).

Horowitz, I. L. (1973), 'Political Terrorism and State Power', *Journal of Political and Military Sociology*, Vol. 1, Los Angeles.

Hyams, E. (1974), *Terrorists and Terrorism*, New York, St Martin's Press.

Iviansky, Z. (1981), 'Individual Terror: Concept and Typology', *Journal of Contemporary History*, Vol. 12, No. 1, London.

Janke, P. (1983), *Guerrilla and Terrorist Organisations: A World Directory and Bibliography*, Brighton, Harvester Press.

Jansen, G. H. (1981), *Militant Islam*, London, Pan Books.

Jenkins, B. M. (1978), 'The Study of Terrorism: Definitional Problems', in Alexander and Gleason (eds) (1981).

Jenkins, B. M. (1977), 'Combatting International Terrorism: The Role of Congress', Santa Monica, Rand.

Jenkins, B. M. (1975), 'International Terrorism. A New Mode of Conflict', California Seminar on Arms Control and Foreign Policy, Los Angeles, Crescent Publications.

Kaplan, A. (1981), 'The Psychodynamics of Terrorism', in Alexander and Gleason (eds) (1981).

Karanovic, M. (1978), 'Pojam Terorizma' (The Concept of Terrorism), *Jugoslovenska Revija za Krimilogiju i Krivicnofravo*, No. 14, Belgrade.

Laqueur, W. (1977), *Terrorism*, London, Weidenfeld & Nicolson.

Laqueur, W. (1977), 'Interpretations of Terrorism – Fact, Fiction and Political Science 1977', *Journal of Contemporary History*, Vol. 12, No. 1, London.

Leiden, C. and Schmitt, K. M. (1968), *The Politics of Violence*, Englewood Cliffs, Prentice Hall.

Leiser, B. M. (1977), 'Terrorism, Guerrilla Warfare and International Morality', *Journal of International Studies*, Vol. 12, Stanford.

Livingston, M. H. (ed.) (1978), *International Terrorism in the Contemporary World*, Westport, Conn., Greenwood Press.

Livingstone, N. (1982), *The War Against Terrorism*, Lexington, Heath.

Lodge, J. (ed.) (1982), *Terrorism: A Challenge to the State*, Oxford, Martin Robertson.

Mallin, J. (1977), 'Terrorism as a Military Weapon', *Air University Review*, Vol. 28, No. 2, Washington DC.

Mallin, J. (1971), *Terror and Urban Guerrillas*, Florida, University of Miami Press.

Marighella, C. (1974), *The Minimanual of the Urban Guerrilla*, Vancouver, Pulp Press.

Marighella, C. (1971), *Teoria y Accion Revolucionaria*, Cuernavaca, Mexico, Editorial Diogenes.

Mickolus, E. (1980), *Transnational Terrorism: A Chronology of Events 1968–1979*, London, Aldwych.

Mickolus, E. (1978), 'Trends in Transnational Terrorism', in Livingston (ed.) (1978).

Milbank, D. L. (1976), *Research Study: International and Transnational Terrorism*, Washington DC, CIA Political Research Department.

Miller, A. H. (1980), *Terrorism and Hostage Negotiations*, Boulder, Colorado, Westview Press.

Morrison, D. G. et al. (1972), *Black Africa. A Comparative Handbook*, New York, The Free Press.

Moss, R. (1971), *Urban Guerrillas: The New Face of Political Violence*, London, Temple Smith.

Moss, R. (1971), *Urban Guerrilla Warfare*, Adelphi Papers, No. 79, London, Institute of Strategic Studies.

Neale, W. D. (1973), 'Terror – Oldest Weapon in the Arsenal', *Army*, August, Washington DC.

Netanyahu, B. (ed.) (1986), *Terrorism: How the West Can Win*, London, Weidenfeld & Nicolson.

Parritt, B. A. H. (ed.) 1986), *Violence at Sea: A Review of Terrorism, Acts of War and Piracy, and Countermeasures to Prevent Terrorism*, Paris, ICC Publishing.

Paust, J. J. (1977), 'A Definitional Focus', in Alexander and Finger (eds) (1977).

Pontara, G. (1979), 'Violenza e Terrorismo. Il Problema della Definizione e della Giustificazione', in Bonanate (ed.) (1979).

Qureshi, S. (1976), 'Political Violence in the South Asia Subcontinent', in Alexander (ed.) (1976).

Rosie, G. (1986), *The Directory of International Terrorism*, Edinburgh, Mainstream Publishing.

Roucek, J. S. (1962), 'Sociological Elements of a Theory of Terror and Violence', *American Journal of Economics and Sociology*, Vol. 21, No. 2.

Schmid, A. P. (1983), *Political Terrorism: A Research Guide to Concepts, Theories, Data Bases and Literature*, USA.

Schwind, H. D. (1978), 'Zur Entwicklung des Terrorismus', in Schwind (ed.), *Ursachen des Terrorismus der Bundesrepublik*, Berlin, Walter de Gruyter.

Sederberg, P. C. (1981), 'Defining Terrorism' (unpublished paper).

Shultz, R. (1978), 'Conceptualising Political Terrorism, A Typology', *Journal of International Affairs*, Vol. 32, No. 1.

Silverman, J. M. and Jackson, P. M. (1970), 'Terror in Insurgency Warfare', *Military Review* Vol. 50, Washington DC.

Silverstein, M. E. (1977), 'Medical Rescue as an Antiterrorist Measure. A Strategist's Cookbook', in Crelinsten (ed.) (1977).

Singh, B. (1977), 'An Overview', in Alexander and Finger (eds) (1977).

Sloan, S. and Shultz, R. (eds) (1980), *Responding to the Terrorist Threat: Prevention and Control*, New York, Pergamon.

Smith, W. H. (1977), 'International Terrorism. A Political Analysis', in *The Year Book of World Affairs, 1977* Vol. 31, London, Stevens.

Sterling, C. (1982), *The Terror Network*, London, Weidenfeld & Nicolson.

Stohl, M. (1981), 'The Three Worlds of Terror' (unpublished paper).

Tromp, H. W. (1979), 'Terrorism and Political Violence', Brussels, AFK/ VVK (unpublished paper).

Waciorsky, J. (1939), *La Terrorisme Politique*, Paris, A. Pedone, as quoted in Crenshaw Hutchinson (1972).

Walter, E. V. (1964), 'Violence and the Process of Terror', *American Sociological Review* Vol. 29, No. 2.

Wardlaw, G. (1982), *Political Terrorism*, Cambridge, Cambridge University Press.

Watson, F. M. (1976), *Political Terrorism: The Threat and the Response*, Washington DC, Robert B. Luce.

Weisband, E. and Roguly, D. (1976), 'Palestinian Terrorism: Violence, Verbal Strategy, and Legitimacy', in Alexander (ed) (1976).

Wilkinson, P. (ed) (1981), *British Perspectives on Terrorism*, London, Allen & Unwin.

Wilkinson, P. (1978), 'Terrorist Movements', in Alexander, Carlton and Wilkinson (eds) (1978).

Wilkinson, P. (1977), *Terrorism and the Liberal State*, London, Macmillan. (Latest edition 1986)

Wilkinson, P. (1976), 'Terrorism versus Liberal Democracy: The Problem of Response', *Conflict Studies* No. 76, London, Institute for the Study of Conflict.

Wilkinson, P. (1974), *Political Terrorism*, London, Macmillan.

Wilkinson, P. (1973), 'Three Questions on Terrorism', *Government and Opposition* Vol. 8, No. 3, London.

Wolf, J. B. (1981), *Fear of Fear. A Survey of Terrorist Operations and Controls in Open Societies*, New York, Plenum Press.

Wolf, J. B. (1976), 'Controlling Political Terrorism in a Free Society', *Orbis* Vol. 19, No. 34, Washington DC.

Zinam, O. (1978), 'Terrorism and Violence in the Light of a Theory of Discontent and Frustration', in Livingston (ed) (1978).

INDEX

Index

296

Index

Index

Index